I0868016

"Oh, they're side by side; they're glorified.
Where the underworld can meet the elite —
Forty-Second Street."

For Dennis Daniel.

A teacher.

An inspiration.

And, most importantly, a friend.

BLOOD SUCKING FREAK

THE LIFE AND FILMS OF THE INCREDIBLE JOEL M. REED

A NOTE FROM THE AUTHOR

I started work on this book in 1998. I was twenty-four-years-old. I had visited New York City a few times prior to that, but by the time 1999 rolled around, I was flying in and out of town on a regular basis. I had made quite a few friends in the city and I leapt at every chance to visit them.

Great memories of those days: late night drinks in bars that never seemed to close. Strange hotels with even stranger inhabitants. Notebooks filled with pages of words—a precautionary measure to ensure documentation in case things went blurry.

One of my friends lived in a small apartment in Midtown. His name was Joel M. Reed.

I had looked up Joel's number in a Manhattan phone book in the winter of 1997. Surprised to find him listed, I decided to give him a call from my room at the Hotel Pennsylvania. Joel answered the phone and we started talking. I asked him a few questions about his infamous film, ***Blood Sucking Freaks***. Joel seemed more than happy to answer any question that I had, so I inquired about setting up a proper interview. "You can always call me," he said. I took that as a yes.

In January of 1998, I boarded a plane at the decrepit Detroit City Airport and wound up in Newark, New Jersey. A late-night bus ride took me under the Hudson River and into Manhattan. Charon might as well have been driving. An entry from one of my notebooks:

"Sitting across from Toothless, the Burro, and his bearded friend."

I don't really remember much about Toothless and company, but they certainly gave me a great feeling of unease. I was still new to New York. My expectations were high, but I remained cautious.

First meeting with Joel at Sam's in 1998. L–R: Brian Krueger, Joel M. Reed, John Szpunar.

Scribbled on the same page:

"Twin Donut."

That, I remember. The place was a fountain of lights, and the splintered images of people who were *not* Toothless, the Burro, or his bearded friend gave me a great sense of comfort. Old men silently drank coffee at the counter as I passed them in the night. The sight of them calmed my nerves, and as the years went on, I made it a point to sit on the same side of every bus out of Newark in order to catch a glimpse of the place. I never recognized a single face, but I'd like to think that the same ambassadors were sitting there, time after time.

On January 10, 1998, I interviewed Joel Reed at a small restaurant called Sam's. As we talked and ate, I knew that I had stumbled onto something special. Joel was full of incredible stories. As the hours flew by, I found myself hypnotized. Whether he was talking about his early days as a New York press agent or about the strange array of misfits that he collaborated with as a filmmaker, I was transfixed. As the sun rose over the city, I boarded my flight back to Detroit and made a pact with myself to return for more. Return I did, and in the pages that follow, I'll tell you all about it.

In those days, I made it a practice to carry a small tape recorder wherever I went. I never knew what kind of mischief or adventures I'd get into, especially in a place like Manhattan. I was young, unstoppable, and, more often than not, full of drink. When the time came to revive this manuscript, I slid cassette after cassette into my old Panasonic Slimline and pressed play. There, ninety minutes at a time, was a choppy yet coherent diary of my misspent youth. Drunken ramblings, laughter with friends, and the voices of strangers. Loud, thumping bass from passing cars, snippets of long-forgotten conversations at restaurants, and music and noise from what was left of the sex shops and dirty bookstores that still haunted Times Square. The place was clean (and going on cleaner) by the time I made it there, but a few old sores were still festering under the whitewash. In some way, this book serves as a document of what was left of the madness.

Filth can find its way into anything, and in a place like Times Square, cleaned up or not, the odds are always in its favor. As I walked up and down the streets, I often found myself inhabiting a ghost world of a million different people, places, and things.

After my initial meeting with Joel, I returned to New York time and time again, sometimes flying sometimes driving. My partner in crime was a guy named Brian Krueger, a friend that I'd known since high school. He shared my love of booze and sleaze, and he made the perfect traveling companion. Every trip—every hour, minute, and second—was an adventure, and together, we staggered through the streets of New York with wide eyes and a wonderful sense of freedom. He was with me on every visit to Joel's apartment, and his presence and influence on the pages of this book cannot be ignored. We were the best of friends, but the passage of time sometimes has a way of tearing friends apart. Here's to you, BK. I hope you're doing well.

I started work on this book in 1998. I was twenty-four-years-old. I last set foot in New York in 2004 and was amazed at how much the city had changed in just a few years. The last gasp of the old Times Square was all but a memory. No danger. No madness. No nothing. Things were clean then and I'm sure that they're even cleaner now.

With that said, a word of warning to those who seek passage today: New York is a city that never sleeps, and neither do its ghosts. Be mindful when you meet them, and enjoy the ride.

—John Szpunar

Detroit, Michigan

The winter before spring, 2017

"When you clean up a city, you kill it."—Charles Bukowski

Photo: David Szpunar

INTRODUCTION

THE CROSSROADS OF THE WORLD

1998

It started off in a bar. A small place two blocks down from Penn Station in New York City. It was half-past midnight, and I knew that I should be asleep. I had a plane to catch in the morning and the last few days had been rough. The bars close at four in the morning in New York, and I had taken full advantage of them. I was tired and hungover. But, against my better judgment, I grabbed my tape recorder, headed out the door of the Hotel Metro, and wound up at a tavern on 34th Street. I was sitting at a small table that wasn't level with the ground. I had to keep my foot on one of the legs so it wouldn't rock too much.

I had flown into town for the weekend to interview Joel M. Reed. I found his number in the phone book a year earlier and called him. We kept in touch, and he told me to visit if I ever came back to New York. Earlier in the day, I met with him at Sam's, a small restaurant on 45th Street. We had dinner and talked for a while about his films. ***Career Bed. Night of the Zombies. Blood Sucking Freaks.***

After eating, we went across the street to Sardi's and drank for quite a while at the upstairs bar. The bartender knew Joel from way back and seemed somewhat shocked that I was paying him any attention. I sipped at my beer and asked Joel what he thought about the recent efforts to sterilize Times Square.

"They cleaned up my city, they ruined it. There's no more black pimps, junkies, fags, transvestites or cheap whores. There's nothing on 42nd Street anymore." He pronounced whores "*who*-ors". Joel's words got me curious. I decided to give Times Square a look, if only to walk along 42nd and Broadway to mourn the loss of something that I would never know. But first, a few drinks were in order.

My foot was resting on the table leg, a whiskey sour in front of me. The bar wasn't very big, and a lot of people were crammed inside. To my left was a bunch of kids, probably only a few days over twenty-one, out for their first big drunk. One of them was named Joe. Joe was having some trouble keeping his head from crashing down on the table. His friends got very loud every time he tried to make his way to the bathroom. But he didn't have anything on the group of men that sat at the back of the room. There were about four of them, and judging by the bottles on their table, they had each consumed a case of beer. They looked like a gang of terrorists. One of the men, a thick beard covering his face, ran a red plastic comb through his hair every few minutes. A guy who worked the bar, a wobbly black man, whose only job seemed to be emptying ashtrays and clearing tables, was somewhat distraught that they refused to let him take their empty bottles. He walked away from them and collapsed in his chair, mumbling to himself. Every once in a while, just as he seemed asleep, he jumped up to make his rounds. The terrorists shot him dirty looks whenever he neared their table, so he walked up to the bar.

The bartender looked exhausted. The black man approached him and began motioning with his hands. The bartender nodded and walked over to the terrorists. His helper followed. Along the way, he bent to grab an empty crate off the floor. When he reached the four angry men, he methodically began throwing their empty bottles into it. The terrorists laughed and ordered another round.

I stuck around for another drink and decided to nurse it. Joel's words were fresh in my mind.

JOEL REED: *They ruined my city. You can't go to 42nd Street anymore. I mean, what if you're a demented faggot from out of town and you want to get a hand job or something? You don't know anyone in the city; you can't go into any of the men's rooms in the new theaters. In the old days, you could walk in, buy your ticket for* *seventy-five cents, make your presence known, walk down the aisle, and three people would follow you to the men's room. You don't have that now. There was obvious feeling toward the common person back then. Now, you've got to pay nine dollars for a ticket. Who are you going to find? Some ancient guy, some seventy-year-old interior decorator, who can't really get it up any more?*

When I finished my drink, I stood up, left a tip, and walked out the door. I rewound my tape and played back my observations. They sounded good. "Kids to my left, drunk as hell. I think Joe is pretty fucked up. He can't even light a cigarette. The girls are young. One of them is staring at me, probably wondering why I'm talking to myself." The tape went on. I heard Joe hit the table and then there was silence. I rounded a corner and pressed the record button. Held the machine up to my mouth and started talking:

"Walking north on Eighth, heading toward 42nd. Not much is happening right now. There must be a garbage strike going on; there's stuff piled everywhere. I must be walking by a police station, there's cop cars up and down the street."

After a few blocks: *"This place is called Fried World. Open twenty-four hours. At the door now."*

The door to Fried World was propped open with a broom handle. The inside was bright with fluorescence. I walked in. Two small Indian men were half-asleep behind the counter. An old Coca-Cola sign hung from the ceiling and slowly swung above their heads. No one else was inside. I walked up to them and scanned the menu. Eggs. That's all I could see. Fried eggs and bacon, fried eggs and Polish sausage, fried eggs and a hamburger patty. Fried eggs and fried steak. I opted for a fried egg sandwich and some iced tea.

"Four dollars," the taller of the Indians said in broken English. I started to hand him the money and then decided to buy a newspaper and some cigarettes.

The sandwich was stale and greasy, but somehow it was what I needed. I opened the paper and lit a cigarette. And looked out at the street.

New York was getting quiet. Fewer and fewer people walked by the window and the lights from the shops across the street slowly went out, one by one. Hunched figures

Times Square

closed the gates in front of the doors and windows as the garbage crew made their rounds, stopping at corners to scoop up glass and cardboard. One of the Indians began humming along with the radio. "My darling, you look wonderful tonight." And the city really did.

I snapped out of my reverie as a small white man of about thirty walked in through the door. Tried to walk in, that is. He was limping pretty badly, and was obviously drunk and insane. He moved over to the corner, his lips moving silently.

"Fuck it," he said. "I knew exactly what I wanted before I walked in here, and now I can't remember what it was."

The Indians stared at him. "Oh yeah. I want a roast beef sandwich with mustard and everything else."

"That's four dollars," the taller Indian said as his silent partner moved closer to the counter. Mr. Roast Beef's left hand slowly slid into his pants and started moving around.

"Four dollars? That ain't cheap." He steadied himself and headed for the door as the Indians broke into laughter. They nodded at me and moved back to their post. I turned my attention back to the paper and finished my meal. Then, I got up and got a coffee.

I was back on the streets by two in the morning, and I pointed myself toward Times Square. I walked into a few sex shops along the way, but they had changed since I'd visited a few years ago. The live girls were long gone, the rows of magazines

Karate Centre on the far right.

replaced by secondhand paperbacks. Most of the stores stocked what they considered "general viewing" near the front of the store. Sealed VHS copies of ***Bad Taste, Ms .45,*** and ***Suspiria***. I was somewhat amused; it was really something to be able to purchase a copy of ***Hidden Pee Volume One*** with an ancient tape of Robert Warmflash's ***Death Promise***. Still, I wondered what the blocks to come would have in store. I walked faster.

It wasn't long before I came face to face with the Karate Center. The place was lit up with the usual neon signs, but there was something strange about them. They didn't promise sex, rather martial arts videos and supplies. I decided to have a look inside.

The front room was stacked wall to wall with old Ocean Shores videos. Titles like ***Green Killer, The Hot, the Cool, and the Vicious***, and ***Blood on the Sun***. Further back was the porn. Piles of it. Bootlegged bestiality tapes. ***Shannon's Enema Show***. Piss and shit films from around the globe. Needless to say, I needed very little coaxing to stay and browse.

The place wasn't very crowded. In fact, the only other people in the store were a balding Indian man in a blue striped shirt and a gangly Italian of questionable virtue. From what I could gather, they were attempting to do business with a distributor from the west coast. "Try to make the order. To see how much they want, what they want. Make a list. Like I want this, this, and this. I come and I give it to you for wholesale." I walked up to them and started talking.

What sells more here, the karate or the sex?

Karate.

Wow, that's weird. I've never seen a store like this...

Karate. Karate store. Karate movie, kung fu.

No one buys any of the sex?

Huh?

No one buys any of this?

There is people, who, you know...

I mean, it's kind of a strange mixture.

There is people. Sometimes when they see one, they buy karate. Or they see sex and buy it with karate. When they come from the nightclub, they pick one karate.

From the nightclub?

I'm cheaper from my neighbors. Where are you from, Europe?

From Detroit.

We've got European movies here, friend. Hold on.

So, do you guys sell a lot of those pregnant videos?

Over there.

How about these dolls?

The recorder. It's working. It's working.

No, this doesn't work...

Please. No recording. Antonio!

I stepped out of Karate Center before Antonio could make his move. Very few people were on the streets. Those who were seemed to be wandering around aimlessly, in semi-straight lines. A drunken couple was looking for their car. "Fuck, here it is," the young man said, as his date brushed past me. She managed to sidestep a pile of phone books on the sidewalk and grabbed onto his arm. She almost brought him down with her as they walked up to their Volvo, the only car in the lot. I kept walking. Further down the road was another sign:

ADULT BOOKS
25 CENTS OPEN 24 HOURS
VIDEO SALES AND RENTAL

The store also promised lottery tickets, cigarettes, and batteries. I felt like a change of pace, so I crossed the street and walked inside.

The first things I noticed were the porno novels. A big rack of them, all going for two dollars a pop. I glanced over the titles. ***Budding Boobs***. ***My Family's Slave***. ***Stud with a Difference***. The cover of ***Bambi Swallows Hard*** caught my eye and I begin to read:

Showworld: Shortly after I took this, I was told to put my camera away.

"I think maybe you want to be alone with me for all the wrong reasons."

"Such as?" Bambi Starr said. He tilted her head and looked naughty.

"Such as because I am a man and you are rapidly becoming a woman."

"Uncle Alexander, I am ashamed of you. That would be incest."

"Oh, my, you are so cute. So very cute," Uncle Alexander said.

I flipped a few pages further. No telling what would happen next.

"I licked by fingers clean after diddling myself," Bambi Starr said.

"I learned to like the taste of my jism the same way," Uncle Alexander said.

"Oh yeah?"

"Uh huh. I licked my fingers clean after yanking Mr. Chicken-neck."

Bambi Starr laughed.

Against my better judgment, I flipped even further.

"Let's get rid of those nasty old clothes," the handsome man said.

"Okay," she replied. She had come to the conclusion that incest wasn't so creepy after all. It wasn't like she was going to be fucked by her father or anything like that.

And further…

"Mind if I eat your cunt?"

"That's the best offer I've had all day. Mind if I ask you one thing?"

"What's that?"

"Your name."

I put the book back on the rack. By this time, a few other people had gathered around the novels. Another couple, this one sober and dressed for the theater, pawed through the books. "I should start reading these instead of the books I'm reading now," the woman laughed. "I think I could probably learn a lot from them." I imagined her boyfriend licking his fingers clean after a bout with Mr. Chicken-neck, had a quick laugh of my own, and walked back outside.

I kept walking. At the corner of 42nd and Eighth, an old black man was dancing around a garbage can, flinging his cane around wildly. I walked up to him. His clothes were unwashed, but weren't filthy, his last stab at a façade of dignity. He carried an old radio that was blasting music and he wanted to talk.

What's your name?

Earl. That's right, Earl.

What are you listening to?

Kiss. AM/FM radio. Listen to me. I was on the ships twenty years. In 1944, I started. I went to India, Bombay, Argentina, Iran, the Pacific.

Now you're in New York.

Yeah. I got court-marshaled. I got court-marshaled. Got shock treatment on East 43rd Street.

You got shock treatment?

Yeah. You know the VA hospital on First Avenue? I got twenty of them there. They took all my teeth. They took them on Staten Island, at the Staten Island Jail.

What were you doing back then?

Living. When I lived on the Bowery, you got drinks for a quarter. In 1945, you got five drinks for a dollar. And on 42nd, you got three tickets for a dollar. A quarter, dollar and a half movies. Five tickets was a dollar and a half.

Where'd you live?

At the halfway houses. In 1934, 1935, you found them a dime a dozen. You ever been to San Francisco? I lived in the Tenderloin. I lived in Fort Worth, Texas for a while. I lived in jail over there. I shot a man. He came at me, wanted to cut my arm. I had a gun, probably saved my life. Shot him right here, in the arm. He wanted nine dollars. Now I got a studio in Harlem. I'm in Harlem now.

You doing OK?

I'm doing all right.

I left Earl at his corner and kept my recorder going. 42nd and Eighth. Times Square was finally upon me. I looked around for something, but there was nothing left. The street wasn't all that crowded, but the people who were out wouldn't have lasted a second twenty years ago. A middle-aged woman walked by me. Her shirt read: "Will Work for Chocolate." It looked as if she did. Young guys in khakis congregated around neon doorways, but I knew that they weren't looking for a blowjob in a theater bathroom. What they *were* looking for, I wasn't sure:

"Don't know why anyone is here. The crossroads of the world is now a dead end street. Things look bad. A fucking Warner Brothers store's here now. What the hell is that? The Times Square Brewery Restaurant? This isn't what I like to see. How charming. A damn ***Lion King*** *sign. I guess you can't have live sex shows next to the* ***Lion King****. At least Show World is still around. Live Girls on Stage; Hot, Hot, Hot. OK. Things are looking up."*

Show World was once the king of the Times Square sex shops. Three floors of porn with great neon signs beckoning the horny, down and out, or just plain curious. A walk inside told me that times had changed. A group of young men, enticed by false promises, walked in with me.

"No live girls," the man behind the counter told them. The young men looked at him, dumbfounded.

"What's upstairs?" I cut in.

"Nothing. Nothing upstairs."

"What about downstairs?"

The man pointed to the back of the store. "No live girls. Only booths, back there."

Show World had been reduced to a handful of peep show booths and a meager selection of tapes for sale. I'd seen better in Detroit. I walked up to the counter and looked under the glass case. There were T-shirts for sale, along with some curious books: ***Surviving in Prison***, ***The Art of Getting Even***, and ***Personal Defense Weapons***. I considered buying the prison book, decided against it, and walked back outside. The Live Girls Guys were gathered on the corner.

"What about that place? They might have live girls." They started off toward a place called The Playpen, and I followed along. A man who looked far worse than Earl was begging for change across the street. I got out my tape recorder and hit record. The Live Girls Guys got to him first.

"So what's your story?" their leader asked. "You homeless?" I got a little closer, hoping that some of the

Peep Land by night.

conversation would pick up. It never got that far. They got a glimpse of my recorder and walked.

"Hey, movie star! Movie star!" the old man wheezed. "Help me out, man!"

"That guy's following me with a fucking tape recorder," said one of the guys. "I'm not sticking around!" He gave me a disgusted look and ducked into The Playpen with his friends. I wondered what they'd find in there…

A few years ago, a friend of mine had gone to a place called Peepland to check out the sights. He came back with wondrous stories.

"I asked the guy behind the counter for a recommendation on the blow up dolls. He couldn't understand me, and he started pulling down these blue dildos off the shelf. There was some guy in there who kept following me around, so I ducked into a booth. I was right next to some Mexican who was shouting at his monitor, 'Oh, bebe! You take it hard, you bitch!' I could hear him through the wall. I put a five into the machine, and when my time was up, he was still going strong."

There was once a time when the theaters of 42nd Street were a direct reflection of the neighborhoods that surrounded them. For better or for worse, things had changed. There was no terror or joy in the night anymore.

I decided to walk back to my room. Speaking softly into the recorder, I watched the street signs slowly fall back to 35th. "The hot dog venders are still going at 3:30 in the morning. I don't think they ever stop. There was about one block of madness left

in Times Square. Sanitized madness."

I suddenly felt nostalgic for something. I wanted to be a part of a block-long line to see ***The Thrill Killers*** at two in the morning. I wanted to see Harry Reems bang Georgina Spelvin on a thirty-foot screen as the rest of the world walked by, oblivious.

JOEL REED: *I really enjoyed those movies. I used to go with a black audience, and they caught every nuance. All of the stupid jokes in* ***Count Yorga, Vampire****. Sid Haig was a major star. You didn't want to sit in front of the balcony back then. You could sit way in front of the balcony because you knew the urine didn't reach out that far, but if you sat under the lip, you were out of luck. The Disney prostitution of Times Square fucked everything up. You have to rent the movies now. There was something real back then. It was a great playground, you could see three movies for a dollar seventy-five. Now it's over. What's open at four anymore? The Duane Reade Drugstore.*

The walk back to the hotel went on forever. My feet hurt like hell as I walked up the stairs and through the glass doors. I flashed my key at the man behind the desk and he waved me on. Up the elevator to the tenth floor, down the hall to room 1017. I fired one last entry into my recorder:

"Back at the Metro. In bed, looking out the window. The sun will be up soon. I'll have to check out."

Checkout time was at eleven AM, so I got to the airport early, sat down at the bar, and had a drink. Then, I waited in line to verify my flight. My plane was delayed. There was nothing else to do but sit down in a small snack bar and chat with the woman behind the counter. The place started to fill up with people and noise, so I found an empty terminal and tried to get some sleep.

Finally, after five hours of waiting, flight 273 arrived. I followed the crowd into the plane and found my seat. I think we were over Pennsylvania when I got out my pen and paper and started to write:

Joel Reed's career has spanned for four decades. Despite the fact that his films are not widely known, he played a major part in the exploitation boom of the '60s and '70s. The list of his acquaintances seems endless: Jerry Gross, Joe Sarno, Vernon Becker, Victor Kanefsky, Jerry Damiano, and Sidney Pink, to name but a few. He gave Georgina Spelvin her first nude role, back in the days when a tit-shot was a revelation. The craziness of this era seems almost innocent now. But Joel was there and he remembers.

And so, we begin our journey into night, neon, sex, and violence. Into the dark world of the 42nd Street sex shops and theaters. But most importantly, into the world of Joel M. Reed, the New York auteur that has stayed with his city for all these years.

Thanks for everything, Joel. This book is for you.

"I could have been the Brad Pitt of my day"—Joel M. Reed

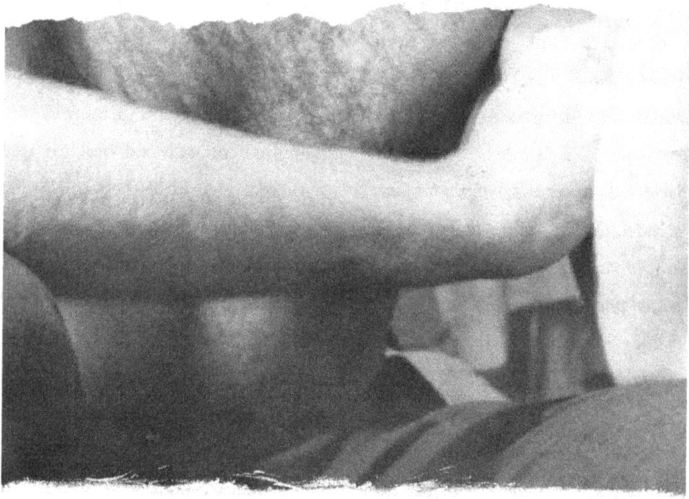

Photo from the collection of Joel M. Reed

CHAPTER ONE

JUST ANOTHER DAY IN THE NAKED CITY

The man in front of me was enormous. Easily 300 pounds. He had walked out of the Tick Tock Diner a few blocks back, smiling, drooling, and wiping his face. His clothes seemed tailor-made and he had a black mustache that looked very unwashed. I turned to Brian, pointed in his direction, and shouted, "Ignatius Riley has found his way to New York!" The man looked back at us, flashed a perverted smile and kept going. He looked at his watch with every third step and slowly made his way along 34th Street. He passed Madison Square Garden and turned left on Broadway. I walked up behind him and smiled as Brian snapped a picture. It was around five o'clock in the afternoon, a surprisingly warm day in January. We were headed to Sam's, a small restaurant in New York City's theater district, to meet up with Joel M. Reed.

The streets were crowded with tourists. They stopped abruptly to look into windows as they cut across the sidewalk, wandering in and out of Macey's with bags and cameras. A young black man sold purses and jewelry on the corner. "Yes, ladies, it's true. Twenty dollars here, but $50 at Macey's. The same bag, ladies. The same bag. Now, there's a *deal*!" We walked past an all-day parking garage. A young Italian, cigarette in mouth, rubbed his stomach as he waved a car in. An old drunk tried his best to get into a taxi that was parked on the side of the road. It was empty. A cab driver in front of the parked car screamed,

"No, man. Over here!" I hadn't been to New York in a while. It felt good to be back on Broadway. I pictured Hal Linden running through the streets like Julie Andrews, singing, "Hey, Big Apple, I'm back!"

It seems as though the world will never forgive Joel Reed for making ***Blood Sucking Freaks***. Tasteless, sexist, violent, and crude, the film is almost impossible to live down. With a 16mm camera and a lifetime in New York behind him, Reed created Sardu, a down-and-out white slavery merchant who uses his Grand Guignol show in Soho as a front for his perverted desires. Women are whipped, chained, butchered, and beaten. A twisted dwarf laughs insanely as he dismembers a blonde ballerina with a chainsaw. He plucks out human eyes and rides women like horses. He's also pretty handy with poison darts. Almost every offense against female flesh imaginable is gleefully celebrated in ***Blood Sucking Freaks***. The film is almost without any redeeming value.

Most of Joel's other films follow suit. His two stabs at the softcore market, ***Career Bed*** and ***Sex by Advertisement*** are sleazy, black and white wet dreams of the most repulsive kind. The only surviving prints are scarred with missing frames and messy splices. But then, that's all part of their charm. While "respectable" exploiters like Joe Sarno and Radley Metzger flirted with an element of style, Joel loaded up the film and let the

Seamus O'Brien as Sardu in *Blood Sucking Freaks*.

camera run through the darkest corners of his mind. Mothers whore their daughters for profit. Old men whip naked women in Central Park. Shaky camerawork, lurid '60s trash music, and butcher knife editing give the films some loose framework. Nobody ever said that sex had to be stylized. With Reed, it was simply rough and dirty.

Joel had told us to meet him at six, but we wanted to get to Sam's early. Might as well have a few drinks before meeting the guy. Probably the best thing to do. We walked past old textile buildings and a store that sold buttons. Two women on our left were discussing breeding dogs with frozen sperm. We dropped back behind them. I reached into my pocket and realized that I was low on cigarettes. I'd have to make a stop someplace in a hurry.

The sign above the door said Marlboro, so I walked inside. A white-hared man with a southern accent was ahead of me in line.

"How much is this tattoo magazine?"

"The price is on the cover."

"Sorry, I didn't see it. Why don't you have a sweater on? You think it's warm outside or something?"

I bought my cigarettes as the man behind the counter followed the old man with narrow eyes. He took my money with a weary smile. I walked back outside. After a few more blocks of commotion and people, Brain pointed across the street. "There it is."

Sam's, at 45th, between Seventh and Eighth Avenue.

We dodged the traffic and went inside. The lights were low, my eyes had trouble adjusting. A young hostess with short black hair and a matching dress met us at the door.

"A table for two?"

"Actually, we're supposed to meet someone here in an hour. I'm going to interview him, he's a filmmaker."

She thought a minute. "You can sit over here. There won't be as much noise." She led us to our table. "Someone will get you some drinks in a minute." Then, she walked back to the door and looked out at the street.

Sam's was a little place with dark brick walls, a low ceiling, and small, square tables with blue and white checkered tablecloths. The people inside were well-dressed and young. The '90s equivalent of Frank Sinatra softly played over the noise of glasses, forks, and plates. I took off my hat and took out a cigarette. The hostess unfolded a paper and began to read. We waited for our waiter to arrive.

I wasn't really sure what Joel would look like. The latest picture I'd seen of him was at least ten-years-old. I kept a close watch on the door. Brian, who had come along for the ride, loaded a new roll of film into his camera and took out some batteries. "You should put in fresh ones, just in case." I took the batteries from him and stopped the tape recorder. It had been recording, almost non-stop, for at least twelve hours.

Our waiter made his way over to us. "What can I get you guys?" he smiled. We smiled back, ordered some beer, and waited. A Picassoesque painting of a ballerina hung on the wall behind me. Most of the artwork on the walls involved ballerinas. A fitting place to meet with Joel.

Joel Reed on the streets of New York.

"I wonder if he'll get here on time." Brian mumbled.

"He'll be here early," I said. No doubt he'd want to get in a few drinks as well. It was 5:30. Joel walked in at 5:45. He was unmistakable. Brian finished off his bottle. "I'll bring him over."

Brian walked up to the bar and came back with Joel M Reed. He was wearing a denim shirt and a leather jacket. His glasses were very thick. His hair was gray and thinning. It was haphazardly pulled back into a ponytail.

"Hello, you must be John. I'm Joel Reed."

Joel took a seat and opened a menu. "The food's pretty good here."

So, this was Joel Reed. I looked at him closely. His face had changed a little over the years, but it was easily recognizable.

Our waiter came over to our table and addressed Joel: "Can I get you something to drink, sir?"

"Glenlivet on the rocks with a splash of water. And give me one of those chicken salads. The thing with the chicken on it."

"The chicken salad?"

"Yeah, give me a grilled chicken salad. With creamy Italian dressing."

The waiter nodded. "Do you guys want to hold onto those menus, or are you on a liquid diet?" Brian and I handed him back the menus and ordered more beer. I moved the tape recorder closer to Joel.

JOEL: OK. Are you on? Hello, this is Joel Reed, I can see that you're reading me. I was born in Brooklyn. Many people in the neighborhood went on to fame and fortune, but Marty Engles is the only one that I can remember.

JOHN: ***When were you born***?

JOEL: December 29, 1933. My father worked at King Karol Records. Marty Engels lived across the Street. Kirk Douglas rented a room in our apartment. I think it was Kirk Douglas. Either him or Burt Lancaster. Which one was the wrestler?

JOHN: ***Kirk Douglas.***

JOEL: I was very little. I don't really remember it. I know we used to rent the rooms out. We were poor. A number of people lived there. Kirk Douglas went to school upstate with my uncle.

A young Joel M. Reed.

We sat in Sam's for about an hour and Joel did his best to keep things entertaining. "I went in to buy a new bed today and the girl at the store was very cute. I asked her if she came with it. She told me no."

We kept drinking and Joel kept talking. His stories were outrageous, crass, and matter of fact. We ordered two more drinks before we moved on.

"Let's go over to Sardi's. We can talk over there."

We made our way outside. The streets were festering with nightlife. The theaters seemed timeless; frozen artifacts from a bygone age. People moved around them, almost oblivious to their presence. Old men in ill-fitting clothes slowly walked along, blind and deaf to everything. Mexicans in T-shirts and jeans, and with mouthfuls of teeth were on the lookout for action. A middle-aged man with a dirty cloth tied around his hand threw a rock into the air, catching it as he made his way toward Seventh Avenue.

It was a short walk to Sardi's. Joel was always a few paces behind us. His leg seemed to be giving him trouble. We reached the corner of 44th Street. Joel stopped at the curb and pointed to a restaurant. "I went into that place a few years ago. I had dinner. A cop walked in with a gun and blew his brains out. They ended up all over the salad bar." Joel adjusted his collar, looked ahead, and smiled.

We continued walking. Sardi's was just ahead. A steady stream of people walked in through open doors. We made it across 44th and joined them.

"They're all here for something to eat before they go to the show. It's really busy here before and after."

Busy and ugly. The faces inside Sardi's were painted and lifeless; tipsy couples talking vacantly in a collected voice. The men looked confident and laughed as if instructed to by subliminal command. Most of their suits were cheap. An older woman hung onto her much younger date, beaming with conquest. Her date's face was indifferent. They found a table by the door and she opened a menu. A younger woman held her purse with bone-white knuckles, smoking a cigarette in great gulps, scanning the crowd for someone. She took a sip of her drink and shifted her feet. A group of four brushed past her, talking loudly. They joined some friends at the far end of the room. It was seven in the evening, going on showtime. Three effeminate men walked in, high on rum and the night. They talked of Chicago and smoked long cigarettes, tapping ashes to the floor in slow, graceful movements. The tourists were hitting New York, swilling overpriced drinks, hoping to catch a glimpse of something. Joel pushed his way through the crowd.

"Let's go upstairs. We can sit at the bar."

We followed him up the stairs. He moved very slowly, using the banister for support. We reached the top and headed for the bar. A young man stood behind it, filling glasses and emptying ashtrays. Joel ordered a chardonnay, we ordered beer. The bartender's name was

Joel at Sardi's.

Frank. The other bartender, Joe, was absent without leave.

BRIAN: I've read that Seamus O'Brien's caricature is hanging up in here. [Sardu, from ***Blood Sucking Freaks***.]

JOEL: Really? I doubt it. I mean, it's possible, from when he was in ***The Fantasticks***. We can ask. [to Frank] Is Max around? The Big Max? The boss?

FRANK: I'm not sure. I saw his wife. I'm not sure if he left.

JOEL: We'll look for him in a while.

FRANK: Did you hear about your friend Lorin Price? He just died a couple of days ago. It was in the paper.

JOEL: Oh, God. I have to look that up.

FRANK: I never met him. It's just that yesterday, some guys who come in here, regulars, were talking about him.

JOEL: Lorin and I were partners. He was the most obnoxious guy to hang out at the bar with. You're a young guy. You didn't know the old guys here, like George Repp and his brother.

FRANK: I never met them.

JOEL: Well, Joe will tell you about them. I was here with Ray. We used to sit here and then we'd go fishing out on Long Island. I'd wait for him, and then we'd go fishing on his boat. Do you remember Ray, or was that before your time?

FRANK: I only met him once. Not on the job, he happened to come in here last year with some people.

JOEL: Ray and I used to go fishing and I'd help him with his garden.

Portrait of the director as a young man.

He would grow all this stuff out on Long Island. I'd come out there and help him hoe the thing.

JOHN: ***Do you want another drink?***

JOEL: I'll have another, thank you. Well, this is Sardi's. I've just started coming here again in the last few months. [to Frank] These guys are from Detroit.

FRANK: Somebody told me there's fifteen feet of snow there right now.

BRIAN: I'd say there's only around two feet.

JOEL (laughing): You've got to have some hot Catholic high school girls around Detroit. I'll come and visit.

The bar was crowded and we were packed up against it, elbow to elbow. I took a look around. A man with a Boston accent was bragging to anyone who would listen about all the plays he'd produced. Not many people were listening. "My old partner doesn't come around here anymore. I run into him now and then. He's got a place in Suffolk now."

An older bartender was caught in the Producer's web. He casually scanned the bar for an out. He caught sight of Joel, excused himself, walked over to us, and leaned up against the bar.

JOEL: Joe!

JOE (thick Italian accent): How are you doing over there?

JOEL: Very good. Is Max around? I want to see if Seamus O'Brien's caricature is hanging up over here.

JOE: Seamus O'Brien?

JOEL: Yeah, he was in ***The Fantasticks***. He might be up there.

JOE: Seamus O'Brien? Who are these friends of yours? Lorin Price—

JOEL: Oh, fuck Lorin. Lorin was good for money—

JOE: Fuck Lorin is right!

JOEL: I could get money from

him, but he was the most obnoxious person in the world. I got a lot of money from Lorin.

JOE: You did, huh?

JOEL: What do you know about making a living in showbusiness?

JOE: I know about as much as you do. You're crazy!

The place began to clear out. Soon, we were about the only people left. We spread out along the bar. Joe walked over and brought us fresh drinks.

JOEL: I've said this before. If I went for older women, I'd be living in the south of France right now. I'll tell you something. Older women want guys who are hard all day long.

JOE: Joel!

JOEL: Don't worry, there's nobody here.

JOE: Yes there is!

JOEL: Relax, there's nobody here. Absolutely nobody here that can hear that. [noticing an older couple sitting to his left] Oh, sorry. But that's what older women want.

JOE: You've got to *respect* these people.

JOEL: I'm sorry. I won't do that anymore. But it's TRUE! They think about sex all the time. Actually... younger girls are a pain in the ass, too.

JOE (to me): Joel is a bad guy. You think Joel's a bad guy?

JOEL: No, I'm a good guy.

JOE: Joel's a good guy. How long you know Joel?

JOHN: ***I just met him today.***

JOE (laughing): Jesus Christ!

I lit a cigarette and nursed it along. The caricatures along the walls stared at each other and at us, as Joel took a sip of wine and looked back at them. Frozen, distorted moments of history. Joe excused himself to go downstairs. Before he left, he refilled our drinks one more time. Joel leaned up against the bar and started talking.

JOEL REED: I've been here a long time. Things have changed a lot. I used to live in Times Square. Forty-eighth Street and Seventh Avenue. There was really nobody there in the days before the big office buildings.

JOHN: ***Where did you go to school at?***

JOEL: I went to public school in Brooklyn and then to Erasmus Hall High School. I dropped out. I think I was in school for about two days. I don't remember going there

The young serviceman.

very much. That was the same High School that Barbra Streisand went to.

JOHN: ***Why did you drop out?***

JOEL: I don't know. I went there about two or three days and decided to become a juvenile delinquent. I hung around with the gang kids in the neighborhood. When I was around thirteen or fourteen, I ran away from home and hitchhiked around the country. I went through the deep south and ended up in Fort Worth, Texas. I bummed around for a while.

JOHN: ***What was that like?***

JOEL: Oh, it was OK. I got a lot of homosexuals picking me up, but it was pretty good. When I was broke, I used to go to the missions. They'd feed me. I met a lot of guys who made their way without spending any money. They'd go back and forth across the country. In fact, in Mississippi, the cops picked me up and bought me a whole bunch of food and let me sleep in the jail over night.

JOHN: ***What year was this?***

JOEL: Nineteen forty-nine or 1950. I got away with a lot down south because I was white. I got a ride in Alabama with some farmer. He turned out to be a Jewish guy from Brooklyn. He had a bull in the back of his truck. It smelled of manure. It was terrible.

JOHN: ***How long did it take you to get to Texas?***

JOEL: Only two or three days. I got rides all along. I got a couple of jobs down there, and then got picked up by the police. The child welfare agency put me into a hotel. I guess I just got bored. So, I came back to New York. I joined the Army and was in the Korean War.

JOHN: ***How long did you serve?***

JOEL: I was in the Army for about four years. I got my high school and college diplomas in the army. I just took the tests. I lucked out. I'm pretty good at those. I just picked the right answers. I did much better on the science questions than anything else.

JOHN: ***Let's hear something about your time in the service.***

JOEL: The Army was actually a very nice place. I had a very good time there. I could have done a lot more. I didn't think about it. I was just floating in the wind. You know, when I got back home from hitchhiking, I joined the Marine Corps. I was sixteen. My parents came and got me out. When I was old enough, I joined the Army. I was sent to Korea, but I was too young for action. Too many seventeen-year-olds were being killed, so they kept me in Japan. They sent me down to Kobe to work on an Army ship. The Army has a big navy. I got on that ship and almost died from sea sickness. I think we were carrying bodies from Korea. I didn't last there, so they sent me to school. It was something about loading ships. Not physical loading, it was on paper. You know, you don't put the ping-pong balls on one end of the ship and the locomotives on the other end so the ship would even out and sail like this. You had to even out the weight. Things about loading cargo. We actually had little model ships. After that, they didn't know what to do with me. My main job was taking the Colonel's daughter to the prom. She went to school over there and never had a date. They got me a tuxedo. The only work I did there, outside of whoring, was the harbor patrol. We had a fleet of little PT boats.

JOHN: ***What was Japan like?***

JOEL: It was wonderful. It was one big brothel. It was 360 yen to the dollar. A carton of cigarettes cost about ninety cents in the PX. Two cartons of cigarettes made you a millionaire. You got laid all weekend. I used to go to the clubs. There were thousands of hookers, very cheap. You'd go out and you'd get beer. Twenty-six cents would get beer and a dinner. Now, it costs you $20 for Kentucky Fried Chicken. The Japanese people were wonderful. When you're seventeen-years-old, it's amazing. I'd go out every weekend and get laid. Usually never with the same girl twice.

JOHN: ***Where were you stationed?***

JOEL: I didn't spend very much time in Tokyo. I spent it in Kobe and Sasebo. I mean, I really didn't do much over there except take the Colonel's daughter to her school dances. It wasn't like the Army, it was like living in a resort. Then, one

Army life.

day, I got in an argument with the Colonel. I bought one of those silk shirts with the dragons on it. After church, all of the senior officers had to have lunch with the whole unit. They all got drunk, and I got in an argument with the Colonel. He ripped my shirt.

JOHN: ***And after that?***

JOEL: After that, I volunteered for Korea and I left within an hour. I was eighteen by then, so I went into combat. I was in the 40th Infantry Division. I forget the regiment.

JOHN: ***Did you see a lot of combat?***

JOEL: There was very little combat. We had patrol actions, but we were mostly in the same place all the time. It was very cold. That was the worst part about Korea. I wasn't worried about bullets or shooting. We were freezing all the time. I spent about nine months in combat.

JOHN: ***What then?***

JOEL: I had three or four months left in the service and was assigned to be First Sergeant of this computer company that I didn't know anything about. It was a school program at Fort Monmouth, New Jersey. I just looked after the students over there. I couldn't yell at anyone, they were all studying so hard. I didn't like the job, I didn't like the company commander at the time. So, I was looking through the paper to get out of this, and I hung around the theater. I saw that they were looking for full-time staff at the post theater. I went over there and they hired me as a set designer. I didn't know anything about designing sets, but I could go to the New York Library and disappear for five days.

JOHN: ***You've said that you knew Ira Levin in those days.***

JOEL: Ira Levin was a student in my platoon. He was going to computer school. He had just finished a book called ***A Kiss before Dying***. He was sort of a celebrity there, getting a lot of time off. I have a funny story about Ira. I went to New York on leave once and this guy that I knew from high school was with me. He was in the Air Force. He said, "Where are you going?" I said, "I'm going to the movies." He said, "I'm going to take out two actresses. Maybe you should come along." I was a young guy, so I went with him. We went to this apartment on the west side. At the time around seven girls lived there. Two of the girls were the Seitz twins. They were in a play called ***Ondine*** with Audrey Hepburn and Mel Ferrer. I went over and we had lunch. I started going out with one of the twins for coffee. She said, "Come over some day and meet us backstage." Well, I was in my uniform when I went back to see them. Audrey Hepburn came over to me. She said, "Oh, you're a soldier." I told Audrey and Mel war stories and they took me out to dinner.

So one day at Fort Monmouth, Ira Levin said, "I'm going in for a press conference for my book. What are you doing?" I told him that Audrey Hepburn invited me to dinner. He said, "You know Audrey Hepburn and Mel Ferrer?" I said, "Yes." I took him over one evening and introduced him around. I think he dated one of the Seitz twins after that.

That inspired me, to some degree, to get into the theater. I never really designed any sets or anything. I knew that I had to get out of the army before anybody caught up to me. They said, "If you sign up for college, you'll get out." So, I signed up for a number of colleges. I think I got into Yale, but I couldn't afford it. Anyway, I attended the American Academy of Dramatic Arts, for lack of anything else to do.

JOHN: ***Who did you study with?***

JOEL: Gina Rowlands was in my class. John Cassavetes had graduated, but he'd wait for her all the time. His father had a travel agency on Eighth Avenue; he'd call me and we'd have coffee. The other guy in my class was really big on Broadway. He's dead now. I can't remember his name. He was doing ***Camelot*** on Broadway. He did a lot of Broadway shows.

JOHN: ***You were studying acting?***

JOEL: Yes. I was in a number of Off-Broadway productions and in a couple of things with television. Actually, I got a lot of calls from people. I never followed up, I was sort of lackadaisical. Who knows, I could have been the Brad Pitt of my day. Then, I started messing around. I went up to the Paramount Building on 1501 Broadway and a guy offered me a job. I'd do their work on the switchboard. At that time, they had a lot of big shots. They had Debbie Reynolds, Gig Young, and Bob Hope. I got to meet all these celebrities.

Then, I went over to MGM and did some publicity work there. I was working for Si Seadler and Howard Dietz, writing captions on the back of pictures. One day, Si Seadler said, "Go over to the Warwick Hotel and pick up Elizabeth Taylor. Take her over to Hicks for lunch." I almost died.

JOHN: ***What was Hicks?***

JOEL: Hicks was a famous coffee shop in New York. It was like a restaurant with a fancy ice cream parlor. That's all gone now. MGM used to take a lot of people there. So I went there with Elizabeth Taylor to meet up with Earl Wilson. He was going to interview her.

JOHN: ***What was he like?***

JOEL: He was very gruff. He couldn't carry on a conversation. He had a distinct lack of personality. Anyway, Si gave me $50 and I went to the hotel. Liz said, "Come upstairs," and I was shaking. I thought, "No, I'd better not."

I sat down with them at Hicks and looked at the prices for lunch and said, "Oh my God." I didn't order anything. After Liz finished the interview, she wanted to do something. I said, "I've got to take you back to the hotel."

I got back to MGM and said, "Si, can I go eat lunch?" He said, "Why didn't you eat lunch there?" I said, "I couldn't afford it." I didn't realize at the time that he had given me expense money. Then he asked me how things went. I said, "She gave me a lot of trouble, but I got her back to her room." He said, "You were supposed to do *whatever* Elizabeth Taylor wanted you to do!" So I got a reputation as the guy who told Elizabeth Taylor to go home. I was young and stupid.

After that, when any starlet came up, they called me to pick them up at the Warwick Hotel. The girls would all say, "Get your ass up here!" You weren't going to reject them.

So I met a lot of people. I can't even remember all of them. I had a great job. Everybody was telling me to come out to Hollywood. But all the girls came to New York, and I was one of the only young guys there.

JOHN: ***How old were you then?***

JOEL: I was a year younger than Elizabeth Taylor. Twenty-two, twenty-three. The same age as Debbie Reynolds.

JOHN: ***Where was the MGM building?***

JOEL: It was at 1540 Broadway. The building is gone now.

JOHN: ***Where else did you work?***

JOEL: I worked for 20th Century Fox for a while. That's now John Jay College. In the old days, I knew around fifteen people in different offices. If I walked down to 42nd Street, I would stop and see three or four people.

JOHN: ***What exactly was your job when you were doing promotion?***

JOEL: I wrote stories and created nonsense about people. I'd submit stuff to the columnists. I'd take celebrities to the clubs. Sometimes, for MGM, I'd take people out just to get them off their nerves. I worked at the office that did publicity for the Copacabana, so I was there for opening night a lot. I saw Nat King Cole, Sammy Davis, Jr., and Johnny Mathis. Jackie Mason used to get up and say, "The women can't live without me. I'm sure that woman over there wants to come up to my dressing room!" All the gangsters used to hang out there. Little Augie Pisano used to be there every opening night. The lounge was full of gangsters.

JOHN: ***What were they like?***

JOEL: They were very gentle people. They'd say, "I love you kid. You see this ring? I can take your eye out with one punch." They all talked like that. But after I left MGM, I got into advertising and sort of drifted away from the film business. I started producing some Off-Broadway shows by accident.

JOHN: ***Any particular titles that you remember?***

JOEL: Oh, the first one was ***Triple Play*** by Randolph Carter. He just died, he was about 100-years-old. We had some names in that. Matthew Cowles was in it, he was just a kid. That was at the Cherry Lane Theater. Then, I produced ***The End of All Things Natural***, which a friend of mine wrote. But I was involved in a lot of productions. I worked, in one capacity or another,

Barbra Streisand and Joel M. Reed in the Village.

on plays like ***Oh, What a Lovely War***. Sometimes, I worked backstage, pulling the curtain. At the Biltmore Theater, we had two plays. ***Barefoot in the Park*** with Robert Redford and Elizabeth Ashley and ***Take Her, She's Mine*** with Art Carney. So, I was hanging around and doing things on Broadway. Do you know who Susan Tyrell is? I remember her when she was only fifteen-years-old. We played strip poker with her one night at somebody's apartment. She was about fourteen or fifteen. She lost her pantyhose and started crying. It was so funny, when you see the parts she plays now. She was a little innocent girl from Connecticut. I know she hangs out at one place down here. I haven't seen her since she was a little girl. Actually, I met her through Art Carney. He was in a play with her, she was one of his daughters in the production. She used to waitress at the Improv. The other waitress that she was working with was Karen Black. She was very snotty. She was going to the American Academy of Dramatic Arts. But, I saw Susan in a movie recently and she's an old grandmother.

JOHN: ***Who else did you run around with back then?***

JOEL: I was friendly with Barbra Streisand when she was doing ***I Can Get It for You Wholesale***. She was hanging around with Elliott Gould. I got friendly with Marty Erlichman, who was her manager. We used to meet for dinner at the Howard Johnson's on Eighth Avenue and 50th Street. They liked to go out for ice cream after the show. I lost touch with Barbra. I never had any business relationship with her, but she was a pleasant enough actress. She was about nineteen when I met her. That was her first big show. I was in touch with Marty for a long time. He wanted to know if I wanted to work with him to promote Barbra. I didn't think much of it. I knew she had a great voice, but what did I know?

JOHN: ***Anyone else?***

JOEL: Actually, one night many years ago, this guy said, "I have a date with two little French girls. Do you want to come out? I'll pick up the tab." I said, "OK." We took out these girls. We went over to the east side. I took them to a party. We took them home and I realized that I'd been out with Catherine Deneuve and her sister Françoise. They were about sixteen or seventeen.

And then one day, I was sitting in a coffee shop on the corner and a whole bunch of dyke looking girls came in. One of them had on about twelve sweaters. She sat next to me and was talking French. She got stuck with the check and she showed it to me. I said, "You're from France." She said, "*Je ne parle pas anglais.*" I said, "What's your name?" I was reading a copy of ***Time*** and she kept pointing to the cover. I looked at the cover and it was Maria Schneider. They had just done ***Last Tango in Paris***. I met with her a couple of times.

I guess, for ten or fifteen years, I was just hanging around in nightclubs. Life was too easy. You didn't have to do very much to survive. At that time, I couldn't help it. I'd go to Europe, and then have to call somebody because I didn't have the fare to get back.

JOHN: ***Where did you go in Europe?***

JOEL: Oh, I went to London a lot. Not for business, I was just messing around. Much later, I went over there for meetings. A play of mine was supposed to be done there. Simon Williams wanted to do it. Nothing ever happened. I wasn't very aggressive. Like I said, I had a lot of offers to go to California in the early days and I didn't do it. MGM wanted me to go.

JOHN: ***Who were some of the big names at MGM?***

JOEL: I was there just after Louis B. Mayor got kicked out. Howard Deitz was the vice president. I think, at the time, they did ***Guys and Dolls***. The guy who got me into MGM was Halsey Raines. He was the publicist there. Jerry Bick was working with me. He married the girl who played the nurse in ***One Flew over the Cuckoo's Nest***. He became a big producer. But he was just a copywriter at MGM. Those were the dying throes of the big studios, when Darryl Zanuck was still around. He was always looking for young girls. He was pretty short; you could spot him six blocks down walking down the street. But Si Seadler was like a grandmotherly-like guy. I assumed that he was gay. He lived down the street. Howard Dietz was very businesslike. I saw Si years later, he lived right on 57th street.

In the late '50s and early '60s, the movie companies almost went broke. That was the time when they stopped with the contract players. They let everybody go. I remember doing some stuff for 20th Century Fox. They had ***Cleopatra*** coming out and everybody was going broke.

JOHN: ***What was a typical night like back then?***

JOEL: There used to be a whole nightclub thing that doesn't exist anymore. When I was a kid, we'd have five or six places to go a night. We'd go to the Copacabana and then to the Stork Club, the Harwyn, El Morocco. We'd wind down at about four in the morning. We couldn't afford to eat at any of those places; we'd stay for one or two drinks and then move on. We'd get hamburgers at P. J. Clarke's.

I used to hang around with a bunch of girls from the Russian Tea Room. I haven't got them all right, but I think one was Diane Ladd and another was Susan Oliver. They were friends of Tammy Allen, who was an actress. She did a lot of plays. They used to tell me all of their problems. Now, they're all playing grandmothers. Susan Oliver died. She did some major movies.

JOHN: ***What was the Russian Tea Room like?***

JOEL: The Russian Tea Room is where all of the power people hung out. We used to go there on Fridays because the drinks were about sixteen cents. They're going to re-open it; it's been empty for five years. Sam Cohen and all of the agents were there. But it's been closed for years. My friend introduced me to Sid, the owner of the place. He died; his wife owns the place now. But it was originally a restaurant-type coffee shop. They had mooncake and caviar. It was fairly inexpensive, then it got to be one of the most expensive places in New York.

I used to hang around at a place called Downey's where I met Marilyn Monroe and Kim Novak. I sat with Marilyn for about two hours. I didn't know it was her. Eddie Bracken and I went over to sit down with Eli Wallach. He was with this girl with this scarf wrapped around her head. She was telling Eddie about the time her car was stuck at the bottom of a hill. Eddie whispered to me, "I'm leaving, this girl's nuts!" Just then, a waiter came over and said, "I'd like your autograph, Miss Monroe." Eddie hadn't recognized her. She was talking about when they were in ***We're Not Married***. Marilyn was very plain, you would never recognize her in person. Every time I saw her, I never took a second look.

JOHN: ***We're at Sardi's now. This was a popular place.***

JOEL: I first came here when I was in the army. It was New Years Eve, 1953. I was still in my uniform. The guys I was with were afraid to go in. It was too ritzy for them. I went in and had a nice New Year's Eve. Everybody bought me drinks at the bar. There were a few Broadway people there who picked up my tab. I didn't spend anything. I looked very young. The first thing somebody told me is that if you go into sleazy bars, they won't let you drink. In a ritzy place, they won't ask for your ID. I've discovered this to be true, wherever you go in the world. I tried to get a drink in a bar in Seattle on my way to Korea and no one would serve me.

Sardi's didn't have this upstairs bar then. A guy named George Repp used to hang around down there. You had to buy him a drink. I used to hesitate, because he'd make such an asshole of himself. He'd start foaming at the mouth, like it was his God given right for a free drink.

JOHN: ***What was his story?***

JOEL: He was one of the characters at the downstairs bar who always thought people owed him a drink. It sort of became kind of a tradition like putting money in a collection box. You went to the bar at Sardi's and bought him a drink. I assume he was very poor, or had no income. I learned later that his brother was an actor on Broadway and was a millionaire. He was somewhat supporting Repp. Repp lived in a furnished room, I think on 86th and Broadway. He either lived on social security or was a part-time hotel clerk. The sad part of the story is that Repp died a week before his older brother and his brother left him a couple million dollars. That did him no good, he was gone already. But he was one of the outstanding characters here.

That's when a lot of people hung out here. There were so many people coming here, I couldn't even start to name them. James Barton, who was getting into his 80s, used to come here. I met him here. All of that's gone now. I did see Natalie Portman here recently. So, some people still show up. There's a bunch of nice chorus girls that hang around. I don't know where the celebrities go any more. The Bowery Bar, I guess. You can't drink there unless you're over sixteen. A lot of underage drinking goes on over there.

JOHN: ***When did these places become exclusive?***

JOEL: Exclusive? Well, I guess in the '50s and '60s. It all sort of disappeared with the coming of the hippies. Downey's closed. P. J. Clarke's was a very exclusive bar on 55th Street. During the week, the place would be packed. I went in there a little while ago and they said, "Oh, God. You're back!" I said, "Do any celebrities come in here?" They said, "Yeah, you just walked in. You're the first one in five years."

I used to like the 21 Club. There was Elaine's. I got into a fight there and they wouldn't let me in for years. But the Stork Club and El Morocco have been closed for years. Near the end, all you needed to get in was a clean suit.

In those places, there was a shortage of young guys. All of these old men were in there with the young girls. So it was pretty easy to meet someone. They had places like that in Hollywood as well. But I don't know where everybody goes now. Maxie's, over here on Seventh Avenue, has some sort of an older crowd. I go over there now and nobody hits on me except these seventy-five year old ladies who want to go to Europe. "Will you take care of my dog?" It would be nice if that's all they had in mind. I was talking to some woman on my block. My friend said, "She has MILLIONS!" She invited me up to dinner and put her hand on my leg. I almost jumped out of the penthouse. She was my age.

JOHN: ***Have you had any luck with anyone a little younger?***

JOEL: I'll tell you my most recent incident. Last year I was in Barnes and Noble. I saw a cute little blonde girl there. I said, "What book are you reading?" She said, "Oh, that's my school book. I go to John Jay." I said, "That's the criminal college." She said, "Yeah, I'm a cop."

So, I was at Virgin Records about a week and a half ago. They have that coffee place downstairs that I like to go to. A cute little Spanish girl was sitting there. I started talking to her and asked her if she went to college. Of course, she goes to John Jay. She was a patrolman. The last two girls I hit on on the street were cops. I guess I'll have to stop hitting on little schoolgirls. Two in a row and two cops. I'm getting to be an old guy. I was reading this article about this guy who was trying to get an interview with D. W. Griffith. Griffith refused to see anybody. Nobody could talk to him for ten years. This film student wanted to do his thesis on him. He said, "I tried to see him. I banged on the door and he wouldn't come out of his room. There was no answer." Somebody told him to take a sixteen-year-old girl to his door and have her knock, but to be real quick because he would pull the girl in and slam the door in his face. The guy tried that. And he got his interview. Maybe I'll be like that [laughs]. I used to get stooped on the street all the time, girls saying, "You must go to the same school as me." That was only about twenty years ago.

JOHN: ***What kind of girls were you dating back in the '50s?***

JOEL: I invited my friend to a birthday party for Marilyn Monroe that I'd been invited to. I brought a girl named Yvonne Craig. It caused quite a riot because she was so cute. Everybody was jumping on her.

JOHN: ***Yvonne Craig?***

JOEL: You know, she was Batgirl on the ***Batman*** TV show. She went to the coast and was discovered by Bing Crosby and the guy who made ***The Young Land***. Bing Crosby met her in LA and was so enamored with her that he put her in ***High Time***. They didn't have a part in the script for her, so they just put her in some scenes. She was the college newspaper editor and she'd run over and say, "Can I have the rest of the story now?" Anyway, she was a nice young girl.

JOHN: ***Anyone else?***

JOEL: I knew a very beautiful girl who once told me that she was gang-raped. She was arrested for kidnapping and murder. She and her bull-dyke friend kidnapped some kid that was madly in love with her in upstate New York. They tied him up and they gagged him too tight. They killed him. They sent out a ransom note to his parents. Of course, they were caught. She spent around fifty years in the can. It was all over the papers. I guess since she was a bull-dyke she was happy in prison. She was a very bitter girl, from what I

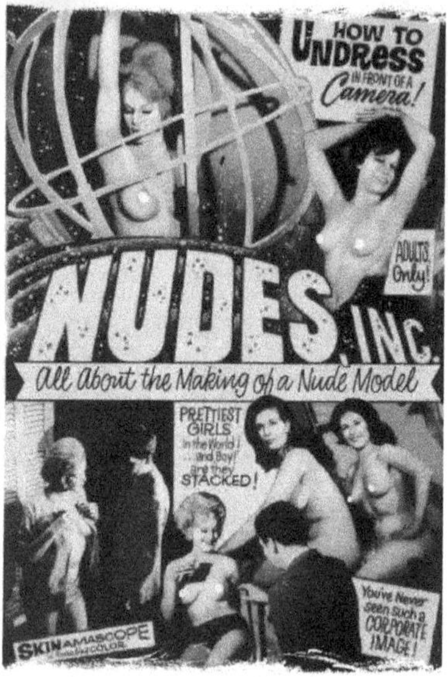

remember. Fortunately, I didn't have a lot of money. She didn't want to have much to do with me.

JOHN: ***I imagine living in New York for your entire life has proved useful for running into some strange characters.***

JOEL: Well, Times Square was a playground. The block I'm on had a lot of whorehouses when I was a kid. Fifty-eighth Street. In the '50s and early '60s, my building had a lot of brothels in it. And in the '70s and early '80s the block was loaded with hookers.

JOHN: ***In the sexploitation days, the industry seemed to be making softcore films like no tomorrow. You were right there in the hub of it all.***

JOEL: Well, those were the softcore days. Some people like Doris Wishman did a whole lot of work. This was about the time when Barry Mahon was the king. He was a great anti-semite. He'd say, "We have to work for these fucking Jews! They put their hands on everything!" But I don't see how he made another movie after ***Nudes, Inc***. That was pretty awful. They had a girl who would come in on an interview to be a model. She'd take her top off, you'd get a quick shot, and they'd bring in another girl. That was the whole movie.

JOHN: ***Well, it drew the people in.***

JOEL: They played them on 42nd Street. I met Barry and he told me to see ***Nudes, Inc***. I went down to the Brandt Theater on 42nd Street. That was the only theater that would play that kind of picture. I went over and the marquee said ***Nudes, Inc***. There were all these pictures in the windows of young models being preyed upon in New York. I went in and sat down and watched some stupid foreign movie with a long shot of this girl's ass. That's all they showed. Then they played some other movie. I went to the manager and asked, "Where's ***Nudes, Inc***?" He said, "The print ripped. You saw a tit, what are you complaining about? Who the hell comes in here to see a specific picture?" Barry laughed about it. He said, "They paid me for my movie, and it's not even playing there!"

JOHN: ***What kind of a crowd did you have to mingle with?***

JOEL: I don't know. Probably dirty old men, but the films weren't very erotic. They were really very boring. I guess tourists would go in to see them. That was just before ***I Am Curious (yellow)***. Barry did ***Cuban Rebel Girls***. I know I met Errol Flynn at the time. He was pretty much a mess. I was at a party at Lorin Price's house and Barry walked in with Errol Flynn. He was shot all to hell. This girl walked in with her friend who was Arthur Godfrey's mistress. Her friend said, "Motherfucking shit! Errol Flynn! I fucked you when I was thirteen-years-old. You've got the smallest dick in the world." He got up, all embarrassed, and ran out. She said, "It's true, you motherfucker!" Then she said, "Everybody take your dicks out! Errol Flynn's got the smallest dick in the world!" It may be true, I don't know. But, I think I saw an obituary for Barry Mahon. He was living up on the west side.

JOHN: ***What other people do you remember from back then?***

JOEL: Jerry Denby. He made some porn pictures. He was a stuck up guy. My friend Marvin Farkas's brother backed him and went broke. I used to hang around with this guy who was 100-years-old in 1956. He used to tell me stories about 1895. He had an artificial nose. He said he got it cut off in a duel.

JOHN: ***Now wait a minute—***

JOEL: I remember hanging around with John Wilkes Booth. I'd say, "John, you'd better stop carrying that gun around." He'd say, "I need it for personal protection." I'd say, "John, you'll blow it off the top one of these days! Lay off the opium!"

"Fade in, fade out . . ."—Vernon Becker

CHAPTER TWO

VERNON BECKER

It was a few months before I saw Joel again. We kept in touch between visits, his ideas for future projects bordering on the surreal:

"I think that the market is ready for another **Mondo Cane,** *but not one of S&M clubs and strange Off-Broadway shows. But the truly wacko that range from green card slaves to would-be filmmakers of all sorts, including Bill Landis and some never approachable subjects as the Man/Boy Love Association and New York necrophiliacs. I have some people interested and somewhat committed—mostly crews. I think financing is at hand. Strangely enough, I see a great market in Germany, as they really go for the off-kilter stuff."*

Finally, in May of 1999, I found a round trip ticket to New Jersey for a very good price. "Let's go see Joel," I said. Brian laughed. "Why not?" He booked the flight, and before we knew it, we were headed back to the city.

The airport in Newark was packed tight. We picked up our bags and walked out into the night. A quick bus trip to Penn Station was all that stood between us and Manhattan. We caught the first bus we could find, checked into the New Yorker on 34th and Seventh, and headed for the bars.

We wound up in the Molly Wee Pub. I'd been there a year before. I had fond memories of annoying the staff and patrons by playing Elton John's "Goodbye, English Rose" ten times in a row on the jukebox. An angry bartender eventually had to reset it, but not before screaming at me, "This isn't funny!"

The Molly Wee wasn't very

The Molly Wee Pub. Nightshift at the thrill factory.

crowded when we arrived. The only people inside were sitting on the far left of the bar. An older man, well on his way to a terrible hangover, had a young blonde cornered against the wall. He kept telling her, "You're just a tease!" He walked over to the jukebox and slid in a five. The Animals' "House of the Rising Sun" began to play. Drink in hand, he serenaded his captive with a crude rendition of the lyrics.

"There is a man. In New Orleans. He called the rising sun."

The blonde got up on a table and began to dance. She moved her hips up and down, inches from her charge's nose. I went up to the bar and ordered them both a shot of whiskey. The bartender automatically poured one for me as well. And then one for himself.

We drank at the Molly Wee until 1:30 AM. The plan was to meet up with Joel on Saturday afternoon, and we wanted to be well-rested. We left our tips on the counter and we headed toward the door. The old man was singing to the bartender. The blonde had left hours ago. A few blocks down to the New Yorker. Then sleep.

We gave Joel a call on Saturday afternoon. I wanted to meet at Sardi's so I could talk to Joe again. Joel had other ideas.

JOEL REED: *Joe hates me. He always says, "You're just like Lorin Price. Always trying to get money from old women." Besides, I can't go out.*

Joel didn't want to drink anything. "Why don't you guys just come over to my place at six?" There was time to kill, it was only a little after four. We decided to get in an early dinner. Down a few blocks and over to a pizza place. A cafeteria-style pizza place. I knew it was a mistake as soon as we walked in. Salsa music was blaring from the radio. Several disfigured pizzas were lined up in crooked rows, baking and rotting under circular heat lamps. They looked like the earliest form of spontaneous generation. The guy in front of me got ahold of the last of anything that looked edible. I decided to brave two slices with sausage. A dirty hand slapped half of the pizza in front of me onto my tray and pointed to the cash register. I picked up a Heineken, paid, and made my way upstairs. Brian followed.

"Maybe we should get some beer for ourselves and bring it to Joel's."

An idea, I thought. "We'll see how things go."

We took a seat at a table. I looked at my food. Free from the light of the heat lamp, it looked even worse. The cheese had hardened and the sausage dripped grease onto my hands. I took a bite, shook my head in disgust, and went downstairs to get another beer. I'd need it.

We were at a table facing the men's room. People walked in on a regular basis and came out with the look of pure terror on their faces. Apparently, someone had made quite a mess in there. Another quick swallow of beer. We ate quickly and were back on the streets by

68th & Broadway: On the way to Joel's.

5:30. It was sixteen blocks to Joel's apartment. We decided to walk rather than pay for a cab.

VERNON BECKER: *Have him tell you the story of how he got into that apartment. He used to live in Times Square, and they started to tear down the old buildings. They just about tore down half of Joel's building, and he was still living there. He wouldn't move. It was crazy, you'd go to visit Joel, and he was the only one left. He cut a deal with the city for them to give him the place he's at now for an incredibly low rate.*

We started walking up Broadway, counting the blocks as we passed them. We had it timed right; at six o'clock, we were standing in front of the brown brick building that Joel M. Reed had lived in for over thirty years. We walked up to the door and scanned the list of names. Four slots down was J. Reed, in room 8-B. I hit the buzzer.

"Hello."

"Hi Joel, this is John."

The door snapped open and we walked in. Down the hall, through another doorway, and past a vacant desk. I looked at the numbers on the doors. 8-B would be on the eighth floor, so I pressed the button on the elevator. Nothing happened. We waited a while and then I pressed the button again. It didn't seem to be working. I decided to look for the stairs. A door at the end of the hall was slightly ajar, so I opened it. A middle-aged woman was hunched over a bed, folding clothes.

"Do you know how I can get to 8-B?"

She stared at me, slightly startled. "End of hall." Her English was poor, she didn't understand what I was asking.

"No, that's 1-B. I have to get to the eighth floor. Are there stairs somewhere around here?"

"End of hall." She walked out of her room and led me to the room closest to the front door. She pointed at the door and smiled. "Room B." Then she went back to her clothes.

Brian looked at the door and shrugged. "That can't be right." He walked over to the elevator and wrenched open the door. The small light by the arrow button lit up. He held it open and we walked inside. Pushed the button marked 8 and waited.

We started going up, pausing for a moment at the sixth floor. I thought

The posters in Joel's apartment

of Henry Spencer's elevator ride in ***Eraserhead***. We got moving again and stopped at 8. Brian slid open the door and we walked out into the hall. 8-B was straight ahead. We walked over to the door and knocked. A few seconds passed before Joel answered. The door swung open and he popped his head out.

"Come on in."

Joel was dressed in a faded denim shirt, unbuttoned and untucked. His jeans were slightly darker and rolled up around his ankles. He was wearing socks and slippers and a felt fedora. As we walked inside his apartment, I noticed the smell of pipe tobacco.

The apartment was small and cluttered. And a virtual shrine to Joel's world. A quick look at the walls revealed framed posters for all of his films. The poster for ***Blood Bath*** caught my eye. Apparently, it had once played a double bill with ***Feast of Flesh***. Next to the one sheet for ***Night of the Zombies*** hung a small bill for something called ***Barry Moses' Bar Mitzvah***.

On the opposite wall were framed pictures of Joel in every get-up imaginable. On the set of ***Wit's End*** with producer Marvin Farkas. Fly fishing somewhere up north. Dressed in a karate outfit, poised to kill. Looking out on the water alongside a suspension bridge.

"They took that one when I was in California a couple of years ago."

Joel walked over to his chair and began to sit down. Then, he sprang back up. "You have to see what

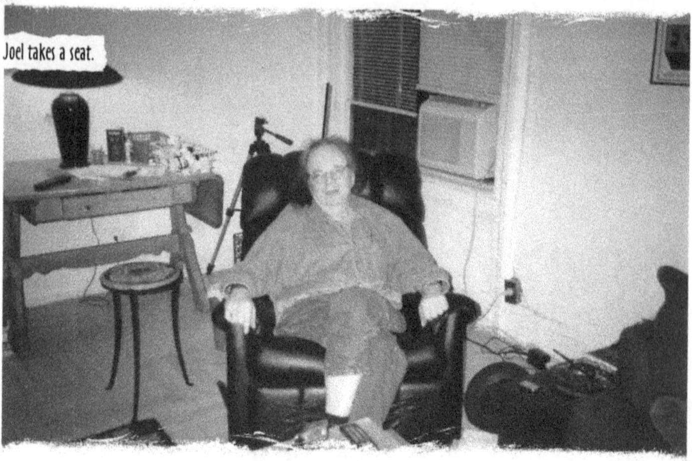

Joel takes a seat.

happened to my bathroom."

We followed Joel down the hall. "A few weeks ago, I was sitting at my computer thinking, 'I had no idea that it was supposed to rain.' I was in here for hours and finally got up to take a piss."

Joel opened the door to his bathroom and we walked inside. The ceiling was a mess of peeling paint and blistered plaster. "Water was leaking from the pipes up there. The contractors at this place are full of shit. It's really going down." We walked back down the hall. "There's my new bed."

I noticed a caricature of Joel hanging on the wall.

"That was done in the '50s by Joe Kaliff. He did a lot of caricatures for Broadway people. He had an office on 47th Street and Broadway. That was a fixture. I used to go up there, the door was always open. It was a big, empty, dirty office. Joe would sit there and draw. He was pretty well known for his work. He was a Lebanese Christian. Danny Thomas used to hang out with him at the bar

and get drunk."

A quick walk down the hall and back to the sitting room. Joel took off his hat and settled in.

JOEL REED: *Darryl Zanuck was hanging around, he used to come into this building. He used to have a woman providing him with girls downstairs. He'd be walking around with these eight-foot tall girls. You can talk to my friend Eddie Jaffe one day if you really want background on Broadway. He's ninety-some-years-old. He'll tell you about the early days. He was roommates with Marlon Brando and all of those people. He had an apartment on 47th Street. The door was never locked and he sometimes had twelve people sleeping there that he didn't even know. I stayed there for a while. People were stacked up to the windows in there. There was this guy who used to come in and take a shower. He'd eat and everything. One day, Eddie said, "Who's that guy?" I said, "I don't know, isn't he your friend?" Eddie didn't know him. He was a complete stranger.*

I hung around with Arlene Sue Farber, the star of those Jerry Gross pictures. I met her through a guy named Joe Russell. One day, Joe said, "I have these two wonderful girls here and they want to meet you. Why don't you come by my apartment?" I went over to get the girls. They said, "Shit, he locked us in." I said, "What do you mean he locked you in?" They said, "We were waiting to come over to your apartment. Vernon Becker said we should stop by. Then Joe grabbed us and said you were going to meet us at his apartment. Then he locked the door. We thought we were going to get murdered." That was Arlene Sue Farber and her friend from Queens. I said to her, "Can I fuck you?" She said, "No, I'm going with Jerry Gross. I'll talk to one of my friends." So she brought her friend over one night. Jerry was about three feet tall and she was about three feet nine. They were a good match. She played the lead in ***Female Animal****. She also played the lead in* ***Girl on a Chain Gang****. I think that film is the funniest picture in the world. It's so bad. They shot it on Long Island. Half the cast sounds like they're from Harvard, the rest have these terrible Brooklyn accents and they're trying to sound like southerners. "I really like black guys, you all." The judge has this Yiddish accent and he's saying, "De black boy iz sleeping wit dis local girl." They're running through Long Island and this truck pulls up. "I've got the hound dogs, man." They let out these*

Joel with some kind of weapon.

French Poodles. I was talking to Nick Demetrolus, Jerry's partner at the time. He said, "We did **not** *have a French Poodle!" He was really defending it. And the movie ends with that classic twist, there just happens to be an FBI agent hanging around.*

But they made **Sweet Sweetback's Baadasssss Song**. *Then Jerry went bust. Nick Demetrolus made out. He sold out Jerry Gross. He made a lot of money; of course the company was totally useless by that time.*

But those were the days. Vernon can tell you stories, he was always hanging around with those kinds of people. He did **Dagmar's Hot Pants, Inc.** *and* **A Man with a Maid**. *The last thing he did was* **Zipperface**. *He produced it and Mansour Pourmand directed it. Pourmand fucked the picture up. He didn't shoot any sex scenes. He'd say, "She took her clothes off, that's too much!" I saw* **Zipperface** *one night at one in the morning. The only decent shots were done by the second unit guy. Car chases and things. It's a fucking awful picture. Vernon got around $200 a week for it. Actually, HBO wanted to buy it, but Mansour wouldn't do it. He wanted ten billion dollars or something. It was released on video.*

Vernon introduced me to Mansour Pourmand around five years ago. He gave me $10,000 to do a play. That was **Barry Moses' Bar Mitzvah**. *The guy came up to me and said, "I was the Steven Spielberg of Iran! Everybody knew me on the street, I won at all the film festivals. Now we do this play! We have three murders, one rape!" I said,*

"You're doing a comedy about a bar mitzvah." He said. "No, in Iran they like rape and murder! You've got too many kids, get rid of the kids!" He opened it up on a Jewish holiday.

I don't even remember how the thing ended up. Mansour wouldn't let me see it. The original story had this thirteen-year-old kid who was trying to make out with this girl. He asks her if she wants to come up to his room to see his Nintendo. She says, "Yes," and he practically pisses in his pants. But that's how I got involved with that guy, through Vernon.

Vernon had a lot of litigation going with Walter Reade. He had the policy of not paying anyone anything. Someone told me that Walter said, "Your picture is doing terrible. I can't get any play dates on it." The guy was driving around and saw his movie at a big drive-in. Walter said, "Oh, they're stealing from me again! They're playing your picture and they don't tell me about it!"

Vernon was involved with people like that. He did one picture called **Dagmar's Hot Pants, Inc***. If I recall correctly, it's about these hookers in Sweden that work on motor scooters or something. It's episodic. They'll go up to this one guy and he'll say, "Take your clothes off," as he then puts them on. It's that old gag, he runs away with their clothes on. Vernon said, "Oh, I don't have an actor to play the lead," so I walked over to this bar where Robert Strauss worked. He was grateful to have a part after all those years of nothing. That was an AIP picture. Vernon talked them into giving him a deal, but after they saw that…*

Then he made **A Man with a Maid***. It had 3D dildos coming at the camera. That's about the only action in the picture. Nothing happens. These girls get undressed and this guy picks up a dildo and points it at the camera.*

One of Vernon's backers came up to me. He'd seen **Blood Sucking Freaks***. He was laughing and he asked me if I really spent $70,000 on it. I asked him, "Haven't you ever seen any of Vernon's pictures?" Have you seen* **A Man with a Maid***? It's all in reverse shots. It looks like it was shot in one day. In one room. Vernon told me, "Well, we had to find this castle. The location was unbelievable!" You watch the movie, and he could have done it with a postcard. And it cost him a lot of money. But those were the old days. Give Vernon a call. He's pretty near dead; he's had three major heart attacks and weighs about 800 pounds. He bought eight pictures and put porn footage into them. It bankrupted him.*

I said, "What do you want to do that for? Everyone wants porn films, not some boring movie with ten shots of action." But you'd better catch Vernon while you can. He'll talk for hours about his pictures.

I talked to Vernon Becker on June 1, 1999. Still alive and kicking in Los Angeles, Vernon talked in length about the early days of New York television, working with Joe Sarno, and of course, about his friend of thirty years, Joel M. Reed.

JOHN: ***You started your career as a writer for television.***

VERNON: I started out as a comedy writer for television, a sketch writer. After a while, I became a television director.

JOHN: ***What year was this?***

VERNON: I refuse to give the year (laughs). In fact, it's so far back, I don't even remember. Except that the studio was lit by men carrying torches. It was the early days of television, I was still in my early twenties.

JOHN: ***What were you working on?***

VERNON: I was a director and a producer of a wide variety of shows; children's shows, quiz shows, circus variety shows, comedy shows with Jerry Lester. Not the original ***Broadway Open House***, though. This was for the ABC network. I did a dramatic show called ***Solo Drama***, which was done with one subjective camera. I did about everything until TV left me and went to California. There was no more live television coming from the networks.

JOHN: ***What did you do when that happened?***

VERNON: I eventually got involved with television again through writing and editing in film. Writing, editing, and eventually directing and producing low budget films. They were mostly documentaries. In the midst of this, I got involved with the first UHF station in New York. I think it was channel 27. That was all put on live. So I went back again to directing everything from the news to gospel programs—everything. All live, the whole time. And then I got back into doing feature documentaries.

JOHN: ***One of which was The Funniest Man in the World.***

VERNON: Yes. That's the most famous one. It was a feature on the life of Charles Chaplin. It was distributed worldwide by MGM. I also did ***The Flame and***

the Fire, which was distributed by Continental Films. That was Walter Reade's company in the United States, but MGM did it worldwide. I did a lot of films that were internationally distributed by MGM. I did one on the great stone face, Buster Keaton. Eventually, I wrote a comedy that Sam Arkoff at AIP liked and I ended up writing, producing, and directing it. It was pretty successful, I still get royalties from it.

JOHN: *Which film was this?*

VERNON: *Dagmar's Hot Pants, Inc*. I did that in Europe. I went to Europe the first time to do an adaptation of a Hans Christian Andersen story. I called it ***The Beggar Prince***. The original title was ***The Swine Herd***, which really doesn't have that magic ring. I did that with Burl Ives who played a traveling minstrel. The rest of the actors were Danish. We shot that on location with all of the castles and everything. So that got me to Europe. I got to do a number of films over there including a 3D film which had almost as many titles as there were shots. Then I came back to the States and worked for a while. I did some cabaret work over here. I never got rich, but very few

pictures, either documentary or dramatic, that I made, lost money. Except for the one thing that is always possible and that is that you're doing business with a thief.

JOHN: *How did you get hooked up with Joe Sarno?*

VERNON: Joe Sarno? Actually, I was over in Europe doing ***The Beggar Prince***. I went over to Sweden because we also imported some pictures. So I was in Sweden and I met him there. He and his wife have had an apartment in Sweden for years. I met them over there. I was in Stockholm, working on another production that I was going to do. It was the early part of June and Stockholm was pretty

empty. Everybody was away on vacation. I bumped into Joe Sarno on the street and we went into this bar to have a drink. You could only have one drink in there because they cost about $45. I had one of the trade papers with me and ***Inga*** was on the back cover. It had taken in five million dollars at the time. And Joe had written and directed it for $5,000. The whole picture cost about $100,000 to make. So he was saying "Can you imagine that?" I said, "I'll tell you what. Let's make a deal. Do you own the rights to it?" He said, "Yeah, I still have all the rights." Some company had sold the American rights to him. I said, "Therefore, you have the rights to make a sequel. I'll tell you what I'm going to do..."

We got some hotel stationary and made a deal that he would write a sequel and transfer the payment of *X* dollars to me for a picture to be called ***Inga 2***. And then he got me in touch with a guy who was a good friend of Marie Liljedahl, who played the lead. He found her for us. This was all done in a space of two hours. She agreed to be in the film. I was offering them telephone numbers, compared to what they got paid before. Marie got $2,000 and I think I was offering her $20,000. Stuff like that. What did I have to loose? If it wasn't a good idea, we wouldn't make the movie.

But I thought it was a sure thing. ***Inga*** was in the top ten in ***Variety*** every week. Everybody thought that Radley Metzger had made it, but he didn't. I think he bought it, although I might be confused with ***I, a Woman***. It's been a long time. They were both almost contemporary. Anyway, I went back and gave a small advance to Joe to write the treatment. With this, I went and got sufficient private money from a financial partner and we announced that we were going to do the film. I had a letter agreement from Marie—it wasn't a contract. She was quite busy at the time; she was making a picture in England. So I met with Joe in June and by September, we were shooting the picture. It was in color, unlike the first one, and it was sold all over the world. MGM even took it to certain markets. And I literally was in the crazy situation of having different distributors bidding against each other while we were shooting. So that's how I met Joe Sarno.

JOHN: ***How long did it take you guys to shoot Inga 2?***

VERNON: We had some trouble with the weather. The winter comes in very fast in Sweden. I think we did it in three or four weeks.

JOHN: ***What kind of a guy was Joe?***

VERNON: He was one of the nicest people I ever knew in movies. He really was a straight guy, he was a Navy fighter pilot. He shot down four Japs and was shot down himself by anti-aircraft fire in the Battle of the Philippine Sea. He was very badly injured. He did aerial films for Republic out on Long Island when they were out there before he got into sex films. He also did industrial documentaries. But he was really a great person.

JOHN: ***He cranked out a lot of films.***

VERNON: Well, it depends on what you call films. He did one for a guy who had been a vice president of a studio. I can't think of his name. Joe shot it for $10,000 or something and it made a fortune. Nobody made porno in those days. It had an R rating, or the equivalent, and it was his first big hit. These were pictures that, like in the time of Roger Corman, you made in five days. But he was paid a good percentage and he sold them all over the world. He made a lot of money out of these black and white films. And he could write. I just read his treatment for ***Inga 2*** not more than a couple of hours ago.

JOHN: *What kind of affect did hardcore porn have on his output?*

VERNON: Well, Joe got involved with a cycle of foreign sex films. When hardcore came in, he was turning them out like one a week. But I wasn't in contact with him then.

JOHN: *What else did you do with Joe?*

VERNON: I did another picture with him that we co-wrote. ***Every Afternoon***. There was this girl who was as big as Georgina Spelvin for a while. She had a part in Joel Reed's ***Career Bed***. Joe and I needed a woman to run this fantastic international whorehouse where they put on these shows. The girls come out as animals and she's the lion tamer. She always wanted to be in the theater so she puts on these shows. And she's the aunt of these two young girls whose mother and father are killed in a crash. She's bringing them up, sort of like ***Gigi***. She's training them to be great kid prostitutes. It sounds horrible, but it's actually a love story, if you can imagine. It has a great romantic ending. But this is just the background. We needed someone to play the aunt. And I called this woman, sent her the outline of the script, and she said, "I'm not doing any sex pictures anymore." That was the girl in ***Career Bed***. I'm the only one who she turned down a sex film for.

JOHN: *Who ended up playing her part?*

VERNON: Diana Dors. It really sounds worse than it is. It's a love story. During the day, when she isn't working, she dresses up as a ballerina. It was supposed to be set in Paris. She goes to this park and she meets this guy who's there every afternoon because he works nights. They tell each other lies. She's studying to be a ballerina, he flies for Air France. He really works for the ground crew. Eventually, through the course of the story, it's somebody's birthday and they guy and his friends go to the whorehouse. It's supposed to be a harem and they're selling off these slave-girls to the buyers. And the two are exposed to each other.

We wrote this thing backwards. And the last scene is in the park by the fountain. She comes to the fountain dressed in the leotards and he's dressed in his Air France jacket. They look at each other for a second and he says, "How was practice today?" She says, "Very hard. Did you fly last night?" And they just go on with their illusion. Because that's the only thing that's worthwhile in their lives. From that scene, we went back and wrote the whole story.

JOHN: *Do you have anything to say about the theaters that these films would play at?*

VERNON: The theaters weren't really my bag. I guess the key theater was the Brandt in Times Square. It was on Broadway and 42nd Street. That was the best place for an exploitation movie, at that time. Harry Brandt owned it.

For a while, I was financed by Walter Reade. He owned Cinema 1 and Cinema 2 on Third Avenue. I was involved with him; he financed and distributed some of my pictures. He had the key first-run houses in all of New York. They were the prestigious houses for European art films to open up at. Films like ***The Lavender Hill Mob***, or Felini's ***8½***.

JOHN: *When did you first meet Joel Reed?*

VERNON: I met him in 1968 at 1780 Broadway. That's where his office was. I was sent over by Irving Wormser. Joel was doing some sex film for Peppercorn-Wormser for about four dollars. When I came to see him, he was doing some promotion, some party promotion. Disco nights with costumes. He was doing happenings. Irving said, "Maybe the two of you can come up with a movie or something." So I got to know him from that.

JOHN: *Joel says that you introduced him to Joe Sarno.*

VERNON: Yeah, I guess I would have. But, you're going back thirty years (laughs). And, there was a lot of activity. He might also have said that I introduced him to Joan Collins and I might even have done that.

JOHN: *What did you think of his films?*

VERNON: Well, let's just say that Joel has a unique vision. Have you read his ***Private School Girls*** novel? You'd never believe reading that that it was written by the same guy who wrote ***Blood Sucking Freaks***. It's a very charming comedy. He is versatile; he's not just Sardu. I was on the set of ***Night of the Zombies*** for a pick-up. The film with Jamie Gillis. A guy's throat was being cut and they had to have the blood gushing out. They had to set up the whole stunt with the false neck. I kept saying, "Forget it, just have him cut his throat, it's cheaper!"

JOHN: ***Is there a reason that you never worked on a film with Joel?***

VERNON: Well, I was quite busy myself. Our schedules were different. I would be back in New York, and he'd be in Hong Kong. Or I'd be over in Sweden and he'd be making something in New York. I mean, those are the only two instances where I was on the set of Joel's own films. I had to be in town when he was doing something. There were some strange people that he's known. There was an awful lot that he told me about, like when he went to Singapore to make that movie [***Wit's End***]. Different funny stories about when he was trying to make that picture for four cents. But we both had busy careers and were in different places.

JOHN: ***Joel's had an unbelievable life.***

VERNON: The strange thing about Joel is that he has a way of cutting through and connecting with upper class people, or people who you would never think he would connect with. You know what I mean? Weather it was because he was a press agent, or what, he can make contact with the most interesting people. It's strange. It's like E.T. hanging around them or something.

JOHN: ***He knew a lot of the old theater people.***

VERNON: At a young age, Joel would befriend people who were a lot older than him. One guy was a PR man who showed Joel the cot that Marlon Brando lived on until he got a job. The guy used to work for Howard Hughes. If he's still alive, he's in his nineties. The guy is like forty-years-older than Joel and they were very good friends. There was another guy, a press agent who was still living in the same rent controlled apartment that he was born in, ninety-some years ago.

JOHN: ***To counter that, he also likes young girls.***

VERNON: He likes them. But, in thirty years, I've never seen him with a young girl. But he loves them, he writes stories about them. I thought the book he wrote about the girls of St. Martha would have made a very charming movie. It was quite witty. But, that's Joel's fixation. How should I say it? That's his fantasy in what he's doing.

"There's a moon out tonight / Let's go strollin' through the park. . ."—The Capris

CHAPTER THREE

MOON OVER NEEDLE PARK

I sat and talked to Joel for a few more hours and decided to call it a night. Joel would have none of it.. "Let's get some coffee, my treat. Do you guys want to go to a fancy place or an ordinary place? There's a place on the Upper West Side called Cafe Lalo. We can go there." Joel lifted himself out of his chair; his mind was made up. I put on my coat. Cafe Lalo sounded fine.

Joel got himself ready, smoothing out his hair and changing his socks. We got on board the elevator and it started its shaky descent to street level. Joel leaned up against the wall.

JOEL: I've been here for thirty-five years. They're turning this into a boutique hotel. If the idiots doing it don't know how to watch their contractor, they're going to go bankrupt. Bob Fosse used to live down the street. He kept eight girls on his floor. At least eight. He had all these apartments filled with girls. I used to try and pick some of them up, but they wouldn't have anything to do with me. I said, "Why don't you give them name tags so I don't make any mistakes?"

The elevator stopped at the third floor. Two Japanese women got in. Joel's eyes lit up. "Come in!" They ignored us and looked at the floor. The elevator doors closed slowly. We all stood in silence as we were lowered to the street.

Saturday, May 15, 1999. Walking up Seventh Avenue toward Broadway. The night was cold. We moved along

Times Square at night.

slowly, taking in everything. The scent of Broadway hung all around us. Steaks, hamburgers, onions, spaghetti, beer, and smoke. Smiling faces looked out at us from the glow of well-lit windows. Music poured out of bars and doorways.

JOHN: *When did all the filth come into Times Square?*

JOEL: During the Depression, the 1930s. The elegant theaters went into Depression and they all became cheap movie houses. Then they started putting in the porn film places. They always had the Brandt Theaters playing carnival-type pictures. Nothing really going on, but they were seedy. There was a big hamburger shop on 42nd and Seventh. Grant's Cafeteria. A lot of ex-convicts, transvestites, and faggot prostitutes were there at any given time of the night. A real scumbag place. You knew your way around. My friends and I used to go there. We'd sit there and we knew we'd get in a fight. I had some friends like that. If the movie wasn't good, they'd beat somebody up. But the people you'd beat up didn't count. You'd go to a movie and some old guy would come over. You'd have to put them in their place. "You put your hands on me and you're dead!" You'd look around and see guys giving people blowjobs. You'd see (laughs)—there was a male prostitute in Show World or someplace. They wrote about this in the ***Village Voice***. The biggest twelve-year-old boy turned out to be a twenty-two-year-old girl. All these guys thought they were getting a twelve-year-old boy. I think that's poetic justice. She'd go around with a little schoolboy outfit on!

JOHN: ***I want my money back!***

JOEL: Yeah! She was getting seventy people a day. She was getting the biggest numbers on the streets. Somebody ratted her out to the ***Village Voice***.

A few steps later:

JOEL: I heard that George C. Scott had a drinking problem. He used to go to all the movies on 42nd Street. He'd get plastered and stay up until seven in the morning. Then he'd fall asleep. On Saturday night, he'd get drunk. My friend used to hang around him. I couldn't go to all those movies.

There was a place called Hubert's Museum on 42nd Street. It was a freak show. They had this room downstairs where this guy kept trained fleas. It was basically a souvenir store. You had to pay a buck or so to get in. They had tattooed people and things like that. Actually, I'm talking with one of the old elevator guys from Sardi's. We want to start a committee to restore 42nd Street. Get Disney out of there and put back the Brandt Theaters. I really think people should get organized and have a freak-in at City Hall. Move the porn theaters back. Actually, things were interesting even before the pornography. Are you staying by 42nd Street?

JOHN: ***No, I'm at the New Yorker.***

JOEL: Oh, by 34th. You know the Sheridan Suite opposite the Pennsylvania? It's loaded with hookers. I went there and they're all cute Russian and Korean girls. My friend's daughter got married there. Her father is about 100-years-old. He went up to see the bride and he got in an elevator with a bunch of them.

One block later, at Seventh and 58th, Joel stopped and pointed to the corner. He smiled to himself and talked into my tape recorder.

JOEL: I was walking over here one day and a bus came by. A woman was standing right here and the bus just squeezed her. Killed her. The guy just came around the corner. You've got to be careful. See that woman [crossing the street] with the baby carriage? She's crazy. She's going to get hit by a bus one of these days.

We started walking again, in and out of crowds of people waiting in line outside of restaurants. Soon, we came upon a place called Freed of London. The windows were filled with frilly gloves and leotards.

JOEL: I'd like to get a job in here. Freed's. This is where all the young girls go. There was this one girl in the neighborhood. One night she stopped me and said she'd been following me since she was thirteen-years-old. She had just gotten married. She said, "Now I have the nerve to tell you! I had this crush on you." A few years later, she rang my bell. She said, "I broke up with my husband, do you want to go out for coffee?" We went out and she said, "I have to get something from Freed's." We went in and I didn't want to leave. I told her I was going to ask the manager for a job. She said, "Oh, God."

Our walk took us closer to Broadway. Joel dropped back behind us, a faraway look in his eyes. We slowed down and soon he was back with us.

JOEL: That's the Coliseum. I had one of my first jobs over there. It's empty now.

JOHN: ***What were you doing over there?***

JOEL: I was doing publicity for the Diners Club. Actually, my office was in that building. That was in 1956. I knew a guy who was the elevator operator. I walked by there a little while ago, and he said, "Hello, Joel!" Amazing.

A horse-drawn carriage raced down the street, almost side-swiping us. A young couple, on a tour of New York, was at the mercy of their driver.

DRIVER: Watch out, guys.

JOHN: ***Almost run down by a horse.***

JOEL: When you're being attacked and charged by somebody on a horse, you put your bayonet out! [strikes an attack pose] I used to have a lot of guns but I sold them all. I should have kept them, they're worth a lot more now. Some black guy sold them to me in the park. I gave him five bucks a piece for them. I eventually sold them to some doctor. I had no use for them.

We slowly approached Central Park. It was filled with a young crowd of tourists.

Joel and John in Central Park.

JOHN: ***When did the park start getting safer?***

JOEL: In the last ten years. Everyone's using it now. It still has its share of rape and murders, but it's pretty safe at night now. They had it closed down for a while. I used to go fishing here at four o'clock in the morning. There was nobody in the park at that hour. Mostly fags. I mean, who would be in the park to mug at that hour anyway? Now, they're jogging. The muggers could make a fortune. We shot some of ***Sex by Advertisement*** over here.

JOHN: ***Did you get any hassles from the police?***

JOEL: No. We were shooting in New Jersey, in the woods there; we had our camera and things. The state police came over saying, "You guys are going to get arrested. You can't shoot here." They followed us for the rest of the day. I said, "We're not shooting anything, we're going over to that diner for lunch." We couldn't shoot over there, so we went to Central Park. I was whipping this nude girl and the cops came up and asked, "Can we watch?" They all came over and we shot the whole thing with police protection. That's the New York cops for you.

JOHN: ***Who was the girl?***

JOEL: Oh, I don't know. There's a good high school over here on 60th Street. I go over here and have coffee and check out the girls. Jennifer Jason Leigh went to school here. The Professional Children's School. I came by the other day to have a look.

A few years ago, this area was very dangerous. You couldn't walk up here at night. They tore all of the old buildings down, they evicted everybody. These are all new buildings. They have a rock-climbing wall over here now. People climb all night. They scramble up and down all the time. Sometimes you can get a glimpse of a few good looking girls.

Seconds later:

JOEL: A few blocks up is where Frank Costello was shot. Have you been to the Dakota?
JOHN: ***No.***
JOEL: We'll have to walk by there tomorrow. That's where John Lennon was shot. It still draws a crowd. They have plenty of ***Blood Sucking Freaks*** tapes at that Tower Records over there. I go in and check. Let's cross to the left. We'll go up Broadway.

And then...

JOEL: Well, here we are. This is upper Broadway. Twenty years ago, there was nothing here. It was all shit. We're going to go by Needle Park. Remember the movie? It's right here. ***The Panic in Needle Park***. It was all street people and drug addicts. Actually, they didn't bother you if you walked by quickly enough. But, you know, you felt a little queasy around here. It was all dark and you'd have some fucking drug addict yelling at you. But, mostly the people were nodded out.

An old woman, babushka over her head, bent down on the sidewalk with a small bag and glove. Her dog, a young beagle, pulled at its leash as several teenagers passed them.

JOEL: See that woman? You have to pick up after your dogs here. We can go straight down over here. That's the new Sony Theater. We're becoming like the midwest, with malls. There's the criminal justice college over here. Sort of an innovation. It's John Jay, the place I was telling you about that had the hot girls. They do forensics studies or something like that. I guess back home in Detroit, you don't have this many people on the streets.
JOHN: ***Not half as many.***
JOEL: This is the big Sony Triplex. They have three floors of theaters, around five theaters a floor.

The street light in front of us turned red. We stopped for a moment and Joel looked around.

Joel at the Cinequest Film Festival, San José, California.

JOEL: Over here is a coffee shop I go to. They give you too much food. You wouldn't believe the amount of food they give you. Back over there is a little low-income area. When the kids come home from school, they have to post cops around. A lot of heroin addicts come out here. Actually, most of the panhandlers you see are on heroin. They're OK. Heroin addicts don't usually get in your face.

JOHN: ***Where do most of the psychos hang out these days?***

JOEL: Well, probably down on the west 20s by the wharf. They got all of those naked hookers hanging out. Hundreds of them. They used to hang out right on my block. At any given time, there was like 100 girls on my corner. The new tourism took them away.

JOHN: ***What do you think about all that?***

JOEL: Well, like I said, they got rid of the cheap whores and brought in the expensive Disney whores. You see, these are all brand new buildings.

JOHN: ***When did they go up?***

JOEL: In the last ten years. Columbus Avenue got really chic. All the stores opened here and then they went down the drain for a while. When we walk up here, you can see where Steven Spielberg and Woody Allen live.

JOHN: ***I meant to ask this before: What were you doing in between films?***

JOEL: I don't know. I was just chasing young girls around. I didn't do enough. Maybe I should have gone to the coast and promoted myself more. Now, this is Needle Park. This little area here. You can't really see it; it goes up the whole way. This is where they shot the movie. This was like the Bowery. It was nothing but bums. Now the new buildings are like cubicles. They spent a fortune on them. Imagine all of these stores all closed up.

JOHN: ***Are you glad you lived in New York all these years?***

JOEL: No, I would have rather lived in LA. I like it over there very much. Oh, they usually have the big hot dog war on this corner! They took the sign down. There are usually two hot dog places over here, selling two hot dogs and a soda for a quarter. They're trying to drive each other out of business. This is 72nd Street. The Dakota is down there.

JOHN: ***How long have you known Joe from Sardi's?***

JOEL: Joe, the bartender there? Way before he came to work there. And I knew all of the guys who worked there before him. He's new. He doesn't like me because I left with some of the girls there.

JOHN: ***How long has he been there?***

JOEL: Oh, a long time. But, I mean, I've been there since 1953. Like I told you, he says, "You're Lorin Price's friend and I hated Lorin." But I don't go hitting on girls for money like Lorin. I was talking to a girl over there from Ohio. She called me one day and said, "Oh, I looked you up in a book. You're really a director. I'm sorry I walked away from you." She never came back again.

JOHN: ***She probably read about Blood Sucking Freaks.***

JOEL: Well, I don't know if she watched it, but she never came back to New York (laughs)! I guess I'll see Brooke Shields wandering around the city again, since she got divorced. She's about eight feet tall. I used to run in to her all the time. I met her in a coffee shop. I said, "You can sit with me, Brooke." She said, "No. I'm not Brooke Shields." I mean, come on. Who else could it be? [To tape recorder:] More theaters. They had a great store over there that sold stones and magic things. Black magic.

Two blocks later:

JOEL: Over here is where Plato's Retreat was. I was over there when Gerry Damiano shot a picture.

JOHN: ***That building?***

JOEL: Over there. Ron Dorfman shot it. He used to ask me to come along. I was interested in the girls.

JOHN: ***What's that building over there?***

JOEL: That used to be the China Club. It moved down to 47th Street. I used to sit here and meet a lot of girls. They'd come out at around two in the morning. It was open twenty-four hours. There was a little balcony over here at that building. This guy was sunbathing. The angle was kind of weird from down here and the cops came over. They put a net out—they thought he was going to kill himself by rolling off. The guy got all upset. He screamed, "What are you guys bothering me for?" These streets over here were 11th and 12th Avenue. During the boom in the '20s, they renamed them to Columbus Avenue and Amsterdam Avenue. They wanted to give them fancier names. Up until the Depression, this was really hot stuff. Then everyone went broke, and the buildings became a lot of rooming houses.

We walked on, passing a loud bar. The music was abrasive and a young crowd tipped back expensive beers.

JOEL: I see the kids are out tonight. There's two bars here where they don't allow anyone in who's over sixteen. If you come in, and you look older, you have to sit in a back room. There's one on the east side and one on the west side. You see a lot of twelve-year-olds. They're famous underage drinking places. There were two murders recently, one at each bar.

A red Mustang plowed through a red light to a chorus of honking horns.

JOEL: Pay no attention to the stoplights of New York. I almost got hit the other day [voice trails off]. Ruby Foo's, over there, is the new 'in' place. It got a lot of write-ups. A lot of celebrities go there.

JOHN: ***What does it cost to live around here?***

JOEL: All of the rents have gone up to $3,000–$4,000 a month here. There's so many people moving into the city. All of the companies want to move out to Denver and Charlotte.

The sound of accordion music hit us full in the face. An unwashed black man, probably sixty, played Cajun music from across the street. Several people gathered around him, stopping to listen. The man was all smiles and

New York's 20th Precinct, the exterior of Tucci's office, *Blood Sucking Freaks.*

he nodded his head up and down, his accordion wrinkling his black wool suit.

MAN WITH ACCORDION: Tell the folks they got a message from the promised land, this is poor boy on the line…

JOEL: You know what happened to me? I got so blasted the week before last. I went to a Russian-Jewish bar mitzvah. Recent immigrants. Do you know what they drink? 195 proof vodka. It has a warning on the bottle not to drink it straight. That's over fifty percent pure alcohol. Like eighty percent, I guess. And they drink and drink. I had two sips, and I almost died. They do shots of the stuff with a pickle chaser. And they eat lousy food.

JOHN: ***How far does Broadway go?***

JOEL: All the way up to Albany. The old Indian trail. If you're in Westchester County and you want to go fishing, there's a Broadway. The same street.

JOHN: ***Do you go fishing a lot?***

JOEL: Not recently. I used to go every day. Do you have these Starbuck's coffee places in Michigan?

JOHN: ***More than you'd ever know.***

JOEL: They should develop a vaccine for them. Awful. I like to go to Lalo because there's a bunch of cute girls in there.

JOHN: ***It's worth the walk?***

JOEL: It's worth the walk.

JOHN: ***How's life outside of show-business treating you?***

JOEL: I was working on something

On the streets.

for IBM the other day. They need charts and all that shit. You see how stupid they are. You walk in with charts, and they shout, "That's terrific!" But, I'm learning a lot of shit about business plans. Look at the demographics! With Joel Reed, you can finally reach out to the freaks! The perverts! You're going to have a core group that you've never approached before!

We finally reached 83th Street. Cafe Lalo stood in front of us, promising something.

JOEL: Let's wait for this light. I don't trust anyone, especially cab drivers.

We walked into Cafe Lalo and were immediately assaulted by laughter and music. I could see why Joel liked to go there. Young girls of every shape and size made up the waitstaff. One girl, who'd obviously dealt with Joel before, gave him a little wave. Joel had some sort of godfather status there. We were in line behind a group of people, but we were offered a table first.

On the way to the table, Joel stopped to look at the various cakes and pastries that were displayed under a glass cover. "You should get something to eat here. This stuff is good."

Conversation at Cafe Lalo, 10:30 PM:

JOEL: They should take these menus from us. Watch out, somebody wants to get through. OK. Let's go. Here are the dark, deep corners of my life that I have unveiled to no one before!

JOHN: ***Go on…***

JOEL: Actually, I have no secrets! I'm a freak for young girls.

Our waitress walked by, taking notice of my tape recorder.

JOEL (switching gears): So, when Alicia Silverstone first saw me… You know what's funny? All the high-class hookers in New York are slaves to the Japanese. The Japanese pay any amount of money. The guys at Sony pay $5,000 a night, the girls were telling me. This goes on in LA as well. They have all these clubs on the east side. A lot of young actresses work there. You can make $500 a night, just being a bargirl. And the girls who work nude make even more. All from the Japanese. But Vietnam is the big place for sex now. According to the ***New York Times***, it's wide open. If poor parents see an American guy over there, they'll pull him in and lock the door and throw their daughters at him.

JOHN: ***This place is pretty busy.***

JOEL: They're doing a lot of business tonight. I think ***Blood Sucking Freaks 2*** should get a grant from the National Endowment of the Arts. I mean, they got a nude ***Romeo and Juliet*** going on Broadway and stuff like that.

JOHN: ***How well did you know Gerard Damiano?***

JOEL: I knew him pretty well. I used to drive his Cadillac around. I think I was his official driver on a picture for a couple of days. He always bought these big Cadillacs.

JOHN: ***What kind of money did he make from his porn films?***

JOEL: He was making some money, but I think the mob was making most of it. He was a very Brooklyn/Italian/Queens sort of guy. He had a building in Queens, a storefront. He made it into a studio and he shot movies there. I like Radley Metzger's stuff a lot better. I like ***The Opening of Misty Beethoven.*** The

Grant's Cafeteria.

scene in the airplane: "Sorry, tourist class passengers are not allowed to give head to first class passengers." In fact, my friend Marvin Farkas was a friend of Metzger. He offered Radley some money to do ***Wit's End*** before I got involved. Metzger wanted too much money.

JOHN: ***Did you know Radley Metzger at all?***

JOEL: Not really. He was from New York and he went to school with Marvin. Vernon Becker used to hang around Linda Lovelace and her husband. But, you know, New York was great for getting to know these people. Times Square was a phenomenon. You had the Loop in Chicago, and that was about it. There were places in Los Angeles, but New York was the biggest city for it. We had 125 theaters at one time in Times Square. We're just recovering now from the Depression. We're booming like in the '20s.

JOHN: ***Let's hear some more about the theaters.***

JOEL: The Brandts were the biggest. They owned about five or six theaters. There were two Brandt Theaters on 42nd Street, facing each other. They're gone now. They started playing the softcore stuff. I already told you about the hamburgers at Grant's. I used to love them. There were the Selwyn theaters. And prior to that, the major studios owned the theaters. I remember Vernon brought in a famous English producer. He was stunned by seeing all of the movie theaters on one block, one after another. They were lined up on both sides of the block. They were playing on 42nd Street between Seventh and Eighth. There was an Army/Navy store that closed and then started selling dirty books. The theaters were open twenty-four hours a day. The Brandts played all the Jerald Intrator films. ***Satan in High Heels*** and things like that. In those days, Jerry would buy a foreign film and put in two reels of nudity. Pierre would be painting or something. "Oh, my beautiful model." And then they'd cut to some girl taking her top off. There'd be like one tit shot in there. It was scandalous. But that's where all the early AIP pictures played. Corman made a bunch of pictures in the Philippines with Sid Haig. I thought they were a riot. I saw all of them. ***The Big Doll House***, ***The Big Bird Cage***.

JOHN: ***I guess it must be strange to go from the world of Barbra Striesand to the world of Sid Haig.***

JOEL: I was just here and things happened. How was I supposed to know—sitting at a coffee shop—that the person next to me would turn out to be a Barbra Striesand, a Joe Sarno, or a Gerry Damiano? You never know. Actually, some guys that I knew from way back are still walking around town with their scripts. They never give up. Most of them hang out with the NAMBLA crowd (laughs). A lot of strange people. My friend Eddie Jaffe was great to be with back then. I was staying at his place when he was in Minnesota. Suddenly, the bell rang and this guy walked in with two beautiful girls. He was dressed like Cecil B. DeMille, with a beret and everything. He said, "Out of my way,

peon! I'm here to see Eddie. I'm the great director. We have to get some rewrites done on the script. We're using this typewriter. You cannot interfere!" I called Eddie up and he said, "This guy's OK." The guy came up to me and said, "You! How about getting us some pizzas!" I said, "OK, give me the money." He said, "Lay it out. Eddie knows I'm good for it. I'm making a twenty-million dollar picture!" It turns out that he walked around pretending he was a director. He broke down crying when I wouldn't pay for his food. I met a lot of people like that. I'll have to ask Eddie, he might still be around.

There was another guy who was putting together a movie, but one of his actors got arrested for murder. When the guy got out, seventeen years later, he made the announcement that he was finally going to make the movie.

JOHN: *Victor Kanefsky was the editor on three of your films. What's he up to these days?*

JOEL: Victor's a funny guy. He did ***Wit's End***, ***Blood Sucking Freaks***, and ***Night of the Zombies***. He's pushing his son's movies now. His son's a nice kid; he did ***There's Nothing Out There***.

JOHN: *You've made six films. Let's hear something about the films that you didn't make, for whatever reason.*

JOEL: There was one called ***The Renegade Ghouls of Kaplan's Swamp***. I still have the script. It's a Civil War thing; it's about a studio like Troma. A studio that doesn't pay anyone anything. In my script, this guy is going to make a movie about Union and Rebel ghouls. So they go to this swamp where these ghouls are supposed to lurk to save money. They say, "We'll spend $32,000 on it, our biggest budget yet." The writer says, "You can't go on location, there's real ghouls over there." They go down to shoot the thing and the ghouls start killing the cast. There's a lot of jokes about extras and things. The company can't afford to pay anyone, so they get these real ghouls to act in the thing.

JOHN: ***Is there a real place called Kaplan's Swamp?***

JOEL: No (laughs). I wrote that for a movie company down in Fort Worth, Texas. This girl called me up, she was in a lot of movies. She said, "I just did a film called ***Mark of the Witch***." That company did two movies. They would give the movie they wanted to do to the lowest bidder. It would be something like, "My God! Did you see what they did to the coed in the bathroom?" And they wouldn't show anything. Anyway, these guys had a script that they copied from Rod Serling. They wanted me to do that, but I refused. I went down there for a meeting. They said, "You know, what we boys like the most here is a touch of the tar brush. That makes a woman real nice, she's got to have a little blackness in her." I couldn't believe it. They wanted me to do this Civil War movie about this octoroon girl in New Orleans. A Yankee Colonel wants to marry her. This causes trouble, so they burn the house down. It was crazy. I told them I didn't like the idea. They took me to this place in east Texas.

One of the guys claimed to be the illegitimate son of Charles Bronson. I said, "What about this nutty film company making a swamp picture?" They paid me $10,000, but they never did it. Later on, they called me and said, "We made our picture, boy!"

One day, I was sitting in a place on 73rd and Broadway and started talking to an airline stewardess at the bar. I told her that I was a director. She said, "I know the movie you made. I went to Southern Methodist University, and they made a movie down there about this girl in the Civil War. You have to be the guy who made it. That was the stupidest movie I ever saw."

So, they actually made that thing. The company was called Presidio Productions. If they would have made ***The Renegade Ghouls***, they would have been all right. They lost a lot of money with their film. But, those good old boys wanted a touch of the tar brush. I never heard that expression before. They took me to some remote place down in Texas. Talk about hillbillies. People were walking around with three dicks hanging out. Shitting in their pants. "We marry our sisters here, isn't that fun?" I think ***The Renegade Ghouls*** hit a little too close to home. I had these two bearded brothers in the script who slept in the same bed and didn't pay anyone for making movies. It had a funny ending, the ghouls take over Hollywood. Now I know a lot more about pictures. If you have the basic elements of a story, you'll sell it. I have another script called ***Teenage Space Girls*** and one called ***The House of All Nations***. That's a Woody Allen/Neil Simon type thing about a disorientated detective trying to find somebody in Asia. Maybe they'll be made.

JOHN: ***Your early films were financed by lawyers. What was going through their minds?***

JOEL: I don't know. They wanted to make money. My first film came about totally by accident. ***Career Bed***. A lawyer put up the cash for that. I didn't know what I was doing.

JOHN: ***That had Georgina Spelvin.***

JOEL: Yeah, as the lesbian talent agent. Her real name was Shelley Ables. It also starred Liza Duran who became better known as Jennifer Welles.

JOHN: ***Do you remember who did the marketing for that film?***

JOEL: Peppercorn and Wormser, the distributors. That was in 1968.

JOHN: ***The year the X rating was born.***

JOEL: That killed us. People could see the real thing. So when ***Career Bed*** and ***Sex by Advertisement*** finally played around, there was nothing left to sell.

JOHN: ***The film works on another level these days.***

JOEL: I don't think there's any market for it, but at least I have one fan. Are you sure you're all there? [Jewish doctor voice] Vell done! You're doing very vell wit your veekend visits to Mr. Reed! We are expecting no more outbursts like vhen you took the gun to vork! Luckily you only wounded eighteen people…

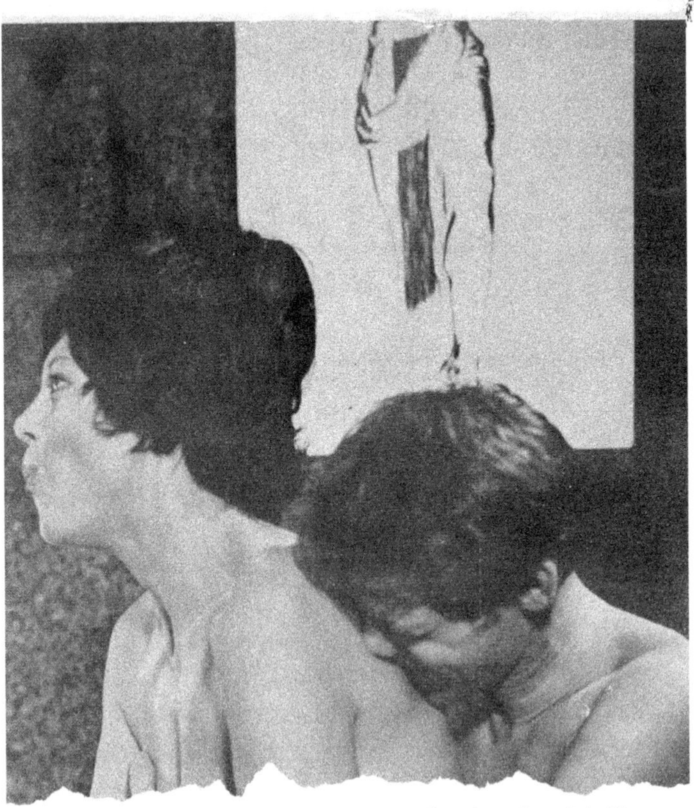

"I used to think that Herschell Gordon Lewis' films were bad. Now I don't know if mine are much better."—Joel M. Reed, after watching *Career Bed*

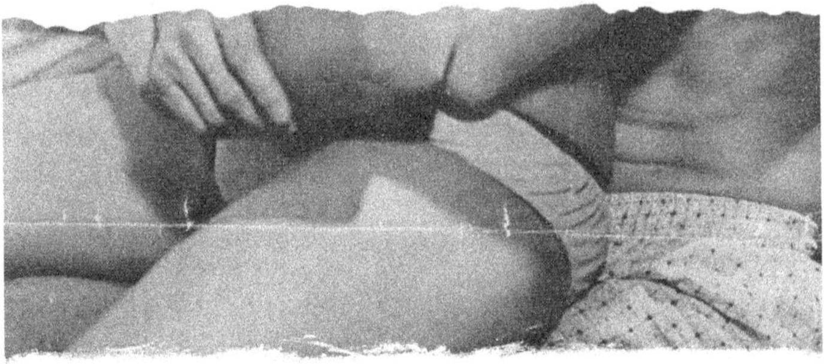

CHAPTER FOUR

CAREER BED

"What Mrs. Robinson did is no comparison to what Mrs. Potter does in this film. A cold-hearted, warm-blooded mother... and her career girl daughter HOT for the big time. Please DO NOT allow your children to see this picture unless they are adults."

So warned the poster for Joel Reed's first film, ***Career Bed***. Shot quickly and on the cheap in 1968, ***Career Bed*** promised it all: sex, depravity, young girls, and dirty old men. This kind of overblown hype was nothing new. The carnival barkers along the grindhouse midway always promised more than they could deliver. But this time, they were dealing with something *different*.

From the very start of ***Career Bed***, good taste is assaulted from every corner. The title sequence seems tailor-made to send shivers up John Waters' spine. The credits appear, written in lipstick on a cheap dressing room mirror. The music itself is dirty; raw '60s rock and roll plays directly from a record, with enough pops and hisses to make Kenneth Anger green with envy. The state of the film print itself seems to reflect the twisted mind and ambition behind it. It is full of scratches and jump cuts from scene to scene, underexposed and overexposed. The dialogue track jumps everywhere, falling in and out of synch at random. The sex is simple and straightforward. Long, leering shots of female flesh haunt the screen as the actors go through their paces, marching to the beat of a drummer whose sense of rhythm

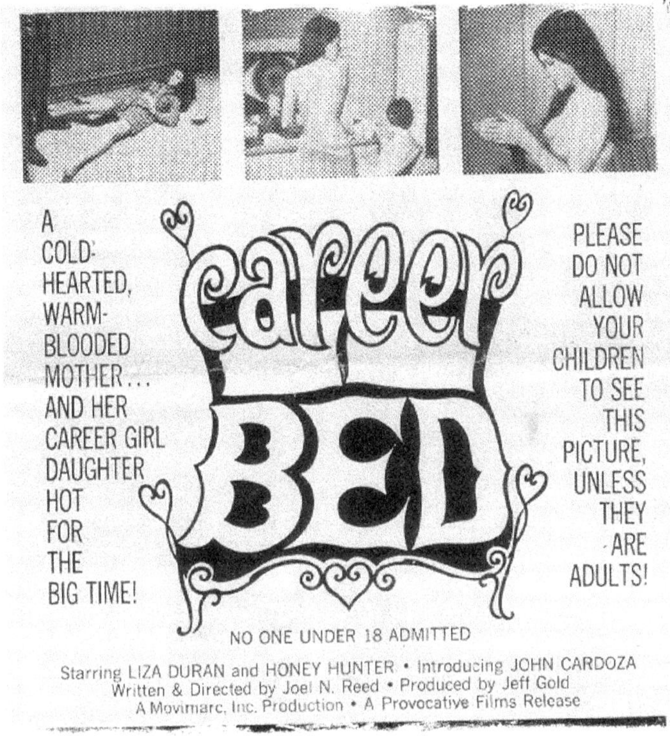

is so warped that it borders on epilepsy. Joel Reed avoided erotic sophistication with the skill and grace of a prizefighter. Class, if anything, was his proverbial four-letter word.

In the spring of 1968, a small notice appeared in the trade paper ***Show Business***. Large block letters announced the casting of a low budget film, ***Career Bed***, tentatively titled here as ***Mother Love***.

Avant-garde Film Casts Actresses

The Entertainment Industry Group is seeking two top caliber actresses for an avant-garde film being directed by Joel M. Reed and filmed in NY at the end of the month. Entitled "Mother Love", it revolves around a theatrical family in NY.

Script includes some nude films. This is, however, not an exploitation film but a "hard hitting drama." Pay above SAG scale.

Mr. Reed is mainly interested in the leads at the present time. They are:

Susan Potter, a groovy teenager

2 More Features For Joel M. Reed

Joel M. Reed, a young film-maker, has completed negotiations to produce and direct two more features this year. Both projects will be in color.

They are "The Strikers" a secret agent type spoof, and a horror script, still untitled, by playwright-critic, Randolph Carter.

The horror film will star a Broadway actress and be shot in its entirety in one of this country's most famous, old mansions.

Mr. Reed just completed an erotic film called, "Motherlove" which is currently being edited and slated for fall release.

He keeps an open casting file and is currently receiving photos by mail only at Rm. 900, 1780 Bway, N.Y. 10019.

with an "out-of-this world body."

Emily Potter, her mother who has a fierce, mature appeal.

For auditions, call Mr. Reed at EIG: 581-0828. Entertainment Industry Group is at 1780 Bway (57).

Entertainment Industry Group, Inc. (EIG) was the brainchild of Joel Reed. He publicly announced its formation in the pages of ***Backstage*** in 1967. EIG specialized in theatrical packaging and talent development, as well as the financing of feature films. On a quiet afternoon, the EIG offices opened their doors to hundreds of young women looking for the lead in ***Mother Love***. Joel sat behind his desk from one to six PM, eyeing each of them.

JOEL REED: Entertainment Industry Group was a company formed to produce live shows for corporations. Trade shows and sales meetings. We did a lot of them for American Express and things like that. That was just before I got to do a movie. I mean, I forgot about EIG when Vernon Becker walked into the office. I decided to do a movie, and ***Career Bed*** just happened like some growth. Like getting a parasitic fungus on your nose. Vernon came up and said, "Let's make a movie." I said, "OK." He said, "Do it with Joe Sarno, he's a brilliant director." I thought ***Inga*** was OK and I wrote ***Career Bed***. It was originally called ***Mother Love***.

JOE SARNO: Back in 1959 or 1960, some guy came to me and said, "Joe, will you make a sex film for me?" The first thing out of my mouth was, "Will I go to jail?" But the stuff became kind of popular. I did a couple of films with Vernon Becker. I worked for him in Europe. I think this was in the late '60s. I was

Georgina Spelvin seduces Jennifer Welles.

living in Sweden at the time. But I met him before that. Listen, I've known Vernon for a long time. He was a very astute filmmaker. We did ***Inga 2***. Vernon was the producer for ***Every Afternoon***. And I guess he introduced me to Joel Reed.

JOEL REED: I envisioned a real movie, not a sex film like Joe was doing. We casted out of the EIG offices. I hired everybody; there was nobody there that wasn't hired by me. We put ads in ***Show Business*** and ***Backstage***. Sylvester Stallone came over. I was thinking of hiring him for the crew. He just didn't come on the right day.

A few days later, the casting of secondary rolls began:

Eight Parts in Feature Film

"Mother Love"

The Entertainment Industry Group Inc., 1780 Bway is still looking for players for the full-length feature film "Mother Love" being shot in June in NY.

Smaller rolls are as follows:

Smith, an advertising executive over forty

Ross, a millionaire over forty

Bob, a young mid-westerner

Gerald Ramer, a far out mod photographer

Jack Landive, a Broadway director, about thirty-five

A very pretty teenage girl for a short scene, fully clothed

JOEL REED: Quite a number of people showed up. We had to get a studio; we had about a couple hundred people come up in one

Jennifer Welles strikes a pose in front of Sardi's.

day. We only casted for a week or so. I saw people before I had the money. Jennifer Welles and Shelley Abels probably came up from casting. Some of the people were friends of Ron Dorfman.

From the ***Career Bed*** pressbook:

After the death of her husband, Emily Potter takes her daughter Susan to New York. Her objective is a theatrical career for Susan and she openly admits she will stop at nothing to insure success. Susan, unhappy in New York, wants to return to Ohio and her boyfriend, Bob Dartfield.

Emily destroys Susan's one dream of happiness when Bob arrives in New York unexpectedly. Emily makes Bob comfortable and then leads him to believe that Susan is having an affair with an older man who will help her career. In revenge, Bob allows himself to be seduced by Emily. Susan discovers them in bed together and her romantic illusions are shattered.

Emily says, "Career first!" and Susan, defeated, complies. A well-known woman agent, Miss Reynolds, offers to open doors for Susan in television. Miss Reynolds seduces Susan with Emily's consent.

A young director named Jack Landive encourages Susan to free herself from the dollar incest her mother has formulated. But Emily has other plans. She insists that Susan date David Smith, a lecherous TV producer. Repelled by the man, Susan packs her bags. Emily attempts suicide. Maternal love takes precedence and Susan becomes Emily's robot, fair game for the roving bands of Smith.

Gerald Ramer, a slimy, sewer-like creature pretending to be a photographer, bolsters his latent homosexuality by making a pass for Susan. Emily intercedes and offers herself as a down payment. Ramer agrees to secure a Hollywood contract for Susan via Ross Miller, a famed producer. His price: Susan.

In actuality, Ramer is an ill-paid procurer. He uses Susan as a lure while begging money from Ross. Ross, an obvious sadist, causes Ramer to debase himself by crawling and barking like a dog. Ross refuses to meet Susan unless he's sure she is perfection. He hides in Ramer's closet, unknown to the girl and Emily, while a revealing photo session is in progress. Entranced by Susan Potter, Ross later slaps the weakling Ramer for touching her.

The Hollywood contract in order, Emily delivers Susan to Ross in payment. Susan, in order to withhold payment of her body to Ramer and to break away from her mother, convinces Ross that she loves him. Ross falls for her approach and marries her. Emily is cast aside.

Susan next turns on Ross. A carbon copy of her mother, she continues to use her body to advance her career. Her first subject is Ross's enemy, the Hollywood director Boris Rachman.

Emily remains in New York and pushes for the big time without Susan. At the close of the film she is found inspecting the body of a teenage actress whom she plans to manage. The girl will have to follow her instructions

Joel's brother Elliott as the waiter in Career Bed.

A seminal moment in *Career Bed.*

very carefully. "Don't be afraid to take your clothes off, especially for certain, important men. I made my daughter a star and I can do the same for you if you do exactly as I say."

Half of the charm of watching ***Career Bed*** lies in the film's bizarre history. Joel Reed made the amazing leap from the lights of Broadway to the sex-charged world of Joe Sarno, Ron Dorfman, Georgina Spelvin, and a host of misfits that would haunt exploitation for the next twenty years. Joe Sarno was originally slated to direct the film. Ron Dorfman went on to work as a cameraman on the Maysles brothers' ***Gimme Shelter***, directed ***Groupies***, and then veered off into the netherworld of hardcore porn. Georgina Spelvin became a household name after starring in Gerard Damiano's ***The Devil in Miss Jones***. But before all of this, Joel Reed had his way with them. This is ***Career Bed***, in all of its perverted glory.

GALE McCARTY: I met Joel in the '60s. He had an office on Seventh Avenue at the time. He was doing some films and wanted some help. I was working for the city, they had a film unit. I'd just come back from Vietnam. I started with Joel on ***Career Bed***. I had a little spot. He needed someone to do a day's worth of work and I played the part of the reporter. That was actually done after the film was made. Joel needed to insert a few scenes. There were about five people involved with that day of shooting. Ron Dorfman was the cameraman. I didn't know him prior to that film. But I worked for Joel after he made that picture. He's one of the best friends I have in New York. I used to get together with him every week for lunch. He started out producing plays. And then he got involved with these films. They're not my cup of tea, but I guess they're ultimately harmless.

JOEL REED: I got the idea to make a softcore porn picture. That turned out to be ***Career Bed***. Vernon Becker introduced me to Joe Sarno and I wrote a script. I started to work on production. When I got things together, I called Joe and he said, "I'm going to Sweden. You direct it." This was at the very last minute. I went ahead and shot the movie. I didn't realize that I'd bitten off more than I could chew.

JOE SARNO: I was never really involved in it. I was asked to direct, but I was busy or something. I may have written the treatment, I'm not sure. I met Joel several times, but we really didn't work together. We were doing different things.

MARK GOLDBERG: I had known Joel for a while. He was in public relations. He was a client of a former law associate of mine. This goes back to the mid-1960s, about 1965. We just sort of struck up a conversational friendship. I thought he was a nice, intelligent, hardworking guy. He had a flair for public relations, which was what he was in back then.

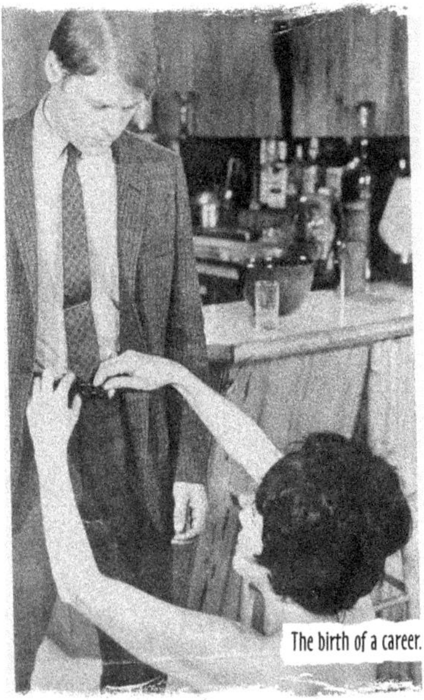
The birth of a career.

JOEL REED: This lawyer said that he'd give me the money for ***Career Bed***. Before we could shoot, he disappeared. I was sitting in my office and thought, "Well, to hell with that." Another lawyer came along. He had met me at a birthday party. I told him I wanted to shoot a little picture but I didn't have any money, the investor copped out. He said, "Well, I'll give you the money."

MARK GOLDBERG: Joel said

Jennifer Welles and Ron Dorfman mingle.

he had this project and asked if I'd be interested in financing it. I told him he was crazy, he was bound to lose money. He said, "Well, go over the numbers." This was in 1968. I'm a lawyer, I do real estate law. At the time that I met Joel, I was doing general practice. I had no real interest in doing anything with film.

JOEL REED: Mark Goldberg produced the film. We had another guy, Jeff Gold. He was a William Morris agent who showed up. He was going to do all these things; raise money and sell the picture. I don't think he did anything, not even show up for meetings. He was a partner for production, but he did nothing. He was there in the beginning, but later—I don't even know if he saw the movie.

MARK GOLDBERG: There was another guy on board named Jeff Gold. I think it was up to him to put a lot of things together. He was represented to me as a producer. As I recall, my involvement with him was very limited. I'm not exactly sure what he did. He would arbitrate some issues between Joel, Ron Dorfman, and myself.

JOEL REED: My brother Elliott is listed as the production manager in the press kit, but I don't think he ever did anything for the film. Mark was involved with a lot of the production.

MARK GOLDBERG: I was pretty much involved with everything. I raised ninety-eight percent of the capital needed. I had an obligation to the people who entrusted me with this money to make sure that it was spent only on the project. I just told people what the budget was—believe it or not, the budget was less than $12,000. I said, "It's not a big risk." People put in $1,000 or $2,000 apiece. If it hit, it would pay off well. The risk was completing it.

JOE SARNO: I worked on salary on most of the films that I did. I think there were one or two that I took some sort of part in. But most of the guys in the business, including Joel, raised the money themselves.

JOEL REED: So there I was. I checked out two books from the library: ***The Five C's of Cinematography*** and a book on editing. We rented a camera from this place, and we didn't know that their cameras never worked. We were ripped off.

MARK GOLDBERG: I saw the script, and I wasn't too impressed. At the time, there were much more restrictions on film. I was sympathetic to Joel's difference. Joel was a little more of a voyeur. My perspective of it was that this was a sexploitation film. And sex, if depicted honestly without physical abuse—there was nothing wrong with it. Lovemaking is a natural thing between two adults. If there was anything dirty about it, it was in the mind of the beholder. It should be viewed. Right after our film came out there were things like ***I am Curious (yellow)*** and ***I am Curious (blue)***. What I mean is that pictures subsequent to ours were much more explicit. That was a problem when our picture played.

JOEL REED: I hired a NYU student, Ron Dorfman, who went on in the business. He shot and edited it. He went on to do ***Groupies***. He did some real classy stuff. But this was his first film.

MARK GOLDBERG: I was on the set on occasion. I met Ron Dorfman. I thought that he was very hard working. He really put in a lot of effort. He was at NYU film school at the time and was interested in earning credits. He went into this thing with little, if any, financial reward. He had a piece of whatever profits we'd take in.

Ample charms.

A future star?

JOEL REED: At this time, Ron didn't know anything. But I guess he was the king of porn for a while. I think he was partners with Joe Sarno.

JOE SARNO: We weren't really partners, but we were friends. He was the cameraman on a couple of my films.

MARK GOLDBERG: I wasn't really involved with the casting. I wanted to see the female star, just to see if she was attractive. I met her before she was cast.

JOEL REED: ***Career Bed*** was the introduction to Jennifer Welles' film career. She went on to be a producer in porn movies. Shelley Abels was also in the picture, before she was known as Georgina Spelvin.

MARK GOLDBERG: As I recall, it took at least a month to finish. We had lots of locations. That was really a hairy part. It came to the point where I was helping Joel set up at various locations. A lot of the locations came from friends that Joel knew. One of them was somebody's loft, believe it or not, on 42nd Street. The building is now gone.

JOEL REED: We shot the thing in a weekend. It would have been a great movie if we'd spent more money on it. But that's how I emerged. The film played around. Carl Peppercorn and Irving Wormser distributed it.

MARK GOLDBERG: I met Peppercorn and Wormser. I thought, based on what Joel told me, that they were suitable to distribute this kind of film. I don't think they did a good job. I don't know how many places they got the film to. I now question their honesty, as far as the money was concerned.

JOEL REED: I got involved with Peppercorn-Wormser through Vernon. He was in the movie business; I think he was with Jerry Lester's show. He worked on all those early shows in the '50s. They distributed the film through Universal Marion, which was Sidney Glazier's company. They had a branch called Provocative Films. They made ***The Twelve Chairs*** and things like that. I was working for them at the time. One of them was the former head of Columbia Pictures. Brandt on 42nd Street offered to buy the picture from them for something like $40,000. That was exclusive to run on 42nd Street. They wouldn't do it. That was like four times what it cost to make the picture. And Brandt used to run the pictures for ten years. They were just old guys; it took them forever to do a poster.

MARK GOLDBERG: I was not very impressed with the finished film. I did think it was kind of sarcastic, but I didn't think it came off that well. We had a screening after it was done at Movielab. We invited all of the investors. The reaction was that we had produced a terrible piece of film.

The film played on 42nd Street. I don't remember how long; this was over thirty years ago.

In the end, I disappointed a lot of the investors, if not all of them. It took up a lot of time and tarnished my reputation. The film didn't make the money back. I couldn't do another film, I had no more credibility.

The following interview with Joel Reed took place in Joel's apartment on November 6, 1999, as we watched **Career Bed**.

The opening credits roll to the sounds of clumsy drumming and a fuzz-tone guitar. Credits written with lipstick on a dressing room mirror.

JOEL REED: OK, this is my picture. That's Moviemarc, the company that I set up to do ***Career Bed***.

JOHN: ***Who did the music?***

JOEL: Vic Spinna. He was friends with Ron Dorfman.

Career Bed

Jerry Krutman, who allowed his studio to be filmed in *Career Bed.*

JOHN: *Ron was the cameraman for this film. What's he up to now?*

JOEL: I don't know what happened to him. I saw a bum in Seattle named Ron. They showed the police rescuing him on some documentary. He looked exactly like Ron Dorfman.

JOHN: *You shot all of the interiors in somebody's apartment?*

JOEL: Yeah, it was shot in my friend Jerry Krutman's photography studio on 42nd Street. He was upset that we used it. He said we'd ruin his reputation. My brother was the assistant director on this. He really did nothing with the picture. The sound guy on this picture was the head of the Miss Universe contest: George Honchar (laughs). I can't believe that these are the opening credits. I don't remember any of this.

JOHN: *Are there a lot of pseudonyms here?*

JOEL: Yeah, I guess. A lot of people didn't want to use their names on this picture. This is great! We wrote the credits with a crayon or something on that mirror.

The camera shakes and jumps as a young man checks a large suitcase into a very small locker. He straightens his tie and walks out onto the street.

JOHN: *OK, this is Eighth Avenue.*

JOEL: Yeah, that's the Port Authority Bus Terminal. We had to ask all the pimps to leave.

JOHN: *The hookers worked the bus stations?*

JOEL: Yes. God, this is so awful. That camera jerks around. Ron didn't know how to run the camera. We had a lot of scenes missing because he pressed the wrong button. We shot on 35mm, by the way. Ron later worked on ***Gimme Shelter***.

JOHN: *He didn't work much in legit features after that, did he?*

JOEL: He never got anything out of it. Some big agency flew him to Hollywood and nothing happened. He was a little crazy.

Susan Potter combs her hair as she watches TV with her mother. She sets down her brush and tests the weight of her breasts. They are held in check by a white bra.

TV ANNOUNCER: *We'll return to* ***The Daily Storm****.*

JOHN: ***How many days did it take to shoot this?***
JOEL: Oh, I think less than a week. Maybe a weekend. We rented the cameras from this guy and they were totally worthless. We were totally ripped off. That was the biggest budget thing, renting cameras. But yeah, these scenes are in Jerry's studio. I forgot what it looked like. The building is still there.
JOHN: ***That's Jennifer Welles as Susan.***
JOEL: Yeah. Her husband was always standing around. Some Cuban guy would go out and buy us food. I asked, "Who is that guy?" It was Jennifer's husband. He was a Cuban guitar player.

A hand lotion commercial plays out over the television, typical satire in Joel Reed's world.

TV ANNOUNCER: *So keep your hands out of trouble by daily use of Lake's Hand Lotion. The lotion designed for the fellow's mind.*

JOHN: ***So you wrote this?***
JOEL: Yeah.
JOHN: ***How long did that take?***
JOEL: As long as it took me to type the words (laughs)! Actually, it started out as an ambitious project. It started out in their suburban house. It was about real stage mothers that I knew. I should have been studying COBOL at the time.

Career Bed—a portrait of a long gone New York.

Gerry Ramer.

I would have been better off.

JOHN: *Who played Mrs. Potter?*

JOEL: Some investment banker's wife. I don't remember much about her. Jennifer Welles was a stripper in Vegas. I don't know why she came to New York. I saw her a couple times after this. She went into hardcore porn.

JOHN: *How did she find her way into Career Bed*?

JOEL: Somebody sent her over one day. Mark Goldberg came over and said, "She's got great tits." She took her top off and Mark was stunned. He was very naive. She had a great body. I think she was twenty-nine at the time. I guess Scorsese started out on a better track than I did. I don't think he was in NYU yet when this film was made. God, this is awful (laughs). And my parents didn't have me committed.

JOHN: *What did they think of this film?*

JOEL: Actually, my father was quite proud of it. He worked at a record store right down the street from where this was shot.

MRS. POTTER: *Don't give up your virginity to some silly boy! It's too important of an asset.*

SUSAN: *What do you mean by that?!?*

JOEL: Oh, God. Well, what more could I do in two days?

JOHN: *When was the last time you watched this?*

JOEL: When we made it. I snuck into the theater on 42nd Street to watch it. We shot everything on Eighth Avenue and 42nd Street.

Rachman's lair.

All of those buildings are gone, it's changed. They'll be taking clips from this to show New York the way it was. It dates the city. In a nutshell, it's a historical perspective of New York. It captures the essence of city that no longer exists—a fleeting moment in eternity.

Bob Dartfield visits Susan with marriage in mind. Susan's mother has ideas of her own.

BOB DARTFIELD: *You know, I always thought that Susan had the prettiest mother in the county. I always thought if I were older, or you were younger —*
MRS. POTTER: *I'd rather have you for myself. Do you like my legs? They're much shapelier than Susan's.*
BOB DARTFIELD: *Mrs. Potter!*

JOEL: It's funny; my friend Jerry was so worried about the reputation of his studio. He had no reputation. And his studio was right in the center of all the porn theaters in Times Square. He's dead now.
JOHN: ***What do you think of this film today?***

JOEL: It would have been a great picture if we would have shot it in color with the original concept. I don't know (laughs). I was taking lithium at the time! I was diagnosed as a manic-depressant. They gave me 500 milligrams instead of my usual 250 milligrams and I made the movie. I wasn't really there!

JOHN: ***Joe Sarno originally had something to do with this film.***
JOEL: He was hired to do this

Mother love...

movie and then he copped out at the last minute. He was a nice, jolly, gray-haired guy. He was wonderful to be with, he had thousands of stories. His daughter was very nice. Joe was a naval pilot in World War II. From what I remember, he would have sunk the submarine that sunk the cruiser Annapolis, but the charges on his plane were faulty. He crashed and had his face all burned. He was called at the war crime trial over here. Some film cameraman was testifying as well. He met up with them and got a job as a cinematographer for this company. He knew nothing about the film business at the time. He probably would have done this even cheaper. My pictures have around 800 percent more dialogue. I was actually trying to do something here. I guess that's the problem with the film.

JOHN: ***How so?***

JOEL: As bad as it is, this film has some very dramatic sequences. That's what they didn't want in the theaters. They just wanted people running around naked. Some tits. Get undressed and go into the next room. That's what people like. Anyway, here's Shelley Abels as Miss Reynolds. She later became Georgina Spelvin. She was great, very nice. When she did the dyke scene that's coming up, she didn't stop. She went to town, she knew what she was doing. That is fascinating to me, two women together. Or two guys and a chicken.

MISS REYNOLDS: *I would be a much better choice than a man. You wouldn't want her pregnant.*

MRS. POTTER: *What's* ***that*** *supposed to mean?*

MISS REYNOLDS: *Must you be so crude? I'm not interested in her... classical virginity. Do I look like a beast?*

JOHN: ***How did people like Shelley handle their lines?***

JOEL: She knew her lines, she was good. She took over Shirley MacLaine's role in ***The Pajama Game***. The others had some trouble.

JOHN: ***How many takes of each scene did you usually shoot?***

JOEL: What, are you kidding? One. We never—who do you think I was, Billy Wilder or something? It's ironic. It seems like hardcore porn started up one day after we finished this film. There was no market for it. We played it for a couple of weeks.

JOHN: ***Where at?***

JOEL: It played in the Brandt Theater, in Times Square. It played the midwest. There were a couple of chains that played this kind of stuff over there. It played in Baltimore, places like that.

JOHN: ***Here's another sequence of street scenes.***

JOEL: You know, this is good to watch to see what was playing on Broadway. I can't believe I was there. That's the Hotel Manhattan. It's the Milford Plaza now. Right on Eighth Avenue. That's close to where Jamie Gillis lived. There's Downey's. That's where it was.

Mrs. Potter and Susan stand in a corner of their apartment. Susan is about to meet with Broadway director Jack Landive. She is subjected to her mother's meticulous inspection.

MRS. POTTER: *Turn around again. Let your mother see. You look so beautiful in your new mini-dress. You're going to drive all the boys wild.*

SUSAN: *Yes, mother.*

MRS. POTTER: *Mr. Landive is a very important man. Be nice to him, within limits. Give him a nice kiss, but don't do anything nasty. Be diplomatic. You'll never get anywhere without diplomacy.*

JOHN: ***OK. This guy, Mr. Landive. Who played him? He's not bad.***

JOEL: That was John Cardoza. He moved to California, I saw him in a lot of movies. He usually plays the Mexican gangster. The last I saw him, he was living in this Mexican

Ramer grovels before the dapper Ross Miller.

neighborhood where they still had little shacks. He was living in poverty. It's funny to see him playing a nice guy. You're right, he's not bad.

JACK LANDIVE: *Would you like some more coffee?*
SUSAN: *No, thank you.*
JACK LANDIVE: *Coffee's about the only thing that keeps me going.*

JOHN: ***Who did the casting for this?***
JOEL: Who do you think? I did. We put a notice in ***Backstage,*** and a bunch of people showed up. I don't remember everybody's real names. You seem to like this picture. Are you sure you're not sedated?
JOHN: ***It's actually pretty funny.***
JOEL: Actually, I see where this could have been a great exploitation picture. The guys who backed it said I should have expanded it and shot it in color. It could have been a great drive-in picture. They wouldn't play black and white at the drive-ins at the time. And this would have been just the picture to play in the drive-ins in the midwest because there's not too much perverted stuff in there. Just enough.
JOHN: ***We're back on Eighth Avenue.***
JOEL: See how few people are in Times Square? Never again. You can't even move around nowadays. These shots remind me of Andy Milligan. He was the king of Eighth Avenue. He'd sit in that cafeteria

holding court. There's my father's record store! It's gone. The Howard Johnson's and the Metropole are still there. I lived just down the street from where this was shot. One block away.

Joe Sarno's pictures were forty percent composed of shots like this. They'd drive somewhere and then get undressed. Oh, God, this is the fountain at Lincoln Center. It's been used in millions of pictures. You'd see lines of would be filmmakers lined up around it, waiting for it to spout so they could put it in their pictures.

JOHN: ***So, this is back in Jerry's Studio?***

JOEL: Yeah. That cut was terrible. Ron wasn't really a good editor. Look at that jump.

JOHN: ***Maybe he was influenced by Godard.***

JOEL: I doubt it.

Susan and her mother decide to pay the perverted photographer Gerald Ramer a visit. Their knock is answered by a high nasal voice.

GERALD RAMER: *Come in, it's open. The King is at work. You can call me Gerry, but my friends call me the King.*

The two enter and Ramer explains his techniques.

GERALD RAMER: *Yes, the king must photograph this lovely girl. Have her take all her clothes off! I don't want to photograph her nude, I just want to look. That will help me when she has her clothes back on.*

JOEL: OK, the guy who played Gerry Ramer was Ron's friend. This was my attempt at humor. There was a photographer named Gerald Kramer who was basically a rapist pimp. I based Ramer's character on him. He used to really do that. He worked for Albert Anastasia; he used to pimp for him. Here's the story. Gerald had this luxurious film studio right down the street. He used to fix him up with girls; he had two-way mirrors in the dressing rooms. Anastasia got shot and Gerald suddenly ran out of money. He ended up in California working in his brother's auto supplies store. Gerry Ramer was based on that.

JOHN: ***I wonder if anyone ever got the joke.***

JOEL: I don't know. I thought it was funny. Now, this is the big scene. There's a picture of a chimpanzee over there. My friend wanted to sue me. The chimp was named Kokomo Junior. My friend thought he was going to make a lot of money selling pictures of chimpanzees, and he thought this would destroy his reputation. He said, "You got to get Kokomo out of your crummy movie!"

JOHN: ***Did he ever make any money selling the pictures?***

JOEL: No (laughs). He had a warehouse full of them. His name was Nick Corrado. He was dying the last time I talked to him. I saw him on television. He had a home for aged chimps. You can't control them once they get older. He made a lot of money from that and got this guy to produce a television series. It was so bad. It was a chimp show, and he couldn't sell it. But his chimps used to climb out the window and try to rape schoolgirls. He had them trained to get him coffee. But he'd leave the house and sneak back in and one chimp would be jerking off, the other would be raiding the liquor cabinet. He'd say, "I got you guys!" and chase them around with a little whip. He scared the shit out of them, beating them up all the time.

Gerry Ramer brings news of Susan Potter to the girl-crazy Ross Miller.

ROSS MILLER: *Call her! Now it's **my** time for enjoyment!*

JOHN: ***Where were the scenes in Ross Miller's apartment shot?***

JOEL: That was my friend Eliot Smith's apartment. I used to call him the Bearded Transvestite from Hell. One day, he came up to me and said, "I have a problem. I like to put women's clothes on." At one time, we were roommates and he'd bring guys home. I'd say, "Eliot, can't you bring quieter people home?" You never knew what was in bed with him. He wore dresses all the time and said, "Don't tell anyone about my problem." Then, I'd bring somebody home and he'd come out in drag. He'd say, "Oh, Jesus! I forgot we had company!" I said, "Eliot, you're really hiding this. Everyone comes over and you answer the door like that." He said, "Well, I'm a little crazy." He got on drugs later and would go out in the street in drag. He went down to the Village to go clubbing and the people at the doors told him they'd kill him if he came in. I mean, he was a disgrace to transvestites. He had a beard. It was insulting.

JOHN: ***So, this was all Eliot's furniture?***

JOEL: Some of it was. Dan Landi,

Boris Rachman meets his match.

who did the set decoration in Eliot's apartment, charged him around $8,000. Then he found out everything was from Woolworth's. You see, Miller's peeking through the wall while Ramer has her model. Like Kramer and Anastasia.

JOHN: *Did the guy who played Miller bring his own clothes?*

JOEL: I think he might have borrowed one of Eliot's dresses. He was more interested in Eliot than any of the girls. Like I said, Eliot was out there. He said he was getting strange phone calls from his neighbors. I said, "Well, you run around in drag all the time." He said, "I only do it sometimes. Nobody sees me. I go by the highway late at night. It's not that." I said, "Well, I think some of your neighbors are aware of this." He said, "They can't see me under the overpass!" He had a collection of dildos; he liked to fuck himself in the ass while he masturbated. He liked to do it in open spaces. I said, "I don't understand why you don't just rent some guy. One of these days, you're going to get rotator cuff syndrome and you won't be able to move your arms back. You'll have a hard time."

JOHN: *Where was this apartment?*

JOEL: Eliot lived at 234 East 66th Street. He thought there were ghosts in there. When he was on drugs, he thought people were sneaking in and taking pictures of him with his dildos. They put him in the nut house. He went away for six months and then got a place on the East Side next to the Dakota, where the windows faced a brick wall. Now he met some girl and they built an $800,000 house and

Gale McCarty as the reporter.

he says they're spying on him again. He's not doing drugs anymore. He's actually a nice guy, but I don't talk to him anymore. I want to do my Eliot Smith trilogy. It's going to be a book or a movie. The first one's going to be called ***Military School Ramrod***. He told me the story of his life, about having his first affair in military school. Oh—Eliot used to dance in his nightgown on that balcony there.

A stereotype newspaper reporter sits at his desk, surrounded by clutter. He talks briefly on the phone with one of Susan Potter's promoters.

JOHN: ***There's Gale McCarty.***
JOEL: Yeah, the reporter. Actually, he's not bad. I think I'm in the next scene.
JOHN: ***Yeah, with Boris Rachman.***
JOEL: Dennis Lord was the guy who played Boris Rachman. He's dead now. He claimed to be a spy in Vietnam. He had a cinnamon plantation over there. He was down and out and visiting New York. He died of cancer a few years ago. He lived most of his life in Vietnam. Supposedly, he was an Intelligence Officer. He was pretty funny. I'd send him some money for him to do things for me in Bangkok and he never did anything. Then when I met him there, he was living in sort of a brothel. We went out to eat and they wouldn't serve us unless we paid them in advance. They didn't

trust him, he didn't have a very good reputation. He picked me up in Bangkok and I wanted to go to a dirty show. He took me to this nightclub. I said, "Dennis, you talk and talk. At least you could have taken me to a sex show." People were brushing up against my head. I didn't realize that I was sitting with my back to the stage. There were these people fucking behind me. The girls came out with their Coke bottles and they were smoking with their cunts. When you're young, those things are interesting. Dennis lived in a whorehouse in Bangkok for six dollars a week. He was pretty good in this film, considering that we basically just picked people up off the street. He actually sounds kind of human.

Director Boris Rachman sits in a darkened theater. He is watching clips from the Susan Potter screen test. The film rolls. Susan fumbles through her lines with a young man with wild hair and a trademark pipe. Joel Reed.

JOHN: ***Here comes your big moment.***

JOEL: Oh, God. I'm in this scene. I look terrible there. I wish I still had that jacket. It was nice. This was shot in my friend Arthur's loft. A woman was living with him. She went out and raised some money and made a movie about her life in this loft with him. He was a neuter, he was an asexual guy. The movie's about her leaving her husband and four kids in Pennsylvania or Kentucky and coming to New York.

Joel Reed ogles Jennifer Welles in Arthur's loft.

Komono Junior surveys the scene.

She's the heroine and she walks out of the house one night leaving the kids crying and screaming for food. Then she moves into this loft and becomes a big star. She wrote all of the music for it, which was awful. When Arthur died, she pretended to be married to him so she could get the loft. It was rent controlled, about $70 a month.

JOHN: ***Dennis got to fuck Jennifer.***

JOEL: Yeah, right. She still has her panties on. The guy who had this loft had diabetes and almost lost his leg. He had a glass of wine, he said, "I read a book that said I can drink this." I said, "There's sugar in there." He died from it, he had a diabetic stroke. That was Arthur. He inherited $750,000 and gave it away in two weeks. He went on welfare. I didn't know he was giving the money away. He said, "If you'll loan me some money, I'll pay you back. Everybody's going to pay me back the money that they borrowed." I said, "No they're not. What are you thinking?"

Boris and Susan roll around on the bed. The camera slowly tracks in on the director's euphoric face through

Susan's spread legs.

JOEL: This was Radley Metzger's specialty, the hands reaching out, the legs entwined. I did OK with it here.

JOHN: ***What do you think of this scene between Dennis and Jennifer?***

JOEL: It's not bad, but it's not even erotic. (Laughs) This was made from an old release print. The tone in the black and white was originally much better. I was studying Eisenstein at the time! I thought of the way he used light to its most effective means. I was trying to bring out the character and motivation of everybody! You can't tell from watching this tape! It's all lost, all lost! God, she had a hot body. And Dennis has inverted nipples. I never noticed that!

Boris Rachman's eyes roll back in their sockets as Susan Potter slowly goes down on him.

BORIS RACHMAN: *Oh—don't stop! You're the devil's own messenger!*

JOEL: That's my line! My line! When you hear that in a picture again, remember!

Gale McCarty sits at his desk in full reporter regalia. He's got a hot story on his hands, a front-pager about a certain mother and daughter showbusiness team.

JOHN: ***Here's Gale again.***

JOEL: Poor Gale had two scenes! He looks so young. He was around thirty-years-old. OK—this girl in the last scene had a crush on my father. She used to hang around my father's store. She took her top off here without being asked to. That's the type of girl I like now, young and innocent.

The film freezes on Mrs. Potter's latest client, her young breasts peeking through her long black hair. The title music plays as the end credits roll.

JOEL: Well, who knows what I was thinking. Not much. I can't believe I have my name on this. Where did they find this print? It's like the search for the Rosetta Stone or something.

JOHN: ***There's probably a better print sitting around somewhere, but I'm glad they found this one. All in all, it's not a bad weekend's work.***

JOEL: If you say so!

"Joel's Hollywood career was ruined by a rent controlled apartment."—Eddie Jaffe

CHAPTER FIVE

EDDIE JAFFE

1999

Something was very wrong with the hotel clerk's hair. Something was very wrong with him in general. He was slouched over the front desk, staring at the world through narrow slits of eyes. His suit was a mess; the collar was filthy and there were ugly white stains on the lapels. It looked like he had just rolled out of bed. His face jumped uncontrollably at times. I leaned back against the wall and watched him. He was arguing with a Korean tourist about the price of a two-night stay.

The Korean's eyes were glued to the desk clerk's hair. So were mine. It looked like a cross between a weave and a wig, and it was dripping with grease and sweat. Brian kicked my foot. "I bet he got that out of the garbage." I had to agree. "Or maybe off of his bedpost."

The clerk was Indian and wasn't very comfortable with English. The Korean was even worse. The Indian twitched his head and snorted. "That $200 for two night."

The Korean held up his hand and extended two fingers. "Two?"

"Yes! Yes! $200! Marathon weekend!"

Another wrinkled brow and another nervous twitch. "Two?"

They went on for a while before the Korean pulled out four fresh bills. The Indian scooped them up and gave him a key. "Room 310. To right. Elevator. 310."

The Korean lumbered off to his left. The Indian didn't make any attempt to stop him. It was 10:30 PM at the Washington Jefferson Hotel.

Louis, the sloppy gatekeeper of the Washington Jefferson Hotel.

The Washington Jefferson was an old brick tenement building on 51st Street and Eighth Avenue in the heart of Hell's Kitchen. The place was a mess, a strange mixture of peeling paint, stained carpets, and burned-out light bulbs. Framed prints of Robert Frank knockoffs haphazardly dotted the walls in a feeble attempt to add an air of sophistication.

A burst of noise caught my attention from across the hall. An old woman was blow-drying her hair, taking in the action from a half-opened door. I turned my attention back to the Indian. A pile of brochures was stacked at his side. I picked one up and began reading:

"At the Washington Jefferson, you are family. Louis greets you with a smile at the reception desk. He knows you by name, as if you've been there before. This is simply a friendly place to stay."

The Korean walked back into the room, looking for the elevator. His face was red and confused. He zoomed past us and kicked the front desk. The Indian scowled. His eyes screamed, "Fuck you!"

Brian and I stepped up and made arrangements for our stay. Louis made no attempt to learn our names. He handed us a key and pointed to the right. "Elevator that way. Room 430."

We made our way through a maze of hallways, took a ride on the elevator, and slowly walked to our room. We were greeted by a ten-by-seven pen: one bed, one sink, one chair.

"I get dibs on the bed," said Brian.

I didn't argue with him. The floor was probably cleaner. I set down my suitcase, walked over to the window, and looked outside. Directly across the street was a mission called Saint Paul's house. A neon cross read, **SIN WILL FIND YOU OUT**. A brown sign hung above the door: **CHRIST LIVES, TRUST HIM**. I tried to open the window for some air, but it was bolted shut. Grimy pipes ran up and down the adjacent wall, from floor to ceiling. They looked like they hadn't been painted in years. The place was full of character. Probably full of bugs as well. I walked over to the sink and risked a glass of water. Brian went out to find the bathroom and I walked down the hall to an open window.

I stepped out on the fire escape for a cigarette. St. Paul's stood before me, a worn down beacon to salvation. A few people were walking on the street below me. One of them was very overweight, his head a mess of bright white hair. He sat down on the steps leading up to the lobby and looked me over. The Washington Jefferson would be my home for the next few days. A friendly place to stay.

Room with a view: St. Paul's House.

It wasn't long before we discovered that the Washington Jefferson doubled as a rooming house. The man who lived across the hall was learning how to play the violin. He practiced the same song hour after hour, climbing scales clumsily with arthritic fingers. An old man with a walker lived down the hall in room 461. He was constantly arguing with his live-in nurse. Their voices rang out above the violin, thundering down the hall and into our room.

MR. 461: You are not doing me a favor! Why don't you clean this room sometime? It's a mess!

NURSE: I can't be here all the time! You have to wait!

MR. 461: You're no good! You're

John outside of room 461.

no good! You never clean!

NURSE: I'm cleaning today!

MR. 461: No, you can't just say you clean! It's not about speaking, it's about action! I want to see action!

NURSE: Be quiet for a minute!

MR. 461: I scream at you because you don't listen! You're never around!

NURSE: I know I'm never around! You always scream at me!

The old man stumbled out of his room like a bullet. Without the walker.

MR. 461: You get out! You're aggravating me! Get out! I don't need you anymore!

NURSE: Oh good, good! You don't need me anymore? You just call some other helpless soul to help you then! You're not nice to anybody! Get back in here, you baby!

MR. 461: Bitch!

NURSE: You're vicious! You're a rotten old egg!

MR. 461: No! Rotten apple!

Sleep would soon prove impossible at the Washington Jefferson. We learned to counter this by spending a lot of time at the bar. The Molly Wee Pub, of "Goodbye, English Rose" fame, would soon become our home away from home.

Stepping into a bar outside of Michigan on a semi-regular basis was strange. The bartenders gave us confused looks of recognition. Paul Schmidt at the Molly Wee was beginning to note our appearance with a smile. Paul was from Ireland. So was everyone else who worked behind the bar. They were friendly enough, and we sat there for hours, watching people come and go, until it was four in the morning. Paul and the others were upset at the large number of tourists that had come in to New York for the marathon weekend. "They just crowd things up. All the fucking tourists."

The drinks were going down

easily. Assorted shots and a lot of beer. Many of them were free. By two o'clock in the morning, things were spinning. I walked over to the jukebox and scanned it. Found Sinatra, put in a five, and walked back to the bar.

Eight hours earlier, Brian and I were walking up Sixth Avenue to Joel's apartment. It was mid-afternoon; a sunny November day. I had called Joel from the Washington Jefferson at noon. "Why don't you come over in a couple hours?" We were back on the elevator in Joel's building by two.

Joel greeted us at the door, pipe in hand. "I was going to enter the marathon, but they didn't want to make special rules for me. I think I could win it if they had the City Marshall chasing me."

We walked inside. Joel's place hadn't changed a bit in eight months. The same pictures on the wall, the same overflowing bookshelves, the same clutter. I set my tape recorder on the coffee table. "Did you talk to Eddie?"

Joel sat down. "Yeah, I called him this morning. I told him we'd get him at seven. Is that too late?"

"No, that's OK. I thought maybe you could tell me a little about him before I met him."

"That's fine." Joel got out his pipe and unbuttoned his shirt. "I don't want to get any hot ashes on it, it's expensive. I told Eddie we'd eat at Hooters, your treat. He's only ninety-seven and he likes the action."

JOEL REED: There was a hotel right near Madison Square Garden that had all of these cowboys in the lobby all the time. They would come over for the rodeo and didn't have the money to go back. They just stayed in New York. Some of them were eighty-years-old. They became New York cowboys. Eddie would know the name of the hotel.

JOHN: ***Is he able to get around?***

JOEL: Yeah, he gets around. He actually broke his hip twice and was using a walker. Now he gets around with a cane. He's a tiny guy. He has a place in Hollywood that he goes to in the winter.

JOHN: ***Where does he live over here?***

JOEL: He lives right by your hotel. 52nd and Eighth. There's a senior citizens' place there; a big building. But he had an apartment on 48th Street between Sixth and Seventh. Nat Hiken lived in the next apartment. He produced ***Car 54, Where Are You?*** And ***The Phil Silvers Show***. Joe Russell lived there, so did Irving Hoffman from 20th Century Fox. Marlon Brando lived with Eddie for a time. The only thing Eddie had against Brando was that he would steal his socks and underwear. He was embarrassed about it; he'd wear it for two weeks and then put it back in the drawer. Eddie would make a good book. He got hired to write a book about himself, but all he wants to talk about is how he advised the presidents of big corporations with stupid ideas. He told the president of Coca-Cola to change the shape of the bottle.

JOHN: ***How did you meet him?***

JOEL: Eddie? Actually, I was taking a bribe to Edna Ferguson, the chief feature writer at the ***New York News***. She did all of the big story interviews. I had a bottle of liquor with me in the elevator, and somebody yanked it out of my hand. It was a guy named Connie Soloyanis, who was Danton Walker's assistant. Connie said, "You're supposed to bring *me* liquor." One day—it was December 29th, my birthday, I arranged a big surprise party for myself at his loft. At the time, I was living in Brooklyn with my parents. I was very tired, I didn't sleep the night before. Connie said, "Why don't you go to sleep at Eddie's? I'll see you at the party." He took me up to Eddie's place. The door was never locked. I went to sleep, and at 12 o'clock at night, this guy tapped me on the shoulder and asked, "Do you want something to eat?" He had no idea who I was. That was Eddie. He sent downstairs to Zucker's for some food. I said, "Come down to the party." Eddie was sort of a recluse back then. He didn't go out. But I started going over to his place after that. At that time, he was the top press agent in New York. That was in the '50s, and he was making over $100,000 a year.

JOHN: ***Who did he handle?***

JOEL: Practically all of the major celebrities were his clients. Joe E. Lewis, the comedian. Nat King Cole, everyone. I broke up with my girlfriend Hope a couple of years later. I didn't have any place to go, so Eddie said, "Stay here." Sidney Beckerman slept at his apartment. He went on to produce ***Marathon Man***. He's a big guy on the coast.

When I stayed at Eddie's, I had this reoccurring dream that a masked bandit was coming in with a hood.

Nobody went to bed there until 4 o'clock, when Eddie went to bed. One day, I woke up at about 4:30. The door opened and this guy came in with a hood. It was very cold. It was Eddie's secretary. He used to come in at five in the morning. He had a job typing. He'd step over all of the bodies and get to work.

There was this guy who was a former fighter-turned-press agent. He did a lot of writing. He was kind of a "dees and dems" type of guy. He used to struggle with the writing. The worst thing in the world was to try to talk to him while he was typing. You'd get punched out. Eddie used to hang around with Joe Gallo, the gangster. ***Look*** magazine did a story about Eddie's apartment. They did a TV special, as well.

JOHN: ***Any other stories about him?***

JOEL: When he lived in that apartment, everybody was using his phone. He got a phone cord about one and a half feet long. They'd have to reach under his bed to use it. That didn't stop anybody. They'd climb over him and pick the phone up.

Eddie had a fountain in the living room of his apartment. It caused a million water bugs to take residence. A press agent named Joe Russell used to steal everything from over there. Eddie was always buying stationary. Whenever we filled up Eddie's refrigerator with food, it would always disappear. One day, I set a tripwire and found Joe in the kitchen. We chased him into his apartment and found four refrigerators filled with Eddie's food. One time, I really got mad. I had a new leather phone book and watch. They disappeared one night and Eddie ran into Joe's apartment. He said, "Give him back his fucking watch!" Joe said, "I'll give it back later." Eddie ripped open his closet and saw all of his stationary. A ten years supply of pens and paper. And my watch and phone book.

Joe Russell was a strange guy. He was determined to make every woman a hooker. He'd scream, "Why are you giving it away for nothing?" He had some money and he gave it to this girl. He introduced her to this guy who bought her an MG, a diamond ring, a fur coat. The guy got arrested the next day and they took away everything. They were running a credit fraud. The sheriff was looking for them for about six months. Joe was crazy. He'd get a dinner invitation and bring about six people along. He took us out to this girl's house on Long Island. He said, "Irving Hoffman invited me to

Eddie Jaffe (center) with boxers Joey Giardello (right) and Rubin Carter, 1964.

dinner. Let's all go. I want him to shit in his pants!" We all walked in and Hoffman went crazy.

JOHN: ***Who was Irving Hoffman?***

JOEL: He was another press agent who talked with this thick Tulsa tone. I didn't know him too well. One day he called me. "Hey Joel, you get along with the women. I want you to introduce me to someone. I'm madly in love with this girl. Meet me on 49th Street, we'll go out to dinner. She works upstairs at the Circus." I said, "That's a porn place, a fuck show!" He said, "Yes! You've got to see her, she's so terrific." We went upstairs and he said, "She'll be out soon, her act is coming on." She got on stage and jumped out into the audience. She was giving blowjobs and jerking guys off. Things were pretty wild in the '60s. People were fingering her and grabbing her tits; she was in this mass of suits. She was collecting money—she was taking bills and jerking guys off, and she never lost count of the cash. It was amazing. Afterward, we went out to eat. She asked what I thought of her act. I said, "Well, I really think it's amazing how you can keep tabs on all the money." But that was Irving. Those were the only times he invited me out.

I look back on those days and can't believe them. It was a different era. I go to Times Square now, and it's crowded. There was nobody there during the day. If it wasn't matinee day, the place was empty. I remember this guy who was the only pornographic salesman in New York. He was a suitcase man; he'd come around, "Do you want to buy some stuff?" This was in the '50s. He was a big fat guy, he sold razor blades. If you got to talk to him, you'd see the goods. Eddie knew this guy who as at the Copa, sitting with Frank Sinatra. He took out a dildo. When you pressed a button, it was like an early Transformer. Wings would come out and it would say, "Fuck you! Fuck you! Fuck you!" Frank said, "I want it, I want it!" The guy said, "I'll get you one, Frank." He said, "No, I want it now! Here's $100." The guy said, "No, I can't sell you this one." Frank offered him $1,000. "Give me the fucking bird!" The guy said, "I can't. It's the prototype from the manufacturer." Eddie said that he was some guy. If you gave him a hamburger, he'd show you his secret pornography collection.

JOHN: ***Did Eddie tell you about anyone else like that?***

JOEL: There was a guy named Maynard Kessler. He had a beautiful townhouse on 62th Street. He'd sell porn if you got friendly with him. A real skinny, dirty old man. He had classical pornography. He had a party every week. He had a big thing for women. He didn't look like the kind of guy who would sleep with anyone. It was a big thing if Maynard took you down to his private gallery. English girls with no clothes on being captured by Arabs. Those were crazy days. And Eddie was a very important person.

JOHN: ***What happened to Eddie in the end?***

JOEL: He met this woman and married her. She cleaned him out. After that, he didn't want to do anything. He gave up his clients and became a consultant for some corporations. He was always giving advice to people anyway. If you were fucking a girl, he'd have something to say about it. One day, Hope called me. She said, "You should do this, and you should do that." I said, "Where are you getting those stupid ideas from?" She said, "I don't want to talk about it." One day Eddie called me. He said, "I've been talking to Hope..."

I was with this girl one day, and Eddie just went on ranting. He didn't know anything about the situation. It just happened to be a girl from the neighborhood. I wasn't fucking her or anything. I was out to dinner with her and her

Joel Reed and a forgotten actress at the opening of a nameless Broadway show.

mother. Eddie came along and said, "I don't know what's going on here, but Joel shouldn't fool around with college girls like you." She said, "I'm twelve-years-old." He said, "That's even worse!"

Time passed quickly. Soon, it was quarter to seven. Joel stood up. "Let's walk over to Eddie's." He buttoned his shirt and grabbed his jacket. I walked across the room to look at his pictures. Joel came up beside me. "That's the girl I told you about who went to jail for murder. It's a good thing she didn't think I had any money. She might have tied the gag too tight on me." I laughed. "What year was the picture taken?"

Joel stared at the picture. "Oh, probably 1956. She was a beautiful girl."

I gathered my things and we walked over to the door. "Let me lock up." Brian and I walked outside and Joel turned off the lights inside. Soon, we were back on the streets, moving along toward 52nd Street, where Eddie Jaffe was waiting for us.

Conversation en route to Eddie's:

JOEL: Look at all the chauffeurs by the Essex House. I think the secret service is here tonight. You can tell—they drive those 4x4s with the weird license plates. The

Essex House is where they have most of the big events.

JOHN: ***OK, we're on 58th Street.***

JOEL: Marlon Brando lived over here when he first came to New York. It was a little hotel with the bedrooms cut off into cubicles. It was like $12 a week to live here then. The Park Savoy. It was a whorehouse after that. This block was all whorehouses.

JOHN: ***It's pretty crowded out here tonight.***

JOEL: Yeah, it's because of the marathon. I can't even find a place to have breakfast in the morning, there's so many people here. You were lucky to find a hotel.

JOHN: ***It was rough.***

JOEL: Let's make a left. There's the Osborne. One of the oldest apartment buildings in New York. It's where Gig Young shot his wife. Look at all the people on the streets. They all want to pay $20 for a hamburger.

We slowly made our way toward Eddie. Joel stopped at 55th and Seventh and pointed.

JOEL: Well, we're walking by where we shot part of ***Career Bed***. There was a loft where this new building is. The building was empty

John and Joel exit Sardi's.

for ten years. A friend of mine called the number and said, "How much are you offering?" He got a whole floor for $60. They never raised his rent or anything.

JOHN: ***It's a shame the place is gone.***

JOEL: They just tore this block down. A friend of mine lived in that apartment there for $3,000 a month. It was smaller than mine. He moved a few years ago. Over here is where Repp's brother lived. He had a penthouse at the Americana Hotel. Let's cross here.

We made our way across the street. The blocks went by quickly and soon we were on Broadway.

JOEL: These places are booming now. They were becoming really seedy. That hotel was all hookers.
JOHN: ***Where are we, 54th and Broadway?***
JOEL: Yeah, I guess so. Well, we have a few more streets yet. Eddie's on 52nd. Think about it, this was once nothing but farms.

Two blocks later, the smell of sirloin hit us full in the face. I looked to my left and watched a group of overweight men frying steak through a giant wall of windows.

JOEL: You get good steaks here, they're really thick.

A large Italian with a heavy beard held up a steak and pointed to it.

ITALIAN: *Really* thick, no?
JOHN: ***So I see.***

We crossed another street and Joel pointed to a gray building with an elaborate façade.

JOEL: That's where I went to school. The American Academy of Dramatic Arts. It was in that studio building. A musician's union was next store, but they moved downtown. Anyway, Eddie's in this building.

We walked up to a giant high-rise that seemed to take up half the block. Joel led the way through a revolving door. The lobby was surprisingly vacant. A skinny man with a black mustache sat behind a long desk. He was chatting with a black woman who was visiting her father. Joel walked up to them and cut in.

"We're here for Eddie Jaffe."

"He just on the street, outside."

"Oh, he's outside?"

"He just walk out."

We walked through the glass doors again. An old man, cane in hand, was perched on the hood of a black sedan, looking out into the night. We walked up to him and Joel called out: "Eddie! We walked right past you! This is John and Brian. They're from Detroit."

Eddie smiled and sat up a little. We got closer and I looked him over. He was wearing a dark blue sport coat with a thin white shirt. Both pieces of clothing looked like they had seen better days. The cuffs of his shirt were gray, the sleeves of the coat worn. A battered hat sat on his head, pushed back, revealing what looked to be a full head of hair.

EDDIE JAFFE: Where is this place located?

JOEL: We'll get a cab and go to Hooters. You wanted to go to Hooters, right?

EDDIE: I'll go anyplace you guys want to go.

JOEL: OK, let's go there. We'd better get a taxi. I was just telling them the dildo story with Frank Sinatra.

EDDIE: You're from Detroit? Everybody I knew from Detroit was in burlesque. This one guy came up with a great idea. He'd hire strippers and then adopt them.

JOHN: ***How long have you known Joel?***

EDDIE: Forty years. How old is he? I've known him since he was a kid. I think he's a genius. I'll tell you why. I saw him on a Thursday and he'd never even seen a movie camera. On Friday he had rented one and over the weekend he shot a picture. He has a great way with words. The only person better was Ernest Lehman. He wrote ***Sweet Smell of Success***.

JOHN: ***The film with Burt Lancaster?***

EDDIE: Yes. Everyone thinks it's about me because he wrote it in my apartment. It's about Winchell and his daughter. It's a classic. The only thing is that they got a director who didn't really know Broadway.

JOHN (thinking): ***Alexander...***

EDDIE: Alexander Mackendrick.

JOHN: ***Do you think he misrepresented Broadway?***

EDDIE: Well, he didn't get some things right. But it's a great story about a press agent who'd do anything for Winchell. You see it rereleased all the time. Did Joel get a cab yet?

Hailing a cab while standing in the middle of 52nd Street was proving to be impossible. Joel walked up the street a way to the corner of Seventh Avenue. The traffic was heavy and most of the cabs were occupied. Joel walked out into the street and held out his arm.

JOHN: ***How long have you been living at this place?***

EDDIE: Since they built it, twelve years ago. Where are you staying?

JOHN: ***The Washington Jefferson.***

EDDIE: That was one of the top whorehouses in the world in my day. How'd you find it?

JOHN: ***It was the only place left, what with the marathon and everything.***

EDDIE: It should be very cheap.

John, Eddie, Joel—Hooters bound.

JOHN: ***Not this weekend. They're making a killing from that race.***

EDDIE: It should be $10! The marathon takes out all the hotels. But I lived across the street from Joel at 48th Street.

JOHN: ***I think we've got a cab here.***

I walked Eddie a few steps over to the curb and we piled into the cab. Joel was arguing with the driver, a man of Middle Eastern descent.

DRIVER: You think I'm crazy?

JOEL: It's on 56th Street. Eddie has trouble walking.

DRIVER: Where are you going? You going where?

JOEL: Hooters, on 56th Street between Broadway and Seventh. Go around the block.

DRIVER: We go up Eighth, that's the only way to get there.

JOEL: OK, that's fine.

DRIVER: I'm just telling you that, and you say I'm nutty.

JOEL: No, Eddie is forty-seven-years-old today, and he has —

EDDIE: No, I'm *forty-eight*!

The driver hit the gas and we headed up 52nd to Eighth. Eddie, Joel, and I sat in back, while Brian kept our driver in check.

EDDIE: I had to wait a half hour for a cab on Eighth Avenue.

JOEL: Well, it's busy. Vernon just moved to an old age home in Florida. I think I'll move down there with him. They've got a bus for senior citizens!

JOHN: ***Did you know Vernon Becker?***

EDDIE: I've met him. It was some experience.

JOHN: ***Joel was telling me about Nat Hiken.***

EDDIE: I think Nat Hiken was the best writer in the history of television. He wrote ***Car 54, Where Are You?*** and ***The Phil Silvers Show***. He lived in the apartment across from me. Joe Russell lived down the hall. My best story is that Joe's apartment caught fire. Rather than spend a dime to call the fire department, he used my phone.

JOEL: Well, that was Joe. He became nicer as he got older.

EDDIE: No, no, no. I went out to lunch today with Ernie Midler, a guy who supported Russell. He gave him everything. I said, "Don't you understand why Russell hated you?" He said he didn't know. I said, "You didn't do enough for him, you should have done more." Russell claimed that Midler owed him money, but it was a *lie*. Ernie's a millionaire. His father left him a million bucks, but the bank has authority of it, and they won't give it to him. Where the hell is this place at?

JOEL: The next block. Now Eddie, hands off the girls in there. Can you get out OK?

The driver let us off and pulled away. I took Eddie's arm and we slowly made our way to the flight of steps that led to Hooters. Joel quickened his stride at the sight of the bright lights ahead. The promise of young waitresses in shorts was thick in the air. Eddie grabbed the banister midway up the stairs. "This is Joel's area!" I smiled. Joel was already inside. The girls at Hooters were in for a surprise.

JOHN: ***Joel said that you knew Joe Gallo.***

EDDIE: I was on his list to be killed. I messed around with his girl.

JOHN: ***So he put a hit on you?***

EDDIE: There was this newspaperman. He called me and said, "Don't leave the house." I said, "What the fuck are you talking about?" He said, "I just came back from Joey Gallo's house, and I noticed that you were on his list to be killed."

JOHN: ***What happened?***

EDDIE: I don't know, but I think I was the only person who fucked Joey Gallo's wife who wasn't murdered! I knew all of the gangsters. Most of them were cheap punks. I lived across the street from where they all hung out.

Eddie Jaffe outside his apartment.

We reached the top of the stairs and opened the door. Joel was smiling and chatting with a hostess. Eddie looked around. "It's kind of noisy in here."

"Jumpin' Jack Flash" was turned up on the radio. As Eddie and I approached Joel, I couldn't help but think of Robert De Niro's slow motion walk in ***Mean Streets***. Eddie signaled to the hostess and pointed to Joel. "He's a technical genius." She let out a confused laugh and led us to a table near the back of the room. I set my tape recorder on the table, close to Eddie. It was time to get down to business.

Eddie Jaffe was reserved and quiet. He said, more than once, "Don't talk about me—let's talk about Joel." He would often argue with Reed over someone's name, or where a particular incident took place.

The following conversation took place at 7:30 PM on November 6, 1999.

JOHN: ***Where are you from originally?***

EDDIE: I was born in 1913 in Duluth, Minnesota.

JOHN: ***What did your parents do?***

EDDIE: My father had a tailor shop. He was also the political boss of the town we lived in. But I grew up… I spent three years in an orphan home in Cleveland, Ohio.

JOHN: ***Joel told me you also spent some time in Texas.***

EDDIE: In 1936, I had some concessions with the World's Fair in Texas.

JOEL: Eddie was down at the World's Fair in Fort Worth and saw all of the strippers and decided to come to New York.

JOHN: ***When did you first come here?***

EDDIE: I came to New York in 1937.

JOHN: ***What were you doing at the time?***

EDDIE: I took any job I could get. I got started as a press agent on Broadway. I worked for all of the major film companies. I worked for Paramount. I was in charge of their column publicity here in New York. We weren't allowed to talk to Paramount in California. I remember when my boss came up to me and said, "Eddie, you can't talk to them." I said, "How will I know what's happening with the pictures?" He said, "You've got to find out somewhere else."

JOHN: ***That sounds a little weird.***

EDDIE: It was a really mixed up thing. It was hard to do publicity like that. The guy said, "Your job is never to bother me." But then I met Joel.

JOEL: And I ruined him. I was saying before that I lived across the street from Eddie. But I met him before that, when I was living with Hope Smith.

EDDIE: He moved in with me. Remember when you tried to steal Joe Russell's girls?

JOEL: I never slept with any of them! Was it ***Life*** or ***Look*** that did that story on you?

EDDIE: ***Look***. They did the ***Tonight Show*** at my apartment, as well. They said, "We'll bring our own girls." I said, "Why can't I use the girls that hang around me?" They said, "They're not pretty enough." Remember that? Earl Wilson brought his own girls.

JOEL: I remember at Eddie's place you could always get laid. If you hung around long enough, some girls would show up. Mainly Kaisha. Remember Kaisha? Joe Russell would run in and say, "What are you fucking this guy for?"

JOHN: ***Who was Kaisha?***

EDDIE: She was a black hooker. She used to work the corner outside our building. Nat Hiken came out and she said, "Nat, do me a favor. I double parked my car..."

JOEL: She went to jail. She once came up to my apartment with another black girl. Kaisha said, "She just came in from out of town. Give her a try, I want to see how she does. I said, "OK. I'll take her up." She said, "No, you have to pick her up on Broadway and argue about money with her. And then she has to see if

Eddie Jaffe (right) and columnist Earl Wilson.

she can get your credit card."

EDDIE: And then there were a lot of orgies going on with top celebrities. The guys needed girls. I did the publicity with Plato's Retreat. That was later on. Joel appreciated that.

JOEL: Well, Jim Moran just died. He had all the orgies.

EDDIE: Yeah. They didn't print any of that in the papers.

JOHN: ***Who was Jim Moran?***

EDDIE: The New York press agent who created the publicity stunt.

JOEL: You can look him up. Jim Moran had this big apartment where he had all these orgies. David Merrick used to come dressed as the Pope. Everything went on.

EDDIE: What scared the shit out of me was the time the guy who wrote all of the top musicals had an orgy. I went to his house and everyone was dressed up in cop uniforms. My friend was with me. Someone came up to him and said, "Did you just fuck my wife?" My friend said, "Why?" And he said, "I want to know how she was."

JOEL: Well, that's true. I went to many orgies like that. I brought a couple of new girls. All the guys would leave their wives and jump on the new girl. I was there with six couples and everyone was fucking my date.

Our waitress appeared with our

menus and I ordered a beer. She soon returned with a pint of lager and I took a sip. "Do you folks need a little more time?" she asked.

I had to wonder what she was thinking. Our table had been loud and conspicuous from the get-go, and our strange conversation had clearly raised a few eyebrows.

"We're still deciding," I said, as Eddie studied the menu.

Joel closed his menu and addressed us: "The Caesar salad's pretty good. Eddie—did you remember to bring your teeth?"

I closed my menu and took a sip of beer. His question was met with a nod. Joel and Eddie started talking, and my mind recalled something that Eddie had said to me earlier in the cab: "Joel was a good press writer. He could imitate anybody's style. He was one of the better guys working. But he fooled around. Joel used to come over to my house to eat when he was broke."

I looked at the two friends as they talked. Joel was now looking after Eddie. The role of father and son had been reversed. I took another sip of beer, smiled, and wondered what kind of person Eddie had been in his prime. I imagined a young Joel M. Reed as he listened and learned from his surrogate father.

The noise of the place brought me back to the present. The table behind us was hosting a birthday party. A bunch of drunks started singing as our waitress walked back to our table.

WAITRESS: Have you folks decided?

EDDIE (looking at menu): I think that the chili's probably the best bet. There aren't many entrees…

JOEL: I'll have the Caesar salad.

EDDIE (to waitress): Miss! You didn't bring our table any water.

WAITRESS: We don't usually bring out water unless you ask for it.

EDDIE: You *always* bring water to the table!

WAITRESS: I'm sorry, sir.

JOEL (to waitress): Watch it! In Eddie's day, he could buy and sell you!

Our waitress scooped up our menus and stormed off toward the kitchen. We all started laughing.

JOEL: Well… at least he's not talking about the president of Coca-Cola!

"I don't think I ever saw *Sex by Advertisement*. If I did, I don't remember it."—Joe Sarno

CHAPTER SIX

SEX BY ADVERTISEMENT

Career Bed might have been a box office disaster, but that didn't stop Peppercorn-Wormser from luring Reed back to the director's chair for another quick and cheap affair. ***Sex by Advertisement*** soon followed, and if anything, the film was even stranger than its predecessor. A good portion of it was shot without sound, resulting in a weird pastiche of mismatched takes and off-camera dialogue. The entire film looks as if it was shot in a week. Don't be fooled. Joel Reed directed the thing over the course of two weekends.

Shelley Abels stars as Dr. Joanne Richfield, the closest thing to a main character that the film can offer. She sits behind her cluttered desk, looks straight into the camera, and starts talking:

DR. JOANNE RICHFIELD: *Prior to the recent sexual revolution, the common… almost universal public acceptance of deviation—advertising for sexual outlets—was done undercover. It was limited to bulletin boards in certain stores, restaurants, and neighborhoods frequented by degenerates. These could be found in almost every major city of the world. But still, they were hidden in coded language… worded so that only the knowing would reply.*

Dr. Richfield's plan is to blow the lid off of Manhattan's sex-scam sewer. She's sent a team of reporters and researchers onto the streets of New York to gather the facts. America loves a good scandal, and ***Sex by Advertisement*** is her shot at the big time.

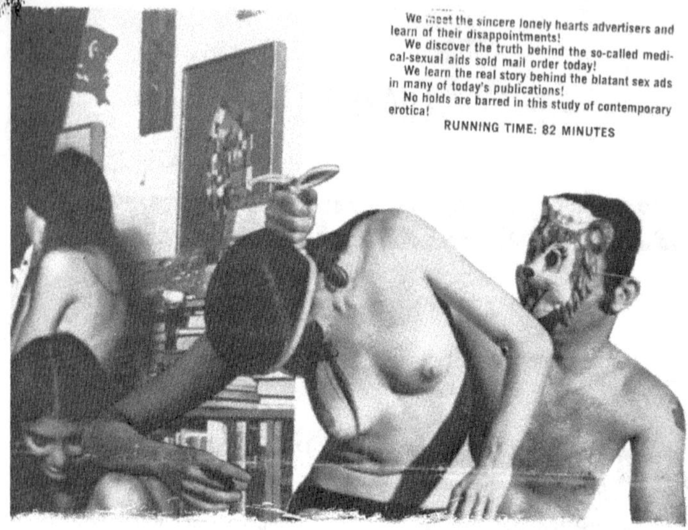

A synopsis from Joel Reed's press clippings collection:

"Our hidden camera reveals actual case histories behind personal ads such as, 'OBEDIENCE COUNSOLER AVALIBLE—SUPPLIES OWN EQUIPMENT.' It visits the office of a New York marriage broker who preys on physical deformity and human misfortune. It rips aside the glamour of showbusiness to depict the procurer posing as a casting director who destroys hundreds of young girls with the promise of a career.

"We visit the manufacturer of torture and fetish equipment, a pornography club, a peeping tom society, figure model studios, a mud fetish perversion establishment, suburban orgy clubs, young marrieds who exchange lewd photos of themselves with other couples, and husbands and wives who prey on babysitters as a hobby.

"We meet the $50,000 a year businessman who can only consummate successful relationships with extremely ugly women and a mad sadist who whips nude, teenage girls as a hobby. We visit a meeting of his organization, whose membership list includes politicians, movie stars, editors, a famed chemist, and a noted philanthropist. We view a sadomasochistic marathon of theirs in which young society girls (including a diplomat's daughter), models, and starlets are abused horribly by every fiendish device imaginable, as it is the only way they can obtain satisfaction."

JOEL REED: Shelley Abels [Georgina Spelvin] was in ***Sex by Advertisement***, as well. She was producing films at JCPenny. She came over, and we shot her scenes in two hours. She was saying, "Oh my God, look at this terrible ad! This is a dirty old man who wants schoolgirls!" I played five characters in the movie; I was the dirty old man. I was also a male hustler, a stud. The trouble with those pictures was that they were too mild. We couldn't go hardcore with them. A major studio wanted to shoot ***Career Bed*** again in color.

It's a pretty safe bet to say that no major studio ever wanted to remake ***Sex by Advertisement***, yet alone in color. The entire endeavor is about as anti-commercial as they come. Virtually plotless, the film is little more than a series of loops strung together by Dr. Richfield's choppy narration. Still—in spite of its flaws—***Sex by Advertisement*** somehow manages to entertain. As crude and rough as its parts may be, the finished product is strangely fascinating.

The following interview was conducted via telephone on February 5, 2016. ***Sex by Advertisement*** played softly in the background as I asked the questions.

A grainy shot of Madison Avenue fills the screen. Deadpan narration crackles over the speakers as midday traffic moves up and down the street.

NARRATOR: *Advertising, headquartered on New York's Madison Avenue, is a multibillion dollar industry. A TV commercial, designed to entice you to buy a 59-cent can of hairspray, may have cost $60,000 to produce, and a million dollars in fees to broadcast. However, due to the liberalization of pornography laws, a new group of publications has sprung up, and their market is sex advertising. The sex by advertisement market operates far from the posh executive suites on Madison and Fifth. Their locale: a garbage-ridden side street. Their masterminds: cruel, anything-for-a buck businessmen, fresh from the sewer. Fiscal degenerates!*

With that, ***Sex by Advertisement*** *begins. White credits slowly rise over a jet-black background as needle-drop music softly plays. The screen reads: 'An Instant Attraction, Inc. Production.'*

FROM TODAYS HEADLINES!
SADO MASOCHIST HIDEOUT RAIDED
SCORES ARRESTED; TORTURE EQUIPMENT CONFISCATED
IMPORTS YOUNG GIRLS FOR LOVE
DOMESTIC JOB OFFERS FRONT FOR PROSTITUTION
SUBURBAN ORGY-CLUB UNCOVERED
YOUNG MARRIEDS CO-MINGLED DAILY
SHOW BIZ AGENT LURES GIRLS
UNSUSPECTING BEAUTIES FORCED INTO SLAVERY
WHIPS NUDE TEEN-AGE GIRL IN PUBLIC PARK
S_X BY ADVERTISEMENT
Featuring LIZA DURAN • VIC QUARANTA • ANN HARRIS
Written & Directed by Joel M. Reed • Produced by William Samek & Elliott R. Reed
An Instant Attraction • A Provocative Films Release

JOHN: ***What was Instant Attractions Division?***

JOEL: That was a corporation that I had in 1968. I started the company about a year before ***Sex by Advertisement*** was made, booking trade shows and private parties. The main thing was instant disco—we had a van with lighting. You'd get a group, a DJ, or you'd get go-go girls. You could rent them for around $500 and up. That was the original Instant Attractions.

JOHN: ***So, it was basically a package that corporations could hire in order to spice up their meetings?***

JOEL: That's right. We did some sweet sixteen parties, too. For the corporate meetings, we'd have this guy who would get up and start reading from actuarial tables and accounting books. He was very dull and dry. Suddenly, he'd rip off his jacket and say, "Oh, screw this!" And then the go-go girls would come out.

JOHN: ***Was Instant Attractions a spin-off of EIG?***

JOEL: Instant Attractions was a part of it, yes.

The music swells as the credits roll.

JOHN: ***So, this was your second film. How soon after Career Bed did you start working on it?***

JOEL: It was within two months. What happened is that Peppercorn-Wormser saw ***Career Bed*** and they told me to make another picture right away. We made a deal for them to release ***Career Bed***, and they said, "Hurry up and make another picture—we'll give you the money." That's how ***Sex by Advertisement*** got made. We shot it in two weekends or something.

JOHN: ***I don't see a credit, but I'm assuming that you wrote the script...***

JOEL: Yes, I wrote the script. I could have been more attentive, but they wanted something fast.

JOHN: ***How long did it take you to write it?***

JOEL: Oh, probably two days. It wasn't much. I just decided to go through all of my friends' experiences. There was the ***East Village Other***, and they had all of those ads in there. They had these photo shoot places where you'd "learn" photography—you'd pay them $10 an hour and they'd give you a broken camera and a nude model.

JOHN: ***I've always meant to***

From today's headlines!

ask if you wrote any scripts prior to Career Bed and Sex by Advertisement.

JOEL: I had written a kung fu script called ***The Tiger and the Dragon***. Everybody thought it was great, but they said, "Who wants to see shit about Chinese people kicking each other?" I gave the thing to Sidney Glazier from Universal Marion. Then one day, I ran into this girl I knew named Jane Ross. She was a madame and a film editor, a really old Jewish lady. I had the script with me. She was holding a paper bag in her hand. I said, "What have you got in the bag, Jane?" She said, "I've got a fart for Arthur P. Jacobs." He was the guy who produced ***Planet of the Apes***. I said, "Well maybe you know somebody who can read my script." She said, "Put it in my bag. I don't want to smell the fart." This is the truth. I called her about a week later and said, "Did Arthur P. Jacobs read the script?" She said, "No, but I gave it to the best director in New York, Joe Sarno."

The credits continue, revealing a familiar name.

JOHN: *Your brother Elliott is credited as a producer. Can you tell me a little about him?*

JOEL: He did a lot of work on this. At that time, he was at Brooklyn College in the television department. He later went to ABC, and he reached high executive status. He was in charge of electronic media. He had a big office with twenty televisions.

JOHN: *You credit another producer. Who was William Samek?*

JOEL: He was one of the investors. He was a young kid—he's in the film.

JOHN: *What part did he play?*

JOEL: Well, let me think... I guess he's the kid with the leather (laughs). I don't even know if he's still alive. But he put $5,000 up for something.

JOHN: *How did you meet him?*

JOEL: I haven't the slightest idea. Somebody introduced me to him, maybe my accountant.

The music fades as Dr. Joanne Richfield takes center-stage via a bizarre barrage of jump cuts.

DR. JOANNE RICHFIELD: *Prior to the recent sexual revolution, the common... almost universal public acceptance of deviation—advertising for sexual outlets—was done undercover...*

JOHN: *I wanted to ask you a little more about Shelley Abels.*

JOEL: Well, she did a lot of production work on ***Career Bed*** and ***Sex by Advertisement***.

JOHN: *How did you ever get to know her in the first place?*

JOEL: She walked into my office. I think she lived on 72nd Street. This is prior to her getting involved in pornography. A year or two later, I called her up and went to visit her. She said that she was in the porn

Shelley Abels, aka Georgina Spelvin.

film racket.

JOHN: ***Did you shoot Sex by Advertisement on 35mm?***

JOEL: Yes. We used to buy short ends.

As Dr. Richfield talks, the screen gives way to a ragged montage of what she describes as "obedience fetish fanciers".

JOHN: ***Did you rent your camera equipment from the same place that you used for Career Bed?***

JOEL: I think so. We rented from Abbey for ***Career Bed***, and they turned out to be a complete disaster. They were really cheap. You know, any price you asked them for, nothing worked. We were stuck for cameras. I went over to F&B Ceco and they said, "Just give them the junk back and we'll give you the equipment. Don't worry about the price."

JOHN: ***F&B Ceco?***

JOEL: Yeah. They were pretty good about it—they were the biggest film equipment rental place in New York. They rented to all of the major features. A lot of people who wanted to get into the union would go to work in one of their departments. Cameramen and electricians. The building was on 43th Street, if I remember.

An obedience fetish fancier rings his shackled hands in ecstasy. An elderly man is whipped with a leather belt. His earlobe is mutilated by an adjustable wrench before his nipples are jolted with electricity. His silent screams make things seem all the more bizarre.

JOHN: ***Not that I want to quote Rex Reed, but where did these people come from?***

JOEL: I met a good portion of these people at the Theater Bar on 44th Street. We used to hang out there and go to all these parties. Joan Mackenzie, my old girlfriend, was rather wealthy. I don't know if she's still alive. She played the cashier in the bodypainting scene. I think she put some money into the picture. Her brother's in there as a bird-watcher. Almost everybody I knew was in the thing.

JOHN: ***You were on a deadline for casting?***

JOEL: We had to work fast.

JOHN: ***Did you shoot at all in your friend Jerry's loft for the film? Some of the sets look familiar.***

JOEL: No. Almost everything was shot in my friend Arthur's loft. It was above the Automat on 55th Street. The building's gone now. Here's a funny anecdote—my brother put a casting notice on a bulletin board at Barnard College. I started dating one of the topless girls in the movie, and I went out with her one night. I remember that she was of Iranian descent and that her father was a diplomat. Anyway, she said to me, "Do you know what I did today? I was in a real porn picture, and I got to fuck!" But we shot most of the picture at Arthur's loft. My friend Gale McCarty shot part of it. He also played the director. I dragged everybody into it. One of the guys was a German/Jewish refugee. He was always getting free meals. He always talked like he was a Prussian Superman: "You vill not address me in that manner! We vill not leave a tip!"

JOHN: ***Was he the old guy in the marriage broker scene?***
JOEL: That's the guy!

A middle-aged woman sits alone at a barren desk. A push-button phone rings, and she reaches down to answer it. She's a marriage broker by trade, an occupation that Dr. Richfield despises.

MARRIAGE BROKER: *Hello, my dearest and prettiest client! How are you today, dear child? I'm so sorry that your date last night didn't go too well—he happens to be a wealthy businessman! Yes, darling... he may have false teeth, but you didn't have to tell him that you lost all your hair when you were a little girl!*

JOEL: You know, we also shot in my office. The marriage broker was the woman who ran the lab next door, this Jewish lady. I said, "Do you want to be in the movie?" She said, "Yes. Can we use your office?" We did some pickup shots over there.

The Prussian Superman sits at the foot of the marriage broker's desk. He is nervous, but his desires ring clear:

PRUSSIAN SUPERMAN: *I... I want to find wife. Young girl.*

Arthur

An orgy for the ages.

MARRIAGE BROKER: *Not so fast! You'll have to fill out an application. That's standard procedure!*

The two of them stumble their way through Reed's rambling dialogue before a deal is made.

PRUSSIAN SUPERMAN: *I have got money. Plenty money. Right… in… bank.*

The marriage broker's eyes light up.

MARRIAGE BROKER: *This certainly looks authentic! I think I have an eighteen-year-old blonde who would be perfect for you!*

The Prussian Superman's Kryptonite is his lust for young girls. He caves in to the marriage broker's demands.

PRUSSIAN SUPERMAN: *I pay, I pay!*

JOEL: What can I say? We were in a hurry.

Satisfied with her findings, Dr. Richfield introduces a new case.

DR. JOANNE RICHFIELD: *Another common cover for sex advertisers is the employment ad seeking young models or would-be starlets. One such adventurer has been operating in Manhattan for years without attracting the attention of the authorities.*

The camera zooms in on a decrepit door to a ramshackle apartment, the residence of Harry Hogar, theatrical manager.

JOHN: *This is one of my favorite segments.*

JOEL: It's not bad. Harry Hogar, the pseudo agent in the movie, was based on a guy named Gene Cogan, a man for the ages. He had a little walk-up apartment and claimed to be the biggest agent in New York.

JOHN: *Did you know him?*

JOEL: Yeah. Every time I'd go visit him, he was on the phone with Darryl Zanuck or Louis B. Mayer. One day I called him up and I said, "Gene, can I come over?" I heard him say, "Just a minute, honey. I'm on the phone with Darryl Zanuck. And he'll tell you himself that "if you don't play along with me, you'll never work in Hollywood." So, I discovered that all of those phone calls were fictional. He was sort of a corpulent guy. He said, "Hey, Darryl! Remember when I was out on the coast and we went to that great hamburger place? I loved those cheeseburgers and the fries!" That was code for what he wanted me to bring up to his apartment.

A phone rings in Harry Hogar's office. He answers the call with a thick New York accent.

HARRY HOGAR: *Yeah, B.J. Linda's here, but she's not cooperating. We'll have to get another girl to fly to Europe for your picture instead.*

LINDA: *Is there really a film?*

HARRY HOGAR: *You can take my word for it. You get your contract in two weeks. But from now on, you take orders from me.*

JOEL: Later on, I was working with some girls for promotion. I brought them over to J. Jay Frankel, the producer of Bing Crosby's ***Cinerama's Russian Adventure***. They think he was thrown off the roof of his building on Park Avenue because he was getting money from the mob and never paid them back. Anyway, there was one girl from Louisiana, and she was dealing with Gene. Bing Crosby saw her, and he said, "Get that girl." I called her up, and I said, "You've got a job to travel with a movie with a couple other girls." She said, "You know, you're full of shit. That wasn't Bing Crosby. I talked to my manager, who's one of the most powerful men in showbusiness." I said, "You mean Gene Cogan?" She said, "See! You know his name!" He was a guy who lived in this dirty, one room apartment. She fell for the story that he was a major manager. "He's going

Bad medicine in Central Park.

to get me in pictures, so don't bullshit me about meeting Bing Crosby!" I ran into her two years later, and she told me to fuck off. Everybody bullshitted her. But—you should have seen this guy (laughs). He weighed around 300 pounds, and he was in this tiny little apartment. And he claimed to control showbusiness. I even believed him for a while. So, I based Hogar on him. I was pretty pissed off.

JOHN: ***Who played Hogar in the movie?***

JOEL: My brother's friend from Brooklyn College (laughs)!

Linda's will finally breaks, and Hogar has his way with her. The crooked agent is eventually beaten and mutilated by a group of thugs, a fitting price to pay for "representing" a girl with mob connections.

JOEL: Hold on a minute, I have to plug in my phone.

A few seconds pass as the film plays on.

JOEL: Are you there?

JOHN: ***Yeah.***

JOEL: OK, I'm back. Anyway, I guess you could call this picture a conglobation of freaks. I just used the people that I had hanging around.

JOHN: ***One of the weirdest things about the film is its lack of sound. It's almost a silent film, save for the narration. I'm guessing that this***

was due to budgetary reasons.

JOEL: Yeah. It was cheaper. You don't have to match dialogue or any of that crap. Go watch some of Joe Sarno's pictures—ninety percent is shot silent.

JOHN: ***Do you remember who edited the film?***

JOEL: Well, ***Career Bed*** was edited by Ron Dorfman. I think I edited ***Sex by Advertisement***. There was a great old editor who started working years and years ago. I rented a room from him, and he helped me with a lot of stuff. He got his start in Brooklyn in the old days. They used to paste film together and put a book on top of it to hold it down.

JOHN: ***To splice it?***

JOEL: Yeah. And then, somebody took off a door hinge and put a clamp on it. It was great for 35mm film. That's how the first splicer was made. Anyway, he taught me how to cut the film. We cut it up in Movielab. I didn't even know how to put the tape on the film. But there's a lot of voiceover. That made it cheap.

NARRATOR: *Dr. Richfield discovered that many seemingly harmless ads for household servants, maids, and other domestics were covers for twisted employers seeking sexual gratification through the abuse of employees.*

A young woman stands before her bathroom mirror, combing her hair. She undresses and settles into a warm bath. Suddenly, the door swings open and a man walks in. She falls to the ground as he assaults her. Choppy voiceover informs us that the woman is a refugee from a foreign shore.

EMPLOYER: *You're in this country illegally. If you open your mouth about this, the both of us will be locked up. Behave from now on and you'll enjoy your job much more.*

JOHN: ***This scene is completely silent except for the sound of a scream.***

JOEL: We may have been doing a little wild sound, but we shot it in no time at all.

Joel M. Reed as the Weird Old Geezer.

Jennifer Welles in Sex by Advertisement.

An older gentlemen walks into a tiny lobby. He approaches a desk clerk and taps her on the shoulder. She looks up from her book, takes the man's money, and directs him to a room across the hall. The man enters the room and is greeted by Jennifer Welles. She is wearing white boots, a short skirt, and a turtleneck sweater.

JOHN: ***I'd like to hear something about the body painting scene. Was that shot in Arthur's loft?***

JOEL: Yes. Actually, he's the guy painting Jennifer Welles.

JOHN: ***What was Arthur's full name?***

JOEL: Arthur Jacobs.

JOHN: ***Arthur Jacobs?***

JOEL: Yes. Not the producer (laughs). He was a very strange character. He inherited a couple of a million dollars. A few years later, he asked me if he could borrow $20. He didn't have any money left. I said, "What did you do with the money?" He'd given it all away. I said, "Why didn't you give me any money?" He said, "You never asked."

JOHN: ***Where did he live?***

JOEL: He started out at the Osborne. I think he came to New York to be a concert pianist. His family owned a meat packing plant in Chicago. He was a little on the fey side, but he was a really horny guy. A real Caspar Milquetoast type, you know? Some people thought he was gay, but he wasn't. He had a fifteen-room apartment that he rented out to twenty girls. There are a lot of famous stories about Jane Russell and a bunch of his other tenants. They'd never pay the rent. Jane Russell was a religious nut. Arthur slept in the living room because he rented out every bit of his apartment. One night, he had to go into the bathroom to take a piss, but the girls had locked the door. He was dying to take a piss because he drank beer all night. He climbed out on the ledge above 57th Street. He crawled over to the next window and started banging on it as Jane Russell was saying her prayers. She said, "Oh, Holy Father Jesus… come to me." She looked up, and there was Arthur in his terrycloth robe, with nothing else on.

Arthur smiles as Jennifer Welles undresses. The camera lovingly follows her hands as she unclasps her bra. When she is finally naked, she gives him a small tray that holds paint and brushes. Arthur goes to work, painting her body with gentle, delicate strokes.

JOHN: ***Do you have any other stories about Arthur?***

JOEL: We went to a New Year's Eve party in Times Square. Arthur kept complaining that he was cold. I said, "Stop it, Arthur. It's not that cold!" I finally looked back at him. He had gone to piss at the party and he didn't button up. His pants were four blocks back in the snow. You could see them in the middle of Seventh Avenue.

Sex by Advertisement *plays on. A young model is sploshed with mud. A young director (Gale McCarty) explains the fine technique of exploitation filmmaking.*

DIRECTOR: *I do the same stuff they do in Hollywood. Only better.*

Dr. Richfield questions his motives.

DR. JOANNE RICHFIELD: *What was your last film?*

DIRECTOR: *Passion on Freak Island—a story of a homosexual, a lesbian, two West Point cadets, and four high school girls thrown together during a storm. It has everything in it but necrophilia.*

DR. JOANNE RICHFIELD: *How does the storyline go?*

DIRECTOR: *Story? You don't understand. Nobody understands!*

The director walks away in disgust. Dr. Richfield smiles and moves on.

JOHN: ***This movie is very self-aware. There's always a lot of satire in your pictures.***

JOEL: Yeah. Most of my stuff is satire. I should have been more serious.

DR. JOANNE RICHFIELD: *I kept my objective viewpoint by avoiding the participating advertisers at first, and speaking only with the vendors of erotic devices and pictures. My first interview was with a young man who made torture instruments. His factory was in a small loft directly opposite New York's Lincoln Center.*

JOHN: ***This is the kid with the leather—William Samek.***

JOEL: Yes. Like I said, he was one of the investors. He got his money back.

KID WITH THE LEATHER: *It's a strict business with me. It's a lot more interesting than my former work as a computer programmer, and many times more lucrative. My father makes leather handbags. And boy—wow—I never thought I'd end up in practically the same business. I estimate that I use 45,000 hides a year in my business—nothing close to the old man's volume. I have a higher markup, though. The plain old leather punishment strap is my biggest seller. I do a big business in leather corsets and underwear. Bondage stuff. Although, my most expensive items are masks and elaborate devices which are all made to order. I have a low price line of whips, but there's quite a demand for my custom made ones. One of my biggest customers, a famous movie director, buys only those of the best leather and made to his specifications. A big surprise in this day and age is the demand for chastity belts. This is a pilot model. I plan to produce and sell them for $125 each. I went into it for money. Two years in the business, and I've already bought a townhouse and a forty-five foot yacht. How I got into it? It was an accident. I was in Central Park one afternoon...*

JOEL: Have I told you the Central Park Story yet?

JOHN: ***About the New Jersey cops? Yeah.***

KID WITH THE LEATHER: *I saw this weird old geezer in the park. He came over to me and started a conversation. I at first thought he was a fag. He asked me if I belonged to his organization. "What club?" I didn't know. Then he asked me where I got*

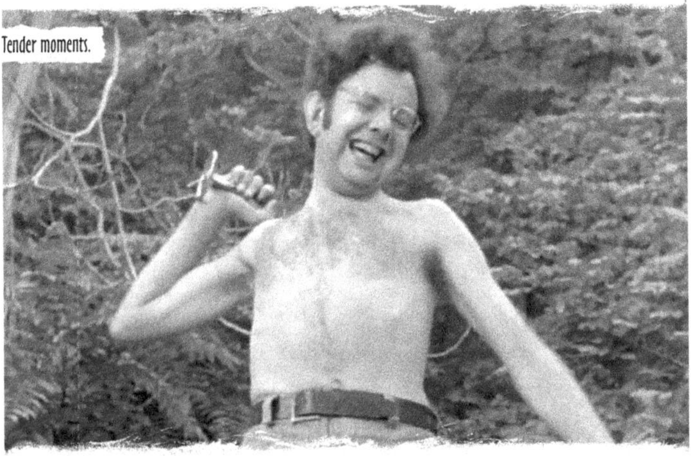

Tender moments.

my leather belt. I told him I made it myself. He wanted to buy it. I turned him down. I wasn't in the belt business at the time. He didn't get nasty—he thanked me for my time and left.

The Weird Old Geezer is played by Joel Reed himself. He is spending a quiet afternoon in the park with one of his sadomasochistic slaves. He soon returns to the Kid with the Leather, offering him $100 for his belt. A transaction is made, and The Weird Old Geezer gets down to business.

JOHN: *Do you remember who played the part of the girl that you were whipping?*

JOEL: Yes. She was living at my apartment. She was from the deep south. I found her wandering the streets. She had taken a bus to New York. And she had a corrected harelip—I didn't know that it went all the way down. She had two vaginal entries.

The Kid with the Leather follows the strange old man and watches in shock as he strips his slave naked. He then begins to whip her with his belt.

JOHN: *Were you surprised that Peppercorn-Wormser distributed Career Bed and Sex by Advertisement?*

JOEL: Yes. I think I told you that Vernon Becker helped to set that up. I was looking for someone to distribute the picture. He said, "I'm having dinner with Peppercorn-Wormser. They don't even take my pictures. They only do major movies." I called them anyway and said, "Mr. Wormser! I hear you're a hard man to get to, but I talked to Vernon Becker. I made a little softcore picture." He said, "What are you doing over there? Why aren't you here?" I said, "Well, I heard that you were hard to get to." He said, "That's why nobody ever comes here! Come over and I'll buy you lunch." So I went over and had lunch with him. He told me how he started in the movies in 1915, or something. And for three days, I had to hear about all the famous old ladies that he fucked.

The Weird Old Geezer invites his newfound friend to bring some samples of his handiwork to his society.

KID WITH THE LEATHER: *He said that there was a possibility of me becoming their official whip maker.*

Bewildered, the young man accepts the offer. The scene that follows is one of the strangest sequences in the history of cinema. The Kid with the Leather knocks on a door and is escorted into a soundproof room. There, the Weird Old Geezer presides over an ugly orgy of sex and violence. All of the participants wear cheap Halloween masks to conceal their identities. Silent footage spools forward without mercy to the tune of an unsettling overdub of groans, barking dogs, and evil laughter. Women sit atop men as if they were horses. Nipples are stimulated with electricity. Men lead women along as if they were dogs. This is ***Sex by Advertisement****'s finest hour, and it is milked for all it's worth.*

JOHN: ***How long did Sex by Advertisement play theatrically?***

JOEL: Not for very long. The trouble with Peppercorn-Wormser is that they gave me money upfront. By the time they got around to releasing the picture, there was hardcore in all the theaters. If they'd released those movies immediately, things would have been different. Brandt wanted to play them on 42nd Street, but then I found out he never paid anybody.

Then—suddenly—as if a switch has been flipped—things return to normal. At least as normal as things can get in a movie like ***Sex by Advertisement****. The Kid with the Leather is introduced as Malcolm. He proudly shows his samples to an adoring crowd.*

Arthur and Jennifer Welles.

MALCOLM: *I received $1,500 in orders that night. All cash. I gave up my regular job.*

The final eighteen minutes of ***Sex by Advertisement*** *stumble toward the finish line, but they never manage to eclipse the filth and frenzy of the S&M scene. Reports of homosexual classified ads, mysophilia, and wife-swapping fail to measure up to the deranged excess of the previous spectacle. Dr. Richfield tries her best to up the ante, but in the end, she sits alone at her desk, addressing a (presumably) empty theater.*

DR. JOANNE RICHFIELD: *The research on sex by advertisement continues. When my book is published, it's sure to reach a wide audience. It is not in my realm to speculate if any one of the governmental agencies or authorities will act on it.*

JOEL: Yeah, it didn't do very well. In fact, I got involved [with some investors] with a picture called ***Eva: Swedish and Underage***. Vernon Becker was a producer. It was a softcore courtroom sex drama. It had the same problem as ***Sex by Advertisement***—they didn't release it until hardcore was out. It actually took about twenty years to earn its money back.

With that, the curtain closes. Not only on ***Sex by Advertisement****, but on the entire softcore film industry itself. The end credits read "FIN", and we can imagine the projectionist packing up his bags and beginning his long walk home…*

"Do you know what was wrong with your film? You let me direct it."—Joel Reed to Marvin Farkas

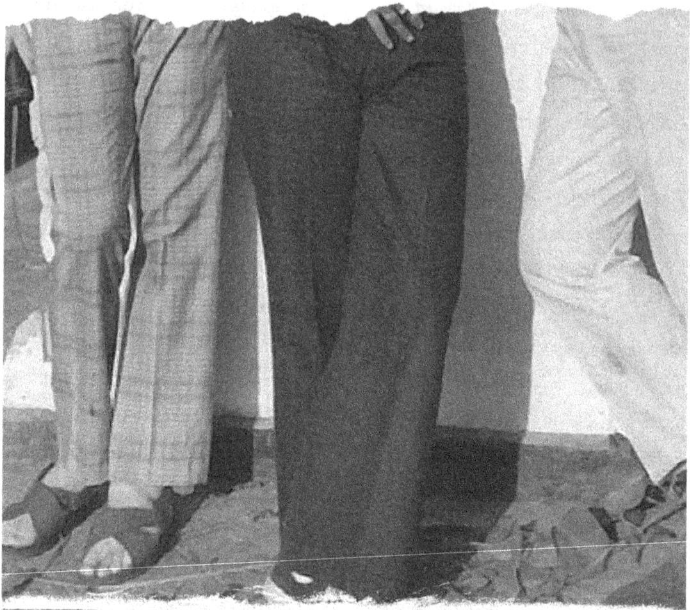

CHAPTER SEVEN

WIT'S END

Million Dollar Spy Film to Be Shot In S'pore

"Singapore, Monday. The tightrope tension of modern Singapore will rip across the screen in a million dollar espionage film being produced here. Mr. Joel M. Reed, director of the Hong Kong based Farkas Productions, has arrived here to shoot every aspect of Singapore's fast living city for the production of the film ***Wit's End****, a story of an ex-American journalist in Singapore who finds himself caught up in a web of women and police.*

"He said Singapore's high rise living, her nonstop traffic, and her dizzy psychedelic night spots would provide the 'ideal' background for the film which will begin shooting on Wednesday. Scouting for local talent is still going on. The film, which is expected to take some five to six weeks to shoot, provides parts for four hundred local extras, many of them women. Tom Keena, well-known stage and television Broadway actor, has arrived to make his first feature film as Dave Dearborn, the lead character.

"Shooting of the entire film, in color, will be confined to Singapore. Mr. Reed, puffing away at his pipe said, 'When we came to Singapore, we knew we would find the ideal city for an espionage plot. Your city is thrilling, and your girls are oh-so-pretty.' The original script of ***Wit's End*** *was written by Keith Lorenz, a correspondent of the Voice of America, who has spent a number of years in Singapore."*

So read the headlines of Singapore's ***Straits Times*** in 1969. Joel Reed and

his crew were "transported from Hollywood and New York" to begin shooting ***Wit's End***, Joel's third feature film. Shot in color over two months in and around Singapore, it was Joel's most ambitious project to date. And, as usual, Joel stumbled into the director's chair completely by accident.

Wit's End is the story of Dave Dearborn (Tom Keena), a former Vietnam war correspondent-cum-nightclub owner. Dave is hired by two intelligence operatives to investigate a triad mob boss that they believe is auctioning off a nuclear scientist to the highest bidder.

Before long, Dave is swept into a labyrinth of violence and sleaze as he encounters Soviet spies, dangerous assassins, corrupt CIA agents (Walter Hill and Chris Ware as Morrison and Jones, two fast talking operatives who will sacrifice Dearborn at a moment's notice), and the infamous homosexual gangster Jacques Dutan.

The following interview took place on January 16, 2000, in Joel Reed's living room as we watched ***Wit's End***. The volume was *loud*…

JOEL: Is your tape going? We can stop and start this thing.

JOHN: ***Yeah. So this is Singapore at the dawn of the '70s...***

Real opium.

Steady camera images flicker on the screen. Faded frames of Kodak Eastmancolor stock play out as Elliot Chiprut's title music erupts from nowhere. A young blonde walks down a crowded street, past children and men selling noodles. An old man sits up in bed, leaning over to grab an opium pipe.

JOEL: That was an opium den with real opium. Everybody had a contact for us.

JOHN: ***You could just go in and film that?***

JOEL: No. We were filming up in a fishing village. All of the houses were on stilts. The police had to be there because we had real opium instruments. I said, "We've got to put tobacco in there." This guy said, "That doesn't look like opium." The police said, "This fisherman will give you some opium." So we used that.

The credits fade in and out as a loud guitar and organ accompany falsetto chants of "Wit's end!"

JOHN: ***What was Lion City Productions?***

JOEL: That was the name of Marvin Farkas' company that he formed to make this picture. Singapore looks nothing like this now. That's Janet

Exotic Singapore.

Wood playing Cindy. This music is from Elliot Chiprut. He had a big hit in the '60s with "Simon Says".

JOHN: ***Who got him for this? Was it Marvin?***

JOEL: No, I think Victor Kanefsky probably did. Keep in mind that I didn't write this script, I tried to clean it up. It was David X. Young's script. It had already changed hands twice by that time. If I had any brains, I would have started over.

A young pimp prowls the streets of Singapore, peddling his wares.

PIMP: *Very clean girl, sir. Practically a virgin. Very special price. $15.*

JOEL: That's Mark Louis, the casting director, playing the pimp. Some of these girls didn't realize that they were playing prostitutes.

Singapore Harbor: Boats filled with fishermen and laborers sail in and out of frame.

JOHN: ***So where was the camera at for this shot?***

JOEL: On another boat. It was a quick scene, we actually shot it pretty easily. You know, David X. Young took his name off this. The original story credit for Keith Lorenz and Ian Ward has nothing to do with this.

JOHN: ***Do you still have their script?***

JOEL: I don't know; it might be

laying around. I don't have David's script. This ship was a nightclub that Keith and Ian owned. Their script also centered on this nightclub. This guy who played Peter was Brian Walden. He's back in New Zealand now. Marvin said he put on a couple of hundred pounds.

A young boat-hand named Peter walks into the nightclub bar. A white parrot chirps maniacally. He stops to pet it.

JOEL: That bird was nice. He died. They set the cage behind the set and forgot about him.

Peter continues to Dave Dearborn's cabin. He stops and knocks on the door.

JOHN: ***Is Tom's room on the junk?***
JOEL: No, this is all in a studio. It was all a built set at Cathay-Keris studio.

PETER: *Dave! Dave! Hey, Dave!*

Dave Dearborn sits up in bed. A white blanket obscures a young woman who is busy earning her keep.

JOEL: This girl in bed with Tom married a French engineer. But this is a set, and this is stupid.

Peter knocks again.

DAVE: *Go away! I don't like to be disturbed while I'm meditating.*

JOHN: ***What did you think of Tom's acting?***
JOEL: It was overdone. I tried to write some new stuff. This is some of my dialogue. This is starting very esoteric and everything and it goes no place.
JOHN: ***How was Marvin to work with behind the camera?***
JOEL: Well, he never read the script. Victor said that we should have used a better cinematographer. And he didn't get along with Tom.

Dave Dearborn prowls around his junk. He is dressed in a flowery silk shirt.

Dave Dearborn

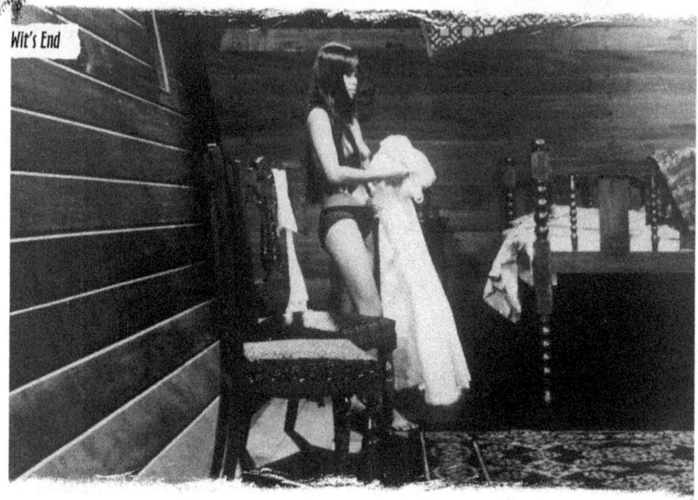

JOHN: ***Who came up with Tom's wardrobe?***

JOEL: Well, it wasn't me. We should have paid more attention to the wardrobe, I guess.

A fat, bucktoothed man in a pith helmet approaches Dearborn, introducing himself as Mr. Plume.

JOHN: ***I like this guy's clothes.***

JOEL: This scene is terrible. He's not an actor. He shouldn't be dressed like that. One of the producers thought it would be funny to put him in that. Nobody dressed like that. In Singapore, they wore jeans, even then. This should have been very subtle and mysterious. It should have been more like ***Alphaville***, with a lot of lights. Marvin didn't care. This guy is out of character.

PLUME: *My card. I want you to do a story for me. I'm interested in the activities of a certain Chinese businessman named Lim.*

DAVE: *I'm retired. Any hack out here can do that job.*

PLUME: *Any hack* ***can't*** *do that job. We want more than just surface information.*

DAVE: *I couldn't get you his phone number.*

PLUME: *You could get a lot more than that. His current concubine, girlfriend, whatever you want to call her, is a woman named Foon Mai Lee. I think you know her. Foon Mai Lee.*

Dave Dearborn's face hardens and his

eyes narrow. He accepts Plume's offer.

JOEL: One of the big problems with this is that Marvin and everyone showed me some old movies of Singapore from the '40s. When I got there, it was a lot more modern than I thought it would be. I've since written another script that takes place in a much more modern city. (Laughing) The A&W Root Beer stand was the hot spot in Singapore at the time.

JOHN: ***So, do you regret filming in Singapore?***

JOEL: If I would have done things correctly, I would have shot this in Hong Kong.

Dearborn and Peter sit on the side of the junk, looking out at the water. Peter knows well Dave's obsession with his former lover.

PETER: *Are you still in love with her?*

DAVE: *Shut up.*

PETER: *Dave…*

DAVE: *All right, I'm still hung on her. When I had her, I hated her. Now she's gone and I miss her. Pete, do me a favor. You go see her. Make sure everything's all right. Tell her I said hello… and don't try to screw her.*

Pete sets off to find Mai Lee and agrees to meet with Dave later in the evening.

Joel Reed, Marvin Farkas, Janet Wood, and Tom Keena.

Tom Keena and Janet Wood.

JOHN: ***This is shot pretty well.***

JOEL: Yeah, but there are too many things going on right now. Too much expository shit. This is Bugis Street, the transvestite area.

JOHN: ***Is this a set?***

JOEL: No, it's another bar about three blocks down from the door they walked in. Everyone in this place is a guy. The transvestites must have a union there!

Elliot Chiprut's "Looking for Love" throbs from the speakers as transvestites of all shapes and sizes dance under colored lights. A blonde American named Cindy walks into the Adonis bar, looking for Dave. She finds him nursing a scotch.

JOEL: That's Janet Wood. I originally fixed that role for my girlfriend. She didn't want to come along.

CINDY: *Hi, Dave.*

DAVE: *Do you follow me because you love me?*

CINDY: *I hoped you'd get around to that. Yes, I love you.*

DAVE: *Do normal American girls visit the object of their affection in a whorehouse? It's not listed in the guidebooks that way, but that's what it is.*

CINDY: *I'm pretty broadminded.*

DAVE: *Broadminded? Aware? Well, then you're aware that this is a whorehouse for homosexuals?*

A spotlight snaps on, revealing a curvy blonde stripper. Dave seems preoccupied.

CINDY: *I thought you said you wanted to talk to Peter.*
DAVE: *I'm waiting for him.*

JOHN: ***I really like this music.***
JOEL: It's OK. That's Angelique Pettyjohn as the stripper.
JOHN: ***Prior to this, she was in that Elvis Presley movie. What was it called? Clambake?***
JOEL: Yes. She was a very funny person. Many stories formed about her in Singapore. Marvin, or somebody must have hired her. I don't think he met her beforehand. He saw a picture of her and he showed it to me. She was fan dancing, and she had her face covered. I said, "You can't even see her face!" But this was a character that David wrote for the script. Bonnie. He based each character on somebody who hung out at Bradley Cunningham's bar.
JOHN: ***That was a jazz place.***
JOEL: Yeah, it was famous. All of the jazz greats hung out there.
JOHN: ***What kind of guy was Bradley?***
JOEL: He was a big, macho guy.

Janet Wood strikes a pose.

Kind of a contrast to David. This was the first scene I shot with Angelique. She was a woman from Utah. She was in a lot of big pictures. She told me that she was doing a love scene with an actor, I don't want to say who, and they actually started to screw. The crew diplomatically turned off the lights and they finished.
JOHN: ***How long did you work on rewriting the script?***
JOEL: Not long. There was really nothing I could do. They were happy to go with the first script. But this is all terrible.

Dave and Cindy make their way back

Angelique Pettyjohn as Bonnie.

to the junk and continue drinking.

JOHN: ***Is this a set?***

JOEL: No, this was shot on the actual boat. These are all kids from the local school. Hey, that's Keith Lorenz dancing! The original screenwriter. People thought he was a CIA agent. He was a good friend of the people who produced ***Blood Bath***.

Dave looks up to see Lim and Bonnie appear through a cloud of smoke. They make eye contact and the lights on the dance floor go out.

JOHN: ***Who played Mr. Lim?***

JOEL: He was a real gangster. He came over, he was the big boss. They said, "Let's use him as the gangster." I came over and everything was supposed to be cast. Nothing was cast. I didn't pick these actors. Marvin's backers, who were doing the business end said, "Oh, we got you this guy for $25 a day. We're not going to hire this other guy." I should have done something about it. Singapore was very poor at this time. People were working in offices for nothing.

JOHN: ***How come you never worked with Marvin again?***

JOEL: I don't think Marvin had any ability to raise any money after this. If he raised money, he wouldn't do it with me. We had a lot of conflicts. You see, what you're supposed to do in these things is a pure tits and ass picture. Not much of a story and a lot of action will make you some money. This tries to say something and it doesn't work. But I don't want to knock Marvin, he's a good friend.

Dave wakes up the next morning to find Peter's body floating in the harbor. He is soon apprehended by the Singapore police as a suspect in the murder.

CHIEF OF POLICE: *We have quite a file on you. 1963, Saigon. Exposing Jacques Dutan, a well-known gangster. Your motives were a little… different.*

JOHN: ***Where was this shot?***
JOEL: In the Cathay-Keris office. This guy was a real English cop. He was all right in this part. We could have played up the bisexual theme more. I guess that was in the original story.

Dave cuts a deal with the police: two days to find Plume and to prove his innocence.

JOEL: You know, David Young was an interesting guy. The one movie he made was very good. You see, all this character shit is in the way. It's not a Joel Reed script. ***Blood Sucking Freaks*** is more my style. Actually, this works in an off the wall way as a character study. Tom's character works. Janet's character doesn't work because we cut out the scenes that gave her any motivation for what she's doing. If we could have developed that, it would have been better.

Dave sits in bed, talking with Cindy. They are interrupted by a knock on the door.

SERVANT: *Mr. Dave! Mr. Dave! The fat man, I saw him at Green Street. He's still there!*

JOEL: OK, I threw in this brothel scene because I thought it was funny.
JOHN: ***Are you tracking with a dolly?***

The bucktoothed Plume.

Transvestite bar.

JOEL: Oh, yeah. We had a dolly. We had tracks. The studio supplied us with everything. This scene is… well, it almost works.

JOHN: ***Did you write this scene?***

JOEL: Yeah, I guess. I was trying to get some kicks in. The funny thing is that the art designer had to put the chamber pot under the bed. He studied some brothels. Someone would bring in a prop and he'd say, "No, they wouldn't be using that!" This is a good scene, really about the only one that works. But it could have been kinkier. It could have been about this guy who prowls through brothels looking for guys.

Dave Dearborn finds the bloated Plume in bed with a young prostitute. He stands at the ready as Plume tries in vain to cover himself.

DAVE: *Hi.*

PROSTITUTE: *Crazy American!*

DAVE: *You wanted some information? I got it.*

PLUME: *I—I—I was going to try and call you this morning. That guy—and Miss Foon Mai Lee—*

Plume leaps from his bed and delivers a sharp kick to Dearborn's balls. He struggles to put on his pants as Dave howls in pain. The music swells; the chase is on.

JOEL: And here's the old Singapore! I used to eat there for a dollar! Lunch was like twelve cents. This bridge is in every movie about

Marvin Farkas (at camera) and Joel Reed.

Singapore.

Dave follows Plume into a public restroom. A sign reads: **MEN ONLY**.

JOEL: I guess I wrote this. My friend was accounting his adventures in the men's rooms of New York subways at the time. I did this scene in honor of him.

Dave smashes Plume into a urinal. Plume screams in agony.

DAVE: *Who killed Peter? Start talking!*

CIA agents Sanford Jones and Greg Morrison burst into the room and knock Dave to the floor. Plume pulls up his pants and hobbles to safety.

JOEL: These two CIA guys remind me a lot of the guys from ***Bring Me the Head of Alfredo Garcia***. This movie seems a little better to me now than when I used to watch it. The whole relationship with Dutan was in the original script. I could have left more of that in and made it more of a gay movie. One of the reasons that it's such a mess is that Marvin was being paid to do the

Dearborn and Bonnie frolic.

movie and I think he wanted to get his paycheck. He didn't care what happened to it. I guess I should have stayed in New York. You see, this is trying to be humorous.

Dearborn wakes up in a strange white room. He slowly sits up.

JONES: *You're a real looser, aren't you, Dave? Down to cruising public toilets.*
DAVE: *Why, are you lonesome?*
MORRISON: *OK, fellows. Sit down.*
JONES: *OK, we've all had our little joke. Now we'd like to buy you. You're still an American. A patriotic one, we hope. Or do you prefer cash?*
DAVE: *Cash…*
JONES: *OK, pervert, we'll talk cash.*
MORRISON: *Let me put it this way, Dave. We need you to get us some information on a gangster named Lim.*
DAVE: *This is beginning to sound like a broken record. Plume wanted the same thing.*
JONES: *Plume?*
DAVE: *The guy I had my hands on when you so rudely interrupted me! He wanted information too.*

Morrison and Jones pitch ***their*** *offer to Dearborn: $25,000 to investigate Lim's involvement with a defector from Red China. Dave rolls his eyes and accepts.*

JOHN: ***Who did the sound for this film?***
JOEL: Marvin's friend from college

did it. It's kind of tinny.

Bonnie lies in bed, deep in sleep. She sucks her finger seductively, a white blanket barely covers her body. Dave enters her room and wakes her.

BONNIE: *Dave, honey! Be my guest! You're in the right position and I'm in the right mood.*
DAVE: *Later. I want you to take a little walk with me.*
BONNIE: *A walk? Dave, where's your sense of timing?*

Bonnie and Dave hit the streets of Singapore. They spot Lim, and Bonnie approaches him.

JOEL: The next scene doesn't work because it tries to be funny. She could have had sex with the gangster or anything else. They could have got into this discussion, "You mean you want me to fuck this old guy?"

Bonnie "trips" over Lim's Leg and flashes him puppy dog eyes. Lim offers to escort the wounded woman home. They get into a rickshaw and ride off into the city.

JOEL: Lim's not bad, he just

Victoria Racimo and Tom Keena pledge undying love.

couldn't talk English. Actually, we broke this rickshaw. This doesn't make sense. But I learned my lesson: cut out the boring shit and give the audience five shoot-outs. That has nothing to do with directing, it has things to do with writing.
JOHN: ***Marvin said that he was in a shot that got cut out.***
JOEL: Yeah, that was the big brothel scene. I forget what happened in that one. I think we had all these girls taking their clothes off. It might have been when Tom fucks Vicky Racimo. Actually, it would have been a very funny scene.

With Lim out of the way, Dave Dearborn pays an unexpected visit to Mai Lee. They argue about the past.

JOHN: ***What nationality is Vicky?***
JOEL: Filipino. I ran into her after

this, she was driving a brand new Cadillac. That was years ago, she was in LA.

MAI LEE: *By the way, who put you into the junk business? One of your* ***men*** *friends?*

JOHN: *How much footage do you think you shot for this film?*

JOEL: Oh, we shot about fifty-thousand feet. You look back in retrospect. I could have made this about a bisexual guy that has to unravel some secret. People are trying to kill him, he might be paranoid about it.

Dearborn leaves Mai Lee. Under the cover of night, he pays her another visit; this time at the mansion of the dangerous Mr. Lim.

JOEL: There were cobras sunning themselves by the pool at this mansion. They had a collection of Asian art in there. And at the back of the place they had a wall to keep the Chinese ghosts out.

Dearborn hides in the shadows as Plume and two Russians bid on the life of the defector.

RUSSIAN: *Why must you wait? I give you four-hundred!*

JOHN: *Who was this guy?*

JOEL: Some actor they hired. He was bad. And Lim stinks because he can't talk.

The Russians leave Lim's mansion with the promise of further talks on a remote island. Talks with Lim and a mysterious American.

MAI LEE: *Where is this information?*
LIM: *That my secret. You never learn it that way.*

JOEL: This is stupid. The next scene is funny. We shot it right next to the McDonald's. It was supposed to be the jungle.
JOHN: *Did Tom like the way this film turned out? It was his first feature.*
JOEL: I might have ruined his career. I didn't see him much in anything after that. He was working in soaps. Now this is next to the McDonald's, or some hamburger place. It was right between that and a car wash. See, Tom came in through the same group of trees that he just left.

DAVE: *Dearborn here! They're trading. Things are going pretty high! There's a Russian involved! The bad guys are meeting at an island…*

JOHN: ***The bad guys?***
JOEL: I was in a hurry to finish the thing!

Dave goes back to his room, exhausted. Bonnie is waiting for him.

BONNIE: *Do I, uh, get a kiss?*
JOHN: ***So, you said that this was a set?***
JOEL: Yeah. That's a set at Cathay-Keris Studios.
JOHN: ***How many walls did it have?***
JOEL: Well, four walls. They were movable. Remember the pan when he came in the door? That door was taken off.

BONNIE: *Why didn't you take your pants off?*

JOEL: Now that's stupid. We had to find out a way to have it so Tom's pants would still be on.

DAVE: *(Sighs) Who had time?*

JOEL: See, they put the wall back

Lim and Mai Lee.

there.

A giant Malay jumps Dearborn from out of the shadows.

JOHN: ***So… where did this guy come from?***
JOEL: He was a professional wrestler. There was a wrestling troupe in Singapore. They had rehearsals, we'd watch them rehearse. And the stupid Chinese would bet on them! It was all rehearsed. The funny story is that we went to a wrestling match and one of the guys hurt his back. The Chinese made out because of the mistake. This is not a bad sequence.
JOHN: ***It's great. He's being attacked by an ape!***

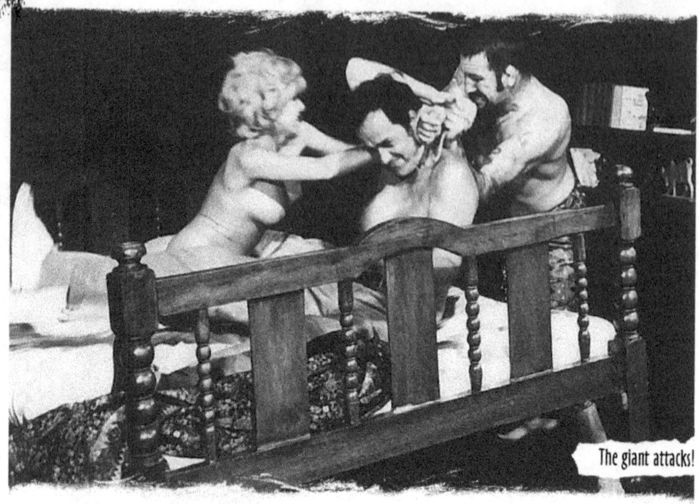

All hell breaks loose as Plume bursts into the room, gun in hand. Bonnie scrambles for Dearborn's gun and takes aim. She is topless.

JOEL: The film board called me up. They said, "We've got to go over this scene." They said, "It's OK to have tits, but you've got forty-two frames in one shot. We've got to take twelve frames from here, and three from there." I think we used the original, we just synched it back so they didn't know any difference. The film board just wanted to say they did something. A funny story is that there was a famous French or Swedish picture. One of the early ones. It takes place on a boat. The film board watched it and this guy's undressing a girl. He kisses her neck and then starts going down. Then they cut away to the boat rocking. The guy from the board said, "We can't have that!" They said, "What's wrong with the shot? Explain it to me. They guy got off the bed and the boat started to rock. There's a blanket covering her." They kept it in there.

JOHN: ***This is a good sequence. This chase.***

JOEL: It's one of the good ones. The whole film should have been this good. Something about this almost works. This island is the place where they actually had opium. These fishermen had real opium.

JOHN: ***Did you guys rent those boats?***

JOEL: The studio had all the latest

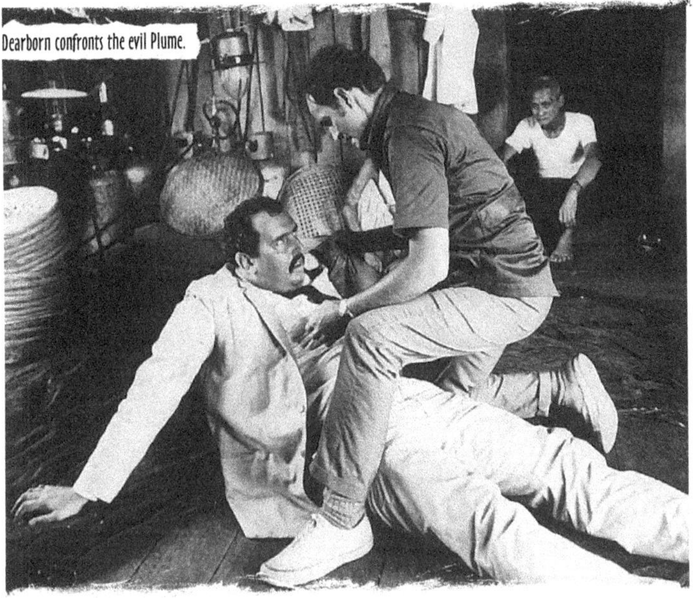
Dearborn confronts the evil Plume.

modern equipment. There were rental places all over the place. This picture is important in the fact that it doesn't reflect Singapore at all. Like I said, we used whatever of the old stuff that was left over. Oh, that's a bad flutter in the lens.

DAVE: *Who's trying to kill me?*
PLUME: *(Gasping for breath) Someone who loves you...*

JOHN: ***Plume looks a little big to dive off the pier like that.***
JOEL: He could swim like a fish. He just ate too much. We worked hard on this. We worked twenty hours at a time. Forty hours for the island sequence. Not only that, but the guy who put up the money for the generators left in the middle of the shoot. The lights went out, and that was it.
JOHN: ***What film did you have the best experience shooting?***
JOEL: ***Blood Sucking Freaks***. I did more or less what I wanted to do there. ***Blood Bath*** was stupid. It almost worked. But I was fighting with everybody here.

Dearborn props up Plume's dead body at Lim's rendezvous point and silently waits for the confusion and shooting to begin.

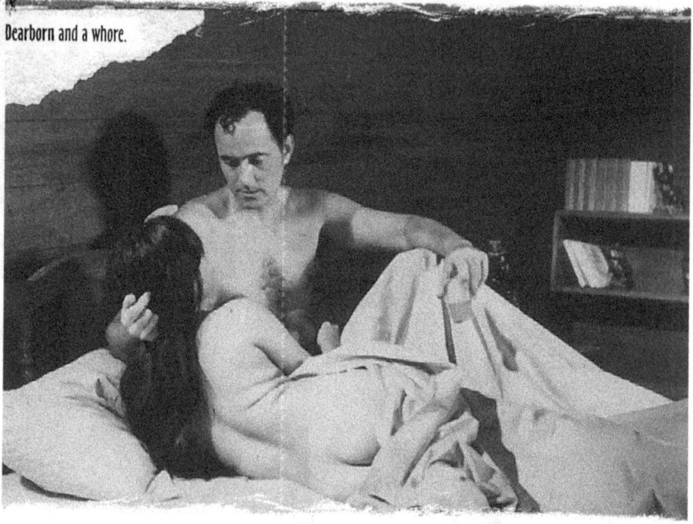

Dearborn and a whore.

JOHN: *Did the police get you the weapons?*

JOEL: Yeah, they provided the weapons. The cops in Singapore are very tough. They hang you over there, they still can. The cops could shoot you dead if you were involved in any kind of armed robbery.

After the smoke clears, Dave and Mai Lee fall into each other's arms among the corpses. As Dave drifts off to sleep, visions of his past haunt him.

JOHN: *Was this sequence Victor's idea?*

JOEL: I don't know. I don't even think we had this scene in the script.

JOHN: *Victor did a lot of fades like this in [Bill Gunn's] Ganja & Hess.*

JOEL: He probably put it in. We probably had to pad the running time.

A deformed, bald giant rises from the rubble and injects Dearborn with a sedative as Mai Lee screams. A giant wearing a small pink vest. Dearborn comes to, bound at the

Dutan holds Dearborn captive.

wrists, hanging from the ceiling in an elegant suite. Dutan stands in front of him, smiling.

JOEL: The costume department came up with these vests. This could have been much kinkier. It could have had a bunch of guys hanging up, we could have built up this whole thing. Marvin had an argument about money. We had an actor that was slated to play a big roll, but he wanted too much money. If I was on top of it, I would have told him, "Fuck it, I want the other actor." That giant was an American school teacher. We could have had a great kinky scene here if we had the balls to do it. We could have had guys totally nude. David Lynch has done stuff like that. I could have broken ground if I had the balls to do it. Dutan's a horrible actor. If we had some real degenerate old faggot, it could have been great.

DUTAN: *Tell me, David. Was she your Saigon girl?*
DAVE: *Yeah, she was my Saigon girl...*

JOHN: ***So where was this set?***
JOEL: In Elizabeth Gay's house.

Dialing down the kink?

I think I told you the story about Marvin and Tom?
JOHN: ***I'm not sure.***
JOEL: Well, remember when Vicky was hanging up? We shot Tom's scene first. Tom wanted to go to dinner with Elizabeth. We said, "Well, let's tie Vicky up while you two go." He came back around four hours later and we shot some of her stuff. Tom came in and said, "You had this wonderful woman tied up for four hours?" We said, "Yeah." Tom grabbed Marvin by the neck. Marvin could have killed him.
JOHN: ***And now for the final***

The very essence of Wit's End.

chase.

Dearborn chases Dutan through the dirty alleys of Singapore. He fires off two shots and Dutan hits the ground. Dearborn staggers through the street in a daze. Dutan fires off a final shot and hits him full in the chest. Dearborn looks up to the sky.

DAVE: *Well, it was fun while it lasted. Or was it?*

The answer to that question would soon lie in the hands of a paying audience. In the meantime, the press in Singapore was having a field day:

Forbidden Locations Used as Actual Backgrounds in Adventure Drama Filmed in Singapore

Wit's End*, an action filled spicy drama of murder, intrigue, and adventure today in SE Asia, was filmed entirely on location with many scenes shot without permission in forbidden areas of the city.*

Marvin Farkas, the producer, who is an old hand in the orient, had to sneak his crews into such locations banned to photographers such as Bugis Street, Coney Island, and Sago Lane, the street of death.

Bugis Street, a notorious hang out for transvestites and seamen, had to be filmed from a camera hidden in the second floor window of a Chinese gambling den, as both the government and the local hoods would have been unhappy if too much publicity was drawn to this sin for sale neighborhood. The camera and sound equipment were smuggled in and out of the area in wicker fish baskets.

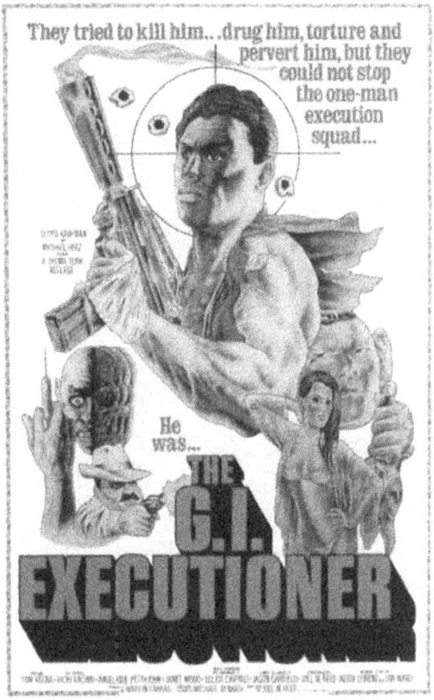

Coney Island, the scene of one of the film's big action scenes was also off-limits. A decaying mansion on the island was one of Malaya's biggest bordellos and natives still dig up the grounds in hope of finding treasure hidden there by gold smugglers who frequented the place. The production crew had to make midnight trips to the island in native dugout canoes to avoid being caught.

Sago Lane, the street of death, has a special guard to prevent even tourists from photographing its morbid funerary homes and undertaking establishments. A camera truck, disguised as a milk van with a two way mirror was used on this location. The van was left in a parking space for two days so that the natives would get used to it.

Sounds simple, but it wasn't, as the film is a drama, and actors, after rehearsing their scene on one location, had to perform in the real place with actual natives, not extras, looking on. Star Tom Keena almost had a fight that wasn't in the script when he knocked over a rather tough looking Malay longshoreman while chasing villain Peter Gernert over a bridge in Singapore River. One scene filmed in a real brothel was interrupted by a fist fight when a drunken English soldier mistook one of the girls in the cast for a prostitute and invited her upstairs.

The filming on Coney Island was complicated by the fact that there were snakes, boars, and a pack of wolf-like wild dogs. Also a small bird attacked the crew every time they turned on the bright lights for the night filming.

Despite its bigger budget and exotic scenery, ***Wit's End*** was not the success that Reed and Farkas had hoped for. The film went through a string of title changes before it was acquired by Troma Entertainment in the early 1980s. Under the Troma umbrella, ***Wit's End*** briefly played theatrically as ***The GI Executioner***.

'Class photo' on the set of *Wit's End.*

TOM KEENA: In 1969, I was doing Off-Broadway plays, doing A.R. Gurney's first play, ***The David Show***. The stage manager there knew Joel Reed. Joel had come into possession of his latest script. I don't know the genesis of how it came about. It was about a bunch of pirates from Hong Kong and Laos. How the hell I ever found my way into it is still a mystery to me. I guess it started when my agent got this call. He came up to me and said, "There's this director who wants to talk to you." That was the first I'd heard of Joel Reed.

GALE McCARTY: I was doing work in Vietnam, I was a cameraman over there. I met a guy named Marvin Farkas out in Hong Kong. I worked with him for a couple of years. He was doing news photography. If somebody came into Hong Kong to do a film, they looked him up because he had the only American film company over there. They'd either use his services or rent his equipment.

MARVIN FARKAS: I was introduced to Joel by Gale McCarty, an old friend from Indonesia who had worked at my company in Hong Kong for a while. He was shooting some of Joel's films at the time. We had a screening at Movielab of ***Sex by Advertisement***. The film was sleazy, but Joel had an ironic sense of humor. He had a very funny tongue in cheek style and that interested me. I really felt he had a talent for making films. I considered Joel more than just a producer of tacky material to shock audiences. He really enjoyed what he was doing and got a big yuk out of it at the expense of the audience. Earnings were not his highest priority.

JOEL REED: Marvin was living in Hong Kong. He's always lived in Hong Kong. At that time, he was doing a lot of shooting of the Vietnam War. He was a cameraman. And then, he would go down and cover Singapore or Bangkok, that whole area. He got involved with two guys, Ian Ward and Keith Lorenz. They wrote the original script for ***Wit's End***. Ian is still there. He was a famous journalist in London. He wrote this piece about the Queen of England, and at that time, you didn't write things like that. He was politely told to leave the country, and he's been in Singapore ever since.

Keith Lorenz was a guy who was pimping for these American service men in Singapore during the Vietnam War; he opened a brothel and would cater to GIs. I think he had a couple of brothels going. The only problem was that Singapore was such a relatively calm place. None of the GIs wanted to go there. They'd rather go to Bangkok, it was a lot louder over there.

MARVIN FARKAS: I covered the wars in Vietnam and Cambodia as a cameraman and correspondent from 1963 until 1975. In the course of my work, I made friends with the London ***Daily Telegraph*** correspondent for Southeast Asia, Ian Ward. One night, while we were sitting around his apartment in Saigon, he asked me what it would take to make our own feature. I told him a decent story would be a start. I was sure I could raise the money if we kept the budget on the low side. He agreed to write a story that took place on the Chinese junk he owned and had anchored in a Singapore harbor. He was operating

Marvin, camera, and Joel.

"He could swim like a fish."—Joel Reed

a bar and discotheque on the junk as a sideline. Ian was always highly materialistic and he tried a lot of things. He said he would be a millionaire in five years. He had a huge ego. A psychoanalyst would probably say it was the result of a low self-image. He could be nasty at times. His views in the things that he wrote were certainly unique. A bit over the edge; right wing. They coincided with the policies of his paper. He was always an interesting guy, though.

JOEL REED: The junk we shot on was Ian Ward's. He was using it as a nightclub and he wrote it into the script. We got there and he didn't tell us that the thing went bankrupt and was hauled away to dry land. We had to get it back for the film.

MARVIN FARKAS: Keith Lorenz was the production manager. He was a nice, seemingly ineffectual character. He had gone to Harvard. He had the look of one of those eligible young bachelors at a debutante ball, but he was also a trifle seedy. Somewhere along the line, he met Ian Ward and they became close friends. Ian was a bit of a megalomaniac. Keith willingly became his semi-slave, doing all the little gopher duties for his Master. I think he was really the one that wrote the original story for the film.

When I first met Keith, he had a restaurant, bar, or whatever, up one of the main klongs in Bangkok. He called it Trader Keith's. I understand it was fairly successful. Keith loved animals and had an eclectic assortment at the place. But he wasn't exactly a neat guy. With rabbits, monkeys and civet cats having free rein, his bar gradually deteriorated to the point of no return. Somehow, he managed to sell it to a German couple who restored it to its original glory. They apparently made a success of it. That was the only real employment Keith had, that I knew of. I did run into him in Phnom Penh, where he told me he was working freelance for the Voice of America doing radio news stories. He never went out of town and got his news from correspondents returning from the field. He echoed what he was told, putting in a few of his own highly inaccurate opinions. He sent them out over the airwaves to the gullible American people waiting for news of the war. The last I heard, he was in Bali, living on the beach and smoking pot most of the day. He was finally evicted by the police. They carried him away on the door of his hut that they had broken down. He was an inoffensive, likable guy. A sharp contrast to the

Movie magic.

On the junk.

brash, opinionated Ian Ward.

JOEL REED: Marvin decided to make a movie. I had just done ***Sex by Advertisement***. I was in the elevator in Movielab and I bumped into him. He said, "Where do I find out about pricing? I'm making a low budget movie in Asia." We got to talking, and I asked him if he wanted to see my movie. He watched it, and he came out saying, "That's a wonderful movie. I should have hired you to direct mine." He gave me the script; it would have cost about 100 million dollars to produce. It had temples and aircraft carriers blowing up, thousands of extras. He'd hired a guy named David X. Young to direct the thing.

DAVID X. YOUNG: Marvin had seen a film I'd done called ***Klaximo***, about a girl fucking a robot. It was the film that shocked the avant-garde. At that time, there were all these Warhol people hanging around who just hated it. I don't know why the gays didn't like the film, I still can't understand it. My film *was* very well made. That might be one reason they didn't want it around!

I shot it in 1963; the last shot in the film was on the day John F. Kennedy was killed. It took me a year to edit it. I showed it around Massachusetts, where I was from, and shocked everybody. This was before X rated films or anything. I brought it to New York, figuring I'd find a hip audience. The gay scene had taken over the underground cinema.

I can't even remember how I got to know Joel in the first place. There was a period back in the '60s where everybody was trying to make a movie. Joel was kind of a journeyman film guy who wrote these scripts; they were awful. What he did to my script was unthinkable.

I gave up shooting the Woodstock festival to work on ***Wit's End***. I would have had Martin Scorsese as my assistant director. But, at the time, there were some terrible personal problems going on in my life. My wife almost killed my daughter with an overdose of vitamins. I found out that there was a doctor in Hong Kong who was a specialist in vitamin A toxicity. Practically the only one in the world.

MARVIN FARKAS: I met David Young through a friend named Lenny Green. He took me to David Young's loft on Canal Street between Chinatown and Soho on the periphery of NY's Greenwich Village. David showed me a 35 minute film called ***Klaximo*** that he had written, shot, and directed. His wife was the star. It was about a girl that constructs a lovemaking machine when she becomes disappointed in the men around her. It was a very good film. I immediately figured that he was the man to do ours.

DAVID X. YOUNG: So Marvin said ***Klaximo*** was one of the greatest films he'd ever seen in his life. He asked me if I'd be interested in coming to Singapore or Hong Kong to make a film. I was caught between a very-high-on-acid Mike Lang, who was yammering about this concert he wanted to film upstate on a farm in New York. I wasn't a rock and roll fan to begin with, so I wasn't interested in that. Then my wife pulled her number and I found out about the doctor in Hong Kong. I accepted the film with Marvin.

MARVIN FARKAS: David was obsessed with Orson Welles and was determined to be innovative no matter how unrealistic and expensive it got. We had a very limited budget and I personally thought David was stretching things.

DAVID X. YOUNG: They sent me the original script, written by these two guys, Keith Lorenz and Ian Ward. It was kind of a celebration of themselves. I think it was all being made on CIA money.

MARVIN FARKAS: The only reference I heard about the CIA being involved with the film was because of one of my partners, Michel Renard. People thought he was a CIA agent but I strongly doubt it. Michel was a very rich guy, about six feet four, who lived on the edge of machismo. He told stories about his adventures in wartime Laos and killing communist agents in the most heroic circumstances. He had all the camera paraphernalia to pretend he was a newsman but I personally think he was just having a good time. I never knew who he was working for.

DAVID X. YOUNG: I went over there and saw what they were trying to do. ***Easy Rider*** had just come out and by that time, I'd heard about what was going on at Woodstock. There I was, in an office in Singapore being interrogated by these two CIA guys! They said, "Look how terrible things are in America," and flopped a ***Time*** magazine down in front of me. There it was, an air shot of the farm at Woodstock. I said, "My God, I could have been there. I'm sitting in this dingy fucking office in Singapore!" I said, "You can't do a pro-war movie. No way. Nobody's going to go see it. It's got to be anti-war." I rewrote the whole damn thing, from scratch, in two weeks. I wrote the thing in twenty days, with no visuals! I just had to get the story down.

David X. Young

MARVIN FARKAS: We brought David to Singapore for pre-production. He told us he planned to shoot the film in chronological order. I don't know if you're acquainted with filmmaking, but films are *not* shot like that. It's completely impractical. For instance, if scenes 12, 44, 58, and 102 take place at the same location, those scenes are shot together and that location is disposed of. We didn't have the time to come back there a dozen times to tell the story, as David said, "Like a home movie."

DAVID X. YOUNG: I wanted to use Bradley Cunningham as the lead actor. He owned a bar in New York and had this great, craggy face. The guys who originally wrote the script wanted a pretty boy. I said, "You don't want to use a pretty boy." Bradley Cunningham had a Bogartish personality. He loved jazz; I was going to have a lot of jazz in the film.

I had the idea of shooting Singapore in thirty frames a second instead of twenty-four. Just for the long shots. It would give it a sort

of dreamy quality, with the little girls and their umbrellas and stuff. I even wrote a song for the film that I didn't leave in the script. It's called "Sing a Song of Singapore." It was very funny, it was to be sung by this stripper.

MARVIN FARKAS: Young was very temperamental and had some weird ideas about making films. First of all, he tried to push a friend of his in as the leading man. That was Bradley Cunningham. He owned a popular bar in the Village near NYU. David made a very nice test with Bradley. He seemed to be a good actor, and in retrospect, I should have discussed him further with David. He might have been an interesting choice. My partners were prejudiced against Bradley because he was a bit of a New York character and didn't fit their stereotyped picture of Dave Dearborn. To avoid making waves, I had to go along with this and eventually fought many battles with David over it.

KEITH LORENZ: [David] came out to Singapore early for script writing, location scouting, hiring, and pre-production with my help. [He'd] just begun to get the ambience of Singapore when he sort of fell apart.[1]

DAVID X. YOUNG: In the long end, I had to go back to fight for the custody of my daughter in court. I

1) Slater, Benjamin, "The Wit's End Story", ***Clearly You've Never Been*** on-line at: http://sporeana.blogspot.com/2012/05/wits-end-story.html (2012)

had no choice. They didn't want to pay for me to go back. In fact, I got demerits for anything I did.

MARVIN FARKAS: Everything about the production was going to hell. The final bit of unreality is when David left Singapore to rush back to NYC because he said his wife had kidnapped his daughter. She had overdosed his baby on vitamin A, and he had to get back there as fast as possible to save the child and get rid of his wife. He left using the other half of the r/t ticket we gave him as part of the contract, with no schedule to return.

DAVID X. YOUNG: They didn't know what the fuck they were doing. I told them, "You're hiring talent. To get the best out of your investment, treat it right. Don't treat it like shit. This is not management of labor."

MARVIN FARKAS: My partners were incredulous. They held me responsible for David and wanted him out of the film. Actually, we didn't have any escape clause to fire him in the contract. That comes from using contracts you can buy in a stationary store.

JOEL REED: Marvin called me from Hong Kong and said, "You've got to help me out. David's disappeared from Singapore. You've got to talk to him for me."

DAVID X. YOUNG: So anyway, they did their thing and I came back to New York. Then, they got the idea of having Joel Reed oversee me to make sure I *behaved*. That was utterly ridiculous! I quit, finally. They didn't give a shit. By that time Farkas had hired Joel Reed. The rest became this unspeakable disaster. I couldn't believe it.

JOEL REED: I went down to see him to try and get him back over to Singapore. He lived on Canal Street, he probably still does. The first thing David showed me was a movie he had made called ***Klaximo***. His ex-wife starred in it. It's about this girl in Cape Cod who all these guys are trying to nail. She ignores all of them. She keeps going to the hardware store to buy bolts and batteries, and levers. Can you guess where this is leading? Anyway, all of the guys wonder why she never goes out, so they sneak up to her house. The electricity is going nuts; she built this big machine. That's about the end of the movie. She keeps going at it and the whole place is shaking. It's not graphic. But anyway, the generator goes out and the entire town blacks out. All of the guys realize that it's a hopeless cause, turn around, and walk back to the bar.

David told me, "I'm not making this fucking movie. I can't stand Marvin." So Marvin said, "Joel, you

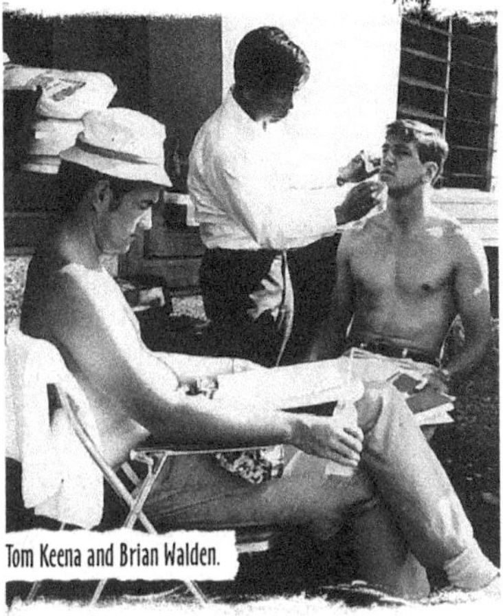

Tom Keena and Brian Walden.

mediate. I'm flying in."

MARVIN FARKAS: I rushed to New York and decided that Joel would be a perfect replacement for David. Joel and I went down to Bradley's place, where David hung out every night. I had to approach the problem delicately to avoid a lawsuit. I used the strategy that I was an insensitive producer and, with my wealthy partners, wanted David back on our own terms. David laughed at me. So did his cronies at Bradley's. I kept firm until David finally quit of his own volition. He turned his back on me and returned to his beer, which I think he got on the cuff by idolizing Bradley Cunningham. Bradley offered drinks all around and asked Joel and me to leave his bar at once.

JOEL REED: We were sitting in

Marvin Farkas

Bradley Cunningham's. One of David's conditions was that he wanted to take everyone from that bar and put them in the movie. He wanted to make Bradley Cunningham the lead. So, we were sitting there and Marvin would say to me, "Tell David that I can get him $5,000 more." And David would say, "Tell Marvin to fuck off." That was the extent of the conversation. I said, "Marvin, I don't think David wants to work with you." He said, "If David proceeds with this attitude, I'll fire him and hire you."

So, I ended up doing that. I had a Broadway play under option that would have most likely been produced, but I ran off and made ***Wit's End***. I shouldn't have done it, I should have stuck with the play. I didn't reach high, but I needed the money at the moment. I guess Radley Metzger wouldn't do it for the price. It was $7,000 upfront.

MARVIN FARKAS: Joel's rewrite of David's script was not a great deal different. Joel put in a couple of very funny touches that were hilarious but somehow they got cut out. One was of a lineup of tarts in Joe's Pleasure Palace. We panned to close-ups of the girls waiting for customers with provocative looks on their faces. Finally the close-up of the last girl on the line is a pre-pubescent female licking an ice cream cone. Joel had a few touches like that, but he didn't mean anything serious by them. He was just trying to be funny.

JOEL REED: I took the script, and in the rush to do it, nobody realized that it was very close to ***Casablanca***. The guy who owned the nightclub, the fascist government, the girl who's trying to smuggle in this atomic scientist...

MARVIN FARKAS: So, that was the end of my relationship with David X. Young. I invited Joel to take up the job and invited him to Westchester for some country dining to celebrate. I seem to remember Joel ending up with diarrhea.

JOEL REED: I went and made the movie. I assumed that there was a production manager over in Singapore. I sent him all these letters to set up the details of the production. So, one day, the bell rang at my old apartment. It was the production manager. I said, "We're shooting in two weeks. I'm going to Singapore." He said, "No, I'm spending a couple of months in America. I have all of your letters, but I haven't had time to read them. In fact, nothing has been done in Singapore."

MARVIN FARKAS: When Joel was in Singapore and Keith was in New York, he agreed to let Keith stay at his apartment. In return for the favor, Keith promised Joel some charming female company from his private, little black book collection in Singapore. Nothing materialized, and I remember an indignant Joel

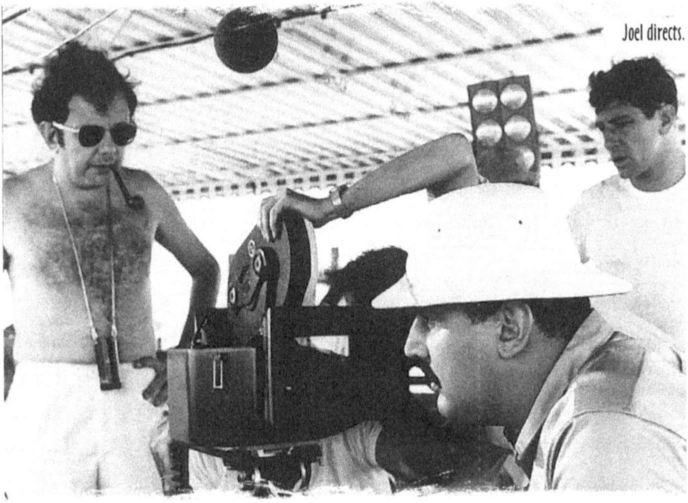

Joel directs.

going to the telegraph office to send a spiteful cable to Keith. He told him, as he had not lived up to his end of the bargain, that he wanted him out of his apartment with all due haste. Otherwise, they got on well together.

JOEL REED: I went over there. Cathay-Pacific helped to set us up. The first thing they said was, "There's no good looking Chinese girls in Singapore." Well, there's millions of them. Singapore is not an exotic city, it's very modern. There was absolutely nothing over there that was close to what we wanted. I was under the assumption that Singapore was some kind of a primitive place. We had to break our backs to find anything that was exotic. We shot half of the scenes next to the Kentucky Fried Chicken. All the trees were there. That's how it came about. We could have shot any other picture.

MARVIN FARKAS: With all things considered, working in Singapore wasn't bad and we got a lot of production value shooting at different locations around town. Lee Kuan Yew had already gotten into office with his People's Action Party on the coattails of the Communists who he later turned against, tossing many of them into Changi prison for subversion. At the time of our production, he hadn't started decimating the colorful old Singapore to replace it with static, colorless, glassed-in skyscrapers, clean streets, and greenery. It's completely devoid of character today. Singapore people are nice, but they seem to have adopted this new way of living and are pretty static and colorless themselves.

JOEL REED: I think that the film was originally called ***Dragon Lady***. It was a big story about these guys who find some hidden land where they have an army of Chinese. You know, MGM was shooting ***Man's Fate*** in Singapore at the time. Nobody would talk to us. Everyone in Singapore said, "No, we're going to work on ***Man's Fate***." We had trouble getting actors. And then MGM went bankrupt. They couldn't pay anyone or give them return tickets, so they all came on board for ***Wit's End***. They had built parts of Shanghai again at the studio there.

MARVIN FARKAS: I didn't know about any other film being made in Singapore at the time, though they did have a pretty busy film industry. In any case, if there was one being made, it had no effect on our production. Ian and Keith originally called our film ***No Visa for Singapore***. The title had almost nothing to do with the plot. But the script outline was what I needed to

raise the $136,000 budget. When David X. Young came into the deal as director, he rewrote the script and called it ***Wit's End*** which also had nothing to do with the story. Finally, when Joel came on the scene, he rewrote it again, keeping the name ***Wit's End***. That was the final script for shooting.

KEITH LORENZ: [Reed] persuaded the cash people to let him make it raunchy and campy, whatever you want to call it. He decided to be both writer as well as director, and got his way. I lost all interest quite soon.[2]

JOEL REED: It was like Marvin never read the script. He'd say, "I'm not shooting this stupid scene. Why

2) Ibid

The Adonis Bar.

do you keep putting these scenes in my movie?" I said, "Marvin, I didn't put it in there, it was in the first script that you threw away. The one you *liked*." He'd say, "I haven't got time to read the thing."

MARVIN FARKAS: With pre-production, we were in Singapore about eight weeks. As I said, the budget started at about $136,000 and ended up about $152,000. We shot with one 35mm Arriflex in a blimp on Eastmancolor negative. We had a new Nagra recorder for live sound. As the cameraman, I was moderately pleased with my work, but the sound was atrocious. The soundman was inept and inexperienced. He made some ridiculous and obvious blunders. David Young's original idea was to have live sound, as he felt post-recording ruined performances. Considering the crappy performances we got, it really made little difference.

JOEL REED: The casting director got me two girls. His name was Mark Louis. He was black, Indian, and American. He was trying to be a procurer. He had a brothel, but the girls would take all of the money from him. He wasn't a very good pimp. He used to buy these young girls from these primitive villages in Borneo and bring them back. He had an exotic animal ring going, and he was trying to raise turkeys on the side. Nobody's seen Mark in years. He played the pimp in the beginning of the picture. It's funny. They were shooting ***The Virgin Soldiers*** right before we came over for our picture. The first time I met Mark Louis, he said, "What is your wish, sir?" I said, "I don't know, are you talking about girls?" He said, "The English people for ***The Virgin Soldiers*** all wanted boys, so I have to be sure about these things."

MARVIN FARKAS: Mark Louis was an all-around guy. A procurer, an actor, an animal trainer, and I don't know what else. He seemed to be a nice guy and arranged a lot of the local cast and the exotic birds and animals we used in the film.

JOEL REED: Singapore is kind of broken up between the Chinese and the Malays. The Chinese people seemed to like women, but the Malays like to go to dance halls staffed by transvestites. We were filming with a Malay crew and we had all these girls running around nude throughout the picture. They didn't even bother looking at them. But when this guy came to lunch, this twelve-year-old boy in shorts, they got all excited. That's the foils of the land, I guess. But, you know, some people like bowling. The Malays threw us the wrap party. They said, "We got you the nicest boy in Singapore." I said, "Very thank you," then got drunk and passed out.

Singapore is noted for its transvestites. There was Bugis Street. At midnight, all of the restaurants would put out tables with white tablecloths and make

Relaxing on the set.

it into a nightclub. There would be this big parade of transvestites. It was very unusual; once in a while you'd see an English soldier come by in full drag. There were only transvestite prostitutes in the area. You couldn't bring in women. This opium addict used to come over to the table and sing opera. It was actually a big hangout for the British forces.

The government decided to clean it up. Then they decided to put it back because there was no other reason to go to Singapore. It used to be about fifteen blocks long. Now it's only two blocks. On the fringes of Bugis Street were all of these old prostitutes with no teeth. One reached out and grabbed my balls one night. I punched the guy. My friend was sitting there laughing.

MARVIN FARKAS: I'm sure Malays enjoy transvestites sometimes, though I don't think it's a particular idiosyncrasy of that race.

JOEL REED: We were over in Singapore for a couple of months. I had a birthday there. I met Elizabeth Gay. She was one of the richest women in Singapore. Her husband was the head of the Singapore stock exchange. She was a dancer in some show in London. That house where we shot the scene with the Chinese gangsters was hers.

MARVIN FARKAS: Elizabeth Gay was the wife of a wealthy businessman. I think she was French. She was looking for a little excitement in her mundane Singapore existence. She hung around our set quite often. Joel gave her a bit part as the wife of a British Gurkha officer that I thought was very funny. Somehow, it got cut out of the film in the editing.

JOEL REED: Elizabeth is in the film, she's dancing in the nightclub. For the disco scene, we just called up a high school and everyone came over. Anyway, we got to meet Lee Kuan Yew; the government was *very* nice there. They were busy tearing down every place that looked interesting! Now it's all condominiums, it looks like Miami Beach. I went back and everything was high-rise buildings and shopping malls.

MARVIN FARKAS: We had permits to shoot wherever we pleased. We also had assistance from the police with guns for filming. We usually always had

Agent Greg Morrison delivers a knockout punch.

policemen on the set watching some of the more torrid scenes with the naked ladies that abounded. They weren't prissy and priggish like they are today. The government helped us where they could and gave us no trouble at all. Permits were reasonably priced. We occasionally hired policemen from the government for crowd control at some locations.

JOEL REED: You always do a little bit of rehearsals for the camera. Some directors do rehearsals for a day. My normal thing was to do a couple of run-throughs with the actors, then we'd do it on the set. When you get on the set, everything changes completely. You can't imagine how different things are. Angelique Pettyjohn got kind of strange during rehearsals. Someone would say their lines: "Nice to see you, what a nice day." Angelique would answer, "You motherfucker, piece of shit!" She knew her lines, she just liked to call people 'piece of shit'. She did all of her scenes perfectly. She used to tell us about all of the great stars she fucked. She said she had Burt Lancaster and Kirk Douglas.

MARVIN FARKAS: It was really unfortunate I did not have a hand in the Singapore casting. I was in Hong Kong on another assignment during pre-production. Our production manager, Joe Zucchero, Joel, our accountant (who was also one of our investors) and

Morrison and Jones question Dearborn.

one or two others did the casting in Singapore. They really picked some clunkers. I think that if I was there at the time, I could have done better, but that's after the fact.

JOEL REED: The guy who played Plume was an oil engineer. When he jumped in the water, he actually threw himself in. It turned out that he was a former diver and a college swimmer. But, he was a pipeline coating specialist. He knew all about the coatings on pipelines. He wasn't an actor.

Dutan was played by an English government worker. We saw him in some local production. He was our second choice. The guy we wanted was involved with ***Man's Fate*** and we didn't get him.

Mr. Lim was the gangster in charge of our district. He came over to shake us down and we gave him a part in the picture. The Russian guy at the end was a retired executioner from Singapore. He was British, he had a thick Cockney accent. He parachuted into Singapore, he was a British agent. He was captured by the Germans when he parachuted into France. He escaped and ended up in Singapore. He'd tell us about the ropes used for hanging people. Sometimes he got the lengths wrong. He said, "Crime was bad, I couldn't measure them all the time." He told us a lot about caning. I think he found the island for us. He hid out there in World War II.

The guy who played the police officer was actually a London Police Inspector. He's now working for the British State Department.

TOM KEENA: My first meeting

Agent Morrison.

for everything was at Joel's apartment. It was convenient, it was easy. He might have had an office, I can't really remember. I'm reaching back. The point is that I walked in, and whatever the hell I was prepared for, there was Joel. He was so far removed from anything I'd ever seen. He said, "*Heeey*, how are you? Good to *see* you!" I thought, "What the hell is this all about?" He said, "Listen, I might be doing a film. People say you're a *good* actor!" I'm thinking, "Oh, Jesus Christ. What the fuck? Where's Singapore?" I didn't know! He said, "Listen. If I bring some *girls* in, would you read with them?" I thought to myself, "Oh, now *wait* a minute!" But Joel brought some girls in and we read together. And that was it. Nothing happened, for a while.

MARVIN FARKAS: Tom Keena was my one choice. I interviewed him in New York. When a soap star dropped out, I insisted on Tom, who I had just met once, to fill the role.

TOM KEENA: I was doing four plays at that time. I did ***An Ordinary Man*** at the Cherry Lane and ***The David Show***. I won an OBIE for that. Then, I went uptown to Broadway to start ***Our Town*** with [Henry] Fonda. So, you know, I was kind of busy. And I didn't hear anything from Joel for a while. I hadn't done that much film. Film intrigued me; I was doing a little prime time television in New York, such as it was, but I came in a little late for what they call the golden age. I was in my early thirties, and was doing very well on the stage. I was about to do ***Our Town***. I was signed on to do that and in rehearsal. My agents called me up and said, "Now listen. We're getting pretty close to a firm offer from this guy from Singapore." I said, "What the hell are you talking about? I'm in a Pulitzer Prize play, I'm headed for Broadway!" They said, "Well, I

Angelique and Tom aboard the junk.

don't know, but here's their offer." Mind you, at this point, there was no script. I had no idea what was going on. Except that the director was this guy who sort of intrigued me, for reasons unknown.

JOEL REED: I might have seen Tom Keena in ***The David Show***. He wasn't my first choice. It was an emergency; we had hired another guy who I'd seen acting a lot. He was on some soap. He was a former priest. His agent wanted a lot of money. I said "Fuck you," and hired Tom. I think I ruined his career! But he was a good actor, he's been in a lot of things. He's getting his pension now from the unions.

TOM KEENA: I got called down and I saw Joel again. I said, "Listen, Mr. Reed. I'm under a contract, I'm doing a play." He said, "No, you're going to *Singapore*. There's gonna be *gorgeous girls*, you're going to be a *star*. We're going to have a lot of *fun*. What's this *play* going to do for you?" I said, "Well, do you have your upfront money?" He said, "Yeah, we're going to deposit half of your salary in the bank, and the other half will be there a little later."

I must tell you, whoever these people were, they lived up to every spec of the contract. I had a very nice time. It was very painful for me to ask for my release from ***Our Town***. The director was gracious enough to grant it to me. So, in November, the lady who would later become my wife drove me to the airport. I got on a plane and some thirty-one air hours later, non-stop, I got there. It was quite a ride. New York, Los Angeles, Honolulu, Guam, Saigon, Manila, and then, "Welcome to Singapore." I was on the set at four o'clock the next morning. I always can keep that straight in my mind, because I toasted in the '70s in Singapore.

MARVIN FARKAS: Angelique Pettyjohn was in the film. I didn't know her very well. Joel found her in Hollywood. She was a pleasant person. I thought quite a good comedienne who didn't reach her potential in our film, what with the bad sound, etc. She claimed she never wore underwear and that she slept with her boyfriend's unwashed, grotty T-shirt (that he had orgasmed in twelve times) under her pillow. She always talked about kinky things, and I understand (though I don't know it to be absolutely true) that she had affairs with several local girls and even a member of the cast. But that's just hearsay.

TOM KEENA: Angelique was a little distant. We were friendly, professionally friendly. I've never fooled around with anyone in my cast in my life. We were pals.

JOEL REED: Marvin met Vicky Racimo at a party or something. She was in an MGM picture, I don't remember the name. It was supposed to be a big hit. The William Morris Agency said, "You can't have her. Well, give us $100,000." I told Vicky, "The William Morris Agency doesn't want us to use you." We finally got to hire her. The picture for MGM died at the box office, by the way. But she went on to do a lot of things. She always plays the Vietnamese mother. She was supposed to play the lead opposite Sinatra in ***Dirty Dingus Magee***, but Sinatra didn't want her.

TOM KEENA: There was Angelique and Vicky Racimo, who played Mai Lee. What they were doing, I don't know. The girls would come over to my quarters every once in a while to chuck me under the chin, but I didn't have any relationships with them. I'm sure there was a lot of fun knocking around. But, that film was a very athletic experience for me! Whatever nonsense was going on, goddamn it, I was rolling! I ran throughout that whole film! I'd say, "Joel, what the fuck is going on?" He'd say, "I don't know!" I said,

"OK, we'll shoot it the best we can."

JOEL REED: I didn't hire Angelique, my friend did. She came over to Singapore and I went into her hotel room. I said, "Hello, Angelique!" She said, "Smell my sweatshirt, my boyfriend came on it six times before I left." She threw it in my face. She was OK. I got along with her, she was very pretty. She became sort of an idol in her own time. She started off as a stripper in Vegas.

TOM KEENA: We were staying at this compound, just slightly outside of Singapore. We kind of took over the whole complex. There was a swimming pool and things. It was like a middle class-upper class Las Vegas hotel. The production office was located out there. There was a dance pavilion. People would dance at night. It was nice, but if I had to listen to those guys try to practice "Hey Jude" one more time in the afternoon…

Marvin Farkas sets up a shot.

JOEL REED: Marvin rented an apartment with a servant. I stayed at the hotel. It was more convenient; everyone was staying there. Marvin seemed to want to stay at the apartment. We were all at the Ocean Park Hotel. It was pretty nice, it was a bungalow-type hotel. Everyone had their own room. Mine was right by the pool. That hotel's gone now, the Singapore government tore it down.

VERNON BECKER: I remember one time Joel sent me a postcard from Hong Kong, or wherever he made that picture. All it said was, "You ought to come over here. They're selling virgins for $200."

JOEL REED: Singapore was a strange place. You couldn't buy ***Playboy*** over there, but you could buy twelve-year-old girls. All of the big shots over there like to fuck twelve-year-old Thai girls.

MARVIN FARKAS: I never heard about $200 virgins for sale. I must ask Joel for details.

JOEL REED: Marvin originally

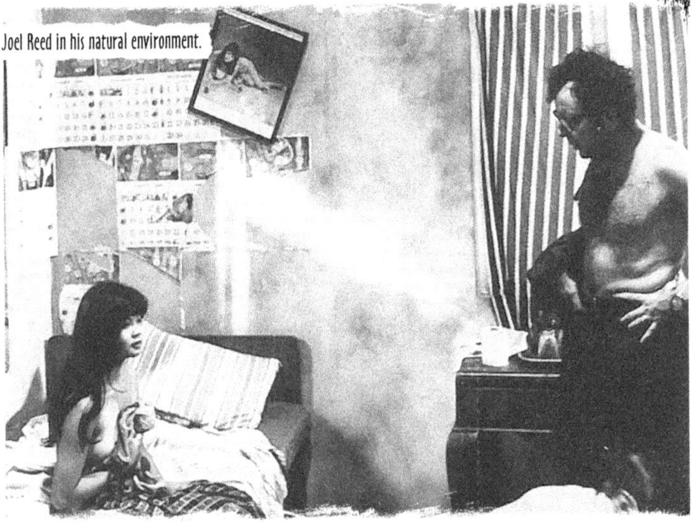

Joel Reed in his natural environment.

said that no Chinese girls would pose nude. That's why we hired Vicky Racimo. Of course, every Chinese girl was taking her clothes off. Marvin was a little naive.

I met a guy on the plane coming in. I ran into him later. He was a real proper English gentleman. "Hello, this is my wife. We must have tea." We used to have tea on the terrace at the Ocean Park Hotel. One day, Mark Louis came over to see me with two girls. I had just ordered a steak sandwich and was sitting with my new friends. I said to the girls, "Do you want some food? I want to eat first." They said, "We're a little embarrassed, sir." The guy's wife said, "For God's sake, these girls came over to get fucked, Joel. Don't be so polite; take them to your room." Wonderful upper class people!

TOM KEENA: I was in every goddamn scene in the movie. I was working like a goddamn horse in 104 degree heat. It didn't take me long to realize that I didn't know what this was all about. There was no script; we'd improvise. But as big as a botch as it was, it was almost an archetypal script for what was to come. This was slightly before all those sword pictures in Taiwan.

JOEL REED: So, we made the picture there and Victor Kanefsky cut it. Victor had worked for Marvin in Hong Kong. He always brags about having cut ***Ganja & Hess***.

FRANCO CARRUBBA PER LA FIRST NATIONAL FILM PRESENTA
vietato ai minori di 18 anni
SINGAPORE: VIOLENZA e SESSO
con TOM KEENA · ANNA LING · VICKI RACIMO · ANGELIQUE PETTYJOHN
PRODOTTO DA MARVIN FARKAS
REGIA DI JOEL M. REED
COLORE

VICTOR KANEFSKY: With ***Ganja & Hess***, I was looking for work. I bumped into an old girlfriend of mine. She said that she'd heard that there was a feature being done—"Why don't you see if you can get it?" That turned out to be the thing for Bill Gunn. She gave me his name, and I sent him a sample of my work. That was after I had cut ***Dragon Lady***, or whatever it was being called at the time.

JOEL REED: I met Victor way before I started doing movies. He was a mutual friend of Gale McCarty. I couldn't afford him for the first couple of films. He started with ***Wit's End***. Marvin wanted to use him.

MARVIN FARKAS: Victor Kanefsky was the best friend of my cousin who touted him as a great and experienced editor.

VICTOR KANEFSKY: I'd gotten fed up with what was happening in New York City. I decided that I was going to go to Europe for a month in order to clear my head. A friend of mine named Marvin Farkas happened to be in Manhattan. When I told him I was going to go to Europe, he said, "Don't go there. Come to Hong Kong." I thought that might be a fun idea, so I booked a ride on a freighter. It took me fifty days to get there. I met with Marvin and cut a couple of films for him. That's really why he wanted me to come—he wanted to work with me. I cut a couple of documentaries and a few commercials. I eventually came back to New York. Meanwhile, Joel Reed had directed a film that Marvin shot. That was ***Dragon Lady***. Joel came back to New York and they chose me as the editor. They didn't know anyone else.

MARVIN FARKAS: I saw a couple of documentaries and commercials that he did and agreed to let him work on our film. This was his first feature. He was paid more than any other single entity in the budget. Frankly, I thought he did a terrible job and just threw the thing together. I asked him to make some simple changes but he quoted some ridiculous figure that we couldn't afford. He kept saying, "Forget it. It's great the way it is." Joel was in New York all the time and was supposed to be the editing supervisor, but Vicky was always so sure of himself that I have no doubt that Joel couldn't get a word in edgewise.

VICTOR KANEFSKY: Joel and I

had a good connection. He never came into the cutting room. He wasn't very proud of the two films that he had done before ***Dragon Lady***. He wanted to do something better.

MARVIN FARKAS: The first time I saw it was at a preview room on Broadway. I nearly slid off my seat in embarrassment. The editing was so choppy that, even as the cameraman, I didn't recognize some of the scenes I had shot.

VICTOR KANEFSKY: I don't know. I considered it a throwaway film when I was cutting it. It didn't turn out too bad, but it wasn't anything special.

DAVID X. YOUNG: I saw the final film at a screening here in New York with Farkas' brother Dick. Joel Reed showed up with a beret, a cigarette holder, a patterned scarf. I think he might have even had a whip—Mr. Movie Director. I saw the fucking film, and there was only one shot that I had planned: a girl hanging in a monkey net, dead. That was the only shot that had anything to do with what I did. As I recall, there was one scene that Reed did with a fat girl undressing. No directorial sense, nothing! I turned to Dick Farkas and said, "I'll sue you guys up through the ass and out through the eyeballs if you put my name on this picture!" It played at a drive-in Missouri for three days and that was the end of it. Had it been done right, it probably would have been a very successful anti-war movie.

JOEL REED: We played it on 42nd Street. All of the blacks were mad that I'd cut out some scenes. I had cut out the part when Tom Keena fucked Janet Wood. They were yelling, "When is he going to fuck her?" It was an awful picture. But ***Variety*** gave it a great review. They said it was one of the great film noirs of all time. I almost fainted when I read that.

MARVIN FARKAS: I do not know very much about the distribution of the film. I only know we were cheated royally by the distributor who charged exorbitant prices for everything. It was distributed in drive-in theatres in the South but that is all I know about it. We never got a penny back on the whole exercise.

LLOYD KAUFMAN: Joel wanted to sell the film. It was sitting in somebody's basement. I guess the distributor wasn't doing anything with it. We thought that Joel was a

good satirist. ***Blood Sucking Freaks*** is very funny. And ***GI Executioner*** is also a very funny film. People don't realize it, but ***GI Executioner*** is a satire. It's sort of a take on a film noir. We didn't expect to make any money on it; we were concerned that the film would just sit, get rotten, and disintegrate.

MARVIN FARKAS: My brother took care of the developing of the negative and all the payments for the services in New York. From our budget, of course. He had complete control of safeguarding the negative. I was shocked one day to read in ***Variety*** that Troma had bought the negative and changed the name to ***The GI Executioner***.

LLOYD KAUFMAN: I don't think I ever met Marvin Farkas. As I recall, it was Joel Reed who thought the film was being wasted and that we should give it a shot. I think we did make some prints of it and played it in some movie theaters. We couldn't get anywhere with it. We did get it out on video in the late '80s.

MARVIN FARKAS: According to the ***Variety*** reviewer, it was some sort of cult film, though I can't see that. The film was more or less dormant for a few years before Troma came along. I don't know how my brother met them. Maybe Joel introduced him. My brother pocketed all of the money from Troma and steadfastly refused to divulge how much he got.

A candid shot at a transvestite bar.

"Pennies!" he said. He claimed that we owed him money from the post-production that he paid for, but according to our books, this was not so. I was really afraid that the shareholders (of which there were about forty, with some investments as low as $1,000) would find out. So, all in all, I was the producer and the cameraman for no pay. I spent about a year and a half of my life bringing it to fruition. My shares weren't worth the paper they were printed on. But, looking back on the experience, I think I had a wonderful time and learned a lot. I'm still alive, healthy, and happy, so who needs money? Frankly, I would do it again at any time, though I *would* like to see a few bucks.

JOEL REED: Once in a while, I run into a couple of the oriental girls from that film. They're grandmothers now. I remember when Sidney Pink got General Electric to back a bunch of his pictures, and he did a film with Tab Hunter. I got a call from the projectionist of this theater. He said, "We're playing one of Sidney Pink's pictures and the audience is tearing the place apart." The film was terrible. Someone is killing all these girls and Tab Hunter is a secret agent. Awful. Sidney Pink was awful. The blacks rioted when they played the one with Tab Hunter. My friend at the theater appeased the crowd with ***Wit's End***.

MARVIN FARKAS: The film did not do well at all. Many films never make it to the final cut. We were proud that ours not only made it to the end, but was actually distributed. As usual in the film industry, I'm sure that the distributor ripped us off. With the copies, the transport, and the advertising we were charged for, we always were behind. One month, I remember getting an accountant. I discovered we had made sixteen cents. That is about the only time I remember being in the black.

TOM KEENA: Joel and I always said, years later, "Considering who we were surrounded with, we should have just made any goddamn fucking film we wanted!" We were *both* trying to deal with his script! Oh, *Jesus*. But then, we started screwing around. We started doing things. Joel did some interesting camera work, given what we had.

MARVIN FARKAS: I really can't say that ***Wit's End*** was one of Joel's greatest cinematic triumphs, but actually he did well. Joel is a prolific writer, he's very original. He definitely has directing talent. There's no doubt that, with the proper vehicle, he could be

Bonnie's routine.

brilliant. Others may argue the point, but I feel that Joel's handling of ***Wit's End*** was sensitive, humorous and innovative. With better sound, acting, and an honest distributor, if such a thing exists, it would have at least been a more viable product. It has colorful Singapore backgrounds and some of the characters are well drawn and worthy of comment. Like the bucktoothed Plume with his tight fitting jungle outfit and pith helmet, Bonnie's nude shoot-out, the ice cream pan that never made it, and Dutan's tattooed wrestler boyfriends dressed in outfits from ***A Thousand and One Nights***. This stuff is funny and original.

LLOYD KAUFMAN: What can I

Joel and Marvin.

say? Joel Reed has definitely got a point of view and a vision. The guy is definitely a filmmaker, he's got something to say. He's definitely *eccentric*. He's one of those artists who has a certain method...

TOM KEENA: It's not a bad little piece of film. It doesn't make any goddamn sense, but what the hell did that came after it? Joel's got that way of cutting right to the core. I don't know whether he knows it, or whether it's unconscious. He's such a reductionist. I've dealt with Joel for a lot of years. He's got these fantasies. Every once in a while, I say, "Oh, just shut up. Just shut up, will you, please?" But at other times, I think about things and say, "Oh, Jesus Christ. He's not far from it, is he? He's not that far from what went down for culture, is he?"

MARVIN FARKAS: A number of Joel's films have reached the silver screen. He's made deals for them all over the world. I guess he's made some money as well. Most of his scripts are about things that happen in the United States, but they could easily be adopted to a Far East location. Since we met, he's shown a great deal of interest in Asia. But basically, Joel is a New York phenomena and no matter where he goes he will always return there. As the Chinese say, "When the leaf falls from the tree, it heads toward the root."

"Actually, I should have worked for the Mafia. You want to get rid of this guy? Put him in one of my movies."—Joel M. Reed

CHAPTER EIGHT

BLOOD BATH

2000

The clerk inside The Playpen was screaming. He came storming down a narrow aisle of videotapes, a copy of ***Amateur First Timers*** in hand. "He did it again!"

I followed him up to the checkout counter, my tape recorder hidden in the pocket of my overcoat. I put on a concerned face, tapped him on the shoulder, and asked, "Did what?"

The clerk spun around. "Some crazy guy comes in here with scissors and cuts out the pictures!" He held up the cardboard box and shook it in front of my face. "What can he possibly do with them? Stick them to the ceiling above his bed and jerk off?"

I took a step back. "Does this happen a lot?"

The clerk threw the box behind the counter. "Once a week, at least!" He pushed me aside and started back down the aisle. "But I'll catch him one day..."

I looked up at the cameras and mirrors that lined the walls and followed him. A greasy kid shifted his weight on a very tall chair, peering down at us like a vulture. Security seemed tight.

"Maybe it's an inside job." The clerk ignored me and made his way toward the booths before I could check to see if *he* was packing scissors. It was a little past one in the morning and things were in full swing at The Playpen.

The Playpen's interior was long and narrow. Bright fluorescent lights illuminated every face like an omniscient spotlight. The place was wired with speakers that blasted

ABBA's "Dancing Queen" at a very high volume. This did little to hide the sounds of sex that rang from the rows of peep booths like a depraved Greek chorus. I rounded a corner. The classic caricature of a New York pervert blocked my path: long black coat, wild gray hair, and three-day stubble. He stood there talking to himself as he ran his fingers along the spines of a row of fetish tapes. I made an attempt to edge past him when Mr. Scissors' voice rang out like an alarm.

"You! Get out! *OUT!*"

I turned around and headed toward his voice. He had two young black kids backed up against the wall.

MR. SCISSORS: *You're underage! You have to leave!*
UNDERAGE PATRON: *Shit, man… come on!*
MR. SCISSORS: *No identification! Out! Come on!*
UNDERAGE PATRON: *Shit, man… everyone's seen a little* ***pussy*** *before!*

Two days earlier, Brian and I were zooming across Route 80, somewhere in Pennsylvania. The radio was playing "One Summer Night" by the Danleers as we made our way east.

"That makes five," Brian said as we passed another dead deer. The poor thing was laid out flat on the side of the road. We had decided to turn the boredom of traveling across the Keystone State into a game. Roadkill was abundant along Route 80—in fact, it was about the only interesting thing in sight. "We're almost out of gas," Brian said. I looked out the window and frowned. I'd been through this before. Brian never seemed to have a handle on the fuel supply of his old Ford Explorer.

We drove on for a few miles, and then a red and yellow sign beckoned to us. The thing read:

MOTEL
COCTAIL LOUNGE
TRAVELER'S DELITE
CABLE-COFFEE-SIX PACKS
TO GO

We pulled into the parking lot, walked into the lobby, and were greeted by a large black poodle that wouldn't shut up. The poodle was named Ted, and his handler scolded him as we attempted to check in.

"Keep quiet, Ted!" said the woman behind the desk. Ted paid her no mind and he barked even louder as

I signed the receipt.

"Ted! Ted! Take it easy," the woman cried. "These boys don't mean you any harm!" The dog calmed down as the woman handed us the keys to room 126.

"You'll have to drive around the cornfield to get to your room," she said. She took out a piece of paper and drew us a crude map. "Pull out of the lot and veer to the left. Follow the lights. You'll see the cabins there."

"Where's the bar?" Brian asked.

"In the next room." She jabbed her thumb to the right.

Brian and I followed her gesture, walked through a doorway, and entered a makeshift cocktail lounge. We were greeted with blank faces. It was as if we had entered a secret club. Men dressed in flannel pants and shirts gave us the once-over as we ordered beer. We sat there for a few minutes before things got too uncomfortable. We ended up taking our six packs over to room 126.

"Jesus Christ," I laughed. "Of all the places we could have stayed..."

Brian smiled. "This place is great! Let's see what's on TV."

We took advantage of the cable, drank our beer, and found a channel that was broadcasting a documentary about spontaneous human combustion.

The next morning, we checked out of the Traveler's Delite and continued toward New York. We parked the Ford in a lot in New Jersey, took a ferry across the river, and found ourselves back in Hell's Kitchen.

The Washington Jefferson hadn't changed much in the past two months. Louis greeted us with a sneer as he handed us the keys to our room. We walked up six flights of stairs, dropped off our bags, and headed down to Times Square. I had my tape recorder with me.

JOHN: ***It's January 15, 2000. We just walked out of The Playpen.***

BRIAN: It's already past midnight.

JOHN: ***OK. Starting over. It's January 16, 2000. The time is... it's 1:15, I guess.***

BRIAN: We should get some food.

JOHN: ***Let's go to that sandwich shop on Spring Street.***

BRIAN: That's too far away. We'll never get down there without a cab. And then we'd have to make it back up to 51st Street.

JOHN: ***Well, OK. We won't go there. I don't know... does McDonald's sound reasonable to you?***

Inside Joel's apartment

We had a late dinner, walked back to the Washington Jefferson, and slept until noon. After a quick breakfast, we were back on the streets. We did some sightseeing and hit a few bars. Before long, it was half-past five.

JOHN: ***OK. We're walking up Eighth. Heading over to Joel's place. Karate Center is gone.***

We arrived at Joel's apartment at six o'clock sharp and took the elevator up to 8-B. Joel invited us in and started talking.

JOEL REED: On 42nd Street you could see all of the real lousy movies. Three for seventy-five cents. That's where I discovered Roger Corman. I saw some great movies there—the Eddie Romero pictures. That was before I got involved in moviemaking.

JOHN: ***How many people did these places hold?***

JOEL: Some of them were 1,200 seat theaters, some were 600. They were full-sized; they were originally Broadway palaces. Some were really big, with multiple balconies. They used to have these huge displays—they'd have all these sexy scenes outside. Basically, one girl would take her top off for a second in the whole movie. They were like come-on places. You've got to get this all down before I kick the bucket.

JOHN: ***Well…***

JOEL: The theaters were originally all by City Hall. If you walk behind City Hall, there's Theater Alley. That's where the first musical comedy played, ***The Black Crook***.

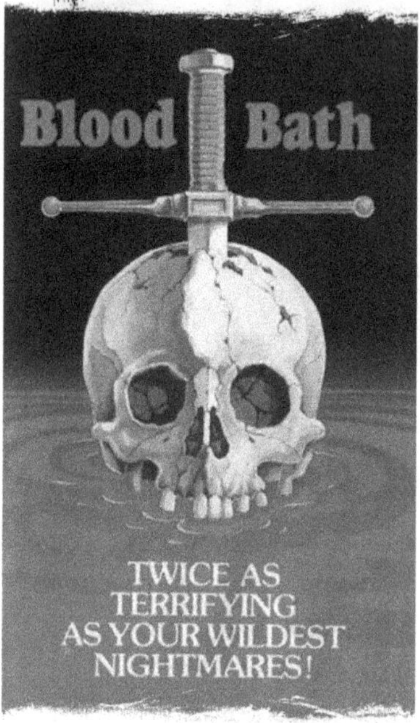

Things gradually expanded to 14th Street, and then to 23rd Street. Then it moved up to Times Square. All the stables were there, the horse places. In fact, they were tearing down some of the buildings and they found some old signs. You know, "Park your horse here for three dollars a month." I wasn't around back then, but I remember when they had the stable on 52nd or 53rd Street. Right on Seventh Avenue. It later became a flea market. People rented out the stalls.

JOHN: ***How old were you back then?***

JOEL: I was a little kid. My father would walk me over to see the horses. Do you guys want some wine? I want to have a glass before we watch this thing.

Joel walked into his kitchen and came back with a bottle. He swiftly uncorked it and turned on the TV. Our plan was to watch his fourth feature film, ***Blood Bath***.

Released in 1976, ***Blood Bath*** is a bizarre horror anthology that borrows equally from ***The Twilight Zone*** and EC Comics. The film is divided into four parts, each segment introduced by a different member of a dinner party.

Nobody in their right mind would ever call ***Blood Bath*** a good movie. Clocking in at a running time of less than 90 minutes, the film all but dares you to stick around long enough to kiss it goodnight. This is strictly PG territory—nudity and bloodshed are nonexistent. The audience is instead treated to an avalanche of exploitation clichés. Still—something about the film almost works.

Come hell or high water, ***Blood Bath*** tackles almost every genre (and subgenre) in the book. It is a world of devil worship, mutant offspring, doomed hitmen, cheating wives,

The blood bath begins...

greedy businessmen, jive-talking ghosts, kung fu fighting, and a Walter Mitty-like shmuck who takes refuge in fantasizing that he's a brave soldier in the French Revolution.

Taken best in small doses, ***Blood Bath*** does boast some solid acting. Harve Presnell, Doris Roberts, and Jerry Lacy are all excellent in their roles. Sonny Landham and P.J. Soles make their screen debuts. The familiar faces of Jack Somack and Stefan Schnabel are given equal time.

Victor Kanefsky returns as the editor, and his trademark touches are easily recognizable. Michael Sahl (who would go on to score ***Blood Sucking Freaks***) delivers a rich tapestry of music that begs to be listened to on its own. Robert Baldwin (who would go on to shoot ***The Exterminator, Basket Case 2,*** and ***Frankenhooker***) does his best as the cinematographer. ***Blood Bath*** looks good, and his contribution to the production should not be ignored.

Blood Bath also boasts a curious credit. Ronald Sullivan (AKA Henri Pachard) is listed as the art director. Best known as a director of hardcore porn, Pachard rocketed to fame in the 1980s with ***The Devil in Miss Jones 2*** and ***Blame it on Ginger***.

The following conversation was recorded on January 16, 2000. Due to the poor quality of the original audiotape, a second interview was conducted in February of 2016.

JOEL: OK, let's put this on. I rewound it. I can put surround sound on if you want...

A Faustian bargain.

A white skull grins down from a black screen. Red credits read, "Trans Orient Entertainment Corporation Presents..."

JOEL: Oh, this is awful.
JOHN: ***How'd this one get started?***
JOEL: I got a call from an exhibitor in the Philippines. He wanted to make a movie. Maybe you should adjust the tracking. It'll adjust itself, won't it?
JOHN: ***Yeah, it should.***

Soft light flickers across the skull, as if it were lit by a candle. A gong sounds as Michael Sahl's score fills the air.

JOHN: ***So, this is your fourth film. Why did it take you so long to do another movie after Wit's End?***
JOEL: I don't know. I'm not an aggressive salesman. I just waited for the next one to come along. ***Blood Bath*** came about on account of ***Wit's End***, actually. A guy named Anthony Fingleton was talking to this guy in the Philippines, and he recommended me.
JOHN: ***Was Fingleton living in New York?***
JOEL: Yes.
JOHN: ***What year are we looking at?***
JOEL: That would have been in 1975. Six months prior to the production of ***Blood Bath***. The picture was released in January of 1976.
JOHN: ***What was preproduction like?***
JOEL: Things went well. We put the deal together in one or two days.

The skull fades into darkness as the opening scene unfolds. An evil priest smiles as he presides over a curious wedding. Credits read: Executive Producer—Philip Dearborn.

JOHN: ***Who was Philip Dearborn?***
JOEL: He was Anthony's friend. He put up the money.

The priest begins the ceremony. Peter Brown (Harve Presnell) seems worried as he gazes at his bride-to-be. Her face is obscured by a white veil. The bride's father, a horned man who bears a striking resemblance to Anton LaVey, smiles. The credits continue.

JOEL: Victor Kanefsky cut this. It's not very good. But I sold this scene to some guy, and he put it in a television series for about three seconds. It almost works. There's Harve Presnell. I don't know who the other people are. I think they were all from soap operas.

Peter stumbles through his lines as he places a ring on his bride's finger. He lifts her veil and leans in for a kiss. Her face is a hideous mess, and he gags as they embrace. The bride's father laughs…

JOHN: ***Did you already have a script ready, or did you have to write one from scratch?***
JOEL: I had one lying around. I don't know when I wrote it. We wanted to do a quick, inexpensive movie that wasn't too gory. Now that I think about it, it was the wrong script to do; I was too naive. I had to do the movie in a hurry. I had another script; I don't know why I didn't do that one. It was called ***I Am the Landlord***. It would have been a much freakier movie.
JOHN: ***Well, anthology movies were somewhat popular at the time. This sort of has an Amicus Productions feel to it.***
JOEL: Yeah, the British made a lot of them. I don't remember this being so dark. Do you think it's the tracking? Wait… it's getting better.

A young virgin is bound, gagged, and strapped to a bed. Peter Brown, suddenly happy with his deal with the devil, prepares her body for sacrifice.

JOEL: This girl said that she was going to sue us if we showed too much of her in the movie. She wouldn't take her clothes off. My friend told me that he shot her in a porn film the next week.

Satan appears to claim his prize, but

Dinner conversation gets lively.

his smile soon turns to rage.

THE DEVIL: *This is not a true maiden!*

He raises a dagger as the woman screams. Suddenly, Peter turns his head to the camera, winks, and bursts into laughter.

PETER BROWN: *Lights, please!*
WOMAN'S VOICE: *Oh, Peter!*

The devil and his would-be sacrifice break character and smile. It turns out that they are only actors in a production that Peter has staged to frighten his friends.

PETER BROWN: *Of course, actors! A show! This is a film studio! Did you actually think I conjured up the devil?*

An elderly man slaps Peter on the back.

JOEL: That's Stefan Schnabel! He was famous for the Yiddish theater. He was on ***The Guiding Light*** for years.

OLD MAN: *Peter, you bastard! Were you trying to frighten us with your cheap tricks?*

JOEL: The trouble with this movie is that it was bland. We should have done ***Guerrilla Girls***, but that's another thing.
JOHN: ***What was Guerrilla Girls?***
JOEL: It was a takeoff on ***The Dirty Dozen***. It was like a Roger Corman thing with a bunch of girls with perfect nail polish and designer shoes. They're recruited to go on this mission to kill all these people. I still

have a copy of the script. We could have shot it for the same amount of money, maybe a little more.

Peter is revealed to be a famous director of horror movies. Champagne is served as he and his friends retire to a dinner table.

JOHN: ***So, where was this film shot?***

JOEL: Oh, here. We shot most of the interiors in some famous painter's loft. I can't remember his name. It was on Lower Broadway and 15th Street. He was one of those impressionistic painters. He had a big loft down there. I don't know if we rented it directly from him, but we rented it from somebody. I think three of the guys in this scene are now major producers. They were interns from NYU. And I just walked by on the left. Did you notice?

JOHN: ***Yeah. With the pipe.***

Two waiters bring dinner to the table as the party settles in.

JOEL: The waiters in this scene are played by Tony Fingleton and Phil Dearborn. Tony Fingleton wrote a book about his life called ***Swimming Upstream***. They made it into a movie in Australia, with Geoffrey Rush playing his father. It's about Tony growing up poor in Brisbane. He was offered a spot on the Australian Olympic swimming team or something like that, but he got a scholarship to Harvard. He went there instead. He and Phil were in the Porcellian Club, which is kind of like the Skull and Bones Society.

JOHN: ***The thing at Yale?***

JOEL: Yeah. They used it in that movie with Angelina Jolie. ***The Good Shepard***. But the Porcellian Club is at Harvard. It's an eating club—they used to roast pigs.

JOHN: ***Are you still in contact with Fingleton?***

JOEL: No. I didn't get along with Tony. He went on to make a series of TV movies of the week. His sister went on to be the first justice of the Supreme Court in Australia to be arrested for bribery. I haven't seen him in a number of years.

Drink in hand, Peter does his best to fend off accusations that he has dabbled with witchcraft in the past.

PETER BROWN: *I do not believe in the supernatural, although I enjoy the black magic world… and make a lot of money on it.*

One of Peter's friends—the actor who played the devil—questions his sincerity.

ACTOR: *It is said that the devil was a female... and that you married her when she last visited the earth. You made a pact with her in exchange for success in films.*

OLD MAN: *We also heard that you had a child by this lady devil.*

Peter rebukes these claims as nonsense—pure publicity stunts, and nothing more. That doesn't stop his curious guests from questioning him further. Before long, the group is swapping stories of the supernatural and arguing about the nature of fate. Pieces in place, ***Blood Bath*** *begins...*

JOEL: Well, this is pretty horrible.

JOHN: ***Didn't Henri Pachard work on this film?***

JOEL: Yes. Ron Sullivan was great. He went on to porn, and I remained friends with him for a long time. He was a general factotum, you know? He was a very hard worker. In fact, he had an office on Broadway in the heart of Times Square.

JOHN: ***Harve Presnell played Peter in the wraparound segments. What was he like?***

JOEL: Well, he was drunk all the time. Can you tell? We had some problems with him. But he was a wonderful guy. He had a beautiful voice and he'd sing throughout the production. He's recently had a resurgence. He played the old guy in ***Fargo***.

The first tale involves the mysterious death of a master hitman named George Lake. We first meet the man as he stands before an old gypsy woman.

Lake, outside of Joel's apartment.

GYPSY WOMAN: *I see evil in the past. Evil in the future! There is evil in this room! You laugh... but the crystal warns of great misfortune on the morrow...*

JOHN: ***Who was the DP on this?***

JOEL: Bob Baldwin shot it. He was sort of a hot photographer at the time; he did some major movies. We didn't get along on the set. He'd say, "I'll direct this for you!" It got on my nerves.

JOHN: ***Whatever happened to him?***

JOEL: He kind of retired. He took some time off—he had millions of dollars. He stopped shooting for a few years, and when he went looking for work again, he couldn't get another job.

George Lake prowls around the city as off-camera narration informs us of his cunning.

NARRATOR: *Lake was a brilliant man. He could have been a surgeon, an inventor... the head of a major corporation. He was cool, accurate, and he thought out every little detail before making a move. Take the Berman case. He made the killing of a labor leader look like a sex murder.*

JOEL: Guess what street that is! See if you can recognize it!

BRIAN: That's right downstairs.

JOEL: Can you guess what building he's going into?

JOHN: ***It's your apartment!***

Lake enters Joel's apartment and walks into the lobby. He is dressed in a white lab coat and he carries a

A killer lurks outside Joel's door.

cardboard box. He walks over to a door, puts on a pair of gloves and takes out a skeleton key.

JOHN: ***Is that your door? It looks a little different.***

JOEL: Is that my door? Look at the number!

JOHN: ***I didn't know if it said 8-B or 8-C.***

JOEL: No, it's my door. I don't know. It looks like my door. No… my lock is on the other side. I think they reversed the print for this shot. OK… that might be my door. But when we go inside, it's the living room of that artist.

JOHN: ***The painter? This is his loft?***

JOEL: Yes. We rented his front room. It was on Broadway and 15th Street. He was really famous. Not like Jackson Pollock, but pretty close.

The camera cuts to a marble statue as Lake enters the room.

JOEL: That was Victor. He was always doing those cutaways.

Lake closes the door behind him and gets down to business. He walks over to a table, sets the box down, and takes out a tape recorder. We cut to a woman in the next room. She is relaxing in her bathtub.

WOMAN IN BATH: *Honey? Whatcha doin' honey?*

JOEL: She was good. She was in a lot of major movies.

Lake's finger presses a red button marked PLAY. A man's voice drifts across the room.

RECORDED VOICE: *How's my little candy doll? I got through a little early today, and my wife is away.*

WOMAN IN BATH: *Did you bring your little baby doll a present?*

JOEL: Oh, well… At least Bob Baldwin's photography was pretty straight-on.

JOHN: ***How long did it take to shoot this thing?***

JOEL: Not more than ten or fifteen days. I mean, the whole thing with shooting a movie is time. It's easier

"She was in a lot of major movies."—Joel Reed

these days with video. I have some good ideas for video, if I could only get the money together.

Lake's game of cat and mouse with the woman in the bath continues. They carry on their "conversation" as he prepares himself for the kill.

JOHN: ***Was this the artist's bathroom?***

JOEL: Yes. This was all shot in his loft.

Lake's tape lures the woman out of the bathroom. She skips out into the living room, naked and vulnerable. He grabs her from behind and slits her throat.

JOEL: Well, this fell apart. I would say the big problem was trying to do something without enough money. And it's another question of nobody reading the script. You get all these rich guys who don't want to read anything.

Satisfied with his kill, Lake sits in wait for his next victim. Before long, the real labor leader enters the apartment. The master hitman strikes, doing him in with an icepick to the neck.

JOHN: ***What kind of budget were you working with?***

JOEL: I think it was close to $200,000. We shot with SAG on 35mm, which is difficult to do these days.

George Lake visits his employers to discuss his next assignment. He opens a briefcase that contains the workings of an intricate time bomb.

GEORGE LAKE: *All miniature. Solid state circuits used in the moon*

The great Sonny Landham makes his film debut.

shot program. Two extremely accurate interlocked clocks. Enough plastic dynamite to blow everyone up in a fifty-foot radius… and reduce his car to little metal scraps. Let his bodyguards search the car. This is an exact replica down to the last scratch of his lawyer's attaché case. They'll think he left it by mistake. It will go off at 11:30 sharp, when he's driving to the meeting.

Lake's insane plan is met with approval, and he disguises himself as a postman. He walks along a country road, the briefcase hidden in his sack. He approaches a sleek luxury car and, as expected, is confronted by a bodyguard.

JOEL: You're going to see this guy in a minute…

GEORGE LAKE (to bodyguard): *Hey, what a boat! Think it would be alright if I… uh… sit in it for a second?*

BODYGUARD: *Yeah, go ahead.*

JOEL: Do you know who that guy is? He doesn't have the mustache anymore, but…

JOHN: ***It's Sonny Landham.***

JOEL: Yes! He was every major villain in every major picture for twenty years after this. He's always the heavy. He was in ***The Warriors*** and ***Predator***. I got him his SAG card with this.

JOHN: ***How did you discover him?***

JOEL: One of the guys that I was working with wanted to hire him because he was very rough looking. He was an unknown—I put him in his first movie.

Lake enters the car and switches briefcases. Everything is going exactly as planned.

JOHN: *Where did you shoot this outdoor stuff?*

JOEL: We shot that at Piping Rock out on Long Island. It was a very exclusive community. Philip Dearborn was the heir to the U.S. Can Corporation. He knew all of these rich people, so this guy let us use the exterior of this beautiful French chateau mansion. This woman from Piping Rock ran out and said, "You're not allowed to shoot a movie here!" They didn't approve of this shit. Bob Baldwin said, "Why don't you take all your grade-A bonds and shove them up your ass before I piss on your face."

Bomb planted and activated, Lake thanks the bodyguard and drives off. He quietly chuckles to himself, but his happy mood soon turns foul. His car sputters to a halt as he rounds a turn. He looks at the dashboard. The fuel gauge reads EMPTY. Lake gathers his belongings, kicks the door in disgust, and begins walking.

GEORGE LAKE: *There must be a telephone!*

Lake's luck goes from bad to worse as a boat of a car pulls up beside him. The driver is a young man in a tie-dyed shirt. He resembles a low-rent Sonny Bono.

JOEL: This is where things fucked up. I had Matthew Cowles in mind for the part.

JOHN: *Who?*

JOEL: Mathew Cowles. He was a pretty big name in movies and on Broadway. He went on to do some big roles as an elderly guy on television, but he had a big following when he was younger. He was kind of like the Brad Pitt of his day. He was in a play that I produced called ***Triple Play***. Every other day, his agent would call me up and say, "You've got to give him another $200." The night before we shot this scene, he said, "I want another $1,000 or he's not coming tomorrow." I said, "Don't send him!" and I hired Dale Whitman to play the part.

JOHN: *Who was he?*

JOEL: A guy from the crew. He was the sound guy.

JOHN: *Didn't Randolph Carter write Triple Play?*

JOEL: He was the guy that wrote it, yes. He did a lot of plays on

Broadway, and he died at ninety-years-old. I was the producer of ***Triple Play***. I should have been the director. Randolph ended up directing. But Matthew was in it. He was the star of the first play. The thing was very gay because Randolph was very gay.

JOHN: *What was it about?*

JOEL: It was three one acts, you know? One was about a male hustler—it should have lasted seven minutes, but it went on for about a half an hour. There was one about a guy who goes to Club 82 and falls in love with a transvestite, but he doesn't know the difference between that and a girl. He's a very naive guy. He kidnaps the transvestite and brings him home to his mother. The guy says, "Get me out of here! Your son doesn't know that I'm not a woman!" The mother says, "Oh, the poor boy. But as long as you're Catholic, it's OK." I remember that joke. It was a big waste of $60,000.

The soundman-turned-actor slows down and offers Lake a ride.

DALE WHITMAN: *Hey, I saw your car back there. You want a lift?*

Lake pauses as his eyes search the car. It looks vaguely familiar, but he can't figure out why.

GEORGE LAKE: *Yeah, sure. How about to the airport?*
DALE WHITMAN: *Huh?*
GEORGE LAKE: *It's worth twenty bucks to you.*

As the two drive off, Lake is filled with unease. He questions the driver.

GEORGE LAKE: *Great car you've got here. Your old man rich?*
DALE WHITMAN: *Rich? Oh yeah… sure, sure.*

The hitman doesn't buy it. His eyes look up and meet a reflection in the rearview mirror. Sure enough, the deadly briefcase is sitting where he left it. He looks at his watch and makes his move.

GEORGE LAKE: *Where'd you get the car? On Meredith Road? You stole it, right? Right?*

The car pulls over to the side of the road. Lake gets out, disgusted. He could have never predicted this. He begins walking and soon finds himself at a place called Tony's Diner.

JOHN: ***Where did you get this diner?***
JOEL: We rented it. We filled it with a lot of the crew.

Lake walks up to a phone booth, dials a number, and orders a cab. He then sits down with a cup of coffee. Suddenly, the front door opens and the young car thief walks over to him.

DALE WHITMAN: *Hey! You left your briefcase in the car!*

Lake looks down at his wristwatch in terror. It is 11:30, sharp. Stock footage of a violent explosion fills the screen as the first chapter of ***Blood Bath*** *draws to a close.*

JOEL: Well, that was just stupid.

Back at the dinner party, Peter Brown is equally unimpressed. He firmly believes that stories of the supernatural are nothing more than fairy tales.

PETER BROWN: *A million to one coincidence. Lake lost to the law of averages.*

The elderly man frowns and does his best to convince Peter otherwise.

OLD MAN: *Now, I know an incident that can only be explained through the occult.*
PETER BROWN: *Impossible. Everything has logic behind it!*
OLD MAN: *No, my dear friend. A housewife had a spat with her husband and he vanished from their apartment. I'm going to tell you everything about this hapless fellow. And then… you tell me that the occult does not exist! Now, his name*

Jerry Lacy dreams...

was Don Savage. He was a man that you might call a dreamer. He lived in a world created by the novels he read...

With those words, the second movement of ***Blood Bath*** *begins.*

JOHN: ***Didn't this movie originally have another name?***
JOEL: Yes. It was originally called ***Terror, Night, and the City***.
JOHN: ***Who decided to change it?***
JOEL: I don't know. Probably Cannon.
JOHN: ***What was it like dealing with the Cannon guys?***
JOEL: Well, let me think. That was before Menahem Golan and his cousin bought the company. Dennis Friedland and Chris Dewey were running it. Were those the guys who had a big hit with ***Joe***?
JOHN: ***The movie with Peter Boyle? From what I can remember, yeah.***
BRIAN: Cannon did ***Joe***.
JOEL: OK. I think they also did some Swedish pictures that Joe Sarno directed. I never met them in person; everything was done through an agent. But I sold the film to them, and they actually paid me. They duplexed it with ***Feast of Flesh*** [AKA ***The Red Queen Kills Seven Times***] with Barbara Bouchet. They actually paid more than our production cost for the film.

Don Savage sits at his desk, lost in a world of make-believe. He imagines a beautiful woman dancing alone in a fog-filled world. She beckons to him, and before long they are in each other's arms. He is smartly dressed in a French general's uniform.

JOEL: This girl was very hot in television commercials and stuff. Boyce Harman was the production manager. He's out in Hollywood now.

JOHN: ***I actually looked him up. He worked on The Exterminator, from what I remember. He's done a lot of TV stuff.***

Don happily kisses the woman, but is soon jolted from his reverie. He looks at his wristwatch, sighs, and gets back to work.

JOHN: ***This segment has a James Thurber feel to it. It also kind of reminds me of Brazil.***

JOEL: I wanted to do something about a guy who got lost in his dreams, but his fantasy turns out to be a nightmare. The guy who played Don is Jerry Lacy.

JOHN: ***He was from Dark Shadows, right?***

JOEL: Yeah, but his big movie was ***Play it Again, Sam***. He played Bogart in the play, too. He looks like Bogart.

JOHN: ***Who did the casting for the movie?***

JOEL: Well, I did. I don't think that we had a particular casting agent for the movie. I know that we used the William Morris Agency. Dorothy Palmer might have been involved—I think she's still in business. We cast it through several agents.

After work, Don visits the strange gypsy woman who predicted George Lake's demise. He nervously asks her for poison. His plan is to murder his wife. The gypsy laughs and chides him.

GYPSY WOMAN: *You go to a druggist for that. We only have talismans and charmed oils.*

JOEL: Actually, if we had dumped this fortune teller, it would have been more interesting. If this was in an office with an occult specialist, it would have been better. Well, that's what you learn from your mistakes. You shoot one person, and you go to jail. You make one bad movie, and it's the same thing. This is awful. It has no zest to it.

Poison out of the question, Don settles on a magic coin. The old crone smiles as she hands it to him.

GYPSY WOMAN: *The possessor of this talisman will be granted any number of wishes.*

Jerry Lacy as Don Savage.

DON SAVAGE: *Really? Could that put me in a different time? A different place?*
GYPSY WOMAN: *Any wish!*
DON SAVAGE: *I'll take it.*

The gypsy woman encourages Don Savage to give the coin to his wife and warns him of its power.

GYPSY WOMAN: *Just a minute! You now own a very dangerous talisman. Don't try to use it yourself. Give it to your wife, and she will wish she's somebody else. And... you'll get rid of her!*

JOHN: ***So, you shot with the unions on this?***
JOEL: Yes.
JOHN: ***What was that like?***
JOEL: Well, I always shot with the union guys. It was no problem, as long as they were aware of the shoot and everybody was willing to participate. At that time, the only people you had trouble with were the from Teamsters union. You know, the drivers. You'd usually just hire one guy, and they'd go away. Later on, it got so that most of the unions would do a low budget picture and not care about it. I even had union guys on ***Career Bed*** and ***Sex by Advertisement***. ***Blood Sucking Freaks*** was SAG.
JOHN: ***That's hilarious.***
JOEL: Yeah. I submitted the script to a guy that I knew, and he called me the next day. He said, "Nobody here has read your script." I said, "What do you mean? They don't want me to do it?" He said, "It's a student film—we don't read student films."
JOHN: ***That's weird.***
JOEL: I said, "What do you mean?" He said, "We don't read student

films. If we read your script, we'd put you in jail!" I still paid SAG rates, but they allowed everybody to be in it.

JOHN: ***Did you have any problems with Blood Bath?***

JOEL: The only pain in the ass was the representative that came around to see if the coffee was hot. And then there was Harve Presnell's agent—Bob Baldwin took him by the neck and threw him off the set.

That evening, Don lies in bed with his wife. He closes his book, pauses for a second, and then speaks.

DON SAVAGE: *Shirley… I got a little present for you.*

SHIRLEY: *It's an old coin! You got gypped by some junk dealer.*

DON SAVAGE: *No! Shirley, this is a magic coin! It will grant you any wish that you want!*

Don tries his best to convince his wife to accept the talisman, but she belittles and mocks him.

SHIRLEY: *Don! I'll not have you raise your voice to me. I am not one of those cheap amoral swingers who work in accounts receivable with you.*

JOHN: ***You know, this is actually pretty funny.***

JOEL: This isn't bad. Can you imagine what this picture would have been like if Jerry Lacy wasn't in it?

Shirley climbs out of bed in disgust. Don gazes at the coin with a faraway look in his eyes.

JOEL: Do you see how bad the lighting in this scene is? This might be a bad print. I guess it's a copy from a ¾ inch tape. [Inflecting German accent] It's like ve could have done Vorld Var II better! Now that I look at all of the newsreels, I know vhy we didn't vin! I know vhy now! Give us a shot back to 1938!

The tape rolls on as Don's domestic troubles reach a pitiful climax.

SHIRLEY: *Don… Don! Don't read in bed! It's ungentleman-like. And don't turn off the lights! I like to make love with the lights on!*

DON SAVAGE: *Shirley… didn't we make love once already tonight?*

SHIRLEY: *Of course we did! I don't make love by timetable! Sometimes, the train arrives more than once!*

Roasting rats.

JOEL: Oh, my God!

Disgusted, Don reaches out for the coin. His wife's words still echo through his brain.

SHIRLEY: *Don... my mother says I should have a personal maid. Don! When are you getting a raise?*

JOHN: ***This scene is hilarious. I really feel for the guy.***
JOEL: Well, this is all based on people I knew. His wife is kind of based on my aunt.

Coin firmly in hand, Don closes his eyes and ignores the gypsy's warning.

DON SAVAGE: *I wish... I wish... I were in Napoleon's cavalry, fighting one of his greatest campaigns. I wish I were a decorated wounded war hero...*

Don opens his eyes to find himself in a dingy bunker. He is dressed in the same uniform that he wore in his dream. He smiles and picks up a sword.

JOEL: That's my sword! I wish I still had it.
JOHN: ***Where was this scene shot?***
JOEL: It's all in the same place. We shot it at the loft. If you have people who study set building in college, they know how to whip these things up. They built this—it's all paper.

Don walks over to a fireplace. A fellow soldier is roasting rats over an open flame.

JOEL: This isn't freaky enough. I should have had shots of people with their teeth rotting away. We should have been roasting arms and legs over the fire.

The mysterious coin.

JOHN: *You can instantly tell that Michael Sahl did the music for this.*

JOEL: Michael was a good friend of Victor's. What's funny about him is that he used to say, "Don't ever tell any people I worked for you. I have a great career as a composer. I don't do that crap anymore, I needed money." Guess what he has on the first page of his website? "The man who composed the music for ***Blood Sucking Freaks***." I talked to him a little while ago. I said, "Don't you want to do another opera?" He said, "No, I want to do more movies." None of his operas received the attention that ***Blood Sucking Freaks*** got.

JOHN: *Well, there's a marketplace for both, but I think the marketplace for horror movies is a little more popular.*

Don soon realizes that life in Napoleon's army is nothing to write home about. Wounded soldiers stagger into the bunker. The food is terrible, and the women are lousy.

SOLDIER: *Some women! That will cheer you up!*

Two ugly whores enter the room. Don looks away, disgusted.

DON SAVAGE: *They're worse than Shirley!*

JOEL: Well, I fucked some girls like that in Korea. I think you guys are the first people to see that this humor was intentional. I'll visit you when they put you in the institution. "We gave them the tranquilizers. They can come down into the day room. Just don't try to get them too upset!"

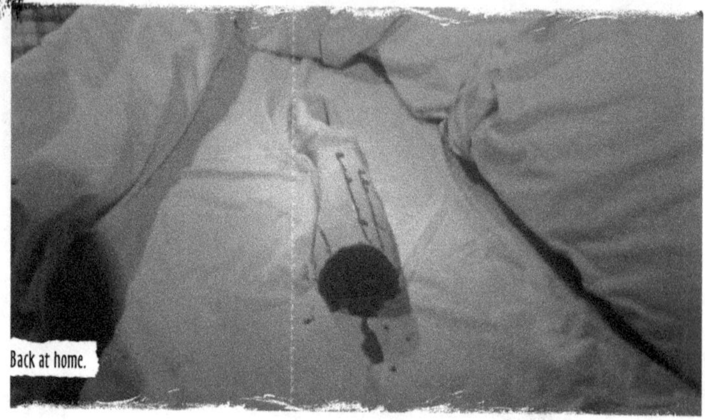

Back at home.

Don takes out his coin and begins to make a wish. One of the whores takes it from him before he can escape. He screams in terror as a cavalry call musters him to action. He is soon engaged in battle, a helpless man on the way to his own bewitched Waterloo.

JOHN: ***This is actually a lot better than I remember it being.***
JOEL: Well, it's sort of a ***Twilight Zone*** kind of thing with humor.

After a violent skirmish, Don stumbles back into the bunker, now a wounded soldier himself.

DON SAVAGE (gasping): *My coin! Where's my coin?*

His friend from the fireplace places the thing in his hand as a surgeon prepares for amputation.

JOEL: You can see where this is headed.

DON SAVAGE: *I wish… I wish I were back home!*

The second segment of ***Blood Bath*** *ends as a bewildered Shirley pulls back the sheets from her bed. Only part of Don is waiting for her. The fingers of his severed left hand slowly open, revealing the powerful and dangerous talisman. Shirley screams as the scene cuts to black.*

JOEL: ***We're back at the party again.***

Indeed we are, and the mood is somber. One of Peter's servants carves a rare side of beef into thin slices. The feast is passed around the table. And then…

ACTOR: *That's the most logical explanation of that case I've heard to date.*
PETER BROWN: *Logical? He just made the whole thing up out of thin air!*
ACTRESS: *Well, I believe in ghosts. My father was done in by a ghost.*
PETER BROWN: *A ghost?*
ACTRESS: *My father was a factor—a semi-respectable loan shark who cared for nothing but money...*

The third chapter of ***Blood Bath*** *opens with a close-up shot of a dingy yellow sign. It reads: "Action Finance Corp. Welfare Checks Cashed! Apartments Rented! Small Loans! Easy Payments!"*

JOEL: The loan officer is based on a guy I knew named Barney. I just saw a picture of him someplace. He was exactly like the guy that Jack Somack played. He had a loan office in Harlem and he did fraudulent receivables for a store that sold televisions. All of his offices were filled with Bowery bums from the street—that's who he was employing. He'd give them a bottle of liquor and $10. He was absolutely awful. He had a nice collection of Yiddish porn, though. I went over to his house in Westchester and he showed it to me. It was pretty funny.

Ralph Lambert, the owner of Action Finance, barks orders into a telephone as his secretary fixes her makeup. Her face is without emotion; she's obviously heard this sort of thing before.

RALPH LAMBERT: *I told you to evict everybody from that Bedford Avenue building! Pay off the City Marshals and toss the furniture into the street!*

JOHN: ***What can you tell me about Jack Somack?***
JOEL: He was pretty popular as a second-level actor. He was on Broadway. Even the girl who played his secretary is pretty good. She had a lot of credits.

RALPH LAMBERT (hanging up phone): *Some lawyer. He's worried about a couple of niggers on welfare.*

We learn that Action Finance is about to shut down for a month, while Ralph Lambert whores around Europe.

SECRETARY: *Did your wife leave yet?*
RALPH LAMBERT: *She's on her way to Paris right now. Maybe I'll meet her in Spain.*

Ralph Lambert (Jack Somack) chats with Earl.

Lambert sings to himself as his secretary readies herself for a vacation of her own. She packs up the things on her desk and walks over to her boss.

SECRETARY: *See you next month!*
RALPH LAMBERT: *Have a good time in Florida. Hey, are you sure everything is turned off? Since we're going to be closed for a month, I don't want to spend a nickel extra on electric.*

JOHN: *You know, Michael Sahl's music is very distinct.*
JOEL: You should call him up and say, "Are you really the guy who did the music for ***Blood Sucking Freaks***?"
JOHN: *I'll really surprise him and ask him if he did the score for Blood Bath!*
JOEL: He was a good composer. I heard some of his other stuff. He was looking down on it at the time. How did he know that it would be his most popular music? What do you know Michael Sahl for now?

Alone in his office, Lambert smiles and pours himself a glass of milk.
RALPH LAMBERT: *I think I'll relax in the safe.*

JOHN: *What did you think of the way Victor Kanefsky handled the editing on this?*
JOEL: It was OK. Whenever Victor started working on a movie, he'd say, "You should see the movie I just cut. It's going to be the single best thing in the world." There was one movie—he told me, "You should learn from these guys!" About five years later, I saw a review of it in ***Variety***. They didn't know why anybody bothered to release it.

Lambert walks over to his safe, unlocks it, and walks inside. It is a cavernous room filled with cash and ledgers.

RALPH LAMBERT: *Everybody owes me! The whole world, almost!*
JOEL: Actually, if this had been released five years later, it would have been better. Now I see what's wrong with it. Look at the lighting. There's no sense of suspense to it. Bob Baldwin was noted for working quickly. If you told him to light a picture in one day, he'd light a picture in one day.

Alone in the safe, Lambert is startled by a noise. He nervously pulls a revolver from his pocket and begins searching for an intruder. Then, out of thin air, the ghost of a young black man named Earl Simmons appears.

EARL SIMMONS: *Booooo!*

Lambert glares at the ghost in disgust.

RALPH LAMBERT: *Look—take ten bucks and get out of here, will ya? If I shoot you, I'll have to spend the whole day in the police station.*

JOEL: Like I said, this movie is personal. I wrote this about Barney.
JOHN: ***How did you meet him?***
JOEL: Let me think. He was trying to be a producer. He had something to do with ***John Paul Jones***; he was Sam Bronston's partner for a while. He actually bought Cathay Pictures. He bought a lot of bankrupt companies, and he had a way of not paying any money. They finally took Cathay away from him.

The ghost walks toward Lambert with a look of hatred in his eyes. In a fit of panic, Ralph fires three rounds into its chest. His act of aggression is met with a laugh. A shot to the head is equally ineffective.

RALPH LAMBERT: *Well, fall down already!*
EARL SIMMONS: *Oh, man! I can't fall down! I've been dead for ten years. I'm a ghost!*

Terror and confusion trickle down Lambert's spine. This is a problem that he can't resolve with his usual means of action.

RALPH LAMBERT: *What do you want to haunt me for, anyway?*
EARL SIMMONS: *Because you caused my death. You repossessed my car and I was too ashamed to tell my*

old lady. She thought I'd scored and paid cash for it. I stuck up a liquor store with a toy gun to get it back. The owner shot me between the eyes.

JOEL: See, this is a revenge piece. If I wanted to, I could write another one about Bill Landis.

JOHN: *Bill Landis? From Sleazoid Express?*

JOEL: Yeah. But I guess I couldn't write anything bad about him. I'm not mad at him.

Earl explains his predicament. Because of his crime, he is serving a sentence in hell. He has been given a chance to right his wrong, but his plan will require Lambert's help.

EARL SIMMONS: *The devil, she said, "If you spook Ralphie into giving you back your registration, you can move on upstairs." Now… you've actually got to buy a '64 T-Bird, call up my old lady, and tell her that it was all a mistake. Tell her that I really paid cash for the car.*

JOHN: *Do you mind talking about Bill Landis for a minute?*

JOEL: He was a mainframe programmer when I met him. He had a suit on. The next day, he quit his job. He said, "I'm going to make a movie with you. I don't want to do that shit anymore." I didn't know anything about computers when I met him. I said, "That's great! You have this good job, and you're writing this magazine." What do you want me to say? I really liked him. He just had problems.

JOHN: *Yeah, I read in one of the clippings that you gave me that you were partners for a while. What movie were you trying to make?*

JOEL: We were going to revive ***The Renegade Ghouls of Kaplan's Swamp***. He raised the money for it, and then he took it all. He was a great promoter. But we're getting away from ***Blood Bath***.

Lambert does his best to rid himself of Earl Simmons, but as time passes, he begins to take a liking to the ghost. Soon, be begins to bore him with business advice.

RALPH LAMBERT: *Earl… I'm a very lonely man! I need company, and I know that you wouldn't let out any of my secrets! I started making my fortune when I was still going to law school. Everybody was too stupid to see that a fortune could be made out of World War II!*

JOEL: The things that he's saying are basically the things that Barney said. He really used to talk like that.

Earl listens to Lambert, cursing his fate. If he can't find a way to get the miser to spring for a new car, he'll be stuck listening to his ramblings for an eternity.

JOEL: Doris Roberts is in here somewhere. She's still going strong.

Suddenly, Lambert's secretary walks back into the office. She rifles through the paperwork on her desk and smiles as she retrieves her airline tickets. As she prepares to leave, she notices that the door to the safe is slightly ajar. She walks over to it and shuts it tight.

EARL SIMMONS: *Ralphie… you're being locked in.*

JOEL: Well, this would have been interesting if the lighting was better. The whole thing is a rip off of Edgar Allan Poe. But Jack Somack was a great actor. He played the Italian guy in the old Alka-Seltzer commercial.

JOHN (thinking): *The spicy meatball thing. Yeah, I guess that's true!*

A month slowly passes, and the doors to Action Finance reopen. Ralph Lambert's secretary rises to greet Mrs. Lambert as she enters the building.

SECRETARY: *Hi, Mrs. Lambert! How was Europe? How's Mr. Lambert?*
MRS. LAMBERT: *I wouldn't know. Isn't he in? I haven't seen him in a month. He loses track of time when he's with that airline stewardess.*

JOEL: There's Doris Roberts! She was famous—she was doing a lot of Broadway and movies. She was quite established. We were actually always trying to do something after this. I had dinner with her and her husband and she said, "I'm trying to get you a deal on television." She had a lot of respect for me.
JOHN: *Who played the secretary?*
JOEL: Sharron Shayne. I wanted to use her in another movie. But this was shot at that same loft. Sets are more convenient than going around to different places.

As the two friends talk, a look of dread creeps across the secretary's face.

SECRETARY: *Oh my God! I think I locked Mr. Lambert up in the safe!*

The miser and his money.

They quickly rush over to the vault. The secretary dials the combination and opens the door. The women gag at what they find inside. An emaciated Ralph Lambert sits cross-legged on the floor, drooling and laughing as he devours what is left of his money.

JOEL: Well, that wasn't very good. ***Guerilla Girls*** would work now, if I did it cheaply enough. [Starts to sing] ***Guerilla Girls***! They'll strike again! Joel M. Reed brings the whole crew back with an original score by Michael Sahl... AND Elliot Chiprut! Harve Presnell stars as the Colonel! P.J. Soles is the grandmother (laughs)! I haven't seen P.J. Soles in here yet. Isn't she in ***Blood Bath***?
JOHN: ***Yeah, in the final segment.***
JOEL: I haven't seen this in a long time.

Back at the party, Peter remains skeptical. His servants pour guests an after-dinner drink as the debate continues.

PETER BROWN: *I didn't know you had such a vivid imagination! He was locked in the safe by accident!*
OLD MAN: *Accident? Just like your marriage to the devil, eh?*
PETER BROWN: *I'm bored. Let's leave it for another time. It's getting late.*

A dark haired girl is seated next to Peter. Silent until now, she finally speaks.

DARK HAIRED GIRL: *I want to tell a story.*

JOEL: That dark haired girl is Deborah Loomis. She was in a movie with Arnold Schwarzenegger

Deborah Loomis, the dark haired girl.

called ***Hercules in New York***. When Schwarzenegger became the Governor of California, there was a big scandal. ***Time*** magazine and the ***New York Times*** started calling me up. They said, "Did you use Deborah Loomis in a movie?" They wanted to know if she had had sex with Arnold Schwarzenegger. They were sure that he had fucked her when they were making ***Hercules in New York***. I mean, it's very possible that he did; who knows? Nobody ever found her.

DARK HAIRED GIRL: *This is the true story of an American kung fu master named Philip Lott, who killed over fifty men with his bare hands and studied the occult—or Hwang's school of kung fu—under master Lu at the Shaolin Monastery on Lantau Island. He was the first foreigner to learn the nine sacred secrets of self-defense, but he was never taught the tenth, or ultimate secret, as his teacher died before the final lesson. Lott, soon after returning to the United States, violated his oath to the monastery by using the secret arts to earn money.*

JOHN: *This is my favorite sequence in Blood Bath. Who played the part of Philp Lott?*

JOEL: You mean you don't know? That's Curt Dawson. He was famous!

JOHN: *I've never seen him in anything besides this.*

JOEL: Curt was on ***As the World Turns***, and he was on Broadway in all the big parts. He died of AIDS when he was 43. He was a very nice guy. We had our choice of people. I don't know what agency he came from, but he thought the part was good.

Philip Lott stands on a makeshift

Philip Lott and his students.

stage as he watches his students practice kung fu.

JOEL: This was shot in the same place. That's just a brick wall in there.

PHILIP LOTT: *As you know, I studied under Master Lu at the Shaolin Monastery on Lantau Island. After ten years of training and meditation, I was the only foreigner allowed to learn the nine ultimate secret techniques of self-defense. There are those of you who have been studying with me for as long as two months… paying the special increased fee. Those students, in my opinion, are now entitled to learn the first. If you wish this priceless information, you must apply to me in private after first fasting for three days, remembering our warrior roles of poverty, chastity, and moderation in all things.*

JOEL: David Niven came over while we were shooting this. His two sons went to school at Harvard with my partner.

We next see Philip Lott as he lounges in bed with a bottle of wine. A young woman pops out from under the sheets.

GIRL IN BED: *I thought kung fu masters weren't supposed to drink or make love.*
PHILIP LOTT: *My old masters at Lantau had a lot of stupid rules about drinking, poverty, and all that. They don't apply here in New York.*

JOEL: That's Illa Howe. She was in ***Blood Sucking Freaks***, as well. She came over on this as a last-minute substitution. She was pregnant or something, so we had to hide her under the blanket. She was Jodie

Illa Howe enjoys a treat.

Foster's stand-in. She opened a big restaurant on 8th Street.

There is a knock on the door. One of Lott's students seeks the answer to the first secret. Philp scrambles around the room in an attempt to hide any evidence of gluttony.

JOHN: *Is this segment based on anything personal?*

JOEL: Yes. I was studying the martial arts, and all these guys were all drinking. This one sensei took out a bottle of scotch. I said, "Sensei, what about your health food?" He said, "That's an endorsement! I get lots of money! I don't eat that crap!" These things were very funny to me, but probably not to the audience.

STUDENT: *I want to learn the first of the ultimate nine secrets of self-defense. I have fasted the required three days.*

PHILIP LOTT: *There is one more requirement. The price of the first secret is $10,000.*

STUDENT: *But, where do I find $10,000?*

Lott gazes over at a golden statue of the Buddha before he looks his student in the eyes.

PHILIP LOTT: *Steal it.*

JOEL: Oh, this is terrible. But I was spoofing kung fu before it was popular.

The scene cuts to a serene landscape. A man dressed in a white robe sits under a tree as he plays his flute. Without warning, he is attacked by four men carrying fighting sticks. Such is life on

Fight to the finish.

the island of Lantau…

JOEL: This guy was my friend, William Chen. He went on to try to get a movie career. He had a martial arts studio on 23rd Street. I used to practice with him a little. He won a lot of contests and he was actually very dangerous. He was a T'ai Chi Ch'uan master and he could barely speak English. But he worked out OK. He was really vicious. If anybody came around, he'd beat them up. He taught a form of fighting Tai Chi.

JOHN: ***What martial arts did you study?***

JOEL: I studied Aikido for a number of years. I also studied Taekwondo. It was very rough, with a lot of kicking and a lot of contact. I studied T'ai Chi Ch'uan. But I never got into any fights or anything. Later on, these kids who were hanging around the apartment actually killed some actor that was going to class. Fortunately, they didn't kill me.

Chen fends off his attackers and wanders through the woods. He finds his master, an armless and legless monk named Lam. He bows and kneels before him.

MR. CHEN: *Excuse this humble practitioner of kung fu for his uncleansed presence in your sanctuary. But for the first time in our history, the sacred rules of the Shaolin Monastery have been violated.*

Chen holds up a newspaper. It reads: "Kung Fu Master Opens Supermarket." The monk scowls.

LAM: *Who did this?*

MR. CHEN: *Philip Lott. An American with round eyes.*

LAM: *He must be defeated and disgraced! The ultimate humility. But… not death.*

JOHN: *Who played the monk?*

JOEL: Lee Moore.

JOHN: *What do you remember about him?*

JOEL: Well, he was teaching acting at some school and I was friendly with him. I met him in a supermarket. I used to eat at his house. I must have hired him earlier for some Broadway thing. I used him for this and for ***Night of the Zombies***.

Meanwhile, back in New York, Philip Lott relaxes in his bed. He is disturbed by another visitor.

PHILIP LOTT: *Who is it?*

MR. CHEN: *I am Chen, servant of Lam, the strongest fighter of the Hwang School!*

Lott's eyes narrow.

PHILIP LOTT: *I'm the strongest fighter!*

JOEL: Actually, in a way this is brilliant.

Lott leaps out of bed as the door to his studio flies off the hinges. Chen advances, and they fight.

JOHN: *Were you a fan of martial arts movies?*

JOEL: Of course. I told you about ***The Tiger and the Dragon***. Nobody wanted to buy the script. They

Free enterprise.

The tenth secret.

didn't like all the oriental stuff.

Their battle ends in a draw. Chen and Lott settle down and begin to talk.

PHILIP LOTT: *You've also been taught the secrets.*
MR. CHEN: *Only nine, like yourself.*
PHILIP LOTT: *Well... let me offer you the hospitality of my humble home.*

As the two men drink tea, Chen carefully sets the bait. He encourages Lott to engage in a fight with Lam, tempting him with the promise of wealth and women: if he defeats the monk, he will inherit the riches of the monastery. Lott is hesitant; Lam may be a cripple, but he fears his tenth secret.

JOHN: ***How long did Blood Bath play in theaters?***
JOEL: It played around. Cannon bought it and released it around the world. It played in a lot of theaters, and then MGM bought it.

Blinded by greed, Lott accepts the challenge, but not without precaution. Before the showdown can even begin, he pulls out a pistol and points it at the monk. Lam laughs.

JOEL: The tenth secret! This guy transforms his mouth into a flame thrower!

In the end, Philip Lott sleeps alone on a hospital bed, defeated and disgraced. He has somehow won the battle, but has lost his body in the process. All that remains is his head, which is kept alive by a clumsy display of medical machinery. He opens his eyes and screams.

JOHN: ***Who did the makeup effects for this thing?***
JOEL: Bob O'Bradovich. He was very good. I hired him again for ***Blood Sucking Freaks***, and he said he'd only do the girls' faces. When he saw all of the naked girls, he was doing all of their makeup. Anyway, we're coming to the end.

Peter Brown says goodbye to his guests, but the dark haired girl remains. It seems as if she'd like to sleep her way to a part in the director's next movie.

Defeated and disgraced.

DARK HAIRED GIRL: *Is this your casting couch?*

PETER BROWN: *No. I've never made love to anybody in this room.*

DARK HAIRED GIRL: *Put me in a movie. I'll sell my soul.*

PETER BROWN: *Oh God, don't say that!*

JOEL: Well, this actually holds the film together. Harve is wearing a full wig, by the way. He was totally bald.

Peter is distracted by a noise. He looks up to see a rattling chain on a locked door.

PETER BROWN: *You'd better get out of here!*

DARK HAIRED GIRL: *Why?*

PETER BROWN: *Never mind. We'll go to my apartment. It's much more comfortable there.*

As Peter leads the would-be-starlet out of the room, a twisted claw breaks through a slat in the door. It finds its way over to the lock and begins to pick it.

JOEL: Again, every character in here is about somebody I knew. The monster in the closet was named after a guy called Conrad. I hated him.

JOHN: ***Can you tell me a little about him?***

JOEL: Conrad was a mutual friend of Eliot Smith. He was always trying to meet girls that I knew. He worked for IBM. He was a pretty heavy drug addict. I never got along with him, because he'd always grab my phone book and start calling girls. He never could get any; he used to get $10 hookers. He was totally obnoxious.

JOHN: ***Whatever happened to him?***

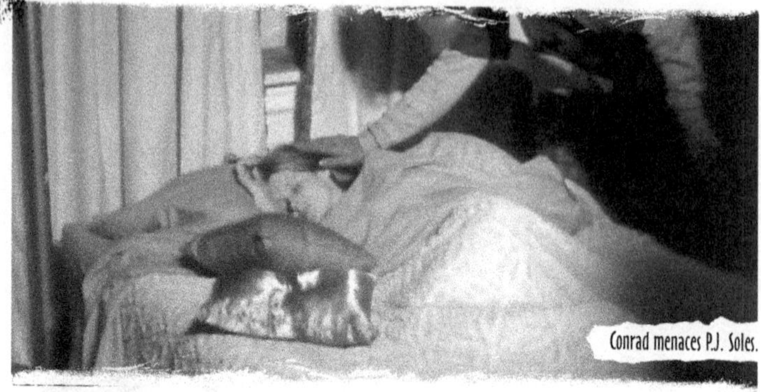

Conrad menaces P.J. Soles.

JOEL: He worked for IBM for thirty years. After ten years, they realized that he was a drug addict, so they gave him these so-so jobs. As soon as he reached his vested interest, they let him go. He was really a mess. That's how I got the idea for it.

Conrad crushes the lock and throws the chain across the room. He bursts out from his prison and begins his reign of terror.

JOHN: ***Did Conrad ever see Blood Bath?***
JOEL: We were going to show him the movie. I don't know if we ever did. Now that I think about it, I don't know why I should have been so mad at him.

Conrad wanders the city streets, killing everyone in sight. His face is hidden in shadows as he breaks into an apartment building. He makes his way into a tiny room where a young woman sleeps alone on her bed.

JOHN: ***Here's P.J. Soles…***
JOEL: Yes. That was her first movie. She'd never acted or did anything before. She went on to do ***Stripes***.
JOHN: ***Oh yeah. She was in Rock 'n' Roll High School, Carrie, and Halloween…***
JOEL: Yes. I first met her in a grocery store on Ninth Avenue. I didn't know she was married, which is another thing…. But she was brought up in Germany. I think her mother was an American girl and her father was Dutch. She denied being in this movie for years. She finally admitted it to somebody.

Peter follows Conrad's trail of destruction and traces him to the bedroom. He breaks down the door to find him menacing P.J. Soles.

JOEL: P.J. kept wrapping her legs around the guy. I said, "P.J., please! He's attacking you!" You know, the interesting thing about this scene is that she originally had her hat on. If you watch every movie she's in, she has on that red hat.

Peter enters the room and pulls out a gun. His voice is stern as he calls out.

PETER BROWN: *Conrad!*

JOEL: See if you can guess the punchline in this one.

Conrad spins around to face the director. Without hesitation, Peter Brown shoots him twice in the head.

JOEL: I guess this came before ***The Elephant Man***. I did the original!

We are finally treated to a full view of Conrad's face. It is a disfigured mess of tumorous flesh and bone. Two small horns protrude from his forehead. His confused eyes well up with tears as he reaches out to his father.

CONRAD: *Why... did you... hurt me... daddy?*

JOEL (sighs): So... that was ***Blood Bath***. We'd better finish this wine, or else it will turn rotten.

Conrad's face grows pale as he falls to the ground. He coughs, gurgles, and spits up blood. The camera lingers on the beast as he takes a dying breath. Then, Conrad—much like ***Blood Bath****—expires. The screen goes black as the end credits roll.*

"Oh, now we're getting the proper reaction!"
—Sardu, *Blood Sucking Freaks*

CHAPTER NINE

BLOOD-SUCKING-FREAKS!

If ***Blood Bath*** was criticized for its self-imposed restraint, Reed's next film would go on to redefine the very notion of excess. In the winter of 1975, Joel began production on what would become his masterpiece. With a $75,000 check and the usual suspects at his side, Reed created a world of demented dwarfs, S&M ballet, castration, cannibalism, poison darts, and eyeball soup. Ron Dorfman eased back into his role as Joel's regular cameraman. Victor Kanefsky was hired as the film's editor. ***Career Bed***'s reporter, Gale McCarty, was on the set daily as a still photographer.

Shot in a little over ten days under the working title ***Sardu: Master of the Screaming Virgins***, the film was retitled ***The Incredible Torture Show*** for its initial release. The trade paper ***BoxOffice*** announced its completion:

> ***Sardu: Master of the Screaming Virgins****, a bizarre horror film written and directed by Joel M. Reed and produced by Alan C. Margolin, has completed principle photography. A tale of a madman who heads an Off-Off-Broadway theater and tortures young girls, it stars many local actors such as Seamus O'Brien, Niles McMaster, Dan Fauci, and Viju Krem.*
>
> *Margolin, a building contractor based here and an active patron of the ballet, is making his film debut with* ***Sardu****. He and Reed are now in pre-production with a second feature based on the works of the Marques de Sade [sic] in the guise of a wealthy industrialist who turns fantasy into reality in his New England castle.*

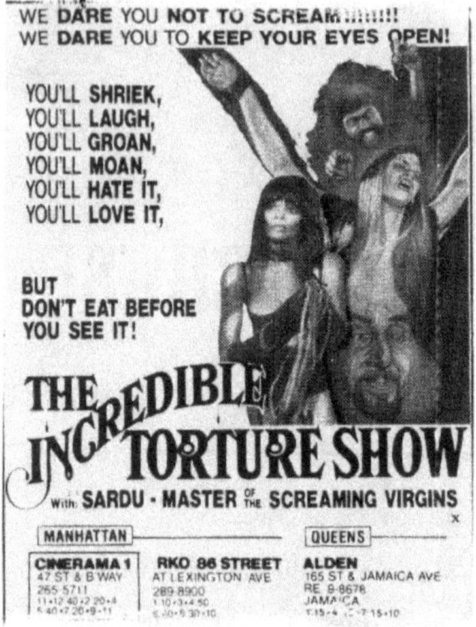

JOEL REED: *When I made* ***Blood Sucking Freaks****, there were things that would have been different if I had complete control of it. I wanted to open it as a cult film. There was a theater down here that played midnight films and I was setting things up. Joel Weinberg, who was responsible for putting up the money, said he wanted to open it up on Broadway at the Cinerama Theater. He spent almost $100,000 opening it up as a full-scale big feature. Everyone walked in, and half the women walked out. Then we had a big sale going in Japan that never happened. Everyone thought it was a drop-dead situation. At that point, the original midnight theater place in New York closed. I had to go into litigation to get the picture back.*

STANLEY BORDEN (original distributor of *The Incredible Torture Show*): *I told them what they did wrong, but you can't tell 'em nothing. They're all experts.*[1]

JOEL REED: *Actually, he—in my opinion—wasted a lot of his own money on it. We were planning to release it ourselves but Weinberg talked me out of it. I'm not very smart.*

A few years after its box office failure, Lloyd Kaufman and Michael Herz of Troma Entertainment acquired the rights to the film and retitled it **Blood Sucking Freaks***. This time the film hit pay dirt, playing to shocked and sickened audiences across America, oftentimes with scandalous results.*

LLOYD KAUFMAN: *It would keep playing. We had several waves. It would go as a midnight movie for many years. We're still booking it. I remember we played a year in Allentown, Pennsylvania. We opened it downtown at the 8th Street Playhouse. The owner was encouraged by the success that it was having. He organized a mock protest. It opened very strong; it would have run for a year on its own steam. But the guy who was managing the theater decided to*

1) Landis, Bill, "Olga's Impresario: Stan Borden Interviewed", ***Sleazoid Express*** (Fall/Winter, 1999): 18-19

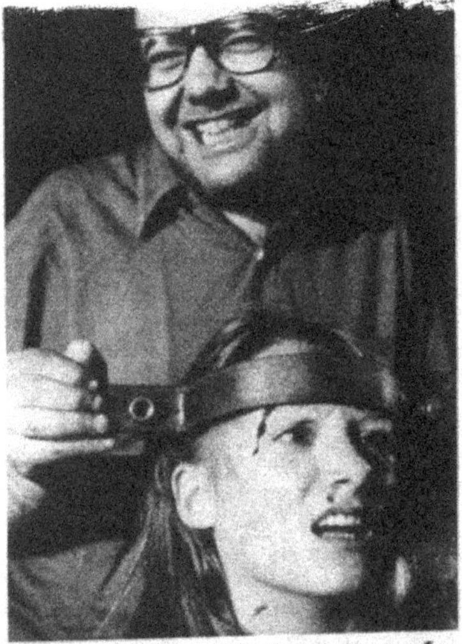

A bloodsucking freak prepares for homestyle brain surgery.

BLOODSUCKING FREAKS: By its title alone, this one will be a must-see for a great many Fangorians. "Dental hijinks, human dartboards and home-style brainsurgery" are plugged by the producers of *Bloodsucking Freaks* as some of its highlights. The story (oh, yes, there's a story, too) concerns a deranged show-biz impressario who stages sado-masochistic entertainments that his audiences believe are faked—needless to say, they aren't. This fellow also keeps a captive hoard of teen-aged girls in cages who perform on command—this group of actresses is billed as "The Caged Sexoids" in the film's ads. Apparently, the Herschell Gordon Lewis revival has arrived!

organize a feminist demonstration. He called them up. He didn't realize that they took it very seriously. They didn't just demonstrate. They called up the board of health, they went after the theater. Like many independent theaters, the 8th Street didn't have a lot of money. They had a lot of violations. The female organization got the violations exposed. The theater was on the verge of going out of business, so they yanked the film.

JOEL REED: *A critic for one of the East Village papers saw it on 42nd Street and gave it rave reviews. It went into midnight showings at the 8th Street Playhouse. It would have run forever if Troma didn't go for publicity and call up Women Against Pornography, saying, "How can you allow this?" Then they came down to picket and there was a clause against pornography. They were trying to evict this guy, Steve, who owned the theater, for years. He had to throw it out. But later, it started to play the midnight shows and I started hearing from people. It played in Allentown, Pennsylvania for a year and a half.*

LLOYD KAUFMAN: *It went all over the country. We had fifty or sixty prints. In those days in the '70s, you could compete theatrically. The majors didn't own the movie theaters. You had a chance. It was no different than today—the major studios were making shit. And any movie that had a little bite to it could compete successfully. This was before the majors were permitted to own the movie theaters. Now they own them and essentially, independent distributors are blackmailed. But* ***Blood Sucking Freaks*** *would always*

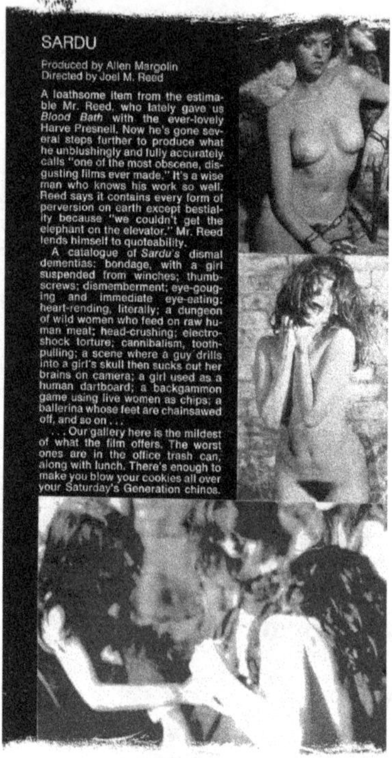

SARDU

Produced by Allen Margolin
Directed by Joel M. Reed

A loathsome item from the estimable Mr. Reed, who lately gave us *Blood Bath* with the ever-lovely Harve Presnell. Now he's gone several steps further to produce what he unblushingly and fully accurately calls "one of the most obscene, disgusting films ever made." It's a wise man who knows his work so well. Reed says it contains every form of perversion on earth except bestiality because "we couldn't get the elephant on the elevator." Mr. Reed lends himself to quoteability.

A catalogue of *Sardu's* dismal dementias: bondage, with a girl suspended from winches; thumbscrews; dismemberment; eye-gouging and immediate eye-eating; heart-rending, literally; a dungeon of wild women who feed on raw human meat; head-crushing; electro-shock torture; cannibalism, tooth-pulling; a scene where a guy drills into a girl's skull then sucks out her brains on camera; a girl used as a human dartboard; a backgammon game using live women as chips; a ballerina whose feet are chainsawed off, and so on . . .

. . . Our gallery here is the mildest of what the film offers. The worst ones are in the office trash can, along with lunch. There's enough to make you blow your cookies all over your Saturday's Generation chinos.

do pretty good business. It was difficult to get theaters, but wherever we could, it did extremely good business.

Violent and sexist, the last word on tastelessness, ***Blood Sucking Freaks*** spooled through theater projectors like a gangrenous sore. The plot was simple enough: The great Sardu (Seamus O'Brien) operates a run-down Soho theater, giving the public a healthy dose of S&M and mutilation. Aided by a dwarf named Ralphus (Luis de Jesus), Sardu tortures and dismembers women of every shape and size. The show is a moderate success, but Sardu has a taste for the big time. He'd love to move his act uptown to Broadway and mingle with high society. After he is insulted by a highbrow critic (Alan Dellay), Sardu begins work on a show guaranteed to bring about the success he desires. He orders his dwarf to kidnap a Lincoln Center ballerina, Natasha D'Natalie (Viju Krem) and begins rehearsal on a new production: ***The Artist: Seduction and Death of a Critic***. This doesn't sit well with Natasha's football star boyfriend Tom Maverick (Niles McMaster). With the help of corrupt NYPD Sergeant John Tucci (Dan Fauci), Tom soon descends into the madness of Sardu's world. A world of caged virgins, white slavery, sadomasochism… and a demented doctor (Ernie Pysher) who just loves to practice a bit of "elective neurosurgery" with a drill and a straw. The violence and misogyny that follows is the stuff of legend.

Watching the cast of ***Blood Sucking Freaks*** march through their twisted paces is morbidly fascinating. The film's ensemble is a great realization of one of the most bizarre collections of misfits to ever grace the silver screen. Seamus O'Brien is perfect as Sardu; his deadpan delivery of some very clumsy dialogue does little to hide the joy in his eyes as he conducts his devious proceedings. Luis de Jesus (infamous as the diminutive star of the mid-'70s sex loop, ***The Anal Dwarf***) tackles the role of Ralphus with sadistic glee. Viju Krem's Natasha D'Natalie prances around naked to the desperate strains of Michael Sahl's score, stumbling through her moves as if just learning how to walk. Ernie Pysher, the brain sucking doctor, plays his role with the gusto (and looks) of a perverted Jim Carrey. Niles McMaster (the male lead in Alfred Sole's ***Communion*** [AKA ***Alice, Sweet Alice***] and the TV soap ***The Edge of Night***) looks as though he'd rather be doing something else. *Anything* else…

The film has had its share of attackers and defenders through the years. John Waters and Andy Kaufman went on record as being rabid fans. Horror film critic Chas. Balun praised ***Blood Sucking Freaks***' tongue in cheek absurdity:

"It spends so much time trying to alienate, disgust, and enrage its audience that by the time it's over, you actually begin to enjoy its guttersnipe defiance."[2] Many others, however, failed to see any value in a film that joyfully called so much attention to its perverted agenda of sex and torture.

ROGER EBERT: ***Blood Sucking Freaks*** is filled wall to wall with screams, with blood, with nudity, with hopelessness, with helplessness, with violence, and most of all, with venomous hatred

2) Balun, Chas., "Movies with Guts", ***Deep Red*** (No. 1, 1987): 26

BLOODSUCKING FREAKS: News recently came to us from Mr. Sleazoid Express himself, Bill Landis, that this picture, reported as a new production in our last "Monster Invasion," is actually a mid-70's release, *The Incredible Torture Show* (*TITS* for short), recut to an R. Nevertheless, we must point out that they have a dandy ad campaign.

of women. I have never seen a movie quite like it.[3]

JOEL REED: *Andy Kaufman used to sit through every performance, so I had one fan out there.*[4]

LLOYD KAUFMAN: *Usually, movies that seem controversial or outrageous become benign with time. The two movies that break that rule, in my opinion, are* **A Clockwork Orange** *and* **Blood Sucking Freaks**. *They're both more outrageous now than when they were made. In those days, it was a different world. When* **A Clockwork Orange** *came out, that rape scene did not look the way it looks now. It's terrible now. I mean the film is a masterpiece, but in those days, nothing was taboo.* **Blood Sucking Freaks** *is really one of the few movies that I've ever encountered that, all these years later, is much more disturbing than when I first saw it. I mean, Michael Herz and I thought it was hilarious. It was one of the first films that Troma bought the rights to. But, it's extremely misogynistic. I suppose, at least personally, that Michael Herz and I have become more sensitive to the place of women in society. I think Troma owns about 500 movies at this point. I do believe that if* **Blood Sucking Freaks** *came to us today, it would give us pause. Of all the movies we've been involved with,*

3) ***Siskel & Ebert & the Movies***, "Video Nasties", 1987

4) Frentzen, Jeff, "'All My Movies are Pretty Crummy': An Interview With Joel M. Reed,"

TROMA: MOVIES OF THE FUTURE

Lloyd Kaufman and Michael Herz present A Troma Team Release

BLOODSUCKING FREAKS

SYNOPSIS

The ultimate GRAND GUIGNOL is now regarded throughout the world as one of the foremost cult classics of our time. Standing proudly along side THE ROCKY HORROR PICTURE SHOW, ERASERHEAD, and NIGHT OF THE LIVING DEAD... BLOODSUCKING FREAKS has earned a world-wide reputation as being a film unlike anything ever seen before in the history of the cinema. It has been held over in certain theatres across the U.S. for over a full year!

BLOODSUCKING FREAKS takes you to a bizarre Off-Broadway theatre of the macabre, operated by a deranged impressario. Inside, sadistic entertainments are staged for his audience's pleasure, including tortures, dismemberments, and other gruesome acts which appear to be faked. When people begin disappearing off the streets of Manhattan, the twisted truth begins to chillingly sink in: these horrifyingly bloodcurdling acts are not theatrical at all. They are real!

You'll be GROSSED OUT by the unique melange of humor and horror as the impressario's horde of beautiful teenage girls, who are kept in cages and "perform" on command, take over the show and devise a tasty game of their own! You'll SCREAM YOUR HEAD OFF as the "fun" climaxes in one of the most unforgettable scenes in movie history!

No audience is left unaffected by the dental hijinks, home-style brain surgery, and human dart boards! No one is immune to the BLOODSUCKING FREAKS!

Director Joel Reed has also directed the significant and highly original action picture, THE G.I. EXECUTIONER.

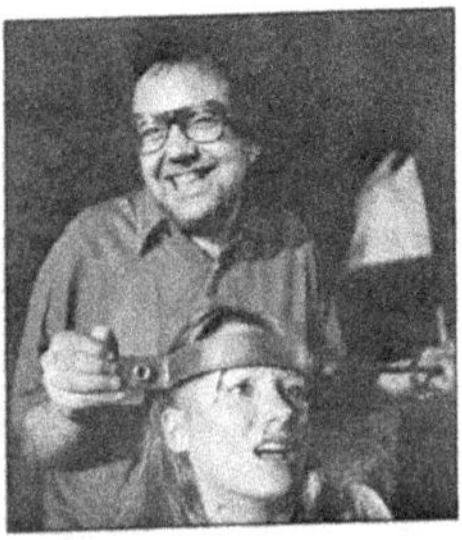

MOVIES OF THE FUTURE

TROMA, INC. 733 Ninth Ave., N.Y., N.Y. 10019 • (212)757-4555 • Telex 645615 TROMA UD

it's the one film that we might think twice about taking on. Although we probably would...

☠

JOEL REED: I didn't want to make ***Blood Sucking Freaks***. That came about totally by accident. I made that film when I was putting together a picture called ***Teen Demon***, which was based on the Oliver Onions story, ***The Beckoning Fair One***. It was about a writer who moves into an old house. He starts hearing a woman's voice; this female spirit visits him every night. Everybody thinks he's totally insane. His girlfriend comes to help him, and he kills her.

Well, I had a conception of doing the story with a writer who moves into a much more modern house. He hears late '50s rock and roll coming through the walls. He finds that someone has gone into his kitchen and taken the milk and the cake out of the refrigerator without putting it back. He's got a teen-aged demon from the '50s on his hands, and she's driving him crazy. Anyway, the writer falls in love with her, and he's having a terrible life. In the end, the police surround the house and they kill him. And in the last scene, there's a '56 Chevy coming up the highway—there he is, with this hot little girl. I wanted to do that; I was pushing the story around.

My partner Alan Margolin was on the board of directors for the Paul Taylor Dance Company. At the time, we were discussing putting together $3– or $4,000 to do this movie. And at that moment, a casting agent named Dorothy Palmer called me and said, "You've got to see this naked S&M ballet company on Spring Street." So I went down, and there was this guy, Gyles Fontaine, and a bunch of girls. They were totally nude, but it was ballet dancing—pretty off the wall. I came back and was at a dinner for the American Ballet Theater or something, and I said, "I saw this freaky ballet down on Spring Street." Everybody said, "Let's go see that. Can you get tickets?" I told them I didn't think they'd want to see it. But I took them all down there and afterward, we went to the Spring Street Bar. They all said, "Joel, forget about this ***Teen Demon*** movie, do a movie about a theater like this." So I wrote a script, and half of the things in it came from other people. These were very big names. I did the script in a week or so, and of course, these other people didn't put a nickel into it. It just happened that this was at the end of the year, and this tax lawyer called me up. He said, "If I send you a check for $75,000, you can make a movie, any movie." So he called me up on a Tuesday and said, "Your check's sitting here." And that's how the movie got made.

VERNON BECKER: Joel went to see a Grand Guignol show in Soho. You know, like in Paris—it looked like they were chopping people's heads off and popping their eyes out. This is the kind of art that appeals to his sensibility. He immediately wrote a story about a ballerina that rejects this guy. He lures her down to this torture show he's doing, which is for real. You know, he rips out eyeballs and has a cage full of kidnapped women. Things like that. Joel used all of the visual stunts that were in the old Grand Guignol—this guy drills a hole in a girl's head and uses a straw to suck out her brains.

JOEL REED: Eddie Jaffe helped raise the money for ***Blood Sucking Freaks*** with Joel Weinberg. Weinberg was an attorney—he and Eddie were friends.

EDDIE JAFFE: That's the only picture I did with Joel. It's a shame. I want Joel to do another one. He's a very talented guy. The problem is, he's too good. If he had gone to Hollywood, he'd be a big shot right now. But the money—it turned out to be an awful amount of money—was a tax write-off. I'm surprised the government allowed it! We had to spend the money before the first of the year to make it.

JOEL REED: Alan [Margolin] was enthusiastic about it, he introduced me to some dance people. We used his apartment to cast the film. He had a beautiful penthouse on 56th Street at the time. I think Oliver Stone was over at the casting call; I know he brought some girls over. Most of the girls were Columbia University students. My brother found them; he put an ad on a bulletin board at Barnard College and at Columbia. We probably cast for two weeks or something like that. Alan was there and we discussed things. We decided on Viju, Seamus, and Niles—the principals.

NILES McMASTER: I started off doing commercials in Chicago in the early '70s. Doing some modeling, commercials, that kind of thing. I was doing it part time initially, and then circumstances happened such that I ended up doing it full time. I was back and forth to New York, LA,

and Chicago; I lived in Chicago and commuted. I went to LA for three years and did some nighttime TV over there. I ended up going to New York and got the lead in Alfred Sole's ***Alice, Sweet Alice***. Then, I went into ***The Edge of Night*** for three years.

Alice, Sweet Alice was shot in Patterson, New Jersey. That was in 1974 or 1975, something like that. It became a cult film in England, from what I understand. It was big over there for quite some time. Actually, that was a pretty good film. I played Brooke Shields' father. There was a guy named Alphonso DeNoble in ***Alice, Sweet Alice*** who was also in ***Blood Sucking Freaks***. He was about 500 pounds. He was a strange character in that film. In real life, he was a strange character.

ALFRED SOLE: [Alphonso] used to get dressed up as a priest and hang around graves in Patterson. And he would watch these old ladies who were by the graves praying for their husbands, and he would go stand next to them. They would say, "Father, can you say a prayer?" He would say a prayer and they would give him a donation after the prayer. And that's how he survived. Then,

5) Sole, Alfred, ***Alice, Sweet Alice*** DVD commentary, Anchor Bay Entertainment (1999)

at night, he dressed in chains and leather. He was a bouncer at a gay bar—Patterson's only gay bar. He was full of fun, full of life.[5]

JOEL REED: Alphonso was in ***Alice Sweet Alice***, that film by Alfred Sole. I worked with him twice, on ***Blood Sucking Freaks*** and on ***Night of the Zombies***. He was funny. He wouldn't eat anything on the set of ***Zombies***. He'd say, "I can't eat! I'm watching my weight." I said to [the cameraman] Ron Dorfman, "Jesus, he's really trying to do it." But I heard he'd sneak out to his car—the entire trunk was filled with food.

NILES McMASTER: I think about a year later, I got a call from an agent about ***Blood Sucking Freaks***. I auditioned for the part. I think it was at the producer's apartment. Alan Margolin's. It was on the West Side somewhere. I read with a few people.

JOEL REED: Ernie Pysher played the part of the doctor with the straw. He was in ***My Fair Lady*** on Broadway. He had a great voice and he made up his whole scene himself. He started singing "The Barber of Seville". That was his idea.

ERNIE PYSHER: I was doing a Broadway show called ***My Fair Lady***. I got a call from my agent. He said, "They're doing a film. Do you want to be in a film?" I said, "Oh sure, I'd like to be in a film." I went downtown to meet some people. I remember that Alan Margolin and Joel were there. I was given the script and I read it. I also was told that there were two other people that I could call—a guy named Seamus, who was then playing the father in ***The Fantastiks***, and a guy called Niles McMaster, who was doing ***Edge of Night***. It's funny—I knew of Niles because we'd gone to the same commercial auditions. Ironically, I did ***Edge of Night*** about a year after him. It was totally unrelated. But, basically, it was a very nice script and we were all very excited about it because it was a good spoof of Off-Broadway. At that time, ***A Chorus Line*** and ***Grease*** had just gone uptown. You have to understand, it was 1975 or something like that; everybody was doing plays. They all wanted to be the next ***Chorus Line***. They were going to make their millions of dollars. And there were big corporations interested in funding Off-Broadway shows and things. It was a very exciting time, and there were some weird, bizarre things going on like the Theater of the Absurd. They were all getting money.

NILES McMASTER: I didn't get a chance to look at the script prior to going down. I really didn't know that much about the film. It was just a job—it wasn't a porno and I wasn't nude in it. Joel Reed was there when I auditioned. I thought he was kind of an odd character. He was pleasant, though, fun to work with. He was pretty focused; he had a good handle on what he wanted. He orchestrated everything pretty well, I felt. I enjoyed the experience. It was kind of *hilarious,* actually, watching everyone...

JOEL REED: Michael Sahl did the music. I think he won some awards for opera. He was an opera composer.

MICHAEL SAHL: I've been a musician ever since I was a child. Remember, I was born in 1934. That makes me more or less Joel's age. I've been a composer right along. I lived in Europe for a while and I got this idea to go back to the States to get into film. I found a friend of mine was an editor. He worked for a company on Madison Avenue that made educational films. I did some work with him back in the '60s. I was doing some people's independent films, but I quickly got into documentaries—industrial and educational stuff. I did a number of those for Victor Kanefsky, who edited ***Blood Sucking Freaks***, but I also did a lot of music editing. Eventually, in 1968, I started to work full time for a music house. I worked for Victor off and on for years. He had his own company called Valkhn, but I met him before that when he worked for ABC or CBS. We go back a while; I think I met him in 1971.

VICTOR KANEFSKY: I stumbled into film when I was in college. I took a film class when I was an Upper Junior and realized that I'd be seeing the world through a camera for the rest of my life. I decided to start at the bottom and learn film editing. I started out

Caged women. *Blood Sucking Freaks.*

doing commercials, but it wasn't something that I liked. I couldn't be proud of selling a bar of soap. I found a job editing documentaries, and I loved it. The problem is that documentaries don't pay very well.

I met Michael Sahl when I was doing some political commercials. He did the music for them. Mike was incredible. He was a very serious composer. When he did his stuff for film, he was always letting you know that it was beneath him. But we were very good friends. I got him the jobs on ***Blood Bath*** and ***Blood Sucking Freaks***.

MICHAEL SAHL: I think I met Joel at Victor's. I remember his terrible suit! I'm not a very fancy dresser, so that's really a strong statement! I got involved with ***Blood Sucking Freaks*** because I'd done ***Terror, Night, and the City*** [AKA ***Blood Bath***] for Joel the year before. Victor introduced me to Joel. He said, "I have a client who does his own stuff and it has to be cheap." The film was already shot. That wasn't true with ***Blood Sucking Freaks***, because with ***Freaks***, I actually came to the set and played piano through certain sequences. It wasn't recorded, but it was part of the shooting. I played piano near the end where the animal women break out and start dancing around Sardu's corpse. That was at the place on Spring Street.

Artwork © Stephen R. Bissette

I got to look at the script for ***Blood Sucking Freaks*** before I started work on it. I was married at the time; I had two children of my own and one stepchild. My reaction to the whole thing was, "This is a gig." I didn't appreciate it for its finer qualities. I didn't really think too much about it, but I could see that there was some originality in it. It was kind of horrible; it wasn't to my taste. I didn't like all the sadomasochism in it, which, of course, is what made it famous. I always prefer my porn to be lyrical. There isn't any real porn in that movie at all.

NILES McMASTER: Most everything was shot in Soho, on Spring Street at someone's residence. It was an old warehouse. My apartment in the film might have been shot at Alan Margolin's apartment. It was a separate location. But we shot at night, for maybe two weeks.

VICTOR KANEFSKY: I was in the movie. I was one of the audience members in the first scene at the theater. It was kind of funny.

ERNIE PYSHER: I shot for one or two days—everything was done in one take. I saw some of the rushes. I sing "Largo" from ***Figaro*** in the film. I made that up as I went along because I happened to be studying it. It was like, "Oh yeah, throw that in there."

JOEL REED: Herve Villechaize from ***Fantasy Island*** was hanging around. We were going to use him for Ralphus. He was pretty big on getting laid. He said, "I can't get laid in New York, I've got to go to Paris to get my tube lubricated." This was before we had any money. Alan finally got things together and we called Herve in Paris. That was like a $12 phone call. Herve said "You've got to send me 400 bucks to get back to New York." Within forty-five minutes, Luis walked in. What's the difference between one crippled dwarf and the next?

VERNON BECKER: Joel shot ***Blood Sucking Freaks*** at the theater

Don't you dare ruin my dinner.

in Soho, making use of the place. I had just come back from Europe, and I was on the set for a scene with a naked girl who was kneeling on all fours. There was a backgammon board on her back and Sardu and the dwarf were playing a game. Now, I'm just telling you what *I* was there for (laughs). If you can imagine walking onto a set and seeing *that*!

JOEL REED: There was one girl [in ***Blood Sucking Freaks***] that I met at the William Morris Agency. We started fooling around and she demanded to be whipped. Her fantasy was a lot of S&M. She was really a freak. I'm not into hanging people up and things like that. One day, she came up to me and said, "Don't touch me, I've got a good shrink." She's actually doing very well in television these days. She's a grandmother now.

MICHAEL SAHL: You see, there were a lot of women over there who had been involved with porn films. They were, I don't know, teasing. There was a woman there named Arlana Blue. It turns out that she was a fan of mine, so she introduced me to the rest of the gang. There was a lot of crossing over between the theater and the porn business at that time. I don't know whether it's still true. It's hard for people to understand. In the '60s and '70s, there were a lot of people who thought that sex would save the world. A lot of them made porn stuff; they didn't think of it as schlock. They made porn stuff in order to keep their communes going, or whatever it was. So the attitude was sort of different. Of

Seamus O'Brien and Viju Krem.

course, everything was technically poorer. By the way, at this time (through Victor, I guess), I was doing music for a number of porn films. They were so quick; it was a day in, a day out. I don't even remember what they were called. But I did one that I later saw on the marquee of a porn theater. That's when there were porn theaters, before everything changed to video. It was called ***Hot Circuit***. The director was Paul Glickler. It was one of those funny films; the music was also funny. I think I did that before I worked with Joel.

JOEL REED: All the girls came down. Some of them were working in porn, and the rest came from Columbia University. One girl was running around naked and her boyfriend was there to protect her. I said, "Get this fucking guy out," so she left. She's in one of the cage shots, but not the rest.

ERNIE PYSHER: It was funny—there were all these women there, and we had read on their resumes that they were porn stars. Well, I didn't see any of that action. In fact, I didn't really see a lot of nudity when I was there. That was all shot at another time. It was certainly titillating to think that something was going to happen, but it was never like that on the set. One girl at the audition was Gyles Fontaine's girlfriend. She looked like the lead in ***The Story of O***.

MICHAEL SAHL: I remember Gyles Fontaine's theater. I said, "Oh, what a great loft! I wish I had a loft like this!" We shot it in the basement. I never figured out what Gyles did for a living, but I gathered he was in some kind of sex related business. He was a French Canadian. For some reason or another, we got to talking about hockey. He told me he'd been a goaltender when he was young. That's all I know about him.

JOEL REED: Gyles used to do that kind of stuff, you know; the girls in his ballet were his actual slaves. I didn't use any of them in the movie. I had Viju. She came over to audition and was around three hours late, which was typical of her. We were having dinner. I said, "Viju, you're going to have to be naked in this picture." She went into another room and came back totally nude. I said, "I think you've got the part. Sit down and finish dinner… but don't put your clothes back on."

MICHAEL SAHL: That Viju Krem, what a pain in the ass she was! A pain in the ass and a prima donna! I was supposed to rehearse with her. She couldn't really do anything, except put on airs. But I was philosophical about it. I didn't pick any fights. I think Gyles Fontaine helped with the choreography. My wife was asked down to help Viju; she was involved with ballet. I don't think she did any choreography.

JOEL REED: [Viju] went to the clink after that. She married this ex-con and got involved in a stock swindle. She came over to my house and asked if she could move in with me for a couple of months. I told her no, which was a very good decision. The FBI was looking for her. They caught up with her and she went to jail. Later, she married this eighty-seven-year-old guy, a millionaire.

NILES McMASTER: The thing I probably remember most about the film was screwing the star (laughs). Viju Krem. We had a little tryst there, after one of the scenes. That was during my first marriage—it doesn't apply to this one! That probably stands out more than anything.

JOEL REED: Luis de Jesus lived on Eighth Avenue. I saw him the first time he fucked Viju. We had a cast party for everyone involved with ***Blood Sucking Freaks***. Viju came in with this Rod Stewart impersonator that was hanging around at the time. The party was at the house of a multimillionaire. One end was devoted to the freaks, with a lot of cocaine. I walked into the freak room before Viju got there and Luis was rolling around on the floor. Everyone was ramming everybody. I was promising to do all the girls there. So Viju walked in with the fake Rod Stewart and said, "We're getting married. What's upstairs?" I told her that it was the freakier part of the party and advised her not to go there. She went up anyway. I walked up to get her out, looked down, and there was Luis doing Viju. Kind of strange. He had a dick about a foot long. Just then, the Rod Stewart impersonator came up behind me and asked, "Have you see my fiancée?" There was like a pile of six people on her. It was very interesting.

NILES McMASTER: The midget was pleasant. I have memories of him bouncing around the set.

JOEL REED: Bob O'Bradovich did the special effects. He worked on thousands of pictures. He's dead now. He was very rough; you would never think he was a makeup guy. I remember when we did ***Blood Sucking Freaks,*** he said, "I'm not going to do any body makeup on these girls. I'm only going to do their hair." When we made the picture, he was putting body makeup on all the nude girls. You couldn't get him to put any on the guys. He'd say, "No! This girl can't go out there like that!"

DONICA O'BRADOVICH: My late father was revered in the makeup industry. If the name doesn't ring a bell, it's because he never could quite bring himself to go Hollywood and make lots of contacts and lots of money. His colleague Dick Smith got all the glory, but it was dad who was the innovator. His other movies include ***Three Days of the Condor, No Way to Treat a Lady*** and Broadway shows such as ***Beatlemania*** and ***Dracula***. He was also the first makeup artist to win an Emmy for his work on ***Hallmark Hall of Fame*** back in the 1950s and '60s.[6]

ERNIE PYSHER: I'm sure I worked with Bob, because I had blood all over me. In fact, I still had the suit up until about a year ago, and it was still red from the blood. But I don't remember him. By the way, the people there were very nice; it was very professionally run. Like I said, it was a nice experience, maybe two nights. A lot of the stuff was improvised.

JOEL REED: Seamus got murdered right after that. I went to his wake and his funeral. They had the body on display and brought

6) Frentzen, "'All My Movies are Pretty Crummy': An Interview With Joel M. Reed," ***Dark Waters*** on-line at http://www.dark-waters.com/features/joel-reed.html (2001)

Luis De Jesus as Ralphus.

music, records, and food. Wine, liquor and beer. They got drunk—it was a real Irish wake. In the old days, they stayed around for days, until the body started to smell, because they weren't really sure it was dead.

NILES McMASTER: Seamus O'Brien was good; very campy. He was a bright guy—that was my feeling when I was watching him do his thing. He was fairly believable.

MICHAEL SAHL: Seamus O'Brien was wonderful. I heard a while later of his death. He was a real, honest-to-God actor; he was probably at one time or another, a Shakespearean actor. He had that style of delivery. He could have done all the old Vincent Price parts. It was a pleasure to see him work. He had a whole bunch of acting credits. He was in little theater. He did serious stuff, literary stuff.

JOEL REED: Some say Seamus came home to the East Village and there was a guy sitting on his steps who stabbed him. Another story is that there was a burglary at his apartment. But he was a great guy, he played in ***The Fantastiks*** for years. He was in ***Marathon Man***.

MICHAEL SAHL: I wrote the score to order by sequence. We even went and recorded it before they started shooting. You see, that's where my ability as a music editor came in. I could write something without having the correct timing. I wrote the score to approximate time, and I wrote it in such a way that I could cut it and make it fit. Now, I made this argument to Joel, and he understood it. It was a lot cheaper for me to go into the studio with an approximate

Ralphus and Sardu.

timing and not have to do takes to time. Most people in the movie business didn't understand that. But, as a music editor, I could make it work. And of course, once I made it work, there would be changes. I'd have to make it work again. So, on ***Blood Sucking Freaks***, my schedule was *yesterday*! I don't know, there was always an emergency.

I didn't use a synthesizer, I used an electric organ and a piano—whatever was in the studio. Various percussion instruments. A percussionist named Cleve Pozar worked with me. He's done some albums of his own. He was very original and resourceful—he could figure out how to do things that couldn't be done. The score sounded like a band. It sounds like a contemporary synthesizer combination.

I'd written a number of operas, starting in 1975. I've always been an opera lover, and the score smells of opera. My wife at that time was a dancer, so there's a lot of ballet music in it as well. There's some funny ballet music in ***Blood Sucking Freaks***. There's the ballet music where Viju warms up, and then there's some funny music where she kicks Creasy Silo to death. That's actually sort of a tango.

It's funny. If I'm known for anything at all, it's for the tango. In 1981, I did an album called ***The Tango Project***. One of the tracks turned up in ***Scent of a Woman***. So I have a little bit of a reputation for that. But I've always been a tango lover. I put a tango in the very first scene of ***Blood Sucking Freaks***. There's a lot of tango stuff in there.

ERNIE PYSHER: You can't imagine how quickly we worked. We had to shoot at night because I was doing a show. So was Sardu. Plus, the cell scene was shot at the place on Spring Street. Well, that's the entrance to the Holland Tunnel. They had to wait until 9 o'clock at night to shoot, or else they'd have all these trucks rumbling by.

JOEL REED: Everybody was cold. It was winter. But they were still in good spirits.

MICHAEL SAHL: Joel was not the type of guy who was easy to work for, because he was always taking over and changing everything. And he probably was right. We had a good cameraman on that picture, Ron Dorfman. He did a lot of good things. I have no idea whatever happened to him.

JOEL REED: The only Ron Dorfman I've heard about lately was a lawyer who shot himself—there were a lot of stories in the paper about it. But that's not the Ron Dorfman we know…

VERNON BECKER: The interesting thing is, since it was low budget, Joel had to submit it to SAG to get a SAG waiver. And SAG read the script and said, "We don't care who plays in this! You can get Marlon Brando. We will not sanction or make a union contract for this script. You can get anyone in the world to work for a penny a day, we don't care. Just keep SAG's seal off the picture!"

VICTOR KANEFSKY: One day, Michael Sahl was late when we were doing the sound mix. I was in charge for a little while, and I got into a discussion with the mixer. His name was Emil Neroda. He was an excellent mixer, by the way. I told him that he should play the music louder. He said, "No, we should take it down." I was protecting Mike. When Mike came in, we had already finished the scene. I said, "Mike, Emil and I had this discussion about the music for this scene. I made it go higher." Mike looked at me and said, "You were wrong. Emil was right." I was trying to capture what I thought Mike would have liked. You're always learning something…

VERNON BECKER: So anyway, he made the picture. Victor Kanefsky cut it.

VICTOR KANEFSKY: When ***Blood Sucking Freaks*** came along, I didn't even know what it was. Joel called me, and I was in bad shape with my company. He said, "We'll pay you in advance." It was very little money, but it was still money. I took the job, and it turned out to be a lot of fun.

VERNON BECKER: I don't know who backed Joel, or what happened, but the picture ended up with Stanley Borden. Quite an interesting character, I must say. He had been a young hood in the late '30s to support his mother. He had worked as a strong-arm man. Although he dressed well, he always sounded like someone from a 1935 movie reporting to Edward G. Robinson. Anyway, he saw ***Blood Sucking Freaks*** and immediately said, "This is art!" He decided to distribute it under the most off-setting title I'd ever heard, ***The Incredible Torture Show***. Even sadists hated the title. I remember being parked with Joel outside the marquee of the theater on Broadway where it opened. We were disgusted, because we sat there for thirty minutes and nobody went inside. And this was with an advertising campaign. Borden had made five prints.

LLOYD KAUFMAN: I met Stanley Borden a couple of times. His wife Loraine designed some posters for us a long time ago. I think we bought the rights to ***Blood Sucking Freaks*** from Stanley Borden's company.

STANLEY BORDEN: So they did this picture. They were showing it around. Nobody wanted it. So what happened—although he denies it now—there was a distributor in New York that loved it. I saw the picture. I took it because I figured the distributor would do something with it. So that was the end of that. Blew a lot of money.[7]

JOEL REED: Joel Weinberg, who arranged financing for the feature, insisted that Stanley release it. I was smart enough to tie up the negative so he could never remove it from the lab. The picture was sold in Japan, but Stanley screwed that up.

STANLEY BORDEN: I blew a lot of money. If the picture didn't sell, I figured I'd work it with something else, a double header or something. They thought they should make a lot of money from it. Everybody I showed it to, nobody wanted it. I did it as a favor. No matter what you did—if the picture made a few hundred thousand—it wasn't enough. Reed conned the guy [Margolin] that it would make a lot of money. The guy was always callin',

7) Landis, Bill, "Olga's Impresario: Stan Borden Interviewed", ***Sleazoid Express*** (Fall/Winter, 1999): 18–19

you know. It was a pain in the neck.[8]

JOEL REED: I didn't con Alan Margolin. If he put any money in, it was minor and he got it back. Joel Weinberg forced Stanley Borden on us. I think Borden was well aware of that. We didn't show it to "everybody" prior to Stanley Borden. Just to Cannon and a top sub-distributor in NY and LA. They wanted it, but we would have to finance prints and advertising.

VERNON BECKER: Years later, I established a relationship with Lloyd Kaufman and Michael Herz of Troma. In fact, Kaufman and Herz had worked with me in the past. We were friends, sort of. Well, they were as friendly as they can get. I was also involved with the early days of cable and video. There was one fantastic year where I bought five pictures from them. Before the end of the year, they bought the same pictures back. It was like the joke; these weren't sardines for eating, these were sardines for buying and selling.

LLOYD KAUFMAN: It's very possible that Vernon Becker brought the film over. I think I met Vernon Becker through Lee Hessel. I was a partner on a movie called ***Cry Uncle***. I was also the production

manager. That was directed by John G. Avildsen. Lee had a company called Cambist and he was phasing out of distribution, kind of retiring from that business. We bought some distribution rights from him, and he was friendly with Vernon.

VERNON BECKER: Lloyd and I got to know each other. There were pictures I bought, mostly from England that had played here and gotten R ratings. We didn't have the prints for the R versions, so I had to bring in the original version and their editor would cut our Rs. So if I sent a film out to a cable station or something, I'd say, "This is the R version." We were never quite sure

8) Ibid

if we'd cut more or less. I was using Troma's people for doing that. We were just generally horsing around on things. Anyway, I forget what happened, but I went over to see Joel. He told me that the lab had foreclosed on the negatives because Borden had never paid the bill for the five prints. It was just a matter where Joel was sort of crying in his beer that his masterpiece would be lost forever. But, he did have a video cassette that Borden had given to him. I said, "Give it to me." I went over to see the boys at Troma and said, "I have a real challenge for you guys." They put it on and were jumping around saying, "This is fantastic!" Most people would have been vomiting at that point. Lloyd said, "What's the deal?" I said, "Well, the deal is first, you pay me ten percent of whatever the acquisition price is." They said, "Well, that's all right," and we went from there. I don't remember the exact deal, but I might have asked for $10,000. $5,000 for Joel, and I got $500 of that. Troma took care of the rest of the stuff. They came up with the title ***Blood Sucking Freaks***, and sold it all over the world.

LLOYD KAUFMAN: My recollection is that ***Blood Sucking Freaks*** came out in an unfinished form, all chopped up. It was called ***The Incredible Torture Show***. Joel indicated a desire to edit the film the way he wanted it. He told us he had a lot of graphic footage and the previous distributors had sort of chickened out. They had cut out all of the wax dripping, the cannibalism, and the penis. None of that was in the version we got. But, we had all the materials. We had the negative, we had everything. I think Joel told us what to put back. It was his vision. Richard Haines was our editor at the time. He went on to edit ***The Toxic Avenger*** and ***Class of Nuke 'em***

High. He put it together the way Joel wanted and created a new trailer. We changed the title to ***Blood Sucking Freaks***. In fact, in the trailer, I think it's Richard Haines' voice that says, "*Blood-Sucking-Freaks*!"

JOEL REED: Troma never edited one foot of the picture. They recently inserted a "lost" scene where Ralphus goes down on Sardu. That was never cut out of the original film. And Troma never had any access to any outtakes. If it wasn't in the other prints, they cut it out to begin with.

ERNIE PYSHER: And then, the film came out. I saw it and wasn't very happy with it. It was edited very… badly. They didn't spend any money on editing, and it came off looking like softcore porn. The jokes of having Creasy Silo instead of Clive Barnes, and Tom Maverick instead of Joe Namath—they didn't do that at all. They just really cared about having a lot of naked people and a lot of sadomasochism and stuff like that.

VICTOR KANEFSKY: I never took those films very seriously. I cut ***Blood Sucking Freaks*** with Joel Herson, and we did what we could with what we had. One day he said, "I can't cut this scene. It nauseates me." That was the brain sucking scene. So, I edited that one. I edited almost everything, anyway. The scene that I really had a good time with was the ballet scene, where [Viju] kicks the critic to death. My wife was a dancer, so I could kind of identify with her.

ERNIE PEYSHR: The major feeling I had was disappointment,

"She will dance!"

because I thought that script had some wonderful possibilities as a commentary. I mean, it was clearly—and we talked about this at a meeting—it was all about the critics making or breaking everything. So what we're going to do is force the critics to write a good review. That's what was intriguing to me. From reading the script, it was clear to me that this could be great satire. Some of the stuff that I saw that was shot—some of the interesting conversations with Sardu about the state of the theater and the whole reason why he does this thing with Creasy Silo—that's what we read and were told about. Alan told us about that, and that's why we sort of got involved in it. I think the fact that there was a Henry Kissinger look-alike was genius. But it was so understated. When it came out, I thought it was kind of just one step above porn. If they had made the film about New York, Off-Broadway—the American scene—who are the blood sucking freaks? Kissinger? Joe Namath? *That's* what the film should have been about. If I was a little disappointed with it, Viju and Niles must have been *really* angry. Joel lost his vision. I think he fell in love with the blood. There's all these nude women who are used as furniture. That was an interesting comment on women, but it came off really tacky. I just felt like they kind of missed it.

LLOYD KAUFMAN: We released the movie in a ninety-one minute version. And I remember we needed to get an R rating. We had to cut it down to fifty-four minutes to get that. Once we had the R, we would accidentally send the ninety-one minute versions to the theaters. At some point, the MPAA caught us and went after us. We got into a lot of trouble. But anyway, Joel had no key art, so we got together some very bizarre people and did a photo shoot. We had this guy with a very strange face. There was a guy named Charles Levey; he was a graphic designer in those days. He helped us put together the photo shoot and design the world famous poster. The dental hijinks and all of that.

ERNIE PYSHER: I wasn't really angry when I saw the finished film, I was more like… amused. I thought, "Well, this is going to die." Little did I know that it would just resurface over and over again. I guess that's a tribute to *something*. I have no regrets at all; I never regret anything. What could I regret? There's nothing—I didn't do anything *wrong* in the movie. I just played it as satire. And I suppose if it had been something really outrageous, I could get myself on ***Biography*** as some star, you know what I mean?

LLOYD KAUFMAN: We got some buyers over the years. Unfortunately, it's the sort of film that's banned in most countries. You can't play it in around ninety percent of the world. But we got deals in Japan. There was a warrant out for our arrest in Germany because we sent the screener to the buyer for the company who had acquired ***Toxic Avenger***. ***Toxic Avenger*** was a huge hit and he asked us for another movie. We sent ***Blood Sucking Freaks***, among others. Apparently, he literally got arrested. He was the buyer for UFA. There were apparently warrants for Michael and me. Just because of the screener. So that's the problem; the film pushes a lot of buttons. But, it has an amazing following, and it's durable. Of its type, it is a major classic. There's no doubt.

VERNON BECKER: It's become a cult movie. Joel was invited to a film festival a few years ago here in California. They played ***Blood Sucking Freaks*** at midnight. Joel said it really shocked them! They had no idea what a picture should be. But he flew over first class. He had a limo, a suite, a cocktail party; all that kind of stuff.

MICHAEL SAHL: You know what Joel's like. He's a bit of a loudmouth, but he's very bright. In some way or another, I identify with him. He had all these deals going in

Singapore—he had a lot of things going. Everything was very cheap. He was remarkable in his ability to get things done quickly. Of course, you had to. He had a certain kind of style. Now, ***Terror, Night, and the City***'s kind of a mess, you know? But it still has some of that style.

ERNIE PYSHER: So, I forgot about it. I didn't think it was going to go anywhere; as I said, I was doing a Broadway show at the time. Then, what made me really forget about it was—well, I was in a mugging, and I got shot. I lost the feeling in my leg. I was recuperating; I was really, totally out of it. I was still working on Broadway, but in a minimal role.

And then, I started to do some other films. A guy named Bernie Styles—he was a casting director who actually was in Woody Allen's picture ***The Front***—he called me. I did some work as an extra; you have to realize that I was on crutches. Bernie arranged for me to be a stand-in. I was a stand-in for Tommy Lee Jones for a bunch of things. That got me my SAG benefits. I was fortunate—I got into ***Deathtrap*** [a stage play written by Ira Levin] for five years, and I did soap operas for a long time. So I totally forgot about that film until I went to Los Angeles. I went up for a movie and the director said, "You're the guy in ***The Incredible Torture Show***!" So apparently, it's become quite a cult film.

MICHAEL SAHL: One day, this kid called me up out of the blue. He said, "Were you the composer for ***Blood Sucking Freaks***? That's such a great score." Then I found out it was a cult film. I walked into Kim's Video, and there it was among the cult movies. I went in there and I said, "Hey, you don't know, but I'm the composer for this film!" The guys at the desk were all impressed.

JOEL REED: Here's something about one of the girls in the backgammon scene. She left her honeymoon to be in the film. Around ten years ago, my friend went to get a job at Reader's Digest International. He walked into an office and had an interview. He noticed that the woman conducting things had the poster for ***Blood Sucking Freaks*** hanging up. She was the vice-president. He asked her about it. It turns out that she was the girl from the backgammon scene. She was proud of the fact.

NILES McMASTER: I saw a screening of the film under its first title. I—(laughs)—I couldn't

believe it! I figured as much when we were doing it. I'm surprised that the film has a cult following today. It's not something I could have used in my career, either. It wasn't something that I would readily use to show to casting directors! Although, I don't have any regrets about doing the film. It's nothing that I'm ashamed of. But I wouldn't do it again...

LLOYD KAUFMAN: I played a joke on my father. In 1980, we re-released the film, starting at the Cannes Film Festival. We made a brand new, pristine print and booked some theaters over there to screen ***Blood Sucking Freaks***. My father happened to come that year. He wasn't a movie person, just an elderly gentleman. He wanted to help, so I said, "OK, you're going to take over on ***Blood Sucking Freaks***. Here are the invitations." They were engraved, very elegant looking. They gave no indication that there was anything unusual about the film. I told my father to hand them

Troma's new title card.

out to people that he met at Cannes to get people into the theater. He did this, and he had a lot of his own friends from the south of France see the first screening of ***Blood Sucking Freaks***. The theater was full of a lot of elderly and distinguished friends of my dad. He was almost killed! They almost killed him, they were pissed. Their wives were all upset. They thought the film was going to be a Joseph Losey kind of thing. My father, until his dying day, would always ask, "How's my film doing?"

The following conversation took place at Joel Reed's apartment in the spring of 2000 as we watched ***Blood Sucking Freaks.*** A follow-up interview was conducted on January 26, 2017. Portions of that interview have been edited into the text.

Michael Sahl's tango-charged score begins to play as a decrepit van drives down a snowy city street. It is well after dark, and the night is awash in a sea of neon.

JOEL REED: Little did I know, when I made this great work that I would create a document that would go down in history with the Magna Carta, the Declaration of Independence, and ***Citizen Kane***!

JOHN: *So where is this shot at right here?*

JOEL: Well, I'm pretty sure this is Union Square. I had just seen ***Alphaville*** again, so I put a lot of strobing lights in the background! This guy driving the van was Telly Savalas' double, and the other guy was Gene Wilder's. It really doesn't come across as it should. If you study the scene, you'll realize that they look like them.

Bold white letters flash across the screen. They read, "BLOOD SUCKING FREAKS."

JOEL: Of course, that's not the original title. It used to say, "THE INCREDIBLE TORTURE SHOW."

JOHN: ***This was shot in the winter.***

JOEL: Yes. It was cold. We had to finish the movie within the year.

JOHN: ***So you guys went out on the streets and shot this from the back of a truck or something?***

JOEL: Yeah, the camera's in the back of a truck. We had two trucks. These are the streets of New York. This looks a lot like the beginning of ***Taxi Driver***. They steal everything from me without credit.

JOHN: ***What kind of film stock was this shot on?***

JOEL: I guess we shot it on 16mm.

The van finally reaches its destination, and "Savalas" and "Wilder" begin to unload its cargo. They stumble through the snow, while attempting to carry a very heavy crate.

JOEL: Anyway, this is the front of Alan Margolin's building. And

that's actually Alan's van for his steamfitting business.

JOHN: ***Who built the crate?***

JOEL: That was just a crate that we had. A lot of this stuff was just lying around. It's a found movie. You see the big door that pulls up? That was where the trucks unloaded their supplies.

The scene cuts. A Hispanic dwarf in a yellow sweater and denim overalls takes a crowbar to the crate. He slowly pries the wooden planks apart as a tall man with an elegant goatee oversees his progress. The dwarf is named Ralphus. The tall man is Sardu. He pets a tiny black cat as Ralphus walks toward him.

RALPHUS: *The new shipment has arrived, Master.*

JOEL: That's Seamus O'Brien with

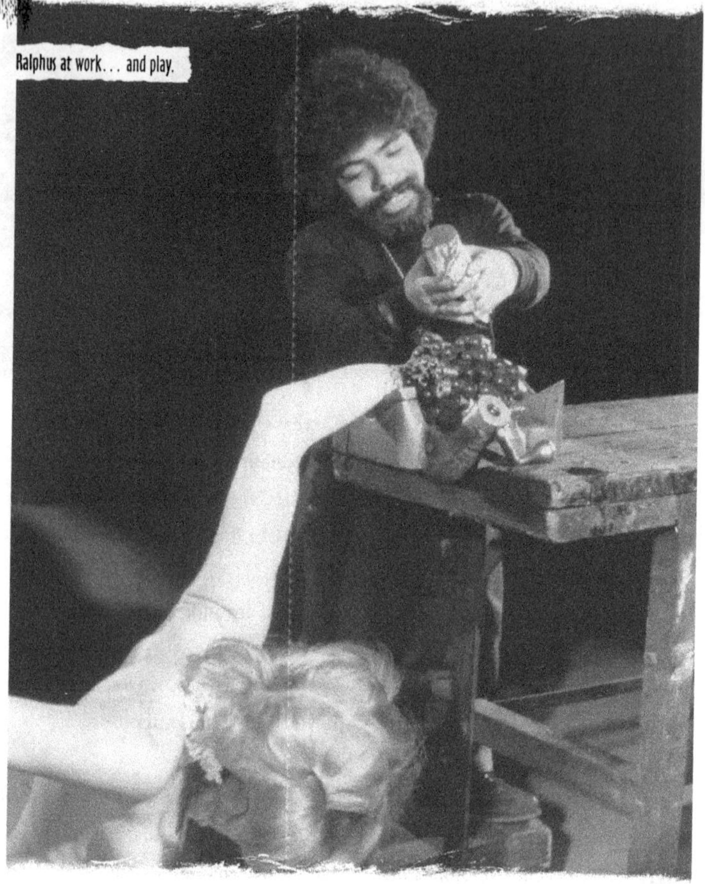

the cat. There's a cut coming up that Victor always brags about. He put in a close up of a cat from another movie. I think Joel Herson did most of the editing on this, but Victor still talks about how he saved the thing with a close up of a cat.

Ralphus returns to the crate and hoists out its contents with a chain and pulley. A naked woman, bound and gagged, is lifted high into the air.

JOEL: That girl was the wife of an FBI agent. That's all I can remember about her. He was standing there while we were shooting. He said, "That's my wife."

JOHN: ***What did he think of the finished film?***

JOEL: He said it was a pretty good movie! Now, this next shot is in

Niles and Viju at the Theatre of the Macabre.

Gyles Fontaine's theater.

The sound of a woman's scream echoes through the room. A young blonde cries out as Ralphus crushes her fingers with a clamp.

JOEL: That's just a thing for cutting pipe. It was just lying around. And that girl was Alan's girlfriend.

A shocked audience watches as the scene unfolds. They clutch one another as Sardu speaks.

SARDU: *What a marvelous, wonderful, attentive audience you are. And, may I add, a brave one.*

JOHN: ***Who are the people watching the show?***

JOEL: One guy is the head of the Drama department at Hunter College. One girl is Lorin Price's ex-wife. One guy was part of the crew; he was from NYU. They're disposable characters—you don't bring them back. Victor Kanefsky's in there. There's Alan Margolin. Gale McCarty is on the right—he's falling asleep.

JOHN: ***Really?***

JOEL: Yeah. He had cancer at the time. He was the still guy, but he didn't take any pictures. There's Michael Sahl—he's the guy with the eyeglasses. There's one guy in this shot who snuck in and didn't sign a release form. He tried to sue us. He made his living trying to sue people; I don't think he ever won a lawsuit.

JOHN: ***Where did Seamus get his outfits?***

Seamus O'Brien

JOEL: I think they're all Gyles' clothes. That's how he used to dress. I didn't have to do anything. There was no wardrobe department.

SARDU: *Those of you who are weak-willed, or are cowards would have fled by now... or regurgitated over the seats in front of you. But why? This is just a theatrical presentation. A show, which offers no reality—not a fraction of reality—and just allows us, you and me, to delve into our grossest fantasies, far beyond erotica. I am Sardu, Master of the Theatre of the Macabre. Tonight, we begin with torture. Again, I warn you—if you find what you see is a little upsetting to your stomachs, then just pretend we're play-acting. But if you are skeptical or bored, then just pretend that what you see is real.*

JOHN: *What kind of coverage did you get for this film?*

JOEL: It's all pre-cut. Close up, medium, and long shots. There was really nothing left to play with.

One member of the audience is skeptical of the torture on display. Football star Tom Maverick sits with his girlfriend, a pretty ballerina named Natasha D'Natalie. He heckles Sardu from afar.

TOM MAVERICK: *It's a trick!*
SARDU: *Who said that? Ahh... Mr. Maverick. The famous football player. Would you like to try it on Miss D'Natalie there, the lovely prima ballerina?*
NATASHA D'NATALIE: *Don't you dare!*
SARDU: *A trick? What you are*

"No true actor would submit to engage in such trash."

about to see now is the second degree of torture: the iron tourniquet.

Ralphus fastens a metal clamp around the young woman's head. She screams in agony as he tightens it.

JOEL: I was trying to get a little Renoir feeling here with the dispersing of the colors.

JOHN: ***How did everyone react when you were shooting this kind of stuff?***

JOEL: It was fun. They were cold. I think we shot all of this on the same day. Luis was a lot of fun, and he rehearsed a lot with Seamus.

JOHN: ***Did they get along?***

JOEL: Yes. Seamus spent a lot of time working with Luis, especially for their scenes together. Some *directors* don't even talk to the actors!

After a curtain call, the jolted audience spills out onto the street. Sardu stands by the exit collecting money.

SARDU: *A donation for the actors, please. None of the actors receive any pay.*

Creasy Silo, a critic from uptown, scoffs at the magician's request.

CREASY SILO: *Actors? No true actor would submit to engage in such trash.*

SARDU: *But you <u>are</u> going to review my show...*

CREASY SILO: *Absolutely not! If I were to review your so called show, even badly, I fear some of my readers might come just out of curiosity. And I do not want to be responsible for keeping your theater open one more day.*

SARDU: *Then we shall see…*

JOEL: This was a twenty-hour day.

JOHN: ***How did the cast handle that?***

JOEL: Everyone was wonderful. I think Viju was a bit disorientated. If you shot her from over the shoulder, she thought she was being cut out of the movie. "What about my face?"

JOHN: ***Was this her first starring role?***

JOEL: No. She was actually in ***Let My Puppets Come*** with Luis. I think that was before this.

JOHN: ***I'd forgotten about that! She was the Sweet Fish girl! What can you tell me about Alan Dellay?***

JOEL: Well, he was doing things on Broadway. He had a lot of acting credits, and he was wonderful. I got along with everybody on ***Blood Sucking Freaks***. Viju was crazy, but what can I say? Alan did all of his stuff in one take. He was great.

Ralphus maneuvers through a dim cavern deep inside Sardu's lair. He carries a torch and a bucket. He reaches a cage filled with prisoners, all women. They yowl at him like cats as he feeds them.

JOEL: That cage was really shaky.

JOHN: ***Where was this scene shot?***

JOEL: This is in the basement. Gyles had a two-level basement.

JOHN: ***How big was his theater?***

JOEL: The theater held maybe 70 or 80 people. He had a big living room. The place was nice.

JOHN: ***What does Luis have in that bucket?***

JOEL: Chopped up meat. We got it from a butcher shop (laughs). One of these girls was living with Jamie Gillis.

JOHN: *Where did you get Luis from, anyway?*

JOEL: The circus. He came in from Ringling Brothers. Whatever happened to him?

JOHN: *He died of a heart attack in 1988. I've read that he and his wife played Ewoks in Return of the Jedi.* [9]

The plot lurches forward. Sardu sits in a pensive mood as he dines alone at a unique table. A submissive woman kneels on all fours as she balances his banquet on her back.

JOEL: The girl that he's eating on was in some Broadway show at the time. She had a great voice; she used to come over and sing for me. But she was really into S&M—she was really out there.

Hot wax drips down from a candle and the young woman screams in pain.

SARDU: *Don't you dare ruin my dinner!*

JOEL: So, this is actually Gyles' living room. Not one thing was changed. He got a great deal on this place. He just rented a basement and fixed it up. He had a dance company there.

JOHN: *Does he appear in this movie at all?*

JOEL: No.

JOHN: *What was his show like?*

JOEL: It consisted of naked men and a couple of girls. They'd whip them and tie them up. His girls were like real slaves to him.

In a fit of rage, Sardu kicks his "table" to the ground. He calls out to Ralphus. A plan is forming in his mind…

SARDU: *I want Creasy Silo brought here!*

RALPHUS: *You want us to kidnap him, Master? I can't do it! It's too dangerous. I'll get caught!*

SARDU: *You must do this for me, Ralphus.*

9) "Trying to cross over into mainstream Hollywood roles, de Jesus was appropriately cast as a hotel guest in ***Under the Rainbow*** (Steve Rash, 1981) a comedy about spies, undercover agents, and midgets who cross paths during the filming of ***Wizard of Oz***. It was while shooting this film that he met his future wife Jean D'Agostino and they appeared together as Ewoks in ***Return of the Jedi***." Milligen, Stephen, "Blood Sucking Freaks, Grand Guignol and America's Crisis in the 1970s", ***Headpress*** 2.6, 2012: 57.

RALPHUS: *Then what will you do for me, Master?*

Sardu rises and fiddles with a set of keys.

JOEL: Well, that's the old bisexual thing with the keychain. I don't think that anyone walks around with their keychains like that.
JOHN: ***What do you mean?***
JOEL: I think if you wore your keys on the left side of your belt you were supposed to be submissive.

RALPHUS: *You've been a very bad boy today.*
SARDU: *Have I really been that bad? Must I be punished?*

Sardu's female assistants seize him and rip the shirt from his body. They force him to his knees and begin to whip him. Ralphus steps up on a stool, unzips his pants, and smiles…

JOHN: ***So, Luis probably got all his clothes from the circus?***
JOEL: Yeah, he brought them over. Alan bought all of the dresses for these girls from the Pleasure Chest or something.

The scene suddenly cuts to an establishing shot of the city.

JOHN: ***Now, where was this location? The exterior. Was it near Lincoln Center?***
JOEL: No, that's right up the street from here.

Creasy Silo walks into a room filled with expressionist paintings. He begins a pompous critique.

CREASY SILO: *Now, I find that this artist makes a very interesting statement.*

JOHN: ***Was this shot at Alan's place?***
JOEL: No, this was right above Gyles' theater. There was an art gallery there. All of these paintings were there.

One of Sardu's assistants seizes the moment and makes a move to distract the critic. She unbuttons her overcoat and flashes him. Her unique body boasts a vagina and a penis.

JOEL: That's a lousy dildo. If she was really a hermaphrodite, it would have looked better.
JOHN: ***What's the story behind Sardu's assistants?***

A match made in heaven.

JOEL: They were in a famous Broadway show at the time. They were dancers.

JOHN: ***Did they have any reservations about appearing in this movie?***

JOEL: No. Nobody had any issues.

Ralphus emerges from the shadows like a bolt of lightning. He shoots a poison dart into Silo's neck. The critic collapses and the two kidnappers scurry off with their prey.

JOHN: ***Did Victor bring Michael Sahl back to score this film?***

JOEL: Yeah, Victor got him. It was a question of money. I mean for a couple of thousand dollars…

Defeated and humiliated, Creasy Silo hangs from the ceiling in Sardu's dungeon. His arms are tightly bound, and his body sways in the darkness.

JOEL: This was shot down in Gyles' basement, right by the cage. Everything was there. I just moved a few things around to accentuate the lighting.

SARDU: *Welcome to the Theatre of the Macabre, Mr. Silo. I think your appreciation of my art shall be greatly enhanced in the next few days.*

CREASY SILO: *I don't believe it. I don't believe it! Sardu? Oh, this is so trite. Kidnapping! So farcical!*

SARDU: *The eminent critic has a sense of humor in times of stress. That won't suffice for what is to follow, my friend. Unless, of course, you agree that my theater is true art and you apologize to me in a most sincere way.*

JOEL: Don't you think it would be horrible if you had a career in acting or cinema and, thirty years later, this was your only claim to fame?

Sardu begins a demonstration of his influence. A disobedient woman is strapped to a dirty gurney and battery cables are clamped to her nipples.

SARDU: *A most modern method of reflex orientation. Ralphus will now induce 500 volts to her nervous system.*

JOEL: That little generator was actually in the cellar of Gyles' theater. It was just sitting in the corner. He had a lot of weird stuff down there.

Ralphus grins and flips a switch. Electricity flows through the young woman's body as she screams in agony.

JOHN: ***Did you ever think you were taking things too far?***

JOEL: No. I always had a humorous approach. The only other thing I wanted to put in was coprophagia, but I didn't shoot it. It was just too much.

JOHN: ***Who is the girl getting shocked?***

JOEL: Jenny Baxter. She was doing a couple of porn films at the time. I think she got raped [on a porn film set], and Alan went down to beat up the guy who was shooting the film.

Exhausted and embarrassed, the young woman finally submits to Sardu's domination.

WOMAN BEING SHOCKED: *Master! Please don't hurt me anymore! Master!*

Ralphus mounts the woman and rides her as if she were a rocking horse.

JOEL: I thought this was cute. And we were lucky that Ralphus had a full wardrobe.

SARDU: *Have you finished your ride, Ralphus? Put her to work in the toilet. Her mouth will make an interesting urinal.*

JOEL: If you look at the urinal scene in ***Fight Club***, you'll see that I was there first.

JOHN: ***I guess that's true.***

JOEL: Remember, most of this was inspired by Alan's friends. They all wanted these scenes in the movie. I mean, I've had girls that liked this kind of thing, but I couldn't even lightly spank them. Not that I wouldn't mind having some people raped by animals.

JOHN: ***What?***

JOEL: Well, I wouldn't find it sexually arousing. But there are certain people in the world that I'd love to see raped by animals. I wouldn't want to have them dismembered; I think that getting raped by a baboon would be enough.

JOHN: ***I'd think so.***

JOEL: I was thinking about this when I was dealing with Bill Landis. Then, I thought, "Well, he might have already done it!" From the stories he told me, who knows?

JOHN: ***How much did it cost you to rent this place?***

JOEL: Alan would probably know better, but I'd say less than $1,000. I guess Gyles was hard up for the money, because I told him off a few times. He was imposing himself on the production. We went back to rent the place for another picture, and he'd been evicted. All of the stuff was gone—they'd cleaned out the space. But, at least we didn't cut anybody's balls off in this movie.

JOHN: ***Well, the girls eat a penis sandwich at the end.***

JOEL: That's right. OK, we did it! I don't remember who brought the dildo.

Creasy Silo scoffs at Sardu's threats. His hands rattle in their chains as he talks through gritted teeth.

Alan Dellay as Creasy Silo.

CREASY SILO: *You haven't the talent to create anything but garbage.*

SARDU: *A ballet is forming in my mind. It will combine two art forms: sadism and dance. The public cannot digest eroticism alone. To display sadism and discipline in its purest form would only lead to imprisonment. But simply disguising it with a story, a minimal plot, and a score will result in my being hailed as a creative genius.*

CREASY SILO: *Kill me! Kill me!*

SARDU: *Oh no, my friend. You're going to be front row center in my triumph. After all… what is the show without the critic?*

JOHN: ***So, you wrote the screenplay for Blood Sucking Freaks in a week or so?***

JOEL: Yes. I thought it was funny; I really have no relation to S&M.

The days roll on, and Sardu goes about his business. He sits in his office and bargains with a white slavery kingpin from the Middle East.

JOHN: ***Here's Alphonso DeNoble.***

Ralphus lazily goes about his day's work. As he packages a new shipment of slave-women, his Master claps his hands and summons him.

SARDU: *Ralphus… be a good little chap and collect Natasha D'Natalie for me.*

JOEL: Well, this actually works as a movie. That's nice framing.

JOHN: ***What did you think about Ron Dorfman's work on this picture?***

JOEL: It was good. I always thought Ron would wind up in Hollywood doing major productions.

JOHN: *Was he pretty easy to work with?*

JOEL: Yeah. But he was a very sensitive guy. Sort of hyper—he had all the cares of the world on his shoulders.

Oblivious to Sardu's plan, Natasha D'Natalie relaxes in bed. She whispers into her boyfriend's ear…

NATASHA D'NATALIE: *Tom… you do everything just so well. Even make love.*

TOM MAVERICK: *Well, no matter what I do, nothing compares to you on a stage. You make Lincoln Center come alive.*

JOEL: I loved Viju's Latvian/Canadian/Brooklyn accent. It was very unique.

JOHN: *Where was this scene shot at?*

JOEL: This was in Alan's apartment. He had a beautiful penthouse. Alan always lived with elegance around him.

Maverick tries to convince Natasha to stay with him a little longer, but the ballerina has responsibilities to tend to.

NATASHA D'NATALIE: *I'll be late for rehearsal!*

TOM MAVERICK: *Will I see you tonight?*

NATASHA D'NATALIE: *Well… after the performance. You know, Tom, if I had time, you would be the only person I would spend it with in this world.*

JOHN: *What do you remember about Niles?*

JOEL: Well, he played Dr. Clay Jordon on ***The Edge of Night***. He was in a swimming pool when some casting director came up and signed him for soap operas. But he was on the threshold of middle-age when we shot this, so he always had to suck in his stomach.

Time quickly passes, and Natasha is forced to leave the loving comfort of Tom's arms. She stands before a row of lockers and sighs as she slowly changes into a leotard.

JOEL: This, of course, was shot in Gyles' theater. All of this stuff was there.

Once again, Ralphus lies in wait—this time hidden in Natasha's locker. He carefully opens the door and surveys the scene. Blowgun in hand, he plans his attack. When the coast is finally clear, he fires a dart into Natasha's shoulder. The ballerina falls to the ground and Ralphus dances with glee.

JOEL: Luis was very gentle. See how they're sliding Viju into the basement at Sardu's theater? That was actually an old coal chute. And there was already a barred door there.

JOHN: ***You've mentioned that Dorothy Palmer did the casting for this. What can you tell me about her?***

JOEL: Well, Dorothy Palmer was a casting agent. She did work for Lincoln Center, and she set up her own agency on West 57th Street. Remember that Woody Allen picture ***Broadway Danny Rose***? She was like that. She had all of these weird people in her office—acrobats, musicians—people like that. And there was always a lot of pretty girls over there. I think she sent Viju over.

JOHN: ***Somebody told me that she worked on a few porn films.***

JOEL: She did, but I don't know if she'd admit to it today. She got into trouble when she was doing that, so she dropped out of it. But, she was a free-form psychedelic agent of the '60s. Her office was a wonderland of weirdos, beautiful women, and future stars.

Now a prisoner in Sardu's lair, Natasha D'Natalie is bound in ropes and chains. Ralphus looks at her body with lust in his eyes.

SARDU: *Do you like?*
RALPHUS: *I like very much, Master.*
SARDU: *Then do what you please with her. Only, don't incapacitate her. She must dance for me.*

JOHN: ***What do you remember about Emil Neroda?***

JOEL: He was our sound mixer. He worked with Victor. He did the mix on ***Ganja & Hess*** and ***The Elephant Man***. In the old days, you used to have to go into a big sound studio. They had these giant tape machines—you'd have the musical score on one tape and the voice track on another. You had to mix them together. He would listen to the tapes and say, "You don't have the sound of the door closing in this scene. Let me put a door in there." He had a big library of sound effects. We paid him something like $100 an hour.

A rare shot of a familiar scene.

As Ralphus has his way with Natasha, Tom Maverick sits alone in his apartment. The telephone rings and he answers it.

TOM MAVERICK: *Natasha? No, she's not here. She did what? She didn't come to the theater? How long has she been missing? Jesus Christ! Why didn't you call me earlier?*

JOHN: ***I'm curious about how you shot this film. Did Ron Dorfman bring his own crew with him?***
JOEL: Yeah, he usually brought the whole crew.
JOHN: ***I was wondering, because a guy named Stephen DeVita is credited as being a gaffer for this movie. He worked on a lot of porn stuff.***
JOEL: Yeah, I knew Steve. He worked on a lot of porn pictures. Our production assistant was named Dan Tieger. He went on to make films as a producer. A lot of the people who worked with Ron went on in the industry. Most of them used fake names for ***Blood Sucking Freaks***. One guy called himself John Caleone—he was from the union. He took the name from ***The Godfather*** or something.

With the first step of his plan firmly in place, Sardu gloats over the weak and cowering Silo.

Virju screams.

SARDU: *Natasha D'Natalie has joined my company.*

CREASY SILO: *Her absence will not be taken lightly. The police will track her here.*

SARDU: *They haven't tracked anyone here yet, and I've been in business for years.*

CREASY SILO: *D'Natalie is a celebrity. The public opinion will force them to come here. She's not your average American high school girl.*

JOHN: ***What kind of lighting setup did you have for this film?***

JOEL: Well, we had about ten or twelve lights. And we had about four or five scrims and reflectors. Ron had a pretty good crew, so I didn't have to bother myself with it. Things went very fast.

JOHN: ***How long did it take you to set up an average shot?***

JOEL: I think around one hour. Around four hours for things that were more elaborate. It took a little more time when we were lighting the theater. But we moved pretty fast. That's the secret of making a low budget movie. You need a good crew—you don't want anybody who's too artistic.

JOHN: ***That makes sense.***

JOEL: You need a big light to fill in all the shadows and you need the key lights. That's basically where you spend all of your time.

JOHN: ***The theater scenes were the most complex?***

JOEL: Yeah. It might have taken six hours to light something. While that's going on, you're just sitting around. Then the actors come out and the scene takes ten minutes.

Natasha hangs from the ceiling. Ralphus circles her, while crashing a pair of cymbals together in a furious attempt to break her will.

JOHN: ***Where did you get this idea from?***

JOEL: Oh, I think there were some musical instruments from the theater lying around. There was a drum set in the corner, and I saw the cymbals. I'm pretty improvisational. And Ralphus was so cute...

JOHN: ***What was Luis like on the set?***

JOEL: He was wonderful! He was friendly; you had to stop him from helping the crew. He was really enjoyable. And he got along well with Seamus. They were rehearsing all day by themselves. When they came on the set, I barely had to tell them anything. They had all of their lines down.

JOHN: ***Did Luis take his role seriously?***

JOEL: Yeah, he took it seriously, but he knew that there was a sense of humor to it. That was important. Herve Villechaize probably would have been much more serious about things. Fortunately, we got Luis instead.

JOHN: ***Where did the idea of an evil dwarf come from in the first place?***

JOEL: I don't know. I guess I saw the hunchback assistant dwarf in a lot of movies. It was just a creative moment. I was thinking about ***Frankenstein*** and ***Bride of Frankenstein***—the scientist always has a deformed assistant with a crippled arm or something. People brought over a lot of S&M comic books that I didn't know existed, and they always had a dwarf in them.

Disgusted by Natasha's reserve, Sardu commiserates with a weary Silo.

SARDU: *She's stronger than we thought. Twenty-four hours without sleep, warmth, or comfort, and she still denies me. Really, I quite admire her for her courage. It's really quite a challenge.*

JOHN: ***Was it difficult to get the look you wanted while shooting on 16mm?***

JOEL: Film is very forgiving. If the scene was too dark, the color corrector could always bring it up. And we had a lot of leeway when it came to focus.

JOHN: ***How does this differ from shooting on video?***

JOEL: You have to be right on target with digital. You can't get blacks, and it's hard to get depth of field. You have to be very careful with that.

JOHN: ***Where did the cameras come from on Blood Sucking Freaks? Did you rent them?***

JOEL: Well, Ron owned the cameras. He had a full set.

JOHN: ***So Ron supplied the equipment?***

JOEL: Yeah, he came with the camera package. Ron had some money through his father who was one of the professors that invented the birth control pill. He was the president of one of those chemical companies. Ron was never short of money.

JOEL: You know what happened to Viju, right?

JOHN: ***You told me that she passed away.***

JOEL: Yes. She was shot by her third husband in a hunting accident in 1983. He told her to walk behind him as he picked up a gun to shoot a deer.

JOHN: ***Oh, man…***

JOEL: He got her right between the eyes. I believe he was innocent, because if you told her to walk this way, she'd walk the other way.

JOHN: ***Wasn't she originally a model?***

JOEL: Yes. In fact she wrote a book called ***How to Become a Successful Model***. She wrote a number of books, but she barely spoke English.

Natasha D'Natalie hangs limp from the ceiling. Ralphus unties the ballerina and leads her to a wheelchair. Sardu checks her pulse and frowns.

RALPHUS: *Is she dead, Master?*

SARDU: *Not quite.*

RALPHUS: *If she dies, no new show.*

SARDU: *I know, idiot. Then all our work would have been in vain. Call the doctor.*

The doctor arrives and examines his patient. His face is grim.

SARDU: *Will she live, doctor?*

DOCTOR: *I've given Ralphus a prescription.*

SARDU: *How much do I owe you?*

DOCTOR: *My malpractice insurance has gone up.*

SARDU: *How about taking it out on trade?*

Sardu and the doctor smile…

The doctor's work begins.

JOHN: *Can you give me an idea of what the layout of Gyles' place was like?*

JOEL: Oh, it was huge. You'd go downstairs, and you'd enter this big reception room. It was decorated like a thrift shop. There was the theater—it held seventy to eighty seats. He had dressing rooms. There was a bedroom. And in the front, under the street, he had a workroom. I would assume that the building was at least seventy-five feet wide and around one-hundred feet long. That's pretty big. He had a giant loft upstairs. I can take you down there tomorrow, if you have the time.

JOHN: *Of course!*

The camera dollies back as a naked woman screams. She is bound to a chair.

JOEL: That's Lynette Sheldon! She's teaching drama in New York now.

The doctor does his best to reassure his new patient that things are under control.

DOCTOR: *I'm not going to hurt you. I'm a doctor. I'm going to cure you... of everything!*

JOHN: *You told me that a lot of these scenes were inspired by S&M comic books. What can you tell me about them?*

JOEL: Well, they were either Dutch or French. If your virgin daughter was a brat, you'd send her to these schools. They never touched them sexually—they'd put chastity belts on them and give them enemas so they'd do their homework. Stuff like that. All of the men were distorted. I had some fiction where these fraternity girls from private schools kidnap the most popular girl. They put her in an attic, and bring all these ugly people from the town to rape her. In fact, I just found a book like that in French. I have the translation. They're bringing in animals and dwarfs.

The doctor laughs as he begins to pull out his patient's teeth. Blood pours as he wrenches them from her mouth. Sardu and Ralphus look on in disgust. Even they have limits.

DOCTOR: *When I was in school, they used to say that I shouldn't do that!*

JOEL: Anyway, the guy playing the doctor is Ernie Pysher. Do you know what he's doing these days?
JOHN: ***When I talked to him, he said that he was working for the public school system in Pennsylvania. I don't know if that's still the case.***

The doctor eyes his prey like a vulture. He begins to sing like a demented Pavarotti. He chuckles and reaches for a drill.

JOHN: ***This scene is kind of out there...***
JOEL: Well, Ernie made all of this up. He just started singing.
JOHN: ***It works, I'll tell you that.***

The doctor plunges the drill into the woman's skull as she shrieks in agony. Bits of bone and flesh fly through the air.

JOHN: ***Bob O'Bradovich did the special effects for this movie. What was he like in person?***
JOEL: Bob was a former boxer. He looked like a professional wrestler, with his big arms and everything.

Without missing a beat, the doctor unveils a long glass straw. He burrows it deep into the woman's skull and begins to suck at her brains.

JOHN: ***The sound for this scene is really disgusting. Come to think of it, what kind of recording equipment did you use for Blood Sucking Freaks?***
JOEL: Oh, we had the best Nagras around. We had a few of them. And we had—what's the name of the famous microphones?
JOHN: ***You've got me there...***
JOEL (thinking): Sennheisers.

We had them on booms, so we had a dolly for the mic. I don't think we ever, ever pinned a mic on anyone. We'd always have the microphone up above them. Sound is very important when you're shooting a picture. You owe it to the audience.

Sardu retires to his study and pours himself a drink. He is obviously unnerved by what he just witnessed. He calls for his dwarf.

SARDU: *Ralphus!*
RALPHUS: *I was just going to see the doctor out, Master.*
SARDU: *Get rid of him. Permanently.*

JOHN: ***What kind of a guy was Gyles Fontaine? Did you get along with him?***
JOEL: Well, he got very mad at me because he had his slaves down there for his show. There were all of these naked girls—they were giving him blowjobs and stuff. He wanted them to star in the movie.
JOHN: ***Were they living there?***
JOEL: He was living with them, yes. I didn't particularly like them. I wasn't very interested in his lead girl—she was very dark and Jewish looking, and I wanted a blonde. He worked on the movie after that, but…

Ralphus leads the doctor down a dark corridor. Things are about to go from bad to worse.

DOCTOR: *Wouldn't it be easier to get the taxi out on Broadway?*
RALPHUS: *No, it's quicker this way. You'll like it!*
DOCTOR: *Ralphus, I need a cab. I don't have time to wait for the subway!*

Ralphus opens a door and forces him into a cage.

JOHN: ***Were these cages in the theater, or did you have to make them?***
JOEL: I think we brought in some of the barred walls. They were made of wood. We painted them to look like metal, and we hung them up there. If you watch this scene closely, you can see them shake.

The doctor cries out in terror as he is surrounded by Sardu's captive women. Before he can attempt to escape, they are upon him. Ralphus jumps with joy as they tear his flesh asunder.

JOEL: Every effect in this movie

A fitting ending for his kind.

was put together by me or Bob. If we needed something, we went to the butcher shop.

Sardu and Ralphus celebrate the doctor's demise with a friendly game of darts. Sardu's eyes narrow as he takes aim at his target.

SARDU: *Bullseye coming up!*

Sardu throws his dart. Sure enough, he strikes a dead hit—right between the buttocks of one of slaves.

JOHN: ***Who was this actress?***
JOEL: She's listed in the credits as Joann Friedman. I'm not sure if that's her real name. Somebody told me that some of these girls became stars.
JOHN (looking through notes): ***Speaking of fake names, what can you tell me about Mayo Gray? Was that a real person?***
JOEL: Mayo Gray was in charge of continuity. Some guy came up to her on the set and said, "I want to marry you." He turned out to be a multimillionaire. She lived in a triplex apartment on Madison Avenue. We had our wrap party there—she sprung for it. Everybody went to the orgy upstairs.
JOHN: ***Yeah, that's where you said you saw Viju and Luis going at it.***

A newspaper headline fills the screen. It reads, "Ballerina Still Missing." John Tucci, a sergeant from the New York Police Department, knocks on Tom Maverick's door. Maverick invites him in, and they begin to talk.

JOHN: ***What can you tell me about the guy who played Tucci?***

JOEL: Dan Fauci went on to become the Vice President at Paramount Television. He all but had a sign in his office that said, "Don't Mention This Picture!"

JOHN: ***What kind of a guy was he? He hasn't returned my calls.***

JOEL: He was easy to get along with. He was a tough-talking know-it-all, but he presented no problems. He sort of had his nose stuck up in the air, but overall he was OK.

TOM MAVERICK: *The D'Natalie case—do you have any leads?*

JOHN TUCCI: *Only you, QB.*

TOM MAVERICK: *Me? I don't understand.*

JOHN TUCCI: *Well, you were sleeping with her. You could have got into an argument or something.*

TOM MAVERICK: *Hey, come on.*

JOHN TUCCI: *Don't worry about it. A little money upfront and I can prove that the mayor did it. You want to be smart, QB? Take some of this money you have and grease the hands of justice.*

JOHN: ***What did Alan Margolin think of the finished movie?***

JOEL: Not much. I mean, he helped to make a deal with Troma against my back. I've told you this before—the main investor went to Stanley Borden at American Film Distribution.

JOHN: ***Joel Weinberg?***

JOEL: Yes. They booked it in Chicago, and they spent a fortune. They spent thousands of dollars on advertising. They thought the picture was going to make millions. It didn't, so they stuck the prints in a warehouse. I had a lien on the movie, so I got it back from them. That's one way of doing things—I learned it from older producers. Vernon Becker produced a movie called ***Flame and the Fire***. It was a documentary. Walter Reade said, "Oh, I couldn't play this picture anyplace! It's dropping dead!" Vernon drove down south, and it was in every drive-in.

Back at the theater, Sardu is at his most persuasive. He addresses Natasha D'Natalie in a domineering tone.

SARDU: *We have a little entertainment planned for you today. Something that may happen to you, if you still insist on not dancing.*

We cut to a wide shot of a young

woman. She is bound, gagged, and strapped to a rack.

SARDU: *The rack. A legitimate form of punishment, legalized by both the church and the state.*

JOHN: ***Who played the girl on the rack?***
JOEL: Jennifer Stock. Everybody's looking for her, but nobody can find her. She was in two other pictures.

Sardu's assistants tear the clothes off their captive and get down to business.

SARDU: *This is going to go far beyond every "stretch" of the imagination.*

JOHN: ***This scene is especially well lit.***
JOEL: You have to know what you're doing with the lights and with the camera. You have to pull focus, and stuff like that. At times, you'd have five lenses. The camera was heavy—you needed three or four people on the camera if you had to move it. You had some guy loading and unloading magazines; you had to take them to the lab.
JOHN: ***Can you explain focus pulling?***
JOEL: You would count off the feet between the actor and the camera, and you had a little white card. It was a round thing that you put around the focus ring. You'd mark the beginning of the shot to the end of the shot. The assistant cameraman would pull the focus knob in time to the movement of the camera. The trouble today is that anyone can shoot a picture. And I see a lot of lousy ones.

Natasha screams in terror as the young woman is torn apart. The gruesome sight is only a sample of what is to come...

SARDU: *Our second demonstration, my dear. Apt punishment for a little girl who refuses to take her dancing lessons.*

A young girl is led to the base of a guillotine.

SARDU: *Due to her tender age, we're being most gentle with her.*

JOEL: This is Illa Howe.
JOHN: ***How did you meet her?***
JOEL: She came in from the William Morris Agency when we were doing ***Blood Bath***. I think she

Illa Howe loses her head.

was discovered by Aram Avakian. She was in a mental institution, and they shot a movie there.

Ralphus unbuttons the girl's blouse as he prepares her for execution.

SARDU: *Now, as long as you do as we tell you, the longer you stay alive.*

JOEL: There was a point when I actually got tired of looking at all of these naked girls.
JOHN: ***Where did this guillotine come from? Was it something that Gyles had in his apartment?***
JOEL: No, we built the guillotine. I think I might have built it myself in Alan's shop. This scene is from a Dutch comic book.

RALPHUS: *Open your mouth. I'm going to put something nice into it!*

The young girl obeys, and Ralphus instructs her to bite down on the rope that holds aloft the guillotine's blade.

SARDU: *Now let's see how long you can go before you open your mouth. Oh… I almost forgot. We're going to cane you for being a very bad little girl.*

Ralphus rips the girl's skirt aside and pulls down her panties. He then begins to flog her.

JOEL: I did some of the caning in this scene!

It doesn't take long for the girl to

scream. She opens her mouth, and the blade falls. Ralphus collects her severed head, and raises it into the air like a trophy. He pauses to kiss it before lowering it to his groin.

JOEL: You know, Niles and I tried to make a movie with William Holden.

JOHN: ***You're kidding!***

JOEL: Well, Niles was doing some soaps, and he said, "William Holden invited us out to Los Angeles! He wants to be in this movie." I can't remember if I wrote the script or if Niles did. But William Holden picked up the tab, and we flew to Los Angeles. Niles was friendly with William Holden's mistress. We met them for dinner, and I said, "Niles, he's drunk. He has no intention of being in this movie. This is all bullshit."

In spite of the horrors on display, Natasha still refuses to dance. Ralphus drags a burlap sack across the floor and opens it in front of her. A young ballerina, confused and afraid, stumbles out into the darkness of the theater.

BALLERINA: *Natasha!*

NATASHA D'NATALIE: *She will not dance for you, either.*

SARDU: *Oh yes, she will. But she'll do a dance of a different kind. I shall now demonstrate to you what shall happen to you if you do not immediately agree to start rehearsal.*

JOEL: I think this girl was Dan Fauci's girlfriend. He was teaching acting at the time.

The sound of a chainsaw fills the air. The girl begins to run as Ralphus gives chase.

JOHN: ***What do you remember about her?***

JOEL: She was waiting around to do her scene. She came up to me and said, "I need some input from the director!" I said, "Well, Luis comes around the corner with a chainsaw. You see him and you run away." Then she said, "What's the name of the character?" I asked her, "Which character?" She said, "My character! The girl who gets her legs cut off!" I asked, "Does she have to have a name?" She said, "I can't play the part unless I know who I am."

JOHN (laughs): ***So, how did you deal with that?***

JOEL: I said, "Your name is Dorothy, and you went to actors school for six years in Ohio." She said, "Boy, you're a lousy director."

JOHN: ***Michael Sahl's music just paid tribute to Tchaikovsky's "Swan Lake." What do you think about the musical score for this movie?***

JOEL: Oh, it's OK. I don't know if Sahl has the tracks anymore, but we should release an original soundtrack album for ***Blood Sucking Freaks***.

Ralphus returns to the scene. He holds two severed feet in his hands. Natasha can take no more.

SARDU: *Now, are you planning to cut short your dancing career?*

NATASHA D'NATALIE: *I will dance!*

JOHN: *Back to Gyles for a moment—was he fond of the basic idea behind Blood Sucking Freaks?*
JOEL: I don't know. He was very stuck up. "I could do better than this! You think you know what you're doing?" Stuff like that.

Sardu decides that a celebration is in order. He groans in ecstasy as his assistants whip his back. He finally climaxes in a frenzy of jubilation.

SARDU: *She shall dance!*

JOHN: *Is this one of Gyles' whips?*
JOEL: I don't know. I think there were some whips in the theater, but it's pretty easy to get ahold of whips. We had people bring their own whips! Some people would come up to me during the shoot and take their clothes off. They'd say, "Do what you want to me! Shit on me! Whatever you want!" I wasn't into that. I won't mention the particular girls.

Sardu confers with the emaciated Creasy Silo. He paces in front of his prisoner, reveling in victory.

SARDU: *You were wrong, Creasy. She shall dance for me.*

Unbeknownst to Sardu, Tom Maverick and Sergeant Tucci are hot on his trail. Tucci holds up a newspaper. The headline is short and to the point.

JOHN TUCCI: *"Ballerina Flips Lid for Freak Show." Your little girlfriend didn't disappear. She just went Off-Broadway. It's right here in* ***Variety****.*
TOM MAVERICK: *Christ, I don't believe it! She wouldn't give up Lincoln Center for that rat hole in Soho!*

JOHN: *Where were the interiors of the police station scenes shot at?*
JOEL: That was all shot at Alan's steamfitting shop. He had a building on the West Side. It had a garage and some offices.

JOHN TUCCI: *Hey—what kind of show does this guy Sardu put on?*
TOM MAVERICK: *A nude one.*
JOHN TUCCI: *I wonder how much he's paying off…*

JOHN: *The last time I talked to Eddie Jaffe, he was saying that he was somehow involved in raising the money for Blood Sucking Freaks.*
JOEL: Yeah. Eddie knew Joel Weinberg, and he called me up to ask if I was doing a movie. He told

Dan Fauci as Tucci.

me that one of Weinberg's clients had to spend some money before January first. I don't know when we shot ***Blood Sucking Freaks***, but it was before the first of the year. So, I called up Weinberg, and he said, "OK. You've got the money." I didn't really know if he was serious. He called up a little later and said, "You didn't come over and pick the money up."

JOHN: *Was Alan Margolin ever involved in the fundraising?*

JOEL: No. He didn't raise any of the money. He was supposed to raise the money for ***Teen Demon***. All of his friends said that they would put in some money if I did a movie about Gyles' theater. I mean, Alan came up with some front money, but Weinberg was the main investor.

Tucci and Maverick decide to pay Sardu a visit. Ralphus greets them in the foyer.

RALPHUS: *Master will be with you in a moment. He's on the telephone with his press agent.*

JOHN TUCCI: *This is some ritzy place. You know something, QB? There's more here than meets the eye. I smell money. I always thought these Off-Off-Broadway gimmicks were a front for something else.*

JOHN: *Where exactly on Spring Street was Gyles' theater?*

JOEL: It was one block west of the Spring Street bar.

JOHN: *Where was the bar?*

JOEL: On Spring Street and Broadway. The upstairs to Gyles' place is still a gallery. I can still recognize the building. When we decided to do this movie, I remembered the address and asked Gyles if we could rent his place. The co-op board got very excited.

JOHN: ***How old was Gyles at the time?***

JOEL: I guess he was in his thirties. He was from a ballet in Canada, and he liked to preform naked on stage with his girls. There was no consummated sex in the act. He'd just tie the girls up and whip them. That was a time when they were having very weird shows Off-Broadway. It was a very big deal to have totally naked people—the nude theater, and all that. I just thought I'd make this as funny as possible.

Sardu descends a staircase and greets his guests. He forces a smile as he shakes Maverick's hand.

TOM MAVERICK: *Listen, I'd like to see Natasha.*

SARDU: *Oh, I'm afraid not. She's exhausted—rehearsal after rehearsal. You know what a perfectionist she is.*

TOM MAVERICK: *Yeah, I know all about that. I just want to see her.*

SARDU: *Why? I mean, we're all going to Sardi's aren't we, afterward, to celebrate?*

JOHN: ***How popular was Sardi's in the mid-1970s?***

JOEL: It was more popular than it is now. I went there a little while ago, and it was geriatric time at the bar. Who played Trixie on the Gleason show?

JOHN: ***I don't know... Jane Kean?***

JOEL: Yeah. She was there. In fact, I told somebody that I knew her. He said, "Can I take her to dinner?" I said, "I'll ask her." I called her, and she said, "How old is the guy?" I said, "Around twenty-five." She was about eighty. She said, "Of course he can take me to dinner!" Anyway, the food there has always been terrible, but the bar was great! Lauren Bacall was always there. She'd say, "Motherfucker! Get me another fucking drink!"

Maverick and Tucci convince Sardu to produce Natasha, but something about her demeanor arouses their suspicion. They vow to visit the theater later in the evening—this time as members of the audience.

JOHN: ***Do you have any more stories about Ron Dorfman? I haven't been able to get in touch***

with him.

JOEL: Ron had a pornographic studio. He had this nine-room apartment, and he was shooting porn there. His little kids were running around. His son walked into a room while this couple was fucking. He said, "Hey dad, are you going to make lunch?" I said, "Ron! You mean your kids are here?" He said, "Well, what am I supposed to do?"

JOHN: ***The last major movie—not a porn film—that I can find him associated with is Night of the Zombies.***

JOEL: Well, Ron and I had a little fight about something, but he was invited out to do major movies. He told them to go fuck themselves. He was getting a lot of offers, and he turned them all down. But, Ron and I were the best of friends. One time, he wanted help with a film he was doing with Gerard Damiano and Sharon Mitchell. He asked me to come in to organize it.

JOHN: ***How did that go?***

JOEL: I didn't get along with Damiano. He was egotistical. I think I quit after one or two days.

JOHN: ***What year was that?***

JOEL: Well, it was after ***Blood Sucking Freaks***. 1978. I'm not into spectator sports, but I've been on porn sets. One time, this guy said, "Hey! You've got to fuck this pussy! She was a man two years ago! That's an artificial pussy! I bet you never fucked one of those!" I said, "No, I haven't. And I'm not interested in fucking this one."

Maverick and Tucci return to the theater. Before the curtain opens, Tucci finds his way backstage.

SARDU: *What are you doing back here? I have a show opening in less than two hours.*

JOHN TUCCI: *Business, Sardu. Monkey business.*

SARDU: *I don't understand.*

JOHN TUCCI: *You've got a record a mile long downtown. Three open murder charges. Now... what's this place a front for?*

SARDU: *I'll cut you in.*

JOHN TUCCI: *Of course, you'll cut me in. But what's going on here, Sardu?*

SARDU: *White slavery...*

JOHN: ***Did you ever supervise Victor when he was cutting Blood Sucking Freaks?***

JOEL: Oh, yeah. But everything was so low budget. We had no alternative takes. What else are you

Opening night.

going to put in there? Victor had an editing shop where he would get a lot of people to do the work for him. The guy that cut this with him, Joel Herson, went on to do some work over at ABC with my brother. He won an Emmy for editing "Music Maestro, Please."

JOHN: *What was that?*

JOEL: It was a segment on [the TV show] ***20.20***. I haven't talked to him in a long time.

Sardu and Tucci cut a deal, and the crooked cop makes his way back to his seat. He quietly fills Maverick in on his discovery.

JOHN TUCCI: *Listen—Sardu is holding Natasha prisoner. He's got a white slavery action—two or three hundred girls a year. He tortures them.*

TOM MAVERICK: *White slavery? In this day and age?*

JOHN TUCCI: *You haul 'em into court, and the judges let them go. You know why? Because they're in on the take like everybody else is.*

TOM MAVERICK: *I don't believe it.*

JOHN TUCCI: *Where do you think half the girls wind up who come into this town to go into showbusiness? Off-Off-Broadway. But this time, Sardu's gone too far, and I'm going to fix him. That freak wants to be a celebrity.*

JOHN: *What do you think of the finished film? I'm talking technically, in terms of the final edit.*

JOEL: I don't know. There are two ways of editing and shooting a picture. In the old days, William Wilder would shoot 700 shots of a scene. The editor had a lot of choices to make. It would take three days to shoot the conversation that we're having. That wasn't a possibility when we were shooting ***Blood Sucking Freaks***.

The lights in the theater dim as Sardu greets his audience. Dressed in a black tuxedo, he introduces his magnum opus.

SARDU: *And now, our prima ballerina Natasha D'Natalie in a composition of my own—"The Artist: Seduction and Death of a Critic."*

A spotlight shines down on Natasha as she clumsily begins to dance. Sardu and Ralphus watch from backstage, euphoric in their moment of triumph.

JOHN: ***Gyles did the choreography for this movie.***

JOEL: Yeah, he did the choreography for the dance sequences. He contributed to that. He helped with some of the sets, but he had his nose stuck up in the air.

JOHN: ***Do you have any other stories about shooting in his theater?***

JOEL: We had some trouble with the owners of the building. They were kind of stuck up, as well. "You won't shoot this movie here!" They called the police and the fire department.

JOHN: ***What?***

JOEL: Yeah. But Alan Margolin was a specialized contractor in steamfitting, and he worked in fire prevention. He was the person you hired if something was wrong.

JOHN: ***You mean if something wasn't up to code?***

JOEL: Yes. The police and the fire department showed up, and they said, "What are you calling us for? You have the top guy in the city right here."

JOHN: ***That's great!***

JOEL: If the city said that you had a blocked exit or a bad door, you had to get an engineer that specialized in fire safety. That's what Alan did. He would say, "Replace the door with a metal one. You can't have anything within twenty feet of that exit." So, when the people tried to throw us out, the fire department came down and said, "You've got the guy right here. He's a fire prevention expert. You're not going to have any trouble."

Natasha slowly disrobes. When she is naked, another spotlight illuminates the far corner of stage right. There, chained to a marble pillar, is Creasy Silo. The ballerina gracefully rears back and proceeds to kick the critic to death.

JOHN: ***Did Gyles Fontaine ever see the movie?***

JOEL: I think he did. Yeah, he was at the screening.

JOHN: ***I was just curious about what the cast thought about it.***

JOEL: Oh, they all liked it. Let me see… most of the girls liked it. And Seamus loved his performance. So did Luis.

The final minutes of **Blood Sucking Freaks** *play out to a morbid tune of cannibalism, necrophilia, S&M, and murder. The climax is hilarious and hopeless. Driven by greed, Tucci is ripped apart by Sardu's female captives. Sardu and Ralphus are beheaded and violated by their prisoners. Natasha kills Maverick with a sledge hammer, shedding no tears as she crawls back to the feet of her eviscerated Master.*

JOHN: ***Was Blood Sucking Freaks influenced at all by Herschell Gordon Lewis?***

JOEL: I hope not. I never heard of his pictures until many years later. And then I saw **Blood Feast** and all of those things.

JOHN: ***Did you ever get the feeling that you were making exploitation film history?***

JOEL: I had no idea. I just wanted it to be funny to myself. I didn't know Herschell Gordon Lewis existed. Years later, all these little kids started running over to my house with videotapes. People would call me on the phone and quote me the lines.

JOHN: ***This film can almost be profound at times. Were you actually trying to say anything with Viju killing the critic in front of a roaring audience?***

JOEL: Well, I hope the film has its moments, but I just liked to put weird things together. I wasn't making a statement. That's what Fred Astaire said—"We're just trying to make a living here."

JOHN: ***I've got to tell you—this is better than anything Herschell Gordon Lewis ever did.***

JOEL: Well, I hope so. I met this guy a few years ago. He stopped me on the street. He said, "I know who you are!" I said, "Who am I?" He said, "You're Herschell Gordon Lewis." I said, "I'm going to punch you right in the mouth!"

"I never met Mr. Reed. That had all happened before I came on the scene. Hate to say it, but to me he was practically a figment of Bill's imagination."—Jimmy McDonough

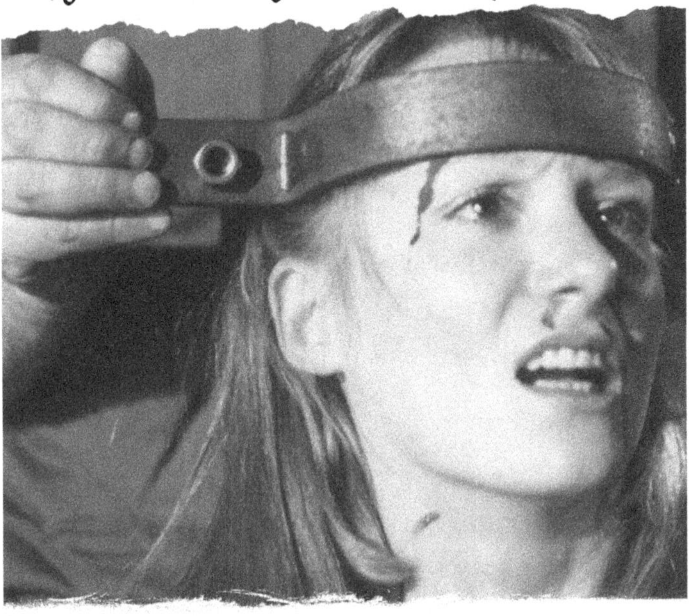

CHAPTER TEN

NEW YORK BABYLON

The next morning found me awake at dawn. I slipped out of room 415 at the Washington Jefferson and slithered down the hallway to find a shower. I remembered what Brian had told me a few days earlier:

"I finally found a clean bathroom! The place has soap, towels, a toilet… it has EVERYTHING! It's right down the hall."

I was understandably tired of the filthy latrine that I had been using.

A clean bathroom?

"What the hell?" I thought. "Let's see what he's been raving about."

I made my way through a narrow maze of corridors and opened a door. There before me stood an immaculate bathroom. At least as immaculate as things could get at the Washington Jefferson. I switched on the light and had a look around. A woman's underclothes were slung over a shower curtain. Perfumes, soaps, and bath oils were haphazardly laid out on the edge of the tub. I ducked back outside and checked the door. Sure enough, a small piece of paper was stuck to the peeling paint. Black handwritten letters read, "PRIVATE."

"Jesus Christ!" I laughed. "Brian has been raiding this place!"

I heard the lazy footsteps of somebody approaching. A middle aged woman greeted me as I backed

The author snaps a photo at the Washington Jefferson Hotel.

away from her chamber. I smiled, excused myself, and walked off to find another place to freshen up.

The plan was to meet up with Joel later in the evening. We were going to take a walk down Spring Street in attempt to pin down the exact location of Gyles Fontaine's old building. It was still early, and Brian wanted to sleep off whatever poison he had ingested the night before. I unlocked the door to room 415 and stuck my head into the room.

"I'm going to grab some breakfast. Do you want anything?"

"No. What time do we have to meet Joel?"

"Around 7:00, I guess. I told him we'd meet him on Spring and Broadway."

Brian nodded. "OK. I'll meet you guys there this evening."

With that, I closed the door, walked down four flights of stairs, and found myself in the heart of Hell's Kitchen. I glanced down at my watch. It was only ten in the morning. With plenty of time to kill, I took a right and headed east. When I got to 51st and Eighth, I started moving south.

JOHN: ***OK. I'm smoking a cigarette and heading down Eighth Avenue. Last night, we went back to the Molly Wee Pub after we talked to Joel. Paul doesn't work there anymore. A new guy named Gareth took his place. We were there until five in the morning. For some reason, he let us hang around and drink beer while he closed.***

It was a very windy morning, and a

sudden gust of air knocked the hat from my head as I talked.

JOHN: ***Shit! That was close! I just bought this thing. Anyway, my brain is still kind of fuzzy. I think I'm going on less than four hours of sleep. Looking for a place to eat breakfast.***

I ended up at a place called The Pig N Whistle. A waiter in clean white clothes brought me a menu, and I ordered a beer. I lit another cigarette and set my tape recorder down in front of me.

JOHN: ***OK… here I am sitting around, eating a hamburger. It's around 11:45 on May 19, 2000. I'm taking my first drink from a pint of Newcastle. What I want to do right now is say something about last night, while it's still fresh in my mind. Times Square is really weird these days. A lot of empty storefronts. I guess they're in the middle of renovating everything. You're always walking under scaffolding, and there's always water dripping down from up above. It's strange.***

TAPE CUTS, THEN STARTS.

JOHN: ***OK, I'm back again. Downed another Newcastle, and now I'm on to Budweiser. This is sort of a ridiculous predicament to be in—I'm running out of money. I should have planned ahead. What else can I say about last night? It's interesting how often the porn shops change their floorplan. A few months ago, certain places like Adult Store and Video had a totally different layout. The wide tables are gone, and it's rather congested. Sort of like a labyrinth of smut. Actually, the place has been repainted. It used to look like Blockbuster Video—the main colors inside were blue and yellow. Now the walls are black. These places now have strange beaded curtains that divide the porn from the rooms that sell regular movies. I caught a glimpse of a few "normal" tapes. They're actually selling Zombie at Adult Store and Video. There's a fine line between exploitation and porn to begin with, and the fact that they have to separate things with beads is sort of funny. My favorite subject when dealing with Times Square is walking down Eighth Avenue and seeing a sign that says, "XXX—Adult Entertainment." The sign itself is somewhat menacing.***

You don't know what to expect when you open the door. You pull it open, and are met with a dead-end that suddenly curves to the left. It zig-zags; you go through a maze of darkness. And suddenly, you're flooded with florescent light. There may be a few rows of shelves of what they consider "general viewing." This mostly consists of exploitation films. In its own way, this is sort of a nice eulogy for what Times Square used to be. What's not available in a theater is now available on a videotape. But, it's no excuse for anything. The only reason the "general viewing" area is there in the first place is because of the mayor's current crusade against pornography. Even the shoddiest stores have a selection of something that is not considered pornographic. But that's almost interesting in itself. I've never seen so many rows of karate films for sale, anywhere. They're bootlegs, no less. I don't know where they get these things from, but they're there. But, OK. You walk past that. Now, a couple places still have the swinging saloon-type door thing as a divider. Most places have beads that hang from the ceiling. And then you see the boxes. Box upon box of porn tapes. They're sometimes laid out for easy viewing, so you can see the covers. More often than not, they're displayed by the spine. I think that's sort of bad for business (laughs). Now... most of the sex shops still have video places—peep booths. The biggest of which, I guess, is still Show World. I think it has 128 selections. At least two places still advertise live girls. That's something I've yet to see. I don't know what I'd do if I ever walked up to see them. I guess I'd like to look into their eyes and try to figure out who they are. I mean, they get up in the morning like I did today, and they go to work. They climb up the stairs and get behind a glass cage. One-on-one fantasy booths, they're advertised as. All walks of life presumably come in to get a look. I wonder what goes on up there...

I finished my burger and continued walking south. The food in my system gave me a renewed sense of energy and I ended up just north of Washington Square Park. I ducked into Footlight Records on 12th Street, looked around for a while, and then walked down to See Hear on 7th. I stopped for a soda at a nearby Wendy's, looked at my watch, and started moving south on Second Avenue. I cut across Houston and had some problems with my whereabouts. I wasn't familiar with the area.

JOHN (mid-conversation with a local): *I'm trying to get to the Shark Bar.*
CONFUSED LOCAL: Shark Bar?
JOHN: *I guess the real name of the place is the Spring Lounge. It's on the corner of Spring and Mulberry.*
CONFUSED LOCAL: Spring and Mulberry is south. You'll pass Prince Street. Spring is the next street down.

I followed the man's directions and found myself in the outskirts of Little Italy. I dashed into a restaurant, ordered a calzone, and took it across the street. I entered the Spring Lounge to find Brian waiting for me.

I had to laugh. "Holy shit! I told you to meet me on Spring Street, but I didn't expect to find you here!"

Brian took a swig of beer. "This is the only place on Spring Street that I know. I figured you'd show up."

I laughed, took a bite out of my sandwich, and ordered a beer of my own. I hadn't been to the Spring Lounge in years. The place had changed—everything in the city was changing—but the shadows in the bar were still familiar.

"Do you think this is the place that Joel went to after seeing that ballet?" asked Brian.

"No. That was on Spring and Broadway. What time is it, anyway?"

Brian looked up at the clock that hung over the bar. "It's just about seven."

"We should go," I said.

With that, we downed our drinks and headed off into the evening.

☠

TAPE STARTS. STATIC FROM THE WIND ON THE STREETS FILLS THE AIR.

JOHN (talking into tape recorder): *OK, we're rolling.*
JOEL: *It's on this corner. Make a left. We'll turn over here.*
JOHN: *OK.*

TAPE STATIC. THEN…

JOEL: Actually, this looks more like it right here. This is the place. You know when we were torturing everybody? This is exactly how it

115 Spring Street

looked.

JOHN: ***This is it, then?***

JOEL: You're looking right at it. It was a cast iron column building. This looks like the same place. The art gallery is still here.

JOHN: ***I've got to get a picture of it.***

JOEL: Is there a vault under the street? I'm trying to remember how you got in—on what side. OK, there's a vault. They took off the grating. What's the address for this place?

JOHN: ***This is 115 Spring Street.***

JOEL: Yeah, this is it. Take a picture here, and then we'll get a wine.

I snapped a picture, and we continued walking down Spring Street. We passed a brightly lit restaurant and paused.

JOEL: They must have a bar inside, but there's nobody in there.

JOHN: ***I guess it's kind of early.***

JOEL: Let's try someplace else.

We doubled back around the block, looking for another bar.

JOEL: This has become a hot spot, down around here.

JOHN: ***Apparently so. I'm not very familiar with this side of town.***

JOEL (pointing): *You see, these are all cast iron buildings. It was the first wave of what you'd call prefabrication. They used to pour these columns and bolt them together.*

We ended up sitting at a small table at a place called Café Bari. A young waitress from Brazil brought us our drinks.

Sardu's Lair.

JOEL: There's some people who've said they interviewed me, and they never interviewed me. I'd like to get my hands on them.

JOHN: ***Really?***

JOEL: I came across something that [I think] Bill Landis [editor of ***Sleazoid Express***] did. It had to be him. Nobody else would write such nasty things about people.

JOHN: *This seems like a good time to talk about him.*

JOEL: He doesn't bother me anymore. I don't have anything against him. It's just—I mean, I don't like it when people jerk off in restaurants, and bring guys that they pick up off the street to my apartment. He thought nothing of taking his dick out.

JOHN (stunned): *Bill did that?*

JOEL: Yes. I mean, I lived with a guy who was a homosexual. I never had a relationship with him, but he used to bring people home. It never bothered me—they'd make too much noise sometimes, but I was never anti-homosexual. Bill got mad at me because I threw him and the guy out of my apartment.

JOHN: *Was Eliot your roommate? The Bearded Transvestite from Hell?*

JOEL: Yeah. I used to share an apartment with him. He'd go down to the transvestite bars with a beard, and they didn't want him there.

JOHN: *It's the kiss of death.*

JOEL: Well, they said that he didn't look good with a beard and a dress. He's still doing that.

JOHN: *Did Bill Landis know him?*

JOEL: Yeah. Bill used to say, "What a schmuck! He wears dresses!"

JOHN: *Did Bill meet most of those*

Searching for the ghost of Gyles Fontaine.

guys? Did he ever meet Eddie Jaffe?

JOEL: Yeah, he met most of those guys.

JOHN: ***See, Bill would be good to talk to. I have to get in contact with him.***

JOEL: Send him an email saying that you're writing a book about me.

JOHN: ***I've done that. I haven't gotten a reply.***

JOEL: Well, I'm sure he's more normal now. He was a very sick guy. Towards the end, he would call me up saying, "I did it again! I'm going to kill myself! I was down in the Village and I did it with five guys." He was just a problem…

JOHN: ***How did you meet him in the first place?***

JOEL: Troma had placed ***Blood Sucking Freaks*** into a theater on 42nd Street. I got a call from Bill Landis saying that it was the greatest American picture ever made. He approached me to talk about the film. He came over. At the time, he was working for Consolidated Edison. He was a small guy, and he was wearing a suit. He said, "I wrote an article about you." I said, "Gee, if you write about all these freaky movies wearing a suit, you'll be

internationally famous!" So, that's how we met.

JOHN: ***Where did that review of Blood Sucking Freaks see print?***

JOEL: *In the* **Soho Weekly News.** It was one of the East Village papers.

JOHN: ***I only ask about Bill in the first place because you've mentioned that you were once partners with him.***

JOEL: Briefly. I really liked him. He started hanging around all the time, and said, "I'd like to make a movie." I said, "Well, you have a nice image."

JOHN: ***So, this was for The Renegade Ghouls of Kaplan's Swamp?***

JOEL: Yeah. I figured that his image with the suit and tie would be beneficial. He said, "I'm going to go ahead and do it." He raised some money with his friend, and he quit his job. The next time I saw him, he was dressed in leather. He said, "I finally quit the fucking job! I can finally be me! I told them to go fuck themselves!" He started going into all of this shit about his life. "My parents are shit! They're dying because I quit my job!" Anyway, he arranged a couple of benefits, but he just spent the money that came in.

JOHN: ***So, you were trying to revive The Renegade Ghouls?***

JOEL: Yes. But nothing ever happened. Bill would say, "I need my rent!" He arranged a big benefit to make money, but it was really for himself. Ken Anger and that guy from Baltimore were there. What's his name?

JOHN: ***John Waters?***

JOEL: Yeah. John Waters said, "I'm honored to be here with Joel Reed." He asked me, "Do you get bags of shit in the mail?" I said, "No." He said, "You're lucky."

JOHN: ***What do you remember about that night?***

JOEL: Well, Bill organized it at some disco in the village. He stood at the door and collected money for himself.

JOHN: ***I saw something in the clippings that you gave me about a fundraising event called the Screaming Cheerleaders Contest.***

JOEL: That was another benefit. Bill had all of these grand ideas. All he did… well, it gave him an excuse to quit Con Edison. He became a leather freak after that. I gave him movie posters that are probably worth a lot of money now. He probably threw them out. I got them from this guy—he had bails of Sam Goldwyn posters.

JOHN: ***Which movies?***

JOEL: Oh, I can't remember, but they were old stone pressed three sheets. I had a stack this big. They were probably worth a fortune…

JOHN: ***Bill is actually one of my favorite writers. The stuff he did in Sleazoid Express was amazing.***

JOEL: I still like him, but he sort of hated everything. I guess he thinks I rejected him—I just couldn't put up with him anymore. What's he doing now?

JOHN: ***He's doing a new magazine with his wife called Metasex. I saw a new issue of Sleazoid Express at See Hear today. I have no idea what he's doing to make a living.***

JOEL: He just went… totally insane. He was picking up guys on the street and jerking off in public. He brought this guy to my apartment. I said, "You can't come up here anymore." Then he started calling me.

JOHN: ***What do you mean?***

JOEL: He was calling thirty times a day. "You're dead! You're dead! You're dead!" I had the phone company tracking him down.

JOHN: ***I take it you know that he acted in some porn films. He called himself Bobby Spector.***

JOEL: Yeah. He did a story in the ***Village Voice*** about it. As usual, he started saying bad things about everyone.

JOHN: ***I'm going to have to talk to him.***

JOEL: He could have done something better with his life. He didn't fully utilize his assets. I just couldn't have him in my house anymore.

Our waitress walked over to our table with another round of drinks. Joel's eyes immediately lit up.

JOEL (to waitress): So, you're from Brazil! Can you teach me the samba? [Starts singing] Caramba! It's the samba, it's the one dance I can't do…

AUTHOR'S NOTE: At this point, I feel an overwhelming need to pause the above conversation in order to interject. In the following months, I did my best to get in touch with Bill Landis. Emails sent to the ***Sleazoid Express*** website went unanswered. In fact, every lead that I happened upon somehow managed to turn sour. I finally got a hold of his number through a mutual friend. Heart racing, I picked up my phone, punched at the buttons, and waited. I was greeted by the listless echo of a female voice. "We're sorry. The number that you have dialed has been disconnected."

I frowned, hung up, and dialed again. This time I stayed on the line until the message played out in full. I had the crazy idea that a human being would eventually answer and give me some information. I was rewarded with a series of high pitched beeps. "That's it," I thought. "I'll never get to talk to the guy."

A few weeks passed. I finally got through to Bill's wife via email. By this time, I was already sowing the seeds for what would eventually become ***Xeroxferox***. We exchanged a few messages. Things seemed to be going smoothly. Would it be possible to interview Bill? Yes. Could we do it over the phone? That sounded fine. And then I mentioned Joel M. Reed.

The tidal wave of hatred that I received from Michelle Clifford's letter was unbelievable. The essence of her vitriol can be summed up in three short sentences: "You have no business writing about Times Square! Bill was there first! Anyone that followed was just cashing in on the trail that he blazed!" Her cruel words went on and on.

My face turned red as I read her letter. I got the feeling that Bill and Michelle wanted nothing to do with me. Still, foolishly, I tried to reestablish a line of communication. I apologized for any misunderstanding—I was, after all, doing research on Bill's writing and on his relationship with Joel Reed. I wasn't trying to tread on his turf. If anything, I wanted to celebrate his writing and set some facts straight about his involvement with Joel. I never received an answer.

"So it goes," I thought. "I can always try again, once whatever the hell just happened has blown over."

Time marched on. By the time 2001 rolled along, I was wallowing knee-deep in what I thought would be the final edits on ***Blood Sucking Freak***. In 2002, Simon & Shuster published ***Sleazoid Express: A Mind-Twisting Tour through the Grindhouse Cinema of Times Square***. I reached out to Bill again. My inquiry was either unheard or ignored. I threw up my arms in defeat and continued working. I wanted to finish my own book by the end of the year.

That didn't happen. The trials of everyday life stepped in, and I was forced to take a break from everything. In retrospect, the respite was much-needed. My candle had all but burned out. "Enough!" I thought. "Rest up. Your day will come."

In 2005, I got my hands on a copy of ***Sleazoid Express*** number 7. It was touted as a special issue, and was subtitled: "The Biography of Joel M. Reed, Director of ***Bloodsucking Freaks***... or Games Con Men Play." I read the thing in one sitting.

The overall tone of Bill's narrative was one of malice. In thirty-eight pages, Bill Landis effectively managed to contradict almost all of the research that I had conducted. The entire thing was overripe with outrageous claims. Nothing added up.

The passage of time has a cruel way of settling scores. The next few years flew by at the speed of light. By the time I finally got around to doing the final edit on this manuscript, Bill Landis had passed away. The man whose words had so intrigued me died of a heart attack in 2008. He was only forty-nine-years-old.

I wanted to interview Bill Landis about ***Sleazoid Express***. I wanted to talk to the man about the weird things he experienced while

pounding the beat in Times Square. I wanted to talk to Bill about his involvement with Joel Reed. I did my best to reach out to him. I never got an answer.

JOEL REED: He was very immature. He had a lot of problems. But I really had nothing against him.

I did manage to talk to Jimmy McDonough, Bill's partner in crime during the autumn years of the first run of ***Sleazoid Express***. A brilliant writer in his own right, McDonough went on to become the celebrated biographer of Andy Milligan, Russ Meyer, and Neil Young. His relationship with Landis was fruitful, if not tumultuous. His memories of Joel M. Reed are all but nonexistent. And his portrait of

SLEAZOID EXPRESS

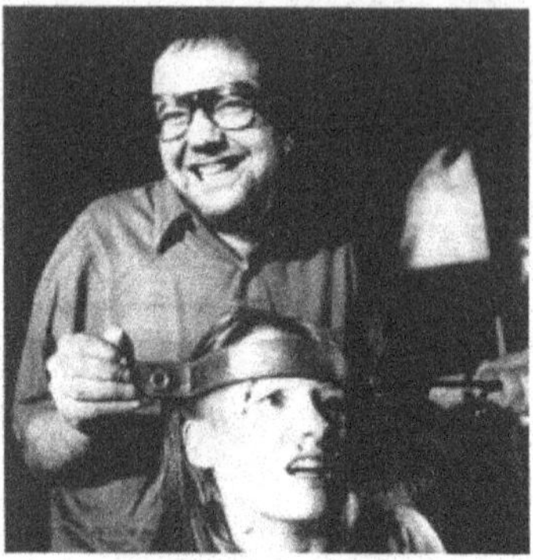

SPECIAL ISSUE:
THE BIOGRAPHY OF JOEL M. REED
DIRECTOR OF "BLOODSUCKING FREAKS"
...or "Games Con Men Play"

Landis is telling:

JIMMY MCDONOUGH: The more vicious or juvenile the sentiment, the more [Bill] enjoyed it. I could do a pretty fair impression of Joel Reed. Bill loved that. He even had me call Reed while I was impersonating him. That was odd. Imagine Joel Reed having an angry conversation with himself. Bill had everybody calling that poor slob, and I do mean everybody. He got calls from around the world! George Payne made the best ones. He'd use that low, nutty psychopath voice of his. At one point, we were going to write a book about the calls simply entitled ***The Caller***. A treatment exists for that somewhere. There were so many things we never got done it was frustrating. Bill and Joel.

Funny. I always thought Bill had more in common with Reed than he cared to admit.

Sleazoid Express number 7 disappeared from the world almost as quickly as it arrived. Just why, I can't say. Was the entire endeavor a quick one-off, designed to slander Joel M. Reed? Did my inquiries about things finally set Bill into a fit of rage? I have no idea. Will the truth behind the story ever be told? Probably not. The fingerprints that once littered the scene of the crime have long since been wiped clean.

The following interview with Joel Reed was conducted via telephone on February 12, 2016. A blizzard had just hit Detroit, and it was slowly making its way east...

JOEL: John Szpunar! How are you?

JOHN: ***I'm doing well, Joel. How are you doing?***

JOEL: Very good.

JOHN: ***How's the weather over there? Have you been hit by the snow yet?***

JOEL: The snow isn't here yet. I have to go out later to pick something up from the store.

JOHN: ***Can you hear me OK? I've***

got my phone hooked up to a new recorder.

JOEL: Yes, I can hear you. It's wonderful. The ghost of Bill Landis is here, circling around. He's saying, "You motherfucker!"

JOHN: ***Yeah, that's who I wanted to talk to you about.***

JOEL: I can talk about him. Just let me grab my eyeglasses. [pauses] Go ahead…

JOHN: ***OK. I just reread the issue of Sleazoid Express that Bill and Michelle did about you. Bill's major point of contention is… well, he claimed that you ripped him off. How did your business relationship with Bill begin?***

JOEL: Well, I met with Bill and his friend John LeMoss. I had some great ideas for making more pictures. The three of us decided to invest $2,500 apiece in a company. I think I mentioned this—I said to Bill, "It's great that you work at Con Edison." A few days later, he told me, "I quit." I said, "The whole idea was that you had a regular job." He had a good image with the suit and everything. He said, "No, fuck everything. I want to make movies." My advice to him was not to quit the job—to only be a freak part time. He went from being a real freak into being just another East Village freak. I asked, "What are you going to do for a living?" He said, "I'm very good at promoting myself." He arranged a show at Danceteria with Kenneth Anger and John Waters.

JOHN: ***Yeah, you told me about that years ago. How did that go?***

JOEL: Well, Bill seemed to be making a lot of money. He was getting five dollars a head. There were a lot of people there. And then, he suddenly became a little Adolf Hitler. He promised Kenneth Anger

money, and when Ken arrived, Bill had no money for him. He said, "You were supposed to do this for free! All the money goes to me!" There was a big blow up, and Bill got up on stage, screaming at Kenneth Anger. But I spoke, and John Waters spoke. John Waters and I got along very well.

JOHN: ***How was Bill making a living at the time?***

JOEL: He had various jobs in the neighborhood. He got a job working in a porn theater right down here on 42nd Street. They were looking to kill him because he was stealing money from the place. He called me one night and said, "They fired me! I left all of my stuff in a bar on West 49th Street! The Westies are going to kill me!" I went down there at four in the morning, and they were nice enough to give me his knapsack.

JOHN: ***How did Bill know John LeMoss?***

JOEL: John was his best friend. They both went to NYU. Bill had this plan to make a movie with me, and he brought John in as an investor.

JOHN: ***So, the three of you put up something like $7,500?***

JOEL: Yeah. And out of that, we spent about $1,200 for stationary and legal fees.

JOHN: ***Bill has publicly admitted that he was taking hard drugs during this time. Were you aware of this?***

JOEL: I didn't know it at first. But, certainly, within our relationship [it became obvious] within a couple of months. Bill kept on spending parts of the money. This is about the time where we broke up. He came up to my apartment, and half of the money was gone. He said to me, "Give me my money back." I said, "Bill, it doesn't work that way. I invested $2,500 and so did John. We've already spent around $2,000. If you want to end everything, you'll get one third of what's left." He said, "No! I want my money back! I'm working with these porn film gangsters, and they're going to come kill you."

In the course of all that, the checkbook was here. Bill was always writing checks. He'd say, "I've got to borrow $300 for my rent." He stole the checkbook and he cleared out the bank account in his name. He also took a check of mine for $700 that he found lying in the apartment. He even admits in the magazine that he was on speedballs at the time. He was pretty much a mess. Those are just some of the troubles that he caused me. Do you remember the Anvil and the Mineshaft?

JOHN: ***No, but I'm assuming they were gay bars?***

JOEL: Yeah, gay bars on the river. He started hanging out over there. These places were very open—guys were sucking each other off. He'd call me and say, "I'm drunk! I think I'm gay!" I said, "I don't give a shit if you're gay." He said, "You hate me! You took my money!" I had to go down to rescue him.

JOHN: ***What?***

JOEL: They didn't want him down there. They actually threw him out. I should have suspected that something was wrong when he started making phone calls from my house. He was calling this woman a cunt, and everything else. I asked, "Who are you talking to like that?" He said, "It's my mother! I'm going to get her, the cunt! Wait until I start calling my father!" He explained that his family was very conservative. His father was a Master Sergeant in the Air Force. He hated his parents, and he loved to cause trouble for them. I really pity them—he was their only child.

JOHN: ***Near the end, he started calling you...***

JOEL: He was calling me day and night. He thought he could disguise his voice. And every restaurant in the neighborhood was delivering meals to my house. And then, I

30 YEARS ON THE DEUCE

THE WICKED DIE SLOW

By Bill Landis

was getting calls from Florida for months.

JOHN: *From Florida?*

JOEL: Yeah, from a mental institution. But, Bill kept threatening to beat me up. I ran into him on 14th Street and said, "Hi, Bill!" He turned around and ran around 800 miles an hour to get away from me. He actually told his wife to attack me a couple of times.

JOHN: *That's insane!*

JOEL: She would run down the street and try to swipe me. She was taking pictures of me, following me on the train. But remember—whatever Bill wrote wasn't... he would tend to write about things that he remembered, you know what I mean?

JOHN: *I think so.*

JOEL: He wrote his version of things.

JOHN: *Well, a lot of the things in Sleazoid Express number 7 don't really add up. He said a lot of weird things about Vernon Becker.*

JOEL: He said that Vernon Becker slept on my couch. That's not true. And I know exactly what conversation he was referring to. Bill was with Vernon Becker and me, and we related a story about Nick Ray. He got things completely confused.

JOHN: *What's the story about Nick Ray?*

JOEL: We told Bill that Nick Ray slept on Fred Mogubgub's couch. I told him the exact anecdote that I'll repeat to you.

JOHN: *Who was Fred Mogubgub?*

JOEL: He was an animator. He was a friend of mine; he had a building in the Village. One day, he said, "Would you do me a favor? Nicholas Ray and his girlfriend are living in my studio, and I want to kick them out. Come by to see them and tell them that you're going to buy them dinner. They're starving. Nick's very careful of his luggage—he has two suitcases. He'll take them with him. I'm going to lock them out." I went down there and said, "I'd love to buy you dinner!" Nick said, "Oh, my God! You have a *face*, Joel! If you were in Hollywood, I could have made something of you!" I took him to this Italian restaurant a couple of blocks away. While we were out there, Fred locked him out of his apartment. So, that was one instance that Vernon and I told Landis about. I mean, I told him stories about myself. He never used anything that was positive. He'd either twist things around or not use them at all.

JOHN: ***Bill said some strange things about Marvin Farkas.***

JOEL: He said that I was using Marvin for money. I would have never considered that. He kept on saying that I was using Marvin as a mark.

JOHN: ***Well, the thing is that you remained friends with Marvin after all these years. Nothing adds up.***

JOEL: Yeah. But if you look at his other writings, he did the same thing. If you read his book about Kenneth Anger…

JOHN: ***I think Anger put a curse on Landis after that book came out.***

JOEL: Bill got mad at Kenneth Anger. This is when I didn't know that he was on drugs. He said, "I'm going to go over to Kenneth Anger's house to get $50. He said, "He likes rough trade." I said, "You're not rough trade, Bill. You look like a little kid." He went over there, and Ken Anger went into hysterics.

JOHN: ***He talked a lot about your friend Eliot, too.***

JOEL: Well, Eliot's dead now. He happened to be a transvestite—so what? He was a nice guy. Bill was always looking for a weakness in everybody's armor. He never said anything nice about anybody.

I used to practice Aikido in a place that was above a leather bar on 18th Street. I used to stop for hamburgers there—they were good. I told Bill about the place. The leather guys all looked like athletes. Bill went down there and he called me up. "You

SCREAMING CHEERLEADER CONTEST FOR FILM GALA

Preliminary eliminations for the first, annual, horror film, "Screaming Cheerleader Contest," will be held at Jay Photography, 351 W. 54 Street, N.Y., N.Y., 10019, on Wednesday, April 14th, between the hours of 3 and 7:30 PM. Entrants should be between the ages of 16 and 21 and be typical, teenage, cheerleader, horror film victim types. The contest is being sponsored by film critic - publisher Bill Landis, Peggy Doyle of Peggy's Restaurant, and John LeMoss of Lanmor Films, Inc. in conjunction with their Alternative Academy Awards gala to be held on April 29th. Among the judges will be such film lumanaries as Joel M. Reed ("Blood Sucking Freaks," "Dragon Lady"), Joe Sarno ("Inga"), Joseph Green ("The Head That Wouldn't Die"), Vernon E. Becker ("Dagmar's Hot Pants"), and Nick Demetroules ("Girl on a Chain Gang," "Teenage Mother."). Winner will receive screen tests and small parts in the Joel M. Reed - John LeMoss Production of the comedy, horror film, "The Renegade Ghouls of Kaplan's Swamp." For further information contact 585-6561.

don't know this leather bar! They threw me out!" I went down to find him. The guys at the bar said, "Is that scrubby guy your friend? He's such an idiot." I found him on the corner in a phone booth. He said, "Help me set the place on fire!"

So, this went on for years. I had the police after him. I had my phone number changed—he was calling me four times a night. And he had his wife call me. She'd show up across the street with a camera.

JOHN: ***That's something I don't understand. Why would she be taking pictures?***

JOEL: Well, he told her to do it. You can ask anybody—I've never had anybody hate me as much as Bill did. A lot of his fans will say that I'm bitter about this, but I'm really not. Bill was bitter. He was very bitter toward his parents, his former bosses, and his former teachers.

JOHN: ***Bill said some things about Eddie Jaffe that I don't understand.***

JOEL: What could he possibly say about Eddie? I introduced them. Eddie liked characters like Bill. I think he took him out to dinner. He might have even given him some money, so what could Bill say about him?

JOHN: ***He said that Eddie was a chicken hawk.***

JOEL (stunned): Eddie wasn't a chicken hawk. Eddie liked women. Chicken hawks like boys. Eddie was very generous. He'd let anybody stay at his place. If you came up, he'd feed you. He had a lot of bad points, but he was a nice guy. He was very charitable.

JOHN: ***The impression that I get, at least with the magazine that he did about you, is that Bill would never let the truth get in the way of a good story.***

JOEL: A lot of my friends were

not angels. If I could delve into their histories… well, they did some nasty things. But Bill Landis managed to get every story wrong. Everything he wrote about was supposed—it was something he'd heard. There were very few facts. He just recreated everything. I think he hated everybody. All of this was a very embarrassing part of my life. And all of it happened right here where I'm sitting. I certainly didn't make any money from him. He said, "Give me all the money! You fucked me! Take John's money and shove it up his ass."

JOHN: ***I wanted to ask you again about the Screaming Cheerleaders Contest. You told me about it a long time ago.***

JOEL: Yeah, that was for promotion. And Bill and John wanted to meet girls. I said, "Well, we'll have a screaming cheerleaders contest. We'll always get a couple dozen girls for that, and we'll get into the ***New York Post***." So, we did it. A bunch of girls were there, and we had somebody playing music. We put a couple of ads in the paper, and a lot of girls showed up. Of course, John LeMoss couldn't talk to the girls; he sat in a corner. We were going to use it as a basis to promote this film…

JOHN: ***This was for The Renegade Ghouls of Kaplan's Swamp?***

JOEL: Yes. But Bill and John scared all the girls away. I was thinking about this—I met this girl who was living at the Evangeline house in Gramercy Park.

JOHN: ***What was that?***

JOEL: It was a girl's residence. Bill said, "You got the best girl out of the whole thing!" I said, "Bill, you can take her out." He made an appointment to go out with her. The next thing I knew, the police told him not to call there anymore. "If that Bill Landis shows up one more time, we're going to have him arrested." He did something to irritate the girl, and she told him to go fuck himself.

JOHN: ***That's kind of weird.***

JOEL: The girl said something like, "I don't want to see you tomorrow. I have a headache." He said, "She's rejecting me!" and he started a campaign against her. I had a friend who was a superintendent on 75th Street. He was a big tough guy. One day, he asked me to look after his daughter. She went to high school on the west side. He wanted me to take her out for pizza or something. I said, "Bill, there's a nice girl over here. Why don't you take her out

for pizza and a normal movie." So he did. After that, her father wouldn't talk to me anymore. Bill kept ringing her bell every five minutes. They had to call the police.

JOHN: ***I'm trying to give this a timeline. Did Bill start harassing you after you fell out with him?***

JOEL: Yes. After the break up, he was on the phone twenty-four hours a day. He had people calling me all the time. And one of them was his wife.

JOHN: ***I know one of his friends from back then. He told me that Bill had him calling you.***

JOEL: Bill was still calling his high school teachers when I knew him.

JOHN: ***Really?***

JOEL: Yeah. He'd say, "I'm going to get this bastard! He gave me a bad mark in high school! You call him, Joel! He wouldn't know your voice!" But anyway, Bill had no case against me. Troma even told him to go fuck himself.

JOHN: ***Yeah, what was that all about?***

JOEL: He wanted to help them release ***Blood Sucking Freaks*** because he was in with all the midnight movies. They told him to fuck off.

JOHN: ***That reminds me—I wanted to ask you about Stanley Borden.***

JOEL: Stanley? What about him? He owned American Film Distributors.

JOHN: ***Well, Bill has quoted Stanley Borden as saying that it was a big waste of time to get involved with Blood Sucking Freaks.***

JOEL: Why was it a waste of his time? He tried to release it as a major picture. He took out full page ads in the ***Times*** and in the ***New York News***. He spent a lot of money releasing it. He and Allan Shackleton thought that my picture would do as good as ***Snuff***. But, like I've told you before, it dropped dead. What did Bill have to do with Stanley Borden?

JOHN: ***I was just wondering if it was an accurate quote. At this***

point, I really don't know.

JOEL: I don't know. Almost everything that Bill said was hearsay. I doubt if he met Stanley Borden. Bill mostly wrote whatever he thought was possible.

JOHN: ***Well, Bill was a big fan of the Olga movies.***

JOEL: Yeah, Stanley released those—the first S&M pictures. They were made for nothing, and they turned out to be film classics. But, see—Bill would repeat things that he heard from others. I don't think he had anything to do with Stanley Borden. He did introduce me to Kenneth Anger.

JOHN: ***What was he like?***

JOEL: Ken Anger was an old queen, but he was very nice to get along with. There was a point in time where he was going to fly me to the coast to do something, and Bill said, "No! No! He's going to rape you!" You could almost write a book about Landis.

JOHN: ***Thankfully, that's not my job.***

JOEL: Well, Bill Landis still has his fans. He wrote that book about 42nd Street. Did you ever get to meet him?

JOHN: ***No. I don't think his wife liked me very much, so I never got the chance to talk to him. I really loved his stuff, especially the early things he did with the first run of Sleazoid Express.***

JOEL: He, his wife, and their baby moved to Chicago. I don't think they wanted to go, but…

JOHN: ***Why do you think he had such a fixation on you?***

JOEL: On me? I don't know. He pestered me for a couple of years, and it was getting on my nerves. And then it went away. He was the only person in the world that ever put me down for anything. Everyone else was very happy with their relationships with me. In the end, I just got tired of defending him. I got tired of going down to the Anvil and the Mineshaft, trying to find him on the docks. He'd call me saying, "Save me, Joel! They're raping me! I'm turning into a woman!" I don't even know if he was on the docks. He could have been anywhere. I'd go down to help him. Whenever I walk down to the lower east side, I still think of him. His building's still there on 14th Street. In the end, Bill didn't get along with normal people. And I think he had a very sad life…

TAPE CUTS.

"There were some attempts at humor in the film."
—Joel M. Reed

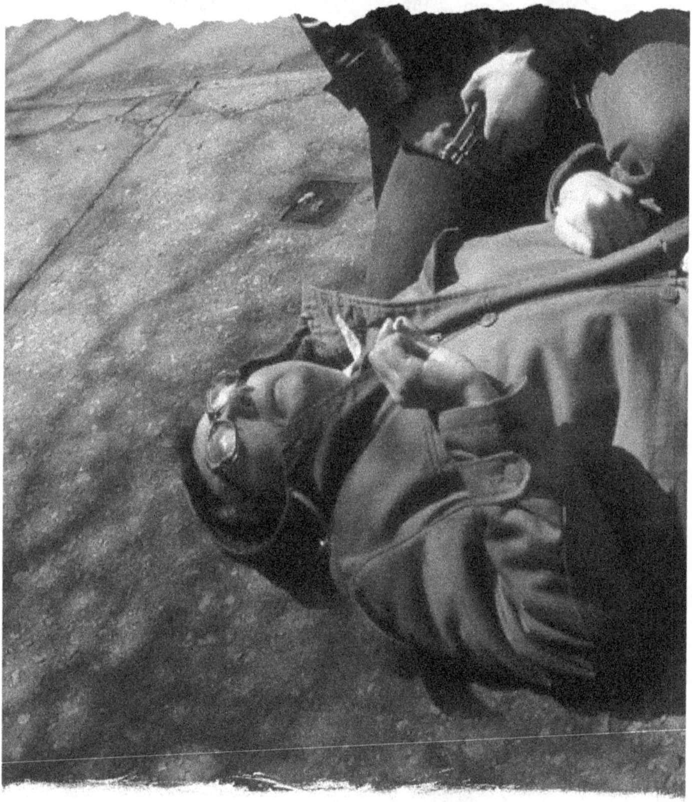

CHAPTER ELEVEN

NIGHT OF THE ZOMBIES

JOHN SZPUNAR: *You've talked a lot about Lorin Price, the producer of Night of the Zombies. What can you tell me about him?*

JOEL REED: *He's dead. I didn't even see his obituary. He called himself Lorin Ellington Price, the third. I called his mother once and said, "Can I talk to Lorin Ellington Price, the third?" She said, "There's no Ellington here and there's no third. There's just Lorin Price." I don't know where he came up with that name.*

Lorin Ellington Price, the third was the son of the head of the New York Merchandise Company. It's still there on 23rd Street. He was born with a silver spoon in his mouth. He was working for his father's company, making about $60,000 a year. This was in the '50s. I met him one night when this girl invited me over for Christmas Eve. There was nobody there for her kids. I went to her house—she lived on Third Avenue. She made dinner and Lorin came in. He said, "This is my girlfriend." He got undressed and put his pajamas on. That's how we met. We became friends.

He'd invite me over to dinner and order Chinese food and go out before it arrived. I'd pay for it and he'd come back. "Oh, you got the Chinese food!" Lorin was always a petty hustler.

I got him interested in theater when I was doing some things Off-Broadway. He got involved, he produced some Broadway shows. **George M.** *was the most successful. He used to have parties at his house all the time. He supposedly saw JFK running through the hall, naked when he was a Senator. I know his limousine was downstairs.*

One day, this press agent said, "Take this girl to a party at Lorin's." Her

EXHIBITOR'S SHOWMANSHIP MANUAL
THE DEAD ARE HUNGRY
and they're coming to eat you alive!
NIGHT OF THE
ZOMBIES
Nicholas Demetroules presents a Lorin E. Price film
in association with Evelyn Wasman
"NIGHT OF THE ZOMBIES"
starring JAMIE GILLIS • RYAN HILLIARD • RON ARMSTRONG and SAMANTHA GREY
Produced by LORIN E. PRICE • Written and Directed by JOEL M. REED • Color by TVC
Released by NMD FILM DISTRIBUTING CO. • Copyright © 1981 NMD Film Distributing Co., Inc. All Rights Reserved
R
THEATRE
NMD Film Distributing Co.
250 West 57th Street, New York, N.Y. 10019 • (212) 581-8011

name was Jane. I went to pick her up and she came to the door, totally nude. I brought her to Lorin's house, and he proposed. I thought they both were crazy. I went home and Lorin called me late in the night. We talked for a while and then he said, "Jane, get on the phone." She said, "You motherfucker! I'm marrying Lorin; he woke a judge up. We're getting married in four hours. Be there. We're going to have a twenty-four hour party." I couldn't believe it.

Well, Lorin really married Jane. He called the judge up, and the judge came over to the apartment. Then they went off on their honeymoon.

One night, Jane called me up and said, "You got to get over to the house, we're having a fucking dispute." So, I went over to their house and Jane was sitting there. She said, "You remember when we got married, we had an agreement that we could have any type of sex we wanted." I said, "I recall something to that effect." She said, "I told Lorin that he could bring girls over at any time." I said, "Yes, I recall that; you woke me up at four in the morning." She said, "Well, I bring these guys over, I bring my girlfriends home, and he doesn't bring anyone home." I said, "What's the problem?" She said, "I brought this big black guy over. He's thick like this. I brought him home and fucked the shit out of him, and I wanted to see him fuck Lorin. And Lorin wouldn't agree. The marriage is over!" I don't know how you can work something like that out.

At the time of all this, they were producing a play together starring Jane. At this point, they were getting divorced. Lorin said to me, "Come down and see the show." It was at the Cherry Lane Theatre. In the middle of the show, Lorin came up to me and said, "You motherfucker, who gave you tickets?" I said, "I don't know, Jane did." He said, "You fuck! You come up to the box office and I'll give you tickets! That piece of shit can't give you tickets!" And Jane said, "What do you mean, you fucking shithead? He's my friend!" They had this big fight while the show was going on and everyone was looking at them. I said, "Listen, this is a little bit too much for me." I went home. Again, at four in the morning, Lorin called me up. He said, "You motherfucker! You turned your back on me and walked out. You're never going to work in Hollywood. You're never going to work on Broadway. You're never going to work Off-Broadway. Lorin Price is going to be the king! You're dead!" About a half hour later, he called back and said, "I forgot to tell you. You'll never

Lorin Price (left) on the set of *Night of the Zombies*.

work in summer stock or regional theatre either!"

Well, that's how Lorin was. He called me up a few years later and said he had invested in some movie. These guys had made some awful movie, and he bought their share of the investment out. Then he started inviting me to his shows. They were all awful. I mean they were major shows with big people, but they were just awful. So Lorin decided to do a movie. He had a couple of my scripts. He actually did a couple of my plays to raise some money. But he always seemed to owe me money. He used to go into Sardi's and get people to give him money there. He'd get married to get money from these old women. One day he said, "I got the money to do this movie. What movie can we do?" I said, "We can shoot **Gamma 693** *in the Philippines. We can shoot part upstate." Someone suggested that we go to Germany with Jamie Gillis instead. Lorin said, "OK, how much do you need?" So we made out a schedule. This week we need this amount of dollars, the next week we need that. I made Lorin pay me all of my money upfront. So, we went to Germany and shot some of the film. Of course, Lorin ran out of money. Ron Dorfman finally got some out of him. Lorin wired me in London saying, "I'm sending you some more money, hang around for a couple of weeks." I assumed that he was full of shit. I came back and said, "Now we're going to do the big shooting. We need $40,000." He said, "This is the seventh week of production, you only need $3,000." That's how he thought. So we went to upstate New York and shot it. It took him a while to come up with*

Lorin, Joel, and Jamie.

the money. Actually, he didn't pay the extras and he didn't pay for the motel. The guy at the motel gave us free meals and we got free gas for the cars. We shot for about two weeks in New York. All of the payroll checks bounced and the unions came in. Lorin said, "Fuck it!" and we finished the picture anyway. I wanted to stop, but the union said that they would work for nothing. Lorin signed the mortgage on the picture. But the only reason this movie was made is because Lorin had hustled the money off somebody. It took him years to get anything back.

I once got this call from an old woman. She said, "How's our movie going?" I said, "What?" She said, "Well, I gave Lorin all this money to give to you to write a script. That was eight months ago, and I haven't seen him since." I ran over to him and said, "You fuck!" He said, "I would have given you some money, but I had to take her to Monte Carlo, and I had to take her to Spain! I invested about $32,000 and I only got around $25,000 back! I'm still down $7,000!"

He was like that. They once barred him from the bar at Sardi's for taking money from people. He was actually running away from a schoolteacher from Alabama. Lorin was married to her; he would marry anyone. He was a terrible person. I used to have a great deal going with him. I liked to eat at the 21 Club. One day I got in a fight with him and he said, "Don't desert me. I'll buy you dinner at the 21." I realized that any time I got mad at him, he'd invite me to dinner at the 21 Club. So when I felt like eating there, I'd tell him, "Lorin, I can't put up with this shit anymore." Because with him,

Script revisions on the set of *Night of the Zombies*.

at any time, he could be completely obnoxious. You'd go out with him to eat dinner and he'd say, "Don't put your salad plate over there." But he was a fantastic character, well-hated by a lot of people. He didn't pay any attention to the quality of anything he produced. I've seen shows that I could have re-wrote or directed and they would have been much better. He had this one show that no one paid any attention to, they just read from the script. Abe Burrows directed it. I think he was banging half the cast, he paid no attention to what was going on. And the show could have been great.

Lorin wasted everything, he went through all of his friends' money. But, he was a good fundraiser, a good salesmen. He'd be on the phone making calls. He'd call anybody. He'd pick up the **New York Times** *and say, "Oh, this guy just sold his company." He'd call him up: "You want to invest in my Broadway show?" And that's the way he was.*

But we made that movie and he lost all of his money. He ended up living in the Edison Hotel in a little rent-controlled room, half the size of this one. For years, he was paying around $72 a month.

One night, I was watching ***America's Funniest Home Videos****. There was some wedding on there. This Rabbi says, "I now pronounce you man and wife. Mrs. Price! How about a big kiss now!" This old woman pushes this old guy away and grabs the Rabbi. I looked closer and it was Lorin. He got married again in Fort Lauderdale, Florida. He was pretty old, he was shaking and everything, but, you know, that was his thing.*

Joel Reed collaborated with Lorin Price on a cheap zombie picture in 1979. The film was shot on location in Munich, Germany and in upstate New York. Originally titled ***Gamma 693***, ***Night of the Zombies*** is probably the most ridiculous film of Joel's career. Press reaction is almost always hostile. If Joel was condemned for going too far with ***Blood Sucking Freaks***, he was criticized for not going far enough with ***Night of the Zombies***.

*"The director of **Blood Sucking Freaks** strikes back with this putrid tale of the CIA vs. a plot to take over the world with Nazi zombies left over from WWII. A lousy rip-off of the above-average cheapie **Shock Waves**, with porn star Jamie Gillis proving he can act better with his clothes off."*

—James O'Neill, ***Terror on Tape***

*"Filmed in 1979 as **Gamma 693**, **Night of the Zombies** is a failed horror film that has an unusual premise, but not enough budget to carry it out. Writer-director Joel M. Reed, whose earlier gore opus **Blood Sucking Freaks** continues in release, has included oddball humor, but doesn't deliver the scares. The picture displays an R rating, but it has never been rated, according to the MPAA."*

—***VARIETY***, *6–20–1983*

No one can argue against their points. Nevertheless, almost in spite of its limitations, ***Night of the Zombies*** carries on, baffling the mind at every turn. The opening credits play out over grainy footage of the Bavarian Alps. Machine gun fire echoes through the trees as "Horst-Wessel-Lied" plays. The credits crawl up the screen. The usual suspects are involved. In fact, almost everyone in Joel's circle of misfits is represented somehow. Victor Kanefsky is the supervising editor. Jamie Gillis is the lead. Ron Dorfman plays the head of the CIA. Lorin Price plays a priest. Alphonso

NIGHT OF THE ZOMBIES

cast

Nick Monroe	JAMIE GILLIS
Dr. Proud	RYAN HILLIARD
Captain Fleck	RON ARMSTRONG
Prostitute	SHOSHANA ASCHER
Man in Bar	DICK CARBALLO
Sergeant Orville Freedman	RICHARD DE FAUT
C.I.A. Agent	ALPHONSE DE NOBLE
Susan	SAMANTHA GREY
G.R.O. Officer	JUNI KULIS
Priest	LORIN E. PRICE
Neo-Nazi	JOEL M. REED
Madam	RENATE SCHLESSINGER
Doorman	KUNO SPONHOLTZ
Zombies	JOHN BARILLA
	MICHAEL CASCONI
	GORDON C. DIXON
	BOB LACONI
	CHARLENE MATUS
	LEE MOORE
	GLEN A. PENCE
	DONALD K. WALLACE
	BILL WILLIAMS
	CARL WOERNER
	KAI WULFF

credits

Produced by	LORIN E. PRICE
Written and Directed by	JOEL M. REED
Edited by	SAMUEL POLLARD
Assistant Cameramen	TODD CRANDALL and JOHN BONNANO
Gaffers	CARL SCHERMAN and STEFAN CZAPSKY
Sound	CHAT GUNTER and ALVAR STUGARD
Grip	DUANE ARTHUR
Best Boy	TIM WALLACE
Make-up	DAVID E. SMITH
Special Effects	PETER KUNZ
Continuity	JANE SCHREIBMAN
Still Photography	JERRY KRUTMAN and JOHN BONANNO
Supervising Editor	VICTOR KANEFSKY
Assistant Editor	DEBORAH JACKSON
Post-Production Services	VALKHN, INC.
Rerecording Mixer	EMIL NERODA
Opticals and Titles	E.U.E./SCREEN GEMS
Costumes	EAVES COSTUMES
Casting	RICHARD CATALDI and DOROTHY PALMER
Production Manager	KENNETH BOWSER
Production Assistants	JAMES T. BULLETT and DANIEL TIEGER
Music and Sound	ONOMATOPOEIA, INC., MATT KAPLOWITZ and MAGGIE NOLIN

Color by TVC

Released by NMD Distributing Co.

DeNoble is a CIA operative. And Joel himself is a neo-Nazi.

Jamie Gillis stars as Nick Monroe, a down and out CIA agent who is sent to the Bavarian Alps when a United States Graves Registration officer is killed under mysterious circumstances. The head of the CIA (Ron Dorfman) believes that his death may be linked to several missing canisters of Gamma 693, an experimental gas that the United States planned to use against Germany in World War II. A very *young* looking biochemist (and WWII vet), Dr. Clarence Proud (Ryan Hilliard) is also interested in the canisters. He and his niece (Samantha Grey) soon join Nick in his investigation.

Things take a bizarre twist as soon as the trio hits the Alps. It seems that a letter was found near the Graves Registration officer's dead body. A letter written by an American GI believed missing in action in 1945. A letter dated 1979.

Soon, Nick finds himself running with a group of neo-Nazis (headed by Joel Reed), unearthing ghastly military secrets, and surviving several zombie attacks from a group of undead GIs who have been hiding in the German countryside for thirty-five years.

Nick learns that 693 was a chemical developed to keep

wounded soldiers alive until they could be taken to a medical unit. Several mortally wounded WWII soldiers hijacked the supply to suit their own needs and are reenacting battles in the desolate Bavarian Alps. Dr. Proud was once one of them, before he was exiled from their camp. He now desperately needs another dose of "the gas" before he begins to rot away.

The film ends with an unintentionally funny looking Proud attacking his niece as she lies in bed. Nick interrupts Proud's meal just in time and saves the day. But there is the slightest hint that Nick is now one of the walking dead himself.

Night of the Zombies is a far cry from the perverted excess of ***Blood Sucking Freaks***, but the film still contains several signature sequences and off the wall performances that hold their own. Reed's cameo as a neo-Nazi leader is a prime example. Joel, dressed in a powder blue sport coat, gives the film's best performance. His interpretation of the German language is beyond terrible, a strange mix of "neins" laced with a New York accent. Alphonso DeNoble's performance as an undercover agent is almost as good. Bloated beyond belief, he struggles with a German accent, but when attacked by Jamie Gillis, he reverts back to New York speak. Ron Dorfman looks like he's reading his lines off a teleprompter. And Ryan Hilliard is more than over the top as Clarence Proud. The camera lingers on a German prostitute as she undresses for Jamie Gillis. She

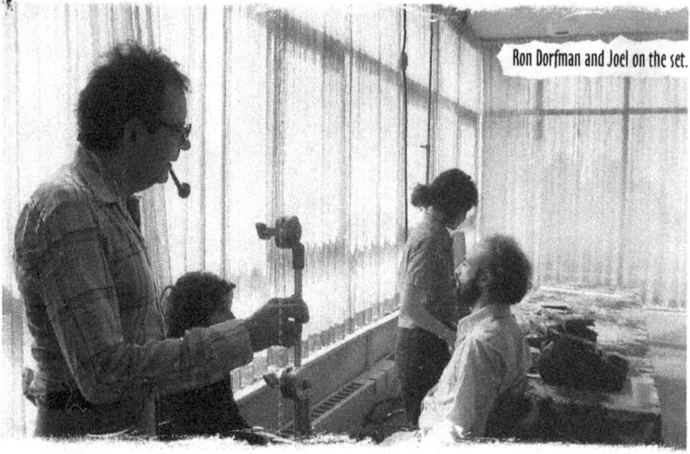

Ron Dorfman and Joel on the set.

might just as well be undressing for Joel. And then, there is Joel's death scene. Stabbed in the back by an unseen assailant, he flops around the streets of Munich like a fish out of water. One of the most memorable scenes has Ron Dorfman examining the blood of a wounded zombie and concluding that it is very similar to vegetable juice. This is ***Night of the Zombies***, Joel Reed's last film to date. An insane mess of priceless dialogue and plot holes, a totally mindless roller-coaster ride to nowhere. This is the film that Lorin Price took a gamble on. The mind wonders what kind of film Joel and Lorin would have come up with if they had worked together again.

JOEL REED: We were supposed to shoot ***Night of the Zombies*** in Asia with Japanese zombies, but I found out I could get air fare to Munich for a lot less. Munich's very much like New York, but it's clean. And on Saturday night, the Germans like to drive on the sidewalk and run people over. The whole town gets very drunk on the weekend. The people were pretty friendly; we'd go to a restaurant and everybody would sort of sit together. I went to Schwabing. A friend asked me if I wanted to go to the hippie part of town. I went over, and the guys had hair that was just a little longer than everyone else's. They didn't have ties on, that was it. I was there during the Fasching. The women run around topless and grab your dick on the street. It's this pre-Lenten carnival. I was tired, I'd been working. This guy wanted to go out

Dorfman gets his makeup.

but I said, "I have to work." By the time I got a chance to do anything it was already Lent. I should have gone out the other nights. They take Lent seriously over there. But it was scary in a way. They would drink a lot and crash their cars. There were so many accidents over there.

I kept asking this girl at our hotel for a date. She said, "I'll meet you in the sauna." I thought she was blowing me off. On the last day, Ron Dorfman asked me if I was going to the sauna. I said, "What the fuck do I want to go to the sauna for?" He said, "They're naked in there." I didn't realize that they had a coed sauna. I rushed over there and the girl who I had my eyes on was there, naked. I got a look at the equipment.

JOHN: ***What part of town did you stay at?***

JOEL: We were close to the Englischer Garten. We were at the Hilton. It was very cheap. Like $35 a night. Then, we went away to Austria. When we came back to Munich, we got a place that was only $15.

JOHN: ***Did you get to see much of the city?***

JOEL: We ate at some restaurants, that's about it. We went to one and it was so expensive I thought it would kill the whole movie budget. We tried to get into this famous coffee shop, but we could never get a reservation.

JOHN: ***How long were your work days for the film?***

JOEL: Twelve hours. You can never sleep when you shoot. In the old days of Hollywood, they used to shoot like it was a regular job.

No one does that anymore. It's like going to war when you're a director. So many stupid things come up.

JOHN: ***What was it like shooting over there?***

JOEL: Actually, it was nice. We got some shots by the Isar River, where all of the ritzy buildings are. That was all bombed flat in the war. They fixed the buildings up to be the same way they were before. I was walking around there once, looking at this beautiful old apartment building. A woman came walking over. I asked her how old the buildings were. She said, "1955." She showed me some pictures of the way things were before. They did a good job.

JOHN: ***Were the interiors shot in New York?***

JOEL: Some of the interiors were shot in Munich. Actually, just the church. We hired this German/Hungarian production manager. I called him up from New York. He said, "I vill have to get der permits in. You cannot shoot in Germany vithout the license." We got over there and he said, "You're shooting stinking picture! I have major movie going right now. You have to vait two veeks, then I get your license. You get arrested in Germany if you try to shoot your picture without the license!" So, Ron and I were sitting in the Hilton. We looked outside and the snow was up to the nose. We said, "We can't shoot anyway. You can't even move out there." Ron said, "Let's just test the camera." We went down to the Marianplatz and started shooting. Some people came up to us and we said, "Americanish TV!" They said, "Oh yes! Shoot, shoot!" The next day, we went to the church with Jamie. We went inside and a priest said, "Halten sie! Aus!" I said, "Americanish TV." He said, "Ohhhhh! Ja, ja!" I told him we were shooting a travelogue. He stopped the service and asked if I wanted to use an altar boy. He made us lunch.

We went out to shoot the chase outside and they got everyone off the street. One little kid came up and said, "You no have the permission, I know." I said, "You no have your balls if you don't shut up." It was a kid about this high. When we were done shooting, the Hungarian guy called me up. He said, "Ahh! This is your production manager! We have to charge you more money! You vill never get the license!" I said, "We shot the whole fucking movie already." He said, "You can't shoot! You vill get arrested!"

JOHN: ***Did you shoot anywhere else in the area?***

JOEL: We went to Austria. We had problems with the snow. It all melted after a few days. An American guy over there told us where to find snow. It's funny. This was the guy who said, "Why do you lock your car all the time? Nobody's going to take anything." He said, "I can't go with you, but just go this way and you'll find some snow. You'll either get to Austria or Italy. And by the way, if they have spaghetti on the menu, you're in Italy. Lock the car." So, we got to this little hotel in Austria. We started unloading the cameras and suddenly we heard, "The mayor wants to see you!" We told him what we were doing and he started picking up the tabs all over town. Ridiculous ski lift tickets; they helped us with everything. Everyone was very nice there. I met all the councilmen from the town. I got back to New York about three weeks later and picked up the ***Times***. All of the guys from that town were wanted by international surveillance. But, we just shot over there, we just winged it.

JOHN: ***You also shot some scenes in New York.***

JOEL: Yeah. Lorin in the church as the priest was done in New York. He didn't go to Germany. We shot a lot in upstate New York, where I'd go fishing. This was when Lorin wouldn't pay any of the bills and I said, "Isn't this great! We can stop shooting." And they said, "No, you can stay in the hotel. He'll pay." All of the restaurants would pay for our food. I said, "You're feeding us." They said, "Oh, Lorin will pay." I said, "No he won't! He's an animal!" And then Lorin bounced everyone's check. The union said, "Well, we might as well finish shooting the picture." SAG said OK, the makeup said OK. So, we shot the movie with no money. And Lorin was so obnoxious that he'd say, "I'm

Jamie and Joel.

a businessman! Just look at my records." If you did even minimal research, you could have him arrested and tortured. But, we shot the rest of that film on 54th Street. Here's something. You know the girl in the film who answers the door to the whorehouse for Jamie? She was Miss Pennsylvania. She got married to Lorin. I walked into PJ Clarke's around ten years later and she was there with him. So Lorin had some faithfulness.

JOHN: ***Didn't you shoot some exteriors at [porn film actor/director] Sean Costello's place?***

JOEL: That's true. We were outdoors in the snow. We rented his place. He had a farmhouse and a big barn.

JOHN: ***What was he like?***

JOEL: He was very obnoxious and insulting. He said, "You'll never have a career like mine! What are you wasting your time shooting this shit for?"

JOHN: ***How did you meet him in the first place?***

JOEL: He was a friend of Ron Dorfman's.

JOHN: ***How was it working with Jamie Gillis?***

JOEL: He was a wonderful guy, very easy to work with. I ran into him on Broadway a few years ago. He got big and fat. He said he was afraid of AIDS. He's a very well educated guy. Highly sexually charged up at times; he'd follow a girl for six weeks before he'd finally meet her. He was pretty good; he could have done much more.

JOHN: ***Do you have any funny stories about Jamie?***

JOEL: We had a lot of fun together when we were shooting in Germany. He said, "I'll get you laid tonight," and he took me to a Turkish leather bar. I said, "That's not my speed." He said, "The reason you don't get laid all the time is because you're too particular." He was very funny.

JOHN: ***Did Lorin end up paying everyone who worked on Night of the Zombies?***

JOEL: I think most everybody eventually got paid. Sean Costello said that he didn't, but Lorin paid him. I don't know what his case is. He might have been stiffed for one day, but I wouldn't know. I didn't have anything to do with the money on that picture. Lorin was the type of guy who would be difficult if you insulted him, and Sean probably insulted him. Jamie Gillis told me that he hated me because he didn't collect a salary.

JOHN: ***Really?***

JOEL: Lorin ran out of money. I knew him very well, so I made him pay me in advance. I hooked up with Jamie just before he died. He said, "You fuck! You never gave me my check." I didn't know about that—I had told Lorin to pay him. Later on, Ron got mad at me. I guess Lorin didn't pay him either. In fact, Ron [Dorfman] wouldn't talk to me after ***Night of the Zombies.***

JOHN: ***That's a shame.***

JOEL: They got into a lawsuit. Ron had the habit of telling people off. Lorin was late in paying him, so he sued him. Lorin and Ron both had a temperament. Like I said, I had learned how to deal with Lorin. If you just walked away from him, he would make amends with you.

JOHN: ***Did you guys try to work together again after Night of the Zombies?***

JOEL: Well, Lorin sort of lost all of his investors. As I recall, he got involved with these guys who made a film. Lorin got around $100,000 from his investors and gave it to these guys. They never finished the film. That ruined him with a lot of his people. He did a couple of Broadway shows after that. None of them were successful. I don't know… I stopped talking to him. He offered me an Off-Broadway play to direct, but he wanted to give me $200. I found out that he had $6,000 in the budget. He found a director who hadn't directed anything since 1940 who was agreeable. Of course, the play lasted one night.

JOHN: ***How did Night of the***

Zombies do theatrically?

JOEL: It played around; it did very well in Germany. It's on television every once in a while. I don't even remember what happened to it…

VICTOR KANEFSKY: I trained Sam Pollard [the editor of ***Clockers*** and ***Jungle Fever***] on ***Night of the Zombies***. That was Sam's first thing. He had never cut a feature before. In other words, I cut that with him—he was in training. I don't know if Joel was even involved with the edit. I don't know if he was with us when we saw the takes. I could be wrong—he might have come in when we were looking at the dailies to give us some suggestions. But he didn't sit in the cutting room and tell us what to do. He might have come in and told us to change something, but that was after we finished the film. He pretty much left us alone. But, ***Night of the Zombies*** was a co-edit. I'd co-edit with everybody. That's how I trained people. I had a training program going on, and I trained well over 200 people. Thirty or forty of them have gone on to really terrific careers in film. I'm pretty happy about that. ***Night of the Zombies*** was one of the movies that we cut. There was nothing particularly worthy about it, as far as I'm concerned.

The following interview was conducted on November 13, 2000, in Joel's apartment as we watched ***Night of the Zombies***.

JOHN: ***The stupid people at Staples gave me AAA batteries instead of AA. I'm going to have to take these back. I think the ones in my tape recorder should hold up pretty good.***

JOEL: Well, I probably have some if they run out. Who owns this picture? Prism?

JOHN: ***They can't be in business***

anymore. I don't know if anyone has the rights to distribute it. I think we have to sit through the Shock Waves trailer first.

JOEL: Oh, fuck that!

A familiar voice narrates a coming attraction for another Prism release. The volume is loud.

SHOCK WAVES TRAILER: *You are now in the deep end of horror!* ***Shock Waves****! Once... they were almost human!*

JOHN: ***Can you turn the volume down a little bit?***

JOEL: Yeah. Actually, as I said, I realized after making this movie that it could have been a great film classic if there were a bunch of teenagers who were World War II veterans in the '80s.

JOHN: ***So the original script for this was called Battalion of the Living Dead?***

JOEL: Yeah. I have a copy of that somewhere. I wrote the script, and Lorin wanted to raise the money for a picture. I think I told you that he wanted to do it in the Philippines with Japanese zombies. He raised the money and said, "Well... could you make it in Germany?" I said, "Yes," and he gave me the money to go to Germany. He said that he had all of the money together—of course, he didn't.

Bright blue credits flicker over a snow-covered landscape. The screen reads: ***Night of the Zombies II****.*

JOHN: ***I've always wondered why they added the 'two' to the title.***

JOEL: I guess they had to retitle it for legal reasons.

JOHN: ***Who was Evelyn Waxman?***

JOEL: She was one of the backers. This would have been a classic picture if I did it straight without any horror makeup.

JOHN: ***Were the shots for the opening credits filmed in New York?***

JOEL: Well, some of the picture was shot upstate, but Ron shot these scenes up in the Alps. There aren't any mountains that look like that over here. This has to be the Alps.

JOHN: ***So, Victor Kanefsky was involved with this one as well...***

JOEL: Yeah. Mainly because he was very cheap.

JOHN: ***Samuel Pollard is credited as the actual editor.***

JOEL: Yeah. He's now doing stuff for Spike Lee. At that time, he was

Victor's apprentice. Now this shot is in upstate New York, where I go fishing.

A man named Captain Fleck zooms across the countryside on a snowmobile. He stops in front of a canvas tent and makes his way inside. He is greeted by two men.

CAPTAIN FLECK: *Guten Tag, meine Herren. Can you tell me what you are doing in this area? It's restricted. Two hikers were murdered on this very spot last year by terrorists. I'll have to ask you to leave.*

JOHN: *Is this guy actually from Germany?*
JOEL: I don't know if he was from Germany, but he spoke fluent German. He was an opera singer.

One of the men stands to greet the Captain. He introduces himself as Orville Friedman.

ORVILLE FRIEDMAN: *We have special permission to remain here. Master Sergeant Orville Friedman, US Army Graves Registration Service.*

Friedman extends his hand as his partner introduces himself.

CLAUDE SCHULLER: *Claude Schuller, Weimar Archive Division.*
CAPTAIN FLECK: *Graves Registration? War memorials? So, you are not tourists...*
ORVILLE FRIEDMAN: *Tourists? No, we're looking for the remains of troops missing in action since World War II.*

JOHN: *Who are these two guys right here?*
JOEL: Well, one guy is an American actor—he's done a lot of shit. He came in from the coast. The guy on the left is actually a German actor. I saw some weird video—like "Ripley's Believe it or Not" or something—I was watching it about a year ago. It had a story about a guy who lived in Cleveland, Ohio. He woke up one day and started speaking fluent German. It was the guy on the left!
JOHN: *Is this set just a painted room or something?*
JOEL: No, it's the inside of the tent. Oh, the tape is muted. Do you want it muted?
JOHN: *We should probably turn it up a little bit so I can hear what's going on when I'm transcribing this. Not too loud, though.*

Fleck tries his best to persuade Friedman and Schuller to spend their nights in town, but his warnings of local bandits fall upon deaf ears. In a last-ditch effort to ensure their safety, he begins to speak of local legend.

CAPTAIN FLECK: *This very grove is supposed to be infested with the living dead. Zombies, I believe you call them?*
ORVILLE FRIEDMAN: *Neither of us believe in zombies. But we do believe that part of a retreating Nazi SS battalion and an American chemical warfare unit ran into one another in these hills… and fought it out to the last man.*

JOEL: This was shot in my friend's studio. They didn't charge him rent for a year. Finally, they asked him to leave.
JOHN: ***Where was that place located?***
JOEL: It was on 54th Street, right opposite the police station. They're tearing down the whole block now. Actually, his old building is still there. It became 100 percent male porn. A big producer of gay magazines had the upstairs floor, and he later took over the bottom floor.
JOHN: ***For some reason, I seem to like this film quite a bit.***
JOEL: Well, it grows on you. You'll be asked to lecture at Harvard on your relationship with me (laughs). But this was a film that I tried to quit. Lorin kept on giving me money.
JOHN: ***What kind of shooting ratio did you have for this?***
JOEL: Oh, never more than four to one. One set up a couple of close-ups. I mean, in the old days of Hollywood, if you shot more than that, you'd be fired. But this could have been a great movie. Just imagine—they go out and they get killed by teenagers. There would have been a bigger mystery.

Friedman and Schuller continue with their investigation. They dig through the snow and uncover a human skull—proof enough to justify their search for undocumented casualties. That night as they relax in their tent, they are startled by the sounds of gunfire.

CLAUDE SCHULLER: *That's a German machine gun! I know a German machine gun when I hear it!*
ORVILLE FRIEDMAN: *Don't tell me you believe that living dead bull!*
CLAUDE SCHULLER: *If they are*

out there... we've got to make sure that they rest in peace!

JOHN: ***How many cameras did Ron have?***

JOEL: You only shoot with one camera, Hollywood style. You can't really light for more than one camera.

JOHN: ***I guess that's true. I've noticed that you never use a zoom lens.***

JOEL: I don't like the zoom lens. It doesn't have the depth of focus. But, this is stupid. If they were young looking Nazis it would have been better. Imagine this scene if they were attacking them on skateboards. Of course, I wasn't thinking. I just wanted to get my money and get out of there.

JOHN: ***Well, you got a trip to Germany out of it.***

JOEL: Yeah, that was nice. This picture cleaned up in Germany. They really liked it.

Schuller ventures out into the night. He is greeted by an army of the living dead and is soon the victim of a German machine gun.

JOHN: ***So, David Smith did the makeup for this.***

JOEL: Yeah. He was Dick Smith's son.

The sound of gunfire grows louder. Concerned for his friend's safety, Friedman decides to investigate. He walks out into the snow and is quickly cut down by a volley of lead.

JOHN: ***Who did the casting for this?***

JOEL: I don't know. Dorothy Palmer and a couple of casting agencies. Lorin fucked some of the girls.

JOHN: ***Do you have any recollection at all about how you got Jamie Gillis?***

New York, not Munich.

JOEL: I met him someplace and thought he'd be good. We didn't have any money. I think I met him at Gerry Damiano's when he was shooting a picture. I had coffee with him, or something.

JOHN: ***Was he pretty easy to work with?***

JOEL: Yeah, he was a wonderful guy. I finally forced him to have a fit, but he was just acting. He was living with [restaurant critic] Gael Greene at the time. I think I still have one of those hats and jackets. Can we auction them off on eBay? I know I have the jacket.

JOHN: ***How long did preproduction take for this film?***

JOEL: Preproduction? There was no preproduction. We flew to Germany and we made the movie. But Ron Dorfman did a lot of work on this. He was like the production manager.

Dawn brings peace to the land as Captain Fleck pulls up to the tent. He is greeted by the dead bodies of Friedman and Schuller.

CAPTAIN FLECK: *I warned them about bandits! Any tracks?*

GERMAN OFFICER: *Only this.*

The officer hands Fleck a letter.

CAPTAIN FLECK: *One of these poor souls probably dropped it. I'll put it into the mail.*

Satisfied with their investigation, Fleck and his men mount their snowmobiles and race off toward town. In their haste, they do not notice that they are being watched. A young man dressed in a SS uniform sits in thought as he observes them from afar…

JOEL: This Nazi fanatic was hanging around. He came to us when we were up there and said, "Do you want to use my uniform and gun? I don't want to pay you too much for it." I said, "We'll use it for free. We'll even put you in the movie." I went to his house and his mother took me aside. She said, "I don't know why he's like this! We sent him to the psychiatrist and everything." It's funny—at the end of the movie, he said, "I don't think I'll be a Nazi anymore. I'll get into films."

An establishing shot of the Pentagon fills the screen. Special Agent Nick Monroe (Jamie Gillis) walks across a hallway and into a briefing room. A man named Collins (Ron Dorfman)—the head of the CIA—is waiting for him.

JOHN: ***So, where was this scene shot at?***
JOEL: At the Best Western Hotel on Ninth Avenue.
JOHN: ***This is Ron and Jamie…***
JOEL: Yeah.
JOHN: ***Whose decision was it to make Ron the head of the CIA?***
JOEL: We didn't have any money, and we needed somebody that day. He's not bad. And Jamie's not a bad actor. He just established himself as a freak. The enema bandit—we'll never know the heights of what he could have done. There's a path of resistance in the movie business.

COLLINS: *I have a piece of puff for you. A minimum exposure assignment.*
NICK MONROE: *Minimum exposure? I've heard that before. I'm still walking around with a couple of slugs from the last minimum exposure assignment. What is this, World War III?*
COLLINS: *Would you believe World War II?*

Collins hands Monroe a top-secret file. Nick pages through it and frowns.

NICK MONROE: *OK… what have we got to do with the Graves Registration team killed in Bavaria?*
COLLINS: *Nick, they don't matter. I want you to go down there and uncover a lead on Special Unit C—a chemical warfare outfit that they were looking for. They were armed with Gamma 693, a lethal gas that the*

United States was going to experiment with on the Germans. Nick—Gamma 693 could be more destructive than any bomb.

NICK MONROE: *I thought this was a minimum exposure assignment.*

COLLINS: *There's a biochemist flying into town who can deactivate the agent for you. If… if you can find it.*

JOHN: ***How long did it take you to write this one?***

JOEL: I don't know. Probably a couple of weeks. I wrote the original script over in the Philippines. For some reason, they wanted to do two or three movies.

JOHN: ***OK, so that explains the press clipping that said you had a deal going over there.***

JOEL: Yeah. They wanted to make some quick pictures.

A bugle call accompanies an exterior shot of the Chemical Warfare Laboratories building at Fort Detrick, Maryland. Nick Monroe sits in a room with Dr. Clarence Proud (Ryan Hilliard), the biochemist that Collins spoke of.

JOHN: ***So where was this place?***

JOEL: This was shot at the same hotel. We just used a conference

Reed Schedules 4 Pix In Philippines

Former Broadway publicist Joel M. Reed, whose fourth feature film, "Wit's End," now is in release, has three more action, adventure, horror films ready to be shot on location in the Philippines.

First is "Guerrilla Girls Against the Viet Cong," a beauty-beast satire of war flicks. Second, "The Curse of the Ghoul Battalions," involves Japanese and American zombies in World War II. Third is "The Tiger and the Dragon," about a group of cutthroat mercenaries in Southeast Asia.

room. All of this was shot in the same day—the last day of shooting.

DR. PROUD: *Excellent! I never thought I'd ever get involved in a James Bond-type caper. I thought you people didn't exist, outside the world of novels.*

NICK MONROE: *Actually, Dr. Proud, our work isn't as glamorous as you may think.*

DR. PROUD: *Nick—may I call you Nick? It is absolutely imperative that we retrieve that gas as soon as possible. The containers may start leaking any day now.*

NICK MONROE: *What happens then?*

DR. PROUD: *Well, the gas may be effective enough to kill two million people. Or, on the other hand, be perfectly harmless. I don't know what, exactly. The scientist who developed it*

Nick Monroe confronts a young GI.

destroyed his notes and himself when he realized we were actually going to use the gas. I was his assistant back in '44.

NICK MONROE: *1944? You don't look that old. Poison gas… no wonder they gave me this assignment.*

DR. PROUD: *I wouldn't worry about it if I were you. We have developed a deactivating foam.*

NICK MONROE: *And what if the stuff doesn't work?*

DR. PROUD: *Well… you didn't expect to live forever, did you?*

JOHN: *What's the story on Ryan Hilliard?*

JOEL: He lived in this big loft in Brooklyn. I went to a party there, and he said that he was trying to be an actor. He's not in Brooklyn anymore?

JOHN: *I really have no idea. I recently saw him in a movie from 1979 called Incoming Freshmen.*

JOEL: You could look him up, if he's still with us. A lot of people have shot themselves after being in my movies.

Nick meets with Collins at the Pentagon. The two compare notes, and Collins produces a familiar letter.

COLLINS: *This was written by a member of Special Unit C to his sister.*

NICK MONROE: *OK, it was dated last month and written with a ballpoint pen.*

COLLINS: *I know that, Nick. His sister received it last week. It was written by a man reported missing in* *action in 1945!*

NICK MONROE: *Collins, the next thing you're going to be telling me is that there's been an entire US chemical warfare outfit hiding out in the Alps for thirty years.*

JOEL: This was shot at the Best Western. That's the stairway of the Best Western on 53rd Street and Ninth Avenue. I don't know what it's called today—it's had several names. We made a deal with them; we rented two rooms.

JOHN: *What kind of insurance did you have when you were shooting?*

JOEL: Well, we had liability insurance on the production, and insurance for errors and omissions.

Time passes. The towers of the Frauenkirche stand tall in the sky.

JOHN: *So, now we're in the heart of Munich.*

JOEL: This is the Marienplatz, yeah. I actually watched a German movie and it had the same shot in it. There's the Glockenspiel—the singing clock. I directed this scene from a nearby coffee shop. It was so cold.

The soothing chimes of the Glockenspiel ring out as Nick Monroe enters an elegant cathedral. He makes his way over to a confessional booth and steps inside.

JOEL: Actually, the shot in the confessional was shot in a church on 40th Street.

JOHN: *So, Lorin didn't actually go to Germany?*

JOEL: No. We shot this in New York. We just bought a little screen to divide them from the hardware store.

An undercover agent posing as a priest (Lorin Price) greets Monroe with a weary smile.

FR. LORIN: *May God save us from the CIA. Nick! What are you doing in town? Starting World War III?*

NICK MONROE: *I'm finishing World War II. I'm looking for deserters.*

FR. LORIN: *Deserters? Deserters from where?*

NICK MONROE: *The US Army.*

FR. LORIN: *You must be kidding! Nick! World War II…*

JOHN: *Is this the only film that Lorin produced?*

JOEL: Well, these two brothers

The mysterious bearded man.

made some films, and Lorin put up a lot of money. They stole it from him. They made a documentary, and they clipped Lorin. They produced about twelve Broadway and Off-Broadway shows.

Later in the evening, Monroe meets with Dr. Proud in a smoke-filled restaurant.

JOEL: This was shot next door at the Japanese restaurant.
JOHN: ***Really? Next door to your apartment?***
JOEL: Yeah, right next door.
JOHN: ***I always figured this for Munich.***
JOEL: You can go and look. They haven't changed the décor in years.

NICK MONROE: *I'm sorry I'm late.*
DR. PROUD: *This is a beautiful restaurant, Nick. You have impeccable taste. You are not as crude as your first impression would lead one to believe.*
NICK MONROE: *I'm glad you feel that way, doc. Now why don't you drop dead?*
DR. PROUD: *Me? I'm going to live forever.*

Proud introduces Nick to his niece Susan (Samantha Grey), and insists that she accompany them on their adventure.

DR. PROUD: *It has been cleared through channels, Nick—all the way to the top.*
NICK MONROE: *Why?*

A quickie for Jamie.

DR. PROUD: *Because they always bring a dumb blonde along on missions like this.*
NICK MONROE: *Who is they?*
DR. PROUD: *The movies!*

JOHN: *Where did you get Samantha Grey from?*
JOEL: I don't know. I only hired her because nobody else showed up.
JOHN: *Believe it or not, I saw her in a movie that Sean Cunningham directed called Here Come the Tigers.*
JOEL: She was terrible. I should have hired somebody else. Actually, I should have went with my first instinct and cut out all of this exposition.

Dr. Proud is distracted as a heavy-set woman walks into the room. The two lock eyes, and the chemist excuses himself. He leaves Monroe and Susan alone at their table as he heads off to pursue her ample charms.

JOHN: *Do you have any idea who this woman is?*
JOEL: Well, Proud likes to eat fat women.
JOHN: *Yeah, but do you remember who she was?*
JOEL: No. She was just there.

Proud approaches the fat woman and makes his move. The two smile at one another as an impromptu 'courtship' begins.

JOHN: *This scene always cracks*

me up.

JOEL: Actually, I based it on my friend from MGM who always liked fat girls. Did I ever tell you the story? We were sitting with Sophia Loren, and everybody was staring at her. This big fat girl came in. My friend left and started talking to her. To each their own.

Monroe and Susan are left alone to chat. Nick wastes no time as he tries to unravel her secrets.

NICK MONROE: *Just what I needed. An absent minded professor.*

SUSAN: *I think he'll surprise you when things get rough. He's totally without fear.*

NICK MONROE: *Are you his "niece", or are you his niece?*

SUSAN: *Uncle Clarence has been looking after me since my father got killed in Vietnam. I'm an Army brat. Why? What did you think? My father was Uncle Clarence's younger brother. Besides, I'm not his type.*

NICK MONROE: *I see. Quantity, not quality.*

JOEL: Oh, God. That's pretty stupid.

JOHN: ***It's a funny movie, though.***

JOEL: Well, in retrospect it is.

JOHN: ***I always thought it would have been great if you would had have made a sequel to this, or didn't kill off Tom at the end of Wit's End. You could have brought Dave Dearborn back for another movie—maybe even teamed him up with Nick Monroe.***

JOEL: Well, Tom calls me once a month…

After dinner, Monroe hits the bars in search of a clue that will lead him to Special Unit C. He strikes up a conversation with a mysterious bearded man.

BEARDED MAN: *World War II? You must be kidding. There are thousands of German war veterans in the city, but no US battalion. You should know better to go looking for people the way you are. They may find you first.*

NICK MONROE: *That's exactly what I want them to do.*

JOHN: ***OK, where's this at? Is it in Europe or in New York?***

JOEL: This is at the same bar. Look across the street. If you look closely, you can see a yellow cab drive by. But, the guy with the beard at the bar committed suicide. He shot

himself in front of everyone at dinner. Right after the movie. He had a townhouse in the Village and a beautiful young wife. He came down to dinner and said, "Fuck it."

Monroe finishes his drink and walks out on the street. A mysterious character follows him as he slowly moves along.

JOEL: This was shot in Munich.
JOHN: ***Do you happen to remember what street it was shot on?***
JOEL: It was just a side street with a lot of bars. I guess you could look at the street signs.

Nick Monroe enters another bar. He is soon joined by his silent pursuer, a neo-Nazi played by Joel M. Reed.

JOHN: ***Where was this scene shot?***
JOEL: This was back at the Best Western. We shot it on the same day as the other scenes.

NEO-NAZI: *You were talking about World War II.*
NICK MONROE: *And you just happened to overhear? I'm looking for American deserters from World War II.*
NEO-NAZI: *So are we. We have a group here in Bavaria that likes to see things done in an old fashioned manner.*

The two men exchange information and agree to meet again.

JOHN: *Do you remember how many feet of film you shot?*
JOEL: What is it, forty feet a minute for 16mm? Probably 21,000 feet of film.

Monroe catches up with the killer and corners him in an alley.

JOEL: This was shot back in the studio where we shot the tent stuff. I just ran into [the guy who plays the assassin] in the supermarket. He does a lot of work as an extra.

The assassin smiles and bursts into laughter.

NICK MONROE: *What's so funny?*

Monroe sneers, shoots the man three times, and clubs him over the head for good measure. Convinced that the killer is dead, he makes his way over to see a local operative.

JOHN: *So, now he's going to go into a camera shop.*
JOEL: That was a Radio Shack on 84th Street. We put the German magazines and posters up. We gave the owner $50.

Monroe enters the camera shop. An obese man named Krieg (Alfonso DeNoble) is there to greet him.

KRIEG: *You work for the company?*
NICK MONROE: *I want to see the local station boss.*
KRIEG: *No. The local station is closed down.*

Monroe grabs the fat man's arm and wrenches it behind his back.

NICK MONROE: *Come on! Where is he?*
KRIEG: *All right! Number 7, Lehderstrasse. Ask for the boss!*

JOHN: *I love the way Alphonso's accent keeps changing throughout this scene.*
JOEL: I think Alphonso killed himself after this movie, too.
JOHN: *Did you know him very well?*
JOEL: Well, I knew him to talk to him.
JOHN: *Was he from Jersey?*
JOEL: Yep.

Monroe storms back outside as Krieg nurses his arm. Before long, another stranger enters the shop. He wastes no time in stabbing Krieg in the stomach.

Jamie Gillis in his element.

The fat man screams and falls to the ground.

JOHN: *What do you remember about the music for this film?*

JOEL: This guy named Matthew Kaplowitz wrote a lot of it. He said he was lowering himself to do this shit.

Nick Monroe wanders over to Weidermeyer Street. He takes out the note that the neo-Nazi gave him. On it is scribbled a name: Schefield. He finds the address and enters an apartment building. He rings a doorbell and a young man answers.

NICK MONROE: *Is your father around?*

SCHEFIELD: *No, not really. He's back in the States. He's been dead a long time.*

NICK MONROE: *Are you a GI?*

SCHEFIELD: *Yeah. So what?*

NICK MONROE: *AWOL?*

SCHEFIELD: *Hell, no. I just live off base. What's up?*

NICK MONROE: *Never mind. Thanks.*

JOEL: This was shot at Ron's apartment building on 83rd Street or something.

Monroe makes his way down to the

lobby. An elderly doorman stands at his post.

NICK MONROE: *How long has he lived here, Schefield?*
DOORMAN: *Three years. Wait—eins, zwei, drei—THIRTY years!*

JOEL: The doorman was a guy named Kuno Sponholz—he was an agent for child actors. He was in ***Radio Days***, the film by Woody Allen.

Monroe walks over to see the station boss on Lehderstrasse. For some inexplicable reason, he is greeted by a madam.

JOEL: Lorin went out with that girl for ten years after this movie. Her mother made her go home to Ohio, and Lorin used to fly out to see her.
JOHN: ***That's not the girl that he married, was it?***
JOEL: No. Now, this is Ron's apartment. He moved the stuff out of his editing room.

MADAM: *You will see the boss later. In the meantime, I'll get you a nice girl.*

The madam quickly returns with a pretty blonde. Nick smiles as she undresses.

JOHN: ***Who's this playing the hooker?***
JOEL: Shoshana Ascher. Everybody was madly in love with her. Her friend was in a lot of movies. They hung around together. People were always sending them fur coats. She finally married a bigshot at Disney or something. She was beautiful.
JOHN: ***Jamie handles this scene well.***
JOEL: Jamie does sex very well. He gets a spontaneous hard-on and he believes in it. Actually, if Jamie had had another start, he could have gone on to medical or dental school. He's just overly-sexed.

The prostitute stands naked in front of Monroe. Before she can service him, he notices a carefully camouflaged two-way mirror on the wall. Nick picks up a chair and smashes it, sending a would-be peeping tom screaming down the hallway.

JOEL: There are moments in this film. You know, the CIA had two whorehouses by the UN. They were photographing everybody. It was in the paper. All of the massage parlors were owned by the CIA.

Monroe and Collins hold a meeting. The head of the CIA is none too pleased with Nick's unorthodox method of investigation.

COLLINS: *He could have lost an eye!*
NICK MONROE: *What was I supposed to do, put on a show for you? Is your job that boring?*
COLLINS: *It was, until you shot up half of Munich.*
NICK MONROE: *You know I don't work that way. This whole thing sounds like a typical company screw up. Who was the guy who got hit in the kidney?*
COLLINS: *A local stoolie.*
NICK MONROE: *He had me on to something. What about the guy in the backyard?*
COLLINS: *I don't know anything about that. What did you do to Krieg?*
NICK MONROE: *I twisted his arm a little.*
COLLINS: *Twisted his arm? The police say that someone killed him and ate him in the back of the camera store.*
NICK MONROE: *Let's go look at the other stiff.*
COLLINS: *Are you planning to save him for breakfast?*

JOHN: *What did Ron think about this movie?*
JOEL: Well, Ron was a guy who was always saying, "I'm going to help you make a great movie." He got all these awards for ***Groupies***, but he was very good at porn.

The two agents return to the alleyway where Monroe shot down the Nazi's assassin. There is no corpse to be found—only a slight trace of red liquid on the ground.

NICK MONROE: *What is that, blood?*
COLLINS: *No, this isn't blood. Vegetable juice.*

Baffled by their find, Monroe, Collins, and Dr. Proud plan their next move.

DR. PROUD: *What does all of this have to do with our assignment?*
COLLINS: *Well, I've done a little reading, and would you gentlemen buy... zombies?*
DR. PROUD: *Why do I have to sit here and listen to this insipid repartee? I am a scientist! Let's get on with it, shall we?*
NICK MONROE: *He's right! We're*

here to find the gas.

JOHN: *Why didn't you ever make another movie after this?*
JOEL: Nobody asked me to. I should have gone to the coast. Everybody told me to go out there.

A Jeep drives down a snow covered street. Monroe, Proud, Susan, and Captain Fleck set up camp in the same area where Friedman and Schuller were murdered.

JOEL: This is back in upstate New York. Strangely enough, all of the farmers up there were German.
JOHN: *How many days did you shoot up there?*
JOEL: Probably two weeks. We stayed in a motel.
JOHN: *How many people went?*
JOEL: Maybe twelve people, if you count the crew. Lorin was there, and we had three or four actors. We picked up extras from the local drama society.
JOHN: *Did Lorin hang around the set a lot?*
JOEL: Not really. He didn't hang around because people wanted to get paid. In fact, at this point, nobody had gotten paid. I think I told you—the guy from the motel was feeding us. I said, "What are you doing? You're keeping this movie going!" He said, "Oh, I like to make movies!"

Monroe and company gather around a table in their tent. Susan excuses herself and walks out into the moonlight. She is soon menaced by one of the living dead—a rotting corpse dressed in a GI uniform. By chance, Nick Monroe hears her screams. He rushes to her rescue and carries her back inside.

DR. PROUD: *Bandits! The police should be more alert!*
NICK MONROE: *I'm not so sure.*
DR. PROUD: *Did you see her attacker?*
NICK MONROE: *It was dark—I'm not sure.*
CAPTAIN FLECK: *Not sure about what?*
NICK MONROE: *If it was human.*

JOHN: *What can you tell me about Nick Demetroules? Didn't he distribute this?*
JOEL: Yeah. He was Jerry Gross' partner. Jerry eventually bought Nick out for a million dollars or something. He immediately went bankrupt, so he started NMD

Pictures.

JOHN: *Was NMD successful?*

JOEL: Yeah, within the range of what he did. Nick made a lot of money. He sort of retired and bought a big house in Westchester. He's dead now.

The night of terror continues. Another group of zombies finds its way to Monroe's camp. They creep through the darkness and enter the tent. It seems as though they have eyes for Susan.

SUSAN: *NO! NO!*

The woman's screams wake the sleeping men. The zombies laugh as they drag their prey out into the darkness.

JOHN: *What were your hopes for this film when you started making it?*

JOEL: The hope was that Lorin would pay me some money. That's the only reason I did it. He probably gave me $20,000, which was more than I was even supposed to get. Lorin never really got ahead of stealing money from people. He just grabbed money and lived on it.

Suddenly, an Army commander appears from the shadows. He orders his battalion of zombies to cease their attack.

ARMY COMMANDER: *Fools! You were ordered to stay away from that camp! We cannot draw attention!*

JOHN: *How long did it take Dave Smith to do the makeup?*

JOEL: I guess he worked on the principal zombies all day.

JOHN: *I'm taking it that most of the night scenes were shot at the same time.*

JOEL: Yeah. We shot the night shots at night and we shot all of the tent shots in the tent. Everything that you see in the tent was shot together so we didn't have to rebuild things. It was continuity of place.

Monroe collects the fragile Susan in his arms and leads her back to the tent. Once inside, she does her best to explain the terror that she faced.

SUSAN: *It wasn't a man! It was a thing!*

NICK MONROE: *A zombie?*

DR. PROUD: *I don't want to hear any more of this zombie drivel! Oh well… that's what you get for bringing a woman along.*

JOHN: ***If you would have decided to shoot this in Asia, do you think Marvin Farkas would have been involved?***

JOEL: No. We would have shot in the Philippines. I wouldn't have shot in Hong Kong. They have plenty of cameramen in the Philippines who would have worked for free. They don't have raw stock, though. We would have had to have brought that over. And they would have probably tried to steal it. Roger Corman made a lot of pictures over there—he would just send the actors and the raw stock.

Dawn breaks and the camp awakens. The sound of cawing crows fills the air as our heroes rise to face the day. Dr. Proud shivers in his cot as Monroe hovers over him.

NICK MONROE: *What's the matter?*

DR. PROUD: *It's just a touch of the fever.*

NICK MONROE: *You look terrible. Want to cancel the hunt for the gas?*

DR. PROUD: *Absolutely not.*

Monroe heads out on his own. He wanders through the countryside and finally comes upon a strange house. It sits high on a hill.

JOEL: This is a cutaway shot of, I think, Korea. The Army gives you free stock material.

The camera cuts to a bird—it silently watches the action from high atop a tree.

JOHN: ***Here's a classic Kanefsky cut-in.***

JOEL: Well, they were cut-ins, but that's why we had them. We shot a lot of cutaways in case we needed them. That's the secret. My friend George Sherman used to shoot these low budget pictures for Colombia. He couldn't shoot twenty to one—he shot whatever he was going to use. They're called safety shots.

JOHN: ***How much time did you spend on that kind of stuff?***

JOEL: Well, Ron wanted to stay there to go skiing, so he spent another two or three days doing things like that.

Nick edges closer to the house and looks through the window. What he sees terrifies him. One of the living dead walks into a room and eases into an Army uniform.

A mystery in the woods.

JOEL: You've got to realize that eighty percent of this movie was shot in the same little space.

Monroe backs away from the house and slowly treks back to camp. He enters the tent and sits down to dinner.

CAPTAIN FLECK: *For a sick man, Dr. Proud, you still have not lost your touch at the stove!*

JOEL: This is torture. You should pay me for watching this.
JOHN: ***It's hilarious.***
JOEL (to John): While you were in the bathroom, I was explaining to Brian that he's your nurse. They let you out of the hospital every couple of weeks to come to New York. They give you lots of pills …

Another night begins. A shadowy figure makes his way into Captain Fleck's room. The intruder unsheathes a knife and proceeds to slit the poor man's throat.

JOHN: ***I think Vernon Becker told me that he was on the set for this.***
JOEL: He probably was. I can't really remember.

Monroe and Proud discover the carnage the next morning. Fleck's cot is awash in a sea of blood.

NICK MONROE: *No zombies?*
DR. PROUD: *If there are, the search for the gas is too important to let anyone or anything hold it up. Let's go.*
NICK MONROE: *I thought you were sick.*
DR. PROUD: *That was yesterday …*

The duo trudges through the snow. They are equipped with strange machines that look like blinking cattle-prods.

JOEL: It was fucking cold out there. You could barely walk on the snow. It was awful.

JOHN: *Who designed these Gamma detectors?*

JOEL: I did (laughs). Listen, they're not as bad as some of the stuff that Herschell Gordon Lewis used.

Proud's Gamma machine suddenly begins to beep at a rapid rate. He calls out to Nick, but is confronted by a skiing zombie.

ZOMBIE ON SKIS: *Hi. Dr. Proud?*

DR. PROUD: *Who are you? What are you doing here?*

ZOMBIE ON SKIS: *Don't you remember me? Think, Dr. Proud. Kelly, sir. Special Unit C. Welcome back, doctor. Welcome back to the US Army!*

Proud screams and races back to camp. The zombie throws his head back and laughs.

JOEL: I think that was Lorin's nephew. Actually, if you redubbed this in German, you could probably fix the story up.

Nick returns to camp, only to find Proud a cowering mess. He calls out for one of Fleck's officers.

NICK MONROE: *All right, I'm going back out there. Can you get me a World War II outfit?*

FLECK'S OFFICER: *Ja, Herr Monroe. But… I thought you couldn't kill zombies.*

NICK MONROE: *Well, if I can't kill them, I'll join them.*

JOEL: That's the guy I told you about—the professional Nazi. He supplied all of the uniforms. We had to give him some money. We basically had to force it on him—he didn't want it. I mean, I always made sure that everybody got paid.

Nick rushes back into the woods. Night has fallen, and he hears the distant echo of machine guns. He follows the sound and crouches down to survey the scene. A large group of zombies, both German and American, dutifully reenact a battle in the moonlight. Nick joins the ranks of the dead Americans and follows them into a bunker.

Samantha Grey as Susan.

JOEL: That's in the same tent. We put crinkly paper up on the walls to make it look like dirt.

Disguised as an American soldier, Monroe sits back as he listens to the voices of the dead.

PRINCIPAL BUNKER ZOMBIE: *Well, well, well. All quiet?*
ZOMBIE GI: *Quiet!*
PRINCIPAL BUNKER ZOMBIE: *Well, don't relax. It's their turn to go on the offensive.*

JOEL: You can interview Don Wallace. He calls me up all the time.
JOHN: ***Who?***
JOEL: The principal zombie. Here he is now.

PRINCIPAL BUNKER ZOMBIE: *OK, guys. Knock it off. You're due your ration of Gamma 693 tomorrow.*

JOHN: ***Yeah, give me his number and I'll call him as soon as I get home.***

Back at camp, Dr. Proud shivers in fever. He calls out for his niece.

DR. PROUD: *Susan…*
SUSAN: *I'm here.*
DR. PROUD: *Susan, there really are zombies.*
SUSAN: *You've had quite a shock. Just relax. Think about something else. Think about something real far away from here… someplace warm. Think about the time right after daddy was killed. Remember? You took me to Atlantic City. Remember all the saltwater taffy we ate?*

JOEL: Oh, God. We cut the original script short so we could get things done. I could have made any other picture. I could have been a great filmmaker.
JOHN: ***Well, this is my favorite scene!***

Susan brings her uncle a glass of water. He gulps it down and looks at his hands. His flesh is beginning to rot away.

DR. PROUD: *The gas. I've got to get the gas! It's almost too late!*

Proud leaps from his cot and runs out into the grove. He pauses long enough to slaughter a bird. Blood runs down his chin as he eats the thing alive.

JOEL: That's Ryan in David Smith's makeup.
JOHN: ***He's attacking a bird (laughs)!***
JOEL (laughs): That is a Chinese Manchu pheasant that you'll never find any place else in the world!
JOHN: ***So, you don't think this works?***
JOEL (laughs): Well, if you think it works, it works.
JOHN: ***I mean, it's sort of ridiculous, but...***
JOEL (laughs): I want you to come to New York or go to Hollywood. Why don't you get a job in Hollywood?

Proud stumbles around in a fit of panic. He finally decides to crawl back to camp. His taste for human flesh has reached an all-time high. Susan screams as he greets her.

JOHN: ***This is Ryan's big moment.***

DR. PROUD: *Susan! This is Uncle Clarence, Susan! I'm not going to hurt you! You don't have to die. I don't have to die. No one has to die! Listen to me! This is your Uncle Clarence, the man who walked on the boardwalk with you. Now, listen to me, please! Did he find the gas? Tell me that! That's all I want to know.*

LISTEN TO ME! I am seventy-seven-years-old! I should have been dead for thirty-five years now, if it wasn't for the gas. Gamma 693 wasn't developed to destroy lives! It was developed to maintain them—to put the wounded in a state of suspended animation so they could be transported to the hospital! Listen to me, please! We have got to preserve our lives. We have got to do that!

I was suffering from an incurable

disease back in 1944. I stole just a little bit of the gas. The scientist who developed it discovered me. I had to kill him! Then, I burned his laboratory in hopes that it would look like an accident. Unfortunately, the formula burned in the fire. I didn't realize how unfortunate it was until a few days later when the flesh began to decay on my body.

JOEL: All of this explanatory shit shouldn't be in here. He shouldn't have to explain all this stuff.

DR. PROUD: *I began to supplement my diet with human flesh in order to maintain a normal appearance. Tell me. Did he find the gas? The gas! Oh my God, it might be too late! I'm falling apart already! I'm hungry!*
SUSAN: *Uncle Clarence, please!*
DR. PROUD: *I thought you had more strength than that!*

Just when all hope seems lost, Monroe bursts into the tent. He wrenches the chemist away from Susan, seconds before he can take a bite of her flesh.

DR. PROUD: *Ahh… Nick. May I call you Nick?*

Proud lunges at Monroe. His attack is countered with a blast of the deactivating foam that he himself invented. Proud slowly melts into a puddle of slime. Susan falls into Monroe's arms.

Snow falls down from the sky and gently covers the bloodstained grove. At last, all is peaceful. At last, all is calm. Or is it? Just what unknown horrors did Nick encounter at the zombie bunker? Is he now himself one of the living dead? The final scene of ***Night of the Zombies*** *finds Monroe talking to Collins. As usual, they argue.*

COLLINS: *Sure. Zombies… dominating the world! Sure, Nick.*
NICK MONROE: *Collins, Gamma 693 is capable of suspending death almost indefinitely. And it can continuously recreate a corpse into a functioning humanoid form.*
COLLINS: *Bull!*
NICK MONROE: *But, Collins, I'm telling you!*
COLLINS: *Don't 'but' me! I just hope the press hasn't gotten wind of this drivel. There is no such thing as zombies! Have you seen Susan lately?*
NICK MONROE: *She went back about an hour ago.*
COLLINS: *That's strange. I didn't pass her on the road.*

NICK MONROE: *Oh... she might have stopped someplace for a bite.*

The end credits roll, offering the viewer a few more seconds to savor Joel M. Reed's last motion picture. And then...

JOEL: And, that's the end of the movie.

JOHN: ***I guess it is. We should watch it again! I really like it.***

JOEL (bewildered): Brian, you must make pretty good money taking care of John! "I don't know. He's been watching these movies since he was four-years-old. I love him—he's my son! But what can you do? We used to keep him locked in the basement, but he has to have some sort of life!"

AUTHOR'S NOTE: *One of the biggest curses of dragging out the boxes of old tapes and files to complete this book was the passage of time. I interviewed Jamie Gillis in the winter of 2000 about his role in* ***Night of the Zombies****. From what I can recall, I talked to the man for about forty-five minutes—the equivalent of one side of a ninety-minute cassette. When I finally sat down to edit this chapter, the thing turned up missing. Only the plastic case remained.*

Whatever happened to the tape? I have no idea. By the time I started working on this book anew, Mr. Gillis had long since passed. Rather than play things by ear (with memory as my guide), I made the decision to exclude any of his 'comments' from the above text. If the tape in question is ever recovered, I will insert his quotes into a future edition of this book. For now, an empty chair is present at the table.

Perhaps Collins can organize a reconnaissance mission. Perhaps a dose of Gamma 693 is in order. At any rate, I now raise a glass to Jamie Gillis. From my limited conversation with him, he seemed to be a very nice man. Rest in peace, Mr. Gillis. Rest in peace, Nick Monroe.

"Nick. Do you mind if I call you Nick?"

Let's play the movie one more time in remembrance...

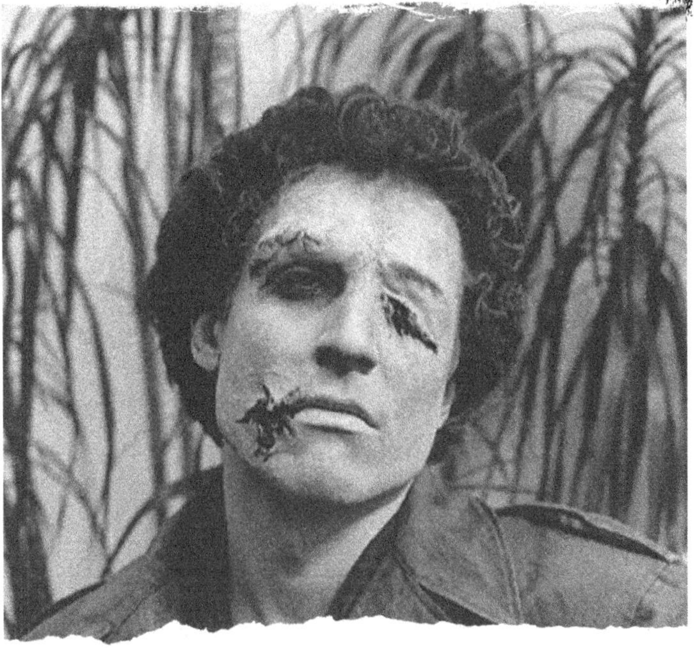

"Be sure to tell Joel that his secrets are safe with me!"—Don Wallace

CHAPTER TWELVE

DON WALLACE, BUNKER ZOMBIE!

If the loss of the Jamie Gillis tape can be considered a curse, the following conversation with Don Wallace can most assuredly be considered a blessing. As I was going through the army of tapes that faced me during the final edit of this book, I came across a conversation that I'd long since forgotten. On the B-side of a cassette labeled "Mark Goldberg," I stumbled upon an interview that I had no memory of conducting. Side two of the thing was labeled (in faded blue magic marker), "Don. Bunker Zombie. Fishing story."

I was very curious as I slid the tape into my old Panasonic Slim Line. Who in the world was Don? Did I actually interview an extra from ***Night of the Zombies***? If so, why couldn't I remember it? What was the fishing story? Would there be anything on the tape at all?

I rewound side B, hit PLAY, and waited. At first, there was only static. A few seconds later, the familiar sound of a phone number being dialed erupted from the machine's tiny speaker. And then, the voices from the past started talking.

"What's this?" I thought. I let the tape play on. And then I remembered. Seconds after the interview ended, I rewound the thing, walked over to my computer, and started typing.

The following conversation took place during the final days of the year 2000. Donald K. Wallace played the part of the "Bunker Zombie" in Joel Reed's last film, ***Night of the Zombies***. I called the

Doctor Proud attacks!

man on a whim—Joel had given me his number a few days earlier while I was visiting New York. This was a cold call. I had no questions ready. I wasn't even sure what to say to the guy. I simply dialed his number and waited for an answer…

DON WALLACE: Hello.
JOHN SZPUNAR: ***Yes, is Don there?***
DON: Yes.
JOHN: ***Hi. My name is John Szpunar. I'm a friend of Joel Reed's.***
DON: Hey! How are you doing?
JOHN: ***Not bad. To tell you the truth, I'm writing a book about Joel. He told me that you had a small part in one of the films that he directed. I guess it was Night of the Zombies.***
DON: He promised me that he would never tell a soul about that (laughs). This is a violation of our agreement!
JOHN: ***Well, do you have any objections to speaking about that?***
DON: Actually, no. What are you looking for?
JOHN: ***Basically just any information that you can give me about what it was like being involved with the film.***
DON: Well, I can tell you that right over the phone. Joel is one of those people who has an innate sense of editing. He knows at the beginning of the day exactly what shots he needs to put a movie together, and he gets them. The first movie that I ever saw that he did—I forget what it was called (and I think I forgot it because it was a Tromatic experience)—was the most

JOHN: ***Do you have any recollections of any of the other cast members that you worked with?***

DON: I seemed to be the only one who could remember lines. I've just always had the ability to remember lines quite easily. They just kept throwing lines to me—if somebody forgot a line, they'd give me that line. I mean, it seemed like the lines that the characters spoke were kind of interchangeable. It didn't matter which character spoke them.

JOHN: ***Did you happen to see the film when it premiered?***

DON: I've never seen it. I was simply helping a friend out who seemed to come up one actor short.

JOHN: ***Any regrets?***

DON: Well, I don't think I was hurt by it (laughs). Basically, I don't think that I do have any regrets about it. It was all pretty much fun. Even menacing Lorin was kind of fun.

JOHN: ***Did you guys have to get on his ass in order to get paid?***

DON: I went down to his office. I walked in and told him that the money that he was withholding from my salary was the money that I used to feed my child, and that people who screwed around with that made me very, very fucking angry. And at the point that I mentioned the word 'angry', my nose was practically touching his nose. Frankly, I didn't like the man. I was just looking for an excuse to yell at him. But, he really screwed us over. And the fact that I had been tipped off that this was a guy who was screwing around with people made me even more hostile. I finally had to go to court to sue the guy.

JOHN: ***I guess you came out on top, then? You finally got paid…***

DON: Yeah. But if you have to resort to that to get paid, you don't come out on top. What are you? Are you an actor, a writer, or what?

JOHN: ***I'm a journalist.***

DON: Well, you know—you write a story for somebody in exchange for money.

JOHN: ***Right.***

DON: That's how you pay the rent, that's how you buy your clothing—that's how you provide for your family. Now, you're accustomed to exerting a certain amount of effort to produce a story. The story is your product. If you have to go to extraordinary lengths to get paid for your product (which you've already delivered), it has nothing to do with the effort of producing that product. That's like a burden. That's a fairly

Inside the bunker.

large burden. You know, write me an article for the ***New Yorker***. Let it be 20,000 words. We'll pay you when you deliver it. You deliver it, and we don't pay you. So, whatever effort you've expended writing the story, you have to at least double in court to get your money. Now, if somebody were to tell you when you delivered that story, "Well, this is nice. Now, I'd like you to write another one… and, we'll send you a check for the first one." You'd kind of like to know—am I getting paid for the second one? Is it your expectation that I just throw that in? What's going on here? For all of those reasons, Lorin was not a nice person. And furthermore… well, I never understood what the movie was really about. I mean, I know that it was about some kind of horror business. But I never really understood if they were trying to make something really good or if they were simply trying to roll the cash over to make a profit. I could never get to the bottom of that.

JOHN: ***From what I've heard about Lorin, it doesn't sound like he was very good at doing either.***

DON: Joel is just a guy who enjoys making films. He just enjoys doing that. I mean, let's face it—it's a fun job to do.

JOHN: ***Right. Have you seen Joel recently?***

DON: I owe him a call. Our friend Tom Keena lost his leg over the Christmas vacation, and so… well, we've been in touch discussing that. And then, we'll call each other sometime within the next month or two to discuss fly fishing. When was

the last time you talked to him?

JOHN: ***A couple of days ago.***

DON: Well, you've talked to him much more recently than I have. Have you actually seen him?

JOHN: ***Oh, yeah. I've been over to his place quite a few times. Like I said, I'm writing a book about him.***

DON: Really? Just about Joel Reed?

JOHN: ***Yeah. Well, about Joel, his films, and whatever else I encounter along the way. I've done so many interviews. It might take me another fifty years to edit everything together (laughs).***

DON: That's amazing.

JOHN: ***Yeah, I guess so. It's been fun, though.***

DON: Well, I know that he has a following. That's terrific. But… is it a large enough following that you'll be able to sell your material?

JOHN: ***Well, I've already got a deal for it, so…***

DON: Oh, cool!

JOHN: ***We'll see what happens. Joel has a lot of great stories.***

DON: Joel never forgets anything. He's an interesting neighborhood character. He's been in the neighborhood so long, and he's been a part of the New York scene for a long time. He's seen a lot of things pass by.

JOHN: ***I've met and talked to a lot of his friends from those days. A lot of them have some crazy stories to tell about showbusiness.***

DON: Well, when people in showbusiness tell me something, particularly when it has to do with their credits, I never quite believe it until I see some kind of cross-referencing. I mean, you and I live in a world where bullshit has been raised to art and beyond. That's just right across the board, no matter what endeavor you happen to be in. Showbusiness is ahead of the rest of the pack in that way (laughs)! I don't really know how one would go about out hyping Microsoft, no matter what business you're in.

JOHN: ***Yeah, that's true.***

DON: But I think that Joel is one of the good guys. And if he ever did a script that I liked, I'd work with him in an instant. Not that he would ask me, but...

JOHN: ***He's one of the most entertaining people that I've ever met.***

DON: He's a funny man. Years ago, Tom and I went down to his house. We were taking a walk in the afternoon, and we dropped by to say hello. Joel sent us back into his bedroom. He had a very early version of a computer set up. I think it was something that he bought from Tandy or somebody. I don't think it was an Amiga, but it was from somewhere around that era. Anyway, he'd written this little program. You'd sit down at the keyboard, and you had to type in your name. Once you did that, the computer started to ask you questions. This early computer maybe had a megabyte of memory. It was text only. It would ask you these questions, and he was quite excited that he'd gotten it to do this. And frankly, Tom and I were both

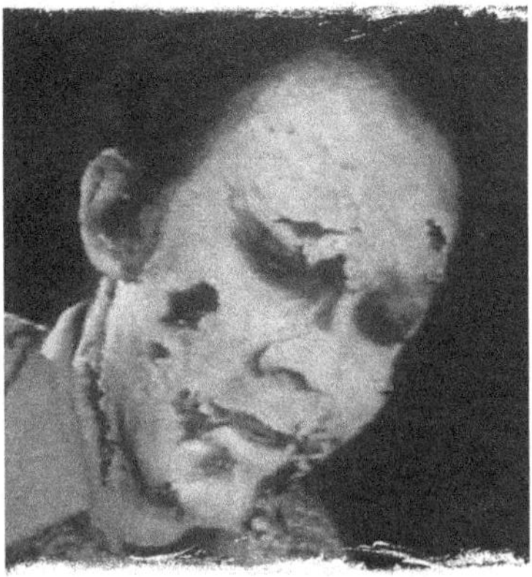

impressed. And looking back on it, I'm still impressed. Joel went from that to being able to write serious code. The guy taught himself software. As I told you before, he might be a genius.

JOHN: ***I've certainly gotten that impression.***

DON: I've just always been amazed at his capacity to absorb information. And he's at the age now where one might expect him to forget a few things here and there. I think he glosses over some of the high spots a little bit, but he's basically pretty amazing. He can tell you the types of hammers that carpenters use, and the purpose they're used for. These are bizarre and antiquated construction implements. I mean, he can go on and on. The guy is just amazing. You know, he comes in and he looks a little demented—he kind

Bunker zombies.

of lurches around.

JOHN (laughs): ***Can you tell me a little about fishing with Joel?***

DON (laughs): Fly fishing with the guy is an experience. Whenever we'd go to the stream, we'd always have to walk through a little bit of woods to get down there. Between the road and the stream, there's always a little bit of woods. And in the woods, there will always be a briar batch or two. We'd leave the car and start walking down toward the stream. Invariably, Joel would always get caught on the briars. He would start cursing. You would hear this voice behind you: "Son of a bitch! Goddamn!" It became like a litany between the car and the stream. In the early days when we fished together... well, on some days, the bugs are coming off the water.

JOHN: ***Right.***

DON: You know what's coming off. You look in your fly box, you pull one out, and tie it on. Then—wham! The action starts! But most of the time, very little, if anything, is coming off the water. You're stuck there beside the river, looking on and wondering what in the hell they might be feeding on. On those occasions, those of us who are serious about producing dinner that evening revert to worms or juicy grubs. Something of that sort. On one such day (laughs), we went up to the shore and we passed Joel. He was working his way upstream. "How you doing, Joel?" "Ahh, not too good. Nothing's happening." I said, "Well, why don't you put a worm on?" The guy's face turned crimson red. He started stomping up and down in the middle of the stream. He said, "I don't fish with worms! I don't date old ladies, and I don't fish with worms!"

JOHN: ***That's great!***

DON: Ever since then, the guy I was with and I have retold that story during dull moments. "I don't date old ladies, and I don't fish with worms!" These are the defining things (laughs). I think if he goes, and if anybody asks me what sentiment should be placed on his tombstone… well, I think I'm going to go for that one. "I don't date old ladies, and I don't fish with worms."

JOHN: ***That would be perfect.***

DON: Joel is certainly interesting and witty. And very studious. I always looked at him and hoped that he would find something of an artier nature to make films about. I always wanted him to do something like ***The Red Balloon*** or ***Sundays and Cybele.*** I always wanted him to direct one of those creative French films like ***The 400 Blows.*** I always had the suspicion that he'd be very good at it. And I've always found it a little bit unfortunate that, for whatever reason, he never really got the chance. Joel has that kind of brain. A lot of directors are good with actors. A lot of directors are good with the technical people. Some can combine both, but the majority of people don't have the kind of brain that Joel has. He's able to compartmentalize and handle all of these different and diverse bits and pieces of information that one has to handle as a director. What's the weather going to do? Can we get our shot? How much time do we have left to shoot? Can we really get everything we need? How many shots do we really need to be covered on this? What do I want the actors to do? It goes on and on. There's a lot of stuff that you've got to keep running in your mind. And there are a lot of asses that you've got to kiss along the way. You've got to keep your producer happy, you've got to keep your money people happy. And you have to keep your talent happy all the way around. Otherwise, everything suffers. If anything can ever be considered an ensemble effort, filmmaking is one of those things. Even more so than legitimate theater. In legitimate theater, the writer can sit down and write a good play. The producer can

Joel with *Night of the Zombies* fans.

stay on his phone and put the thing together. Ultimately, in legit theater, it's really up to the director and the actors to tie it all together. But with film, you've got the camerawork, you've got the prop people, you've got the electricians, you've got the carpenters, you've got the grips. And the goddamn unions each have a different set of rules. You've got to deal with all of this stuff, in addition to temperamental people. Some people are wondering where their money is going. Joel has the kind of brain that can deal with that. And he seems to do it with much less effort than the rest of us. And he's always kind of interested me in that regard.

And, the other thing is this: Joel has never ever lied to or bullshitted me on a serious basis. I think that's probably the reason that we've been friends for so many years. So… does that answer all of your questions?

JOHN: ***Yes, it does.***

DON: I've probably told you more than you wanted to know (laughs).

JOHN: ***Too much is never enough. Thanks again for your time.***

DON: My pleasure. And let me know if you need anything else.

JOHN: **Will do. Have a good evening.**

DON: You do the same…

"I know my way around town/Used to Live around here . . ."—Pere Ubu

CHAPTER THIRTEEN

ELIOT SMITH

It isn't very often that one gets to talk to a man who carries the nickname the Bearded Transvestite from Hell. Yet, talk to the man I did. In another case of fatigue-inflicted amnesia, I'd all but forgotten about the following conversation. In fact, had I not made a last-ditch effort to go through my library of unlabeled audiotapes that might in some way be related to this book, the following interview might have very well remained buried in a sea of dust.

I talked to Joel Reed's good friend Eliot Smith at some point in 2004. The only reason that I am able to pinpoint a date is because we compared notes on the (then) new John Waters film, ***A Dirty Shame***.

From what I can remember, I called Eliot early in the morning. He was up for an interview, but he asked me if I could call him back at a later hour. I happily agreed, and spent the rest of the afternoon trying to come up with some questions.

I wasn't really sure how to approach things. Any friend of Joel's was likely to be very open and nonchalant about his particular proclivities, but I decided to address Eliot with an air of caution. I didn't want to insult the man, and to tell you the truth, his tenure as a bearded transvestite didn't really interest me. I was more concerned with talking to the man about his friendship with Joel.

I started the interview with a fair degree of anxiety. Within five minutes, it became clear that everything I wanted to discuss was fair game. Eliot Smith was a very funny and intelligent man, and I found myself wishing that I could travel back in time to roam the streets of Times Square with him. God only knows what we would have encountered...

A young Eliot Smith.

JOHN SZPUNAR: ***OK, here we go. This is the Eliot Smith interview, take two...***

ELIOT SMITH: Hello.

JOHN: ***Hi, Eliot. This is John calling back. Is now a good time to talk?***

ELIOT: Sure. How are you?

JOHN: ***I'm doing just fine. I think I have some basic questions in order. If you have the time, could I run them by you?***

ELIOT: Yeah. I've got the time, and I've got the energy.

JOHN: ***Sounds great. When did you first meet Joel?***

ELIOT: I think I met him in 1959. It was very close to that year, at least—he was less than thirty-years-old at the time.

JOHN: ***Where did you meet him?***

ELIOT: We met by chance. There was a photographer on 58th Street. I think I met him over there. A lot of this is fuzzy. It was a long time ago. But I'm pretty sure it was at the studio of a guy named Jerry Krutman.

JOHN: ***No kidding? Joel used his studio loft as a location in Career Bed.***

ELIOT: Yeah. He was a photographer.

JOHN: ***What was Joel doing back in 1959 to make a living?***

ELIOT: He was doing press at the time. He was a press agent.

JOHN: ***Do you remember your first impression of him when you met him?***

ELIOT: Well, I don't know. I liked him. He was interesting.

JOHN: ***Was he pretty much the same character that he is today back in those days?***

ELIOT: Yes.

JOHN: ***What were you doing at the time?***

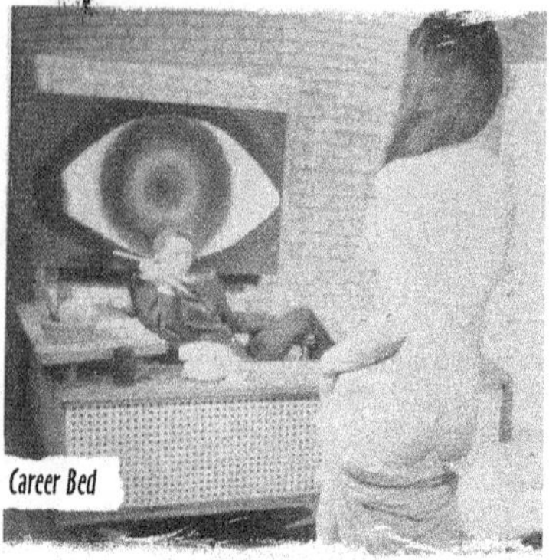

Career Bed

ELIOT: I was working in a family business. Machinery.

JOHN: ***OK. What I want to do is… well, I have a list of names in front of me. I'm going to run some of them by you. Do you remember a guy named Ron Dorfman?***

ELIOT: Yes. He was the cameraman for a lot of Joel's movies. I met him, but I don't really know him. Anything that I have to say about him would probably be the same stories that Joel told you.

JOHN: ***Fair enough. Joel told me that he shot a lot of Career Bed in your apartment.***

ELIOT: Yeah, that was at my apartment. I regretted it afterword, but when you're young, you do things that you think will be interesting.

JOHN: ***Why did you regret it?***

ELIOT: Because they left a bit of a mess (laughs).

JOHN: ***How many people were on the set?***

ELIOT: Well, at times… up to ten, I guess.

JOHN: ***Do you remember how many days everybody was there?***

ELIOT: Not really. It all started to blend together.

JOHN: ***What thoughts crossed your mind when you first saw Joel directing?***

ELIOT: I didn't have a very good fix on any of it. I'd never experienced anything like it, that's for sure.

JOHN: ***Do you have any memories of the actors?***

ELIOT: Jennifer Welles, the porno actress was there. She didn't want me in the bedroom (laughs).

JOHN: ***Really?***

ELIOT: Yeah. And she was one of the reasons that I got involved with the thing in the first place—I was kind of hot for her.

JOHN: ***That's understandable (laughs).***

ELIOT: Yeah. So there were times when they would ask me to get out of the bedroom when the scenes were being shot, whatever they were. I can't remember—it was such a bad movie in the first place (laughs). Anyway, [***Career Bed***] left no impression on me. But I did get impressions of Joel's capacity when he made ***Blood Sucking Freaks***.

JOHN: *What did you think about that film?*

ELIOT: Well, I could see that he was very capable.

JOHN: *Were you actually hanging around the set for that movie?*

ELIOT: Yes. That was much later on, but I was on the set for a couple of days. In that case, I just came in and sat around in the background. I watched what they did.

JOHN: *Were you down on Spring Street?*

ELIOT: I can't remember just where it was filmed. I've forgotten.

JOHN: *Do you remember any particular scenes that you were there for?*

ELIOT: Well, I remember the most interesting part. And this is only subjective, as far as I'm concerned. I didn't know any of the people, except Alan Margolin. I actually knew him pretty well. I had a small role in that film, in the sense that I loaned Alan a book that was pretty sadomasochistic. It had a lot of pictures—it was kind of the porno stuff of the day. One of them struck me as particularly gruesome.

JOHN: *What was that?*

ELIOT: A girl had to hold a

Jennifer Welles ignores Eliot.

guillotine rope in her mouth while she got whacked on the ass. And if she let go of the rope, she'd be killed. That was in the movie.

JOHN (giggling): *That came from one of your books?*

ELIOT: Yeah, that was from one of my books. And that was my contribution to the film, so to speak. I loaned Alan the book, and he still owes it to me (laughs). Joel just spoke to him the other day. I told him to tell him that he still owes me the book, and he did. Alan said, "Oh, I'll look for it."

Eliot Smith prom pic.

JOHN: ***Did you meet Alan through Joel?***

ELIOT: I really can't remember. But, he was a really good looking guy. He was kind of unstable. Well, no—I don't mean that. He wasn't unstable, but he wasn't that swift with the money.

JOHN: ***Did you know Gale McCarty?***

ELIOT: Oh yeah. I knew him through Joel. McCarty was… oh, let's say that he was really a weak sister. He was just a nice, bumbling guy who was just fated to do himself in, so to speak.

JOHN: ***Joel told me that he was the still photographer for Blood Sucking Freaks.***

ELIOT: I wasn't aware of that. But, Joel and I had some wild times together.

JOHN: ***Can you elaborate on that?***

ELIOT: Well, the Annie Sprinkle story is a good one. She was a famous porno girl. She's on the lecture circuit now.

JOHN: ***Yeah, I know who she is.***

ELIOT: We did a number on her. I took her up to Joel's apartment. I thought we'd both receive a good oral fixative because I led her to believe that we'd be able to do things for her. She was looking for beauty work. We took her out to dinner, and everything was fine. A little while later… well, I guess she found out that our word was not as good as it should have been. She got pissed off.

JOHN: ***I've never heard that story before, and I've heard some good ones from Joel.***

ELIOT: Yeah, well that was a good one because I was there (laughs)!

JOHN: ***Speaking of porn, did you get to meet Jamie Gillis when Joel was shooting Night of the Zombies?***

ELIOT: No, I never met him. But I looked up some of the stuff about Bill Landis that Joel was telling me about. What I really know about Joel in a general way is that I've always found him to be so much smarter than he would ever appear on the outside. He's the perfect uncultured genius type of guy. That's why I stayed friends with him for so long. He was always impressing me with his memory. And he was generally a man of integrity. He never did me any harm, at least not consciously. I lost a bit of money on an investment he talked me into making, but I know how it came about that I got swindled. It wasn't through Joel.

JOHN: ***I don't know you at all, so stop me if this is out of line. Joel once told me that you were once known as the Bearded Transvestite from Hell.***

ELLIOT: No, that's OK. I've been down that road. I mean, it always came back to haunt me, but I'm fine with it.

JOHN: ***I don't want to step on any toes…***

ELIOT: You can relax. There's no pressure. But, I'll tell you—Joel sort of got me in trouble (laughs).

JOHN: ***What do you mean?***

ELIOT: He put me into one of his columns—I can't remember if it was with Walter Winchell, or what. I was supposed to be this tycoon going out with a famous star of the day. I mean, it was just nonsense. And I can't really blame Joel because I was his pal. He just went and did it. But it turned out to be a big problem for me. My uncle called me up and started yelling at me.

JOHN: ***I can understand how that might have been rather strange...***

ELIOT: I don't really care about that anymore. I don't know who'd even care about it these days. The only person who could ever make use of it would be Bill Landis.

JOHN: ***Did you ever meet Bill?***

ELIOT: I met him. I remember

Eliot flexes muscle.

what he looked like. But I never had any real relation with him. I mean—I can deduce what finally happened between Bill and Joel. Joel threw him out one day, and I'm sure that Bill was consumed with the somewhat insane rage that people get when they get shat upon and can't do anything about it. I mean, he's still evidentially on the same kick.

JOHN: ***Yeah, I can't quite figure that guy out, myself. I contacted his wife a while back, and she went berserk.***

ELIOT: Did you tell her that you knew Reed?

JOHN: ***Yeah.***

ELIOT: Well, I'm sure that probably drove Bill through the roof.

JOHN: ***I guess it pretty much did.***

ELIOT: Yeah, I can see that happening.

JOHN: ***So, how long did you actually live in New York?***

ELIOT: For all of those years, up until twelve years ago.

JOHN: ***What can you tell me about the sleazy days of Times Square? It seems as if it was pretty intense and insane.***

ELIOT: Well, it's always been like that. Have things really changed all that much?

JOHN: ***Things are pretty sterile now. I was there a few months ago, and I was amazed. Kind of saddened, actually.***

ELIOT: I used to go into the theaters. I used to see a couple of movies a day when I had nothing else to do. When I didn't have any money.

JOHN: ***Right. Do you remember what the atmosphere was like back then?***

ELIOT: It was seedy. But listen—there are plenty of seedy places elsewhere.

JOHN: ***I guess that's true.***

ELIOT: Of course it is. And they really are the same. I went to Germany around seven years ago. I was in Munich, and I had time to kill. It's a beautiful city, by the way. But, I went into a theater that was

The last gasp of Times Square.

off the beaten path. I guess it was a porno theater of some kind.

JOHN: ***What was it like?***

ELIOT: Well, I never saw anything like that in the United States! People were exhibiting themselves and giving each other blowjobs. And, at my age, they were even after me (laughs)! That was the most extreme thing that I've ever seen, including anything on Times Square.

JOHN: ***What was the difference?***

ELIOT: Over here, it wasn't as obvious. Over there it was almost as if they had a right to do whatever they wanted to do. I just mention this because it was new—even for me—to see things go that far.

JOHN: ***How did that scene compare to places like Plato's Retreat?***

ELIOT: Plato's Retreat? Well, I was there a couple of times. That was pretty crazy, as well.

JOHN: ***What do you remember about it?***

ELIOT: Well, I remember Bette Midler and how insane she was. I didn't know who she was. I went there another time with a girl, and we got naked. They had the orgy mats in the middle. Plato's Retreat was all what they say it was. It was kind of fun (laughs). That scene was very famous for a while.

JOHN: ***Do you have good memories of those days?***

ELIOT: I don't know. To me, this conversation is kind of like going back in time. And Bill Landis is talking about this stuff as if it's still happening now.

JOHN: ***Well, it's certainly a history***

"And something flickered for a minute and then it vanished and was gone."—Lou Reed

Photo: John Szpunar

CHAPTER FOURTEEN

GOODBYE 42nd STREET

2016

JOEL REED: *I have some great ideas now [for movies] that the people would enjoy more. They're more cutting. I have one called* **Four Tales from A Men's Room**. *It's really funny. One is about two gay guys reuniting in a men's room in the Village where they first met. It's not graphic; it has a surprise ending. Another one takes place in Germany, near the end of World War II. The Nazis are desperate, so they have a transvestite club. The joke is that a cop comes in and an alarm goes off. Everybody throws off their drag clothing and puts on uniforms. Another story is about the guy who invented the glory hole. He's a multimillionaire and he's illiterate (laughs). It's a quasi-documentary: "For the first time, I can tell you what I invented. When I got out of the institution, I got a job cleaning men's rooms…" The other story is about a film company on 42nd Street that runs its business in a men's room, which is pretty close to how some of those companies were. This guy is invited to sell him a script, and he can't find them. He goes down to a men's room in one of these shitty theaters. They've taken over one of the booths. It's very funny, I think. I have incisive things now.*

But my New York disappeared. Times Square has been gentrified. It's a big tourist attraction. People are walking around dressed as costumed movie characters. You can't even walk down the street. I don't know why anybody would go there anymore. All of the restaurants are disappearing. Sardi's is still there, but most of the old hangouts are gone.

Joel prepares dinner.

I go to the Village, and it's all gone. All the coffee shops I used to go to are gone. Everything is very stuck up. All of the restaurants are now $50 a pop. You go to Tompkins Square Park, and there's no more drug addicts. Just nannies and yuppies with cell phones. People are jogging. It used to be nice with the rats and people begging for heroin. I don't know what the fuck they did to it. New York has changed...

2000

Near the end, Brian and I made a habit of driving to New York. There was something comforting about watching the familiar landscape roll along as we slowly made our way east. We'd take our time, often stopping in Mill Hall, Pennsylvania, to stay at the Traveler's Delite. The place never seemed to change. Ted, the giant poodle, would never fail to acknowledge us as we walked into the lobby. The old woman who stood behind the front desk always drew us a map to the cabins, even when we told her we'd stayed there before. By this time, we'd learned not to set foot in the cocktail lounge; the place was strange, even for us.

Nine times out of ten, we were handed the keys to the same room.

We started to get the feeling that nobody else ever stayed there. "It's like something out of a David Lynch movie," I'd say as I turned on the coffee maker. An ancient Airstream trailer served as the quarters for the housekeeping staff. They never seemed to go home. Late at night, you could catch a glimpse of the glowing embers of lit cigarettes as they circled the trailer like fireflies.

We gradually learned to take the NY Waterway Ferry in Weehawken, New Jersey into Manhattan. We once made the mistake of driving into the city via the George Washington Bridge. After battling traffic for over an hour, we finally ended up in Manhattan only to be rerouted in the opposite direction.

If the landscape on the way to New York didn't change much, the city itself certainly did. Regular haunts and landmarks began dropping like flies. The Washington Jefferson was still our hotel of choice, but the rates were slowly going up. Times Square was becoming unrecognizable, even to a newcomer like me.

It's hard for me to pinpoint the last time I visited New York with the sole purpose of interviewing Joel Reed in mind. The last surviving tapes from those days are labeled November 11–15, 2000. Unless something surfaces in the future, those dates will forever serve as the point of reference for the final chapter in this book.

JOHN: *We're on our way to the airport. We're not driving this time. We got some really cheap plane tickets that we couldn't pass up. The Detroit City airport is pretty much closed, so we're flying out of Detroit Metro. I wonder if Ted is still alive. I guess I'll never know. Going to interview Joel about Night of the Zombies. Don't know what I'm going to do after this.*

We touched down at Newark, took a bus to Manhattan, and checked into the Washington Jefferson. Little did I know that this would be the last time that I'd ever set foot in the place.

JOHN: *OK. We're sitting here in our room on the sixth floor of the Washington Jefferson. I'm going to explain what happened when we checked in. First of all, let it be said that we froze our asses off. It's only November, but it's pretty cold outside. We got off the bus at roughly 34th and Eighth and*

made our way up to 51st. For some reason, we refused to take a transfer to another bus. We made our way north (laughs) and we passed Show World. The sign outside promised twenty-four hour karate movies on the third floor, but we didn't stop to watch them. It was really late—our plane was delayed—but the front door at the hotel was unlocked. We made our way in. A really bulky and obviously drunk black man was propped up against the wall. He was reading a newspaper. He asked us if we had reservations. We said, "Yes," and he proceeded to ring up a clerk. At least that's what I think he was doing. He picked up a phone and then put it down. He said nothing. Very odd. After ten minutes of sitting there, Louis finally walked down the stairs. It looked as if he'd just been aroused from deep slumber. Louis—that's the guy with the toupee—he had on the same dirty suit. His collar was askew, and his necktie was wrong. Everything about him was wrong. After a few minutes of trying to reason with him, we got the keys to our room on the sixth floor. We had to take the stairs because there was a sign on the elevator that said, "Out of Order." I think our room number is 642, but I'll have to check on that. It's a big room this time, with two beds. We're overlooking 50th Street. This room was obviously once a small apartment. It has a tiled floor. The stove has been ripped out and there's a refrigerator in its place. It's a nice place to sit and relax. So that's the Washington Jefferson. Same pictures on the walls, same narrow corridors, same stairway, same elevator, same everything. We took a look at the fourth floor as we made our way up here. It was suspiciously vacant. Not a soul was there. The guy with a violin might have been sleeping. We didn't hear him. His walker was gone. For all I know, he was evicted. Come to think of it, he might be dead. A little side note: as we were waiting for Louis to come down, someone bolted down the stairs and popped his head into the lobby area. He was asking about… well, in his words, "Excuse me. Is there a place around here where I can get a couple of beers to bring back to my room?" The black man hesitated for not a second before saying, "Down the street." The guy took off and was back with his beer before the idiot Louis came down to show us to our

This is the end, beautiful friend…

room. About the inhabitants this time: I think I heard a dog barking somewhere on the fifth floor. And, actually, on the first floor (laughs) a very strange obese woman was wearing a bikini. Well, I guess it was just underwear. She had no robe, no towel—no cloth to cover her. She didn't care. She made her way to the bathroom down the hall.

BRIAN: Talk about the mail.

JOHN: *Oh, yeah. The black guy in the lobby also screens the mail with the eye of an eagle. One of the tenants came down and asked him for his mail. The black guy went to a little cubbyhole and handed it to him parcel by parcel. It took him a long time, because he kept double checking the address. Anything else about the Washington Jefferson this time? The mission is still here. St. Paul's House. But, that's about it. That's what happened at the Washington Jefferson.*

Joel had invited us down to his place for dinner. The following afternoon, we walked north toward 58th Street. Things had changed even more in the past few months. In fact, they seemed to be changing with every step we took.

JOHN: *I guess that I should give a street report of what I'm witnessing. I see all of the old buildings, all of the old bricks, all of the old sidewalks, and the same old tiles in the subway stations. But things*

are different. I can't explain it. It probably wouldn't be as noticeable if I actually lived here. I'd probably be used to it. And that's not even taking into account what Times Square is like. What's left of those blocks is a total nightmare.

We finally arrived at Joel's apartment. He greeted us with a smile.

JOEL: I didn't know Brian was going to be here! I'll have to set another place at the table. I'm baking some chicken. Do you guys like squash?

Joel scurried around his kitchen as he prepared the feast. Brian smiled as he took a few pictures. Joel turned out to be a meticulous cook. He took his time with things as Brian and I waited in the living room.

JOEL: I can make a salad. Do you guys like salad?
JOHN: ***Yeah, that's great. Thank you, by the way. We haven't had anything to eat since breakfast.***
JOEL: Well, Brian's really putting it on. Must be all the beer!

We were soon sitting at a makeshift table in the living room. Joel brought over our feast, and we began to talk.

JOEL: So, where are you guys staying?
JOHN: ***We're still at the Washington Jefferson. The price has gone up, but it's reasonable. It's $70 a night. That's not bad, but it's not as cheap as it used to be.***
JOEL: No, that's OK. There are still some values to be had in New York. But, they just had an article in the paper about the rents around here.
JOHN: ***I guessing that they're out of control.***
JOEL: Yeah. When I got my first apartment, it was basically $17 a month.
JOHN: ***Where was that at?***
JOEL: It was actually on 45th Street between First and Second, I think. The building's still there. In those days, if you got a real cheap apartment, they were called cold water flats. They were $17.50 without heat, but with hot water. The bathtub was in the kitchen. It was $37 a month with heat. You could get an apartment on Park Avenue for $100 a month. That was a lot of money back then. You used to be able to park in New

York—there was regular parking everyplace. The city is overcrowded now.

JOHN: ***What was your place like when you were growing up?***

JOEL: We lived in a tenement. You had to go out to the backyard to take a shit—you had to walk down four flights of stairs. When my father made some money, we actually had a toilet in the apartment.

JOHN: ***What can you tell me about your parents?***

JOEL: Well, they're dead. What do you want to know? My parents were poor. My father always worked in record shops at close to the minimum wage. He had no ambition or drive. My mother used to yell at him all the time. She got a good job at Bergdorf Goodman, but then she got cancer. I never got along much with her. But, my father was a very good singer. He had a job to sing on the radio, and then I was born. He had to find a different job. He always blamed me for that.

JOHN: ***Do you have any stories about visiting Los Angeles?***

JOEL: My friend George Sherman directed many major features. He used to be John Wayne's roommate. He started with Mack Sennett in Brooklyn. He was a wonderful guy. He was very short, about five feet tall.

JOHN: ***George Sherman? How did you meet him?***

A pinch of salt.

Uncorking the wine.

JOEL: His brother was my accountant. He said, "When you get out to the coast, go see George." When I finally went out there, I talked to him on the phone. He said, "I'll be over in an hour." He called back and said, "I'll be over in two hours!" I took a shower and he finally rang. I said, "Come up to the room." He walked in and I said, "How are you doing, George?" I had to look down, he was so tiny. I said, "What happened, George?" He said, "My wife had the Rolls-Royce. I couldn't drive another director around in a shitty second car." So I hung out with him and he gave me a tour of Hollywood and introduced me to John Wayne. He did ***Big Jake*** with him. We drove out to his house and all I remember is George saying, "You don't call him John Wayne. This is not his name. His name is Duke."

George told me many stories of working for Harry Cohn at Columbia Pictures. They never paid George much attention because he did B pictures. He would get the leftover short ends to shoot with. They wouldn't give him professional film. One day, he needed an extra 1,000 feet. Well, George was tiny, so he climbed into the locker and stole two cans of film. Harry Cohn said, "You did a terrific job with this movie, but you little bastard! Where did you get the extra film?"

One time, George was shooting and he didn't have enough light. The set was being used as a day set. They had everything locked up, but he stole two 1000 watt tungsten bulbs that they used to use in the old days. They were about $100 apiece. He just took them from the supply room and turned them on. Harry Cohn was on Mulholland Drive with some starlet. He looked down toward Gower Gulch, and he suddenly saw those lights come on. He said, "George is doing it again!" He drove all the way back to the studio and turned the lights off. "The picture is over!"

George wanted me to join his production company, and I should have. He said, "I'm too old, but a young guy like you could get a lot of deals."

JOHN: ***You told me that you enjoyed staying in LA. I never cared for the place all that much.***

JOEL: The trouble with Los Angeles is that you have to drive an hour to get to anyplace. And you can't have too many drinks because you'll be driving back.

JOHN: ***True. Plus, it's so hot over there.***

JOEL: You were there at the wrong time of the year. I like it, but you have to know where to go. You would have liked going to Boardner's. It's the bar where Robert Mitchum got busted for smoking pot. It's right downtown on Hollywood Boulevard.

JOHN: ***Where have you been going lately in New York?***

JOEL: I've been going to Café Reggio a lot. There's a waiter there who writes screenplays. He keeps on giving them to me.

JOHN: ***Are they any good?***

JOEL: No, they're awful. He wrote a screenplay about a coffee shortage. I mean (laughs)...

JOHN: ***Have you been to Sardi's lately?***

JOEL: Not really. I don't think I've been there in a couple of months.

JOHN: ***Is Joe still over there?***

JOEL: Oh, I guess he is. I only go there on Wednesdays, when the girls are there with their mothers. There's nobody there anymore. Is the food OK?

JOHN: ***Yeah, it's great. What can you tell me about the books that you've written?***

JOEL: I wrote a book about Donald Trump [***Donald Trump: The Man, The Myth, The Scandal***]. I've written a lot of Victorian novels. I can't even remember the names. I used to write a novel in three days.

JOHN: ***Who published the Trump book?***

JOEL: Masquerade Books. It came out in 1990.

JOHN: ***What kind of fiction were***

An after dinner treat.

some of your scripts?

JOEL: Yeah, there's been some renewed interest. I'm doing some stuff with Showtime, which I'm falling behind on. Some people up in Canada seem to want to do one of my scripts called ***The House of All Nations***. It's a comedy film noir. I have a friend over in Europe who was kicking around some ideas in France. I read a script that I wrote thirty or forty years ago. It's absolutely awful.

JOHN: ***What script is that?***

JOEL: It's called ***Love Greek Style***. It's basically a story about the small villages there. If you kidnap a girl, you have to marry her. Years ago, a guy named Alfredo Maruchi optioned [the script]. I had originally sent it to the William Morris Agency. The agent there said no one would be interested in it. Then, a guy that owned a big color lab here in New York took the script back to his home in London to read on the plane.

This guy, Alfredo, noticed the script and asked to read it. He called me from Rome and said he wanted to produce it—all he was getting from William Morris was crap. I entered into a short-term option with him. William Morris' opinion of the script changed.

JOHN: ***Who was the agent from William Morris?***

JOEL: I don't remember his name. I met him briefly a few months later—he was living in a luxurious East Side apartment, and was married to a girl I'd once dated. He wanted the script as a vehicle for her.

Years later, I got a call from a bank. They said they owned my script, but didn't have a copy of it. Alfredo gave me a year's option for about 5,000 bucks, but had reported that he had purchased the script for $50,000. The bank had a list of his properties, which included a townhouse, film equipment, and two movies. They seized the negatives.

JOHN: *What kind of movies were they?*

JOEL: They were Italian Westerns. Anyway, they couldn't find him. The townhouse deed was phony, and they asked me if I could sell the pictures for them at a percentage.

JOHN: *What happened?*

JOEL: I arranged for some big guys in the movie industry to screen the film. Just before the screening, the bankers wanted me to sign a paper—they wanted me to give away my commission for $500 cash. I refused to sign it, and I showed it to my friends. As they all made to leave the screening room, the bank started to relent, but the guys there said, "We wouldn't buy a dildo from these pieces of shit." Carl Peppercorn and Irving Wormser stayed and said, "Let's look at this crap." Within fifteen minutes, we were all doubled up in hysterics. It was hysterical. And it cost a fortune. Over the years, I have been approached by different agencies seeking Alfredo—he conned people out of millions. They traced some of his assets to Israel.

JOHN: *How many scripts do you think you've written?*

JOEL: Oh, not that many. Ten or fifteen at the most. They're all pretty silly.

JOHN: *You told me that Marvin Farkas was in town recently. Is he doing better? You said that he had a stroke.*

JOEL: He has a problem with words. I think it took a lot out of him. But, he married a girl from China. He must be pushing eighty, but he still jogs. He's a very tough guy.

JOHN: *How's Vernon Becker doing these days?*

JOEL: Vernon seems to be very good. He's back in showbusiness—he's calling Bingo on Saturdays. He's in a senior citizens place in Florida. I call him once in a while. Anyway, I was up at Scott Rudin's apartment recently. Somebody said, "Can you help my friend with his computer?" I didn't recognize him when I went up there. If I knew he was Scott

"She was a beautiful girl."

Rudin, I would have pursued things. But, I'm very good at coding.

JOHN: ***Actually, how did you get into that? I don't think I ever asked you.***

JOEL: I bought a computer from Radio Shack and I started playing with it. I taught myself assembly language. I didn't go to sleep for three months—I was doing all of that. Then, people started paying me to do it.

JOHN: ***Where have you worked?***

JOEL: Mainly Fortune 500 companies like American Express, Morgan Stanley, and Prudential. I haven't really worked for the new dot-coms. They only want people who are twelve-years-old.

JOHN: ***What's it like working for big corporations?***

JOEL: I'm very good with putting a suit on and going to meetings. You only have to pretend that you're alert! "I'm going to write a memo on that later."

You should marry a girl with a good job. Are you leaving tomorrow morning?

JOHN: ***Yeah. It's back to normal life for a while.***

JOEL: Well, you've got to go back to work.

JOHN: ***Unfortunately.***

JOEL: Well, you've got to pursue this book! You'll be reviewing the stuff you did with me twenty years from now! You'll say, "How the fuck could I have done that! I could have interviewed anybody in the world, but I interviewed Joel Reed!"

Time passed quickly. Soon, it was time to say goodbye.

JOEL: Well, keep on working on the book. You'll be going on the interview shows, saying, "I never thought I'd win a Pulitzer Prize for this." Anyway, with that… I guess I'll see you guys later. Ciao.

Brian and I hit the streets and started walking south. I took out my tape recorder and made another entry:

JOHN: ***I'm trying to think about how to sum all of this up. I can't see what else I can add at this point. Once I cut everything together, the book should make some kind of sense. At least, I hope it does. What do you think I should say right now?***

BRIAN: Just keep talking.

JOHN: ***OK. Joel Reed has always lived in New York. He's seen the city change, and he's worked here for all these years. You could call him a New York icon—he's been here forever. People are looking at me like I'm crazy. "Why is that guy talking to himself?" Well, a lot of people might say that if somebody talks to themselves, they're totally insane. I think in some cases, it's just the opposite. I have a lot on my mind, so I figure that I might just as well get it on tape to see what this actually sounds like afterward. It might be somewhat useful for the last chapter or something.***

We continued walking and we hit Hell's Kitchen. For some reason, a hasty retreat to the Washington Jefferson didn't seem like a proper sendoff to the evening. We slowly made our way over to Broadway and 52nd. A gentleman's club called Flashdancers lit up the night. We walked up to the door and paused. The muffled strains of Phil Collins' "In the Air Tonight" echoed out onto the street.

JOHN: ***I remember this place! Do you want to go inside?***

BRIAN: I don't know. It's probably going to be pretty expensive.

A decrepit black man suddenly cut in front of us. His pupils were wide, and he wasted no time in introducing himself.

ANDRE: I'm Andre. What's your name? You and the other dude.

BRIAN: My name is Brian. We're just walking around.

ANDRE: You don't like the name of the movie?

JOHN: ***What? What movie?***

ANDRE: ***Flashdance***!

BRIAN: ***Flashdance***?

ANDRE: Flash-DANCERS! ***Flashdance***!

BRIAN: Have you ever been inside this place?

ANDRE: Yeah! ***Flashdance***! I like to go to Tower Records. Are you the guy that killed Kennedy?

Brian and I edged away from Andre

The legendary Playpen, once known as the Adonis and the Cameo. Demolished in 2007.

and kept moving. Before long, a man named Anthony approached us. He held out his hand as a gesture of good will.

ANTHONY: Hey, white boy! Help me out! I just got hit by the subway train! My arm is broken!
JOHN: ***Here's a dollar. I'd rather give it to you than that other guy.***
ANTHONY: God bless you! After all these years, I still have faith in the Lord!

We kept walking, and then—without fanfare—the lights of Times Square shone down upon us. Most of them advertised Samsung, Budweiser, and Coca-Cola.

JOHN: ***Walk around Times Square today, and you see no seedy theaters playing anything. All that's left is a handful of sex shops on Eighth Avenue. Forty-second Street is pretty much dead. If you walk over a ways, there's the place with the eye. Peep Land, I think it's called. It's over by the Kinko's. Most everything else is gone. I'll tell you this much, though—I'm hungry. I don't know what time it is, but I'm hungry.***
BRIAN: Let's take one last look inside the Playpen.

We pushed open the door to the Playpen and walked inside. The music was even louder than usual. Cher's voice bleated out the lyrics to "If I Could Turn Back Time" as we sidestepped a stack of porno mags and made our way over to the booths. A young woman stood in front of them. She gave us the once-over as we stumbled past her.

JOHN: ***Have you ever been inside one of these things?***
YOUNG WOMAN (laughing): No.
JOHN: ***I haven't either.***
YOUNG WOMAN: You want to go in there? It's fifty cents.
BRIAN: You can go in together.
YOUNG WOMAN (laughing): I don't want to go into this one! It's all girls!

A loud Pakistani accent ruined the moment. A greasy old man in a flowered shirt stumbled over to us and issued a stern warning.

PLAYPEN CLERK: Only one person per booth allowed!

Flashbacks of Antonio's mop attack at the Karate Center flooded my mind, and I made a break for the door. Brian, however, had other ideas. He scooped up a few magazines and walked over to the checkout counter.

PLAYPEN CLERK: You almost done in here?
BRIAN: Do you have any Patrick Collins movies? He's a famous director.
PLAYPEN CLERK: No.
BRIAN: Nothing by Patrick Collins? He directed ***Buttwoman Does Budapest***.
PLAYPEN CLERK: No.
BRIAN: OK. I'll just get these, then. Maybe I'll come back in a few months or something…

With that, we started walking back to the Washington Jefferson. Brian wanted to turn in early. I continued to talk into my tape recorder as our footsteps echoed in the night.

JOHN: ***Many a time, I have wanted to take a picture of the person who wields the mop at the Playpen. Or, at least of the little janitors' closet where the works are kept. The works meaning the mop, the detergent, and the bucket—usually a rickety yellow thing on wheels.***
BRIAN: Talk about the booths.
JOHN: ***Well, the peep booths themselves have menus—marquees, if you will, on their sides. They mostly play standard sex stuff, but watersports are big in***

some places. It might be interesting to note that the Playpen and a few other places like Empire Video have a wide array of bestiality films for sale. This really boggles my mind, because they're on public display—you walk in and you can't miss them. These places must be controlled by some kind of organized crime. At first, you would think, "Who the hell would want to watch this stuff?" But they've got to be producing these tapes for next to nothing. They've got to be duping them—they don't sell the box. And they must sell enough of them to justify this. Some sick fucks are into sex with animals, and they just keep churning them out. They probably have somebody working in a back room taping them all day long. Step into one of these places, and you can unravel a lot of mysteries about humanity by simply browsing through the aisles. You can encounter a side of man that should remain buried by at least thirty layers of limestone. The fact of the matter is, you don't have to dig that deep. These are the last days of Pompeii in New York City. And as castrated as Times Square is, it can still be a playground.

Brian and I ended up at a bodega across the street from St. Paul's house. We bought a few prepackaged sandwiches and walked up to our room.

JOHN: *Back at the Washington Jefferson, sitting on a chair. I'm eating an Italian sandwich with a lot of dressing. I'm sort of hampered by my suitcase. It's taking up all my space, so I'll move it over. Setting the recorder down...*

BRIAN: We'll have to be awake pretty early tomorrow. Well, before checkout time at least. Do you have any last words (laughs)?

JOHN: *Yes. If I could go back in time to even 1984, I'd gladly take the trip. I guess the ideal thing would be to go back in time to 1977 or something because the streets today are totally unrecognizable from what I've seen in movies like Taxi Driver or even Basket Case. It's a totally different place. A lot of the landmarks are gone—the strange theaters showing Texas Chain Saw Massacre or Cannibal Ferox—that sort of thing is totally history, and I don't think it will ever show up again. The new theaters have taken over what used to be there. For my money, that was*

Last stand at the Molly Wee.

a time that should have existed forever. A lot of people think that the sanitizing of Times Square is a good thing. I'm personally very against it. I think it sort of sucked the blood out of something that was definitely real. Times Square gradually evolved into what it was. For the city to hack it off and sweep it under the rug—I think that's a sin. At least they're attempting to restore the theaters. That's about the only good that I can see coming from any of this.

Brian started snoring on his bed, but I remained restless. I decided to take a walk. I skipped down the steps of the Washington Jefferson and walked back out into the cool November air.

I wound up at the Molly Wee Pub, but after a few drinks I decided to start moving again. I had no real plans in mind, and found myself walking down Eighth Avenue. I walked past block after block of brick buildings and stopped at a red light. It was still rather early. I wanted to cheat a few more hours out of the city. I looked at my watch. It was only a little past midnight. I decided to take a cab down to Spring Street.

The driver let me off at the corner of Spring and Mulberry. I stumbled out, crossed the street, and made my way into the Spring Lounge. The place was crowded, but I managed to get a drink and a seat against the wall. I was facing the front door. I took a sip of my beer and looked out at the street, watching the people walk by. An old man stopped at the front window, using it as a mirror. He took out a plastic comb and began fixing what was left of his hair. A young couple walked past, bumping into him. He gave them an icy stare, shuffled across the street, and walked into an apartment building.

The couple walked into the Spring and pushed their way up to the bar. They got their drinks more quickly than I did and found a space to sit at an already crowded table. The couple next to them asked for their help in snapping a picture. A camera was exchanged and the flash went off with a torrent of smiles.

I first walked into the Spring Lounge in January of 1997. A few of us were walking along Spring Street, trying to find a place to drink. There seemed to be a drought of neon signs that night. Finally, the word BAR flashed in front of our eyes and we walked inside.

It was nowhere near as crowded that night. In fact, the only other people inside were spread out along the bar itself; a strange collection of old men and young Italians. A short young man, easily 250 pounds made regular trips to the jukebox, feeding it with enough money to play "Love Child" ten times in a row. One of his friends, tall and thin, pulled the sleeves of his wool suit up on a regular basis and kept reshaping the brim of his gray felt hat. The phone rang periodically and the bartender answered it in a rough voice: "Spring." The phone was intercepted by Love Child, who snapped his fingers at two of the older men. They walked outside and waited for a giant white car to appear. I scanned the place for Eddie Egan, or at least a look-alike, but came up empty.

I'll never be able to figure out what kind of strange interactions were going on in the white limousine, but the Spring Lounge was cozy that night. I played Dion and the Belmonts on the jukebox and my selection was met by a round of applause. The bartender handed me a Heineken as "Teenager in Love" drifted through the air. My friends looked at me in amazement. It appeared as if real gangsters were buying me drinks, and from what I could tell, they were. Life was perfect at that moment. But things have a way of changing.

In fact, things in The Spring Lounge had changed in just a few years. Even I was able to notice that.

It seemed as if the city itself was a living, breathing thing—evolving, and unaware of its past.

The Spring Lounge of late 2000 was filled with college kids playing backgammon. They chatted aimlessly, and the music of the day all but drowned out their conversations. All I could hear was the ticking of my watch as I finished off my beer.

I decided to have one more drink, but after a few sips, I realized that it wasn't one of my smarter plans. Not if I wanted to catch my flight. I flagged down a cab, ordered the thing over to the Washington Jefferson, and quickly fell asleep.

The next morning was rough, but Brian and I managed to make it to the airport on time. The plane to Detroit was late, but I really didn't care. I sat on a hard seat in the terminal for a while, and then decided that I needed food. I was halfway through what passed as a pastrami sandwich when I heard that my flight was boarding. I shuffled along to the gate and found my seat by the window.

We started down the runway, lifted, and the plane tilted. A female voice announced that refreshments would soon be served. And 30,000 feet below me, crowds of people walked through the streets with all of the ghosts that they chose to acknowledge or ignore. For some strange reason, I suddenly knew that the sounds and smells of old New York would follow them into restaurants, bars, theaters, and hotels. I smiled and said goodbye to them. "Keep a light on for me," I thought as I looked out the window. I closed my eyes, but down below, the lights were still shining.

END

CAST OF CHARACTERS

The Washington Jefferson is now a boutique hotel with tiny rooms that command over $300 a night. It's safe to say that Louis and his tenants have long since vacated. **VICTOR KANEFSKY** still lives in New York. He recently directed the award-winning documentary ***Art Bastard***. **GALE MCCARTY** passed away on October 28, 2009, at the age of eighty-three. **JOE SARNO** passed away on April 26, 2010. There will never be another like him. **TOM KEENA** sadly set sail for whatever adventures await him in the afterlife. **LLOYD KAUFMAN** is still the president of Troma Entertainment. His latest film as producer/director was the ill-advised ***Return to Return to Class of Nuke 'Em High AKA Volume 2***. **MICHAEL SAHL** passed away on March 29, 2018. His most recent album, ***Civilization and Its Discontents***, was released in 2012. **NILES MCMASTER** now lives in Wisconsin and makes his living as a fine artist. **ERNIE PYSHER** is an assistant principal at Midwood High School at Brooklyn College. Truth is indeed stranger than fiction. **EDDIE JAFFE** passed away on March 25, 2003, at the age of eighty-nine. **ELIOT SMITH** is sadly no longer with us. **DON WALLACE** is alive and well in New York. **MARVIN FARKAS** passed away in April of 2016 at the age of eighty-nine. **BILL LANDIS** passed away on December 20, 2008. His ghost now haunts Times Square. **MARK GOLDBERG** still resides in New York. **DAVID X. YOUNG** passed away on May 22, 2001, at the age of seventy-one. His work as a painter and as a jazz enthusiast is detailed in the book ***The Jazz Loft Project: Photographs and Tapes of W. Eugene Smith from 821 Sixth Avenue, 1957–1965*** (Knopf, 2009). **VERNON BECKER** passed away on January 10, 2017. The circle slowly closes. **JOEL M. REED** is alive and well. In recent

Joel M. Reed and Joe at Sardi's, 1998.

years, he has appeared as an actor in a handful of low budget movies. He has also written several novels, and is the author of ***Remembrances of Things Jamie Gillis*** (Filmrage, 2016). He still lives in the same apartment on 58th Street, although, as he puts it, "It's kind of a mess these days..."

SPECIAL THANKS

Thank you: Joel M. Reed, David Kerekes, Scott R. Miller, Mike McPadden, Jimmy McDonough, Graham Rae, Mike Hunchback, Donald Farmer, Chris Poggiali, William Wilson, Bruce Holecheck, Eli Roth, Rolfe Kanefsky, Kris Gilpin, Art Ettinger, JR Bruun, Stephen Milligen, John Harrison, Jamie Chimino, Charles Kilgore, Stephen R. Bissette, Greg Goodsell, Darrin Venticinque, Keith Crocker, Tom Skulan, Brian Krueger, Melanie Dante, Jeff Cleveringa, David Edward Szpunar, Liz Guzman, Matthew Vanker, Kim Menzel, Chris Switzer, and the staff and tenants of New York's Washington Jefferson Hotel.

A HEADPRESS BOOK
First published by Headpress in 2018

{e} headoffice@headpress.com

BLOOD SUCKING FREAK
The Life and Films of the Incredible Joel M. Reed

Book design: Mark Critchell <mark.critchell@googlemail.com>

A CIP catalogue record for this book is available from the British Library

ISBN 978-1-909394-52-0 (paperback)
ISBN 978-1-909394-53-7 (ebook)
NO-ISBN (hardback)

Headpress. B**k publisher. Pop and Unpop Culture.

Exclusive NO-ISBN special edition hardbacks and other items of interest are available at HEADPRESS.COM

CPSIA information can be obtained
at www.ICGtesting.com
Printed in the USA
FSHW012057130720
71470FS

9 781909 394520